Rule-Governed Behavior

Cognition, Contingencies, and Instructional Control

Rule-Governed Behavior

Cognition, Contingencies, and Instructional Control

Edited by

Steven C. Hayes
University of Nevada
Reno, Nevada

Plenum Press • New York and London

Library of Congress Cataloging in Publication Data

Rule-governed behavior: cognition, contigencies, and instructional control / edited by Steven C. Hayes.
p. cm.
Includes bibliographies and index.
ISBN 978-1-4757-0449-5 ISBN 978-1-4757-0447-1 (eBook)
DOI 10.1007/978-1-4757-0447-1
1. Verbal behavior. 2. Behavioral assessment. I. Hayes, Steven C.
BF455.R844 1989 89-35845
153–dc20 CIP

Softcover reprint of the hardcover 1st edition 1989

A Division of Plenum Publishing Corporation
233 Spring Street, New York, N.Y. 10013

To the memory of Aaron J. Brownstein
One of the best we had to offer

Contributors

A. CHARLES CATANIA Department of Psychology, University of Maryland Baltimore County, Catonsville, Maryland 21228

LINDA J. HAYES Department of Psychology, University of Nevada—Reno, Reno, Nevada 89557

STEVEN C. HAYES Department of Psychology, University of Nevada—Reno, Reno, Nevada 89557

PHILIP N. HINELINE Department of Psychology, Temple University, Philadelphia, Pennsylvania 19122

BARBARA S. KOHLENBERG Department of Psychology, University of Nevada—Reno, Reno, Nevada 89557

RICHARD W. MALOTT Department of Psychology, Western Michigan University, Kalamazoo, Michigan 49008

BYRON A. MATTHEWS Department of Sociology, University of Maryland Baltimore County, Catonsville, Maryland 21228

SUSAN M. MELANCON Department of Psychology, University of Nevada—Reno, Reno, Nevada 89557

ROGER L. POPPEN Behavior Analysis and Therapy Program, Rehabilitation Institute, Southern Illinois University, Carbondale, Illinois 62901

HAYNE W. REESE Department of Psychology, West Virginia University, Morgantown, West Virginia 26506

IRWIN ROSENFARB Department of Psychology, Auburn University, Auburn, Alabama 36849

ELIOT SHIMOFF Department of Psychology, University of Maryland Baltimore County, Catonsville, Maryland 21228

B. F. SKINNER Department of Psychology, Harvard University, Cambridge, Massachusetts 02138

MARGARET VAUGHAN Department of Psychology, Salem State College, Salem, Massachusetts 01970

BARBARA A. WANCHISEN Department of Psychology, Baldwin-Wallace College, Berea, Ohio 44017

ROBERT D. ZETTLE Department of Psychology, Wichita State University, Wichita, Kansas 67208

Preface

Animal learning and human learning traditions have been distinguishable within psychology since the start of the discipline and are to this day. The human learning wing was interested in the development of psychological functions in human organisms and proceeded directly to their examination. The animal learning wing was not distinguished by a corresponding interest in animal behavior *per se*. Rather, the animal learners studied animal behavior in order to identify principles of behavior of relevance to humans as well as other organisms. The two traditions, in other words, did not differ so much on goals as on strategies.

It is not by accident that so many techniques of modern applied psychology have emerged from the animal laboratory. That was one of the ultimate purposes of this work from the very beginning. The envisioned extension to humans was not just technological, however. Many animal researchers, B. F. Skinner most prominently among them, recognized that direct basic research with humans might ultimately be needed in certain areas but that it was wise first to build a strong foundation in the controlled environment of the animal laboratory. In a sense, animal learning was always in part a human research program in development.

Modern-day cognitive psychology is the major current heir to the human learning tradition—a tradition that has grown noticeably in strength over the last two decades. Conversely, animal learning has weakened noticeably and has split into several small groups. Some of these groups really *are* interested primarily in animal behavior, not learning processes that might be relevant to humans. Some are still true to the original vision.

One of the major modern heirs of the animal *learning* tradition is behavior analysis. Applied work with humans was always an emphasis of behavior analysis and is a major source of its current strength but not basic human research. Just within the last decade, however, behavior analysis has apparently reached a point where direct basic research on human action is possible, respectable, and most significantly of all, thought to be of fundamental importance. Over the last decade human experimental research in this group has increased severalfold. Dozens of behavioral laboratories across the country have begun to emphasize basic human research.

The biggest intellectual reason for the change is this: The experimental analysis of verbal functions is now on the agenda. For that topic, direct human work seems needed, and it has proceeded. The work has focused in particular on the impact of verbal stimuli on human reactions to environmental contingencies. It has included basic work on stimulus class formation in human beings: stimulus equivalence, exclusion, and related phenomena.

The rubric for much of this work has been an interest in rule-governed behavior. Rule-governed behavior in this sense does not refer to general strategies of performance that can be stated in rule form. Rather, it is behavior that is directly impacted by verbal formulae. What that means, how to conceptualize it, how to study it, how it fits in with other psychological processes, what it means for clinical interventions with adult humans—these are the topics dealt with in this volume.

1. DESCRIPTION OF THE VOLUME

The present volume spans a wide variety of topics and perspectives. The book starts with Hayne Reese's scholarly analysis of rules as understood by behavioral and cognitive perspectives. Hayne is one of those rare psychologists respected by both groups and with a deep understanding of both perspectives. His chapter places the current volume in the larger intellectual context of contemporary psychology.

A chapter by B. F. Skinner follows. Skinner's distinction between contingency-shaped and rule-governed behavior has vitalized much of the work in this book. His chapter analyzes the effect of verbal stimuli on listeners as a general context for rule-governance.

Margaret Vaughan's chapter summarizes the history of the concept of rule-governance within the behavioral community, both theoretically and empirically. She shows how the contingency-shaped/rule-governed distinction emerged from a historical context and developed in response developments within psychology. She also reviews some of the kinds of research that have emerged in the attempt to analyze rule-governance.

The team of Charles Catania, Eliot Shimoff, and Byron Matthews has done some of the more important work on rule-governed behavior within the behavior analytic community. Their chapter is an excellent example of research strategies being used to assess the nature and impact of rules.

The first four chapters, then, give a view of current behavioral theory and research on rule-governance and place this work into a larger historical and intellectual context. The four chapters that follow are more speculative and theoretical.

The chapter by Linda Hayes and me attempts to relate the literature on stimulus equivalence and related phenomena to the nature and function of verbal stimuli. An analysis is developed of the verbal action of the listener and of rule-governance that leads in turn to a different view of verbal behavior itself.

The chapter by Robert Zettle, Irwin Rosenfarb, and me extends the issue of rule understanding to rule-following. In particular, it focuses on the listener's motivation to follow a rule and develops a contingency analysis of rule-following.

The chapter by Philip Hineline and Barbara Wanchisen deals in detail with cognitivist and behaviorist interpretations of rules. Not simply a summary of differences, the chapter identifies areas of contemporary cognitive psychology of relevance to rule-governance and areas of overlap between behavioral and cognitive accounts.

Richard Malott analyzes the relevance of rule-governance to behavior with delayed or improbable consequences. His account relies heavily on principles of self-control to explain the effects of rules.

The final two chapters deal with the implications of rule-governance for applied psychology. Roger Poppen shows how the concept can help make sense of existing research in cognitive therapy and the theories that underlie it. A final chapter by Barbara Kohlenberg, Susan Melancon, and me shows how research on rule-governance and stimulus equivalence can be the basis for a variety of new clinical procedures that have as their basis avoiding or altering rule-control. The chapter also argues that contemporary behavior therapy does not always fit very well with much of what we have learned about verbal control in humans.

2. THE ROAD AHEAD

The book does not so much present answers as show a wing of psychology in the middle of an attempt to properly frame the question. The attempt involves difficulties and challenges: philosophical, conceptual, methodological, and empirical. Work on all of these areas is proceeding simultaneously but at times unevenly. There is a sense of vigor and excitement to the area, but there is also much to be humble about. Many of the analyses are tentative and uncertain. Human research in behavior analysis is walking a fine line between a complete break with its past on the one side or a collapse into conventionality on the other.

The former result would be of no use to anyone. There are many other honorable legacies at work in psychology. Whatever value they bring to the field is already there. The animal learning tradition must maintain a contact with its past as it confronts human learning issues to have anything unique to contribute. The work in this volume reveals that contact in the embrace of functionalistic, monistic, contextualistic, and pragmatic analyses of human organisms. Although it is difficult at times to connect across the chasm of research paradigms, the qualities reflected in the work in this volume could be of value to cognitive psychologists and others interested in a basic analysis of human functioning—precisely because it is a bit different.

The latter reaction is also unhelpful. The very reason for the growth of human research in behavior analysis is that researchers have come to the conclusion that there may be something of fundamental importance—something new—to be found there. A reversion to conventionality is a direct challenge to this perception and literally cuts the heart out of the work. Basic research on human functioning cannot be driven by an attempt to show that human learning is no different than animal learning. Given such a belief, there is no *basic* need to study humans at all. Human research would then be only of applied interest.

But a basic analysis *is* needed. We have a great deal to learn about human functioning. Particularly when it comes to verbal interactions, additional psychological processes seem to be involved. It is the task of psychology to determine if that is the case, and if so, to understand those processes. Doing so does not require that we abandon hard-won knowledge—but it does require that we be open to what we may find.

Steven C. Hayes

Lake Tahoe, Nevada

Contents

I. THE NATURE AND PLACE OF BEHAVIORAL ANALYSES OF RULE-GOVERNED BEHAVIOR

II. THE NEW DIRECTIONS IN THE ANALYSIS OF RULE-GOVERNED BEHAVIOR

PART I

THE NATURE AND PLACE OF BEHAVIORAL ANALYSES OF RULE-GOVERNED BEHAVIOR

CHAPTER 1

Rules and Rule-Governance

Cognitive and Behavioristic Views

HAYNE W. REESE

1. INTRODUCTION

The major purpose of this chapter is to analyze cognitive views of rules and rule-governance, but major aspects of behavioristic views of rules and rule-governance are also analyzed. These views are analyzed herein from their own perspectives because criticizing a cognitive view for being nonbehavioristic or a behavioristic view for being noncognitive would be at best self-congratulatory and would not promote understanding of the views.

Between the introduction and the summary, the chapter is divided into five major sections, beginning with a brief rationale for studying rules, proceeding to a summary of cognitive approaches to rules, followed by a discussion of the meanings of *rule,* then rules as causes, and ending with criteria for inferring rule use.

Although I refer frequently to *cognitive views, cognitive approaches,* and *cognitive psychologists* without further distinction, I have limited the relevant coverage almost entirely to the information-processing approach and its practitioners. The "structural" cognitive approach—best represented by the work of Jean Piaget and his followers—is mentioned occasionally but not really discussed. Also, to avoid cluttering the chapter with adjectives, I use *behavior analysis* and its cognates to refer to versions of behaviorism that are based on or consistent with Skinner's behaviorism. I refer to other versions of behaviorism as *stimulus–response learning theory,* but when the distinction makes no difference, I refer generically to *behaviorism.* I use *behaviorial* to refer to behavior, rather than approaches to behavior.

HAYNE W. REESE • Department of Psychology, West Virginia University, Morgantown, West Virginia 26506.

2. WHY STUDY RULES?

Can cognitive psychologists learn anything useful about rules from behaviorism? Can behaviorists learn anything useful about rules from cognitive psychology? I think the answer to both questions is *yes*. Behavior analysis focuses on performance, and cognitive psychology focuses on competence. Performance *must* reflect competence, however poorly, and cognitive psychology may advance more rapidly if cognitivists approach the competence-performance relation as a research topic rather than as a source of error variance. Performance is a distorted reflection of competence, but the distortion should be considered lawful until proved otherwise, and behavior analysis has plenty of laws relating performance to noncognitive variables.

I agree with Overton and Newman (1982) that most behaviorists view cognitive psychology as at best a source of as-yet untested hypotheses. As such, it can benefit behavior analysis by providing hypotheses that can be tested. The hypotheses are about private events of a specific kind—those resulting from experiences with tasks, or in a word, *rules*. The hypotheses may turn out to be blind alleys, but they may turn out to lead to new breakthroughs that will keep behavior analysis vital and progressive.

Exploring these hypotheses will require more emphasis on theory than has been typical in behaviorisms based on Skinner's approach The atheoretical stance of many behavior analysts is a "Baconian oversimplification"—and the top-heavy theoretical structure of cognitivism is a "Cartesian oversimplification":

> The Baconian oversimplification rests on the doctrine that the activity of *collecting facts* is, if not the be-all and end-all, at any rate—in John Austin's phrase—the "begin-all" of any new science . . . The Cartesian oversimplification rests on the rival doctrine that, as a preface to anything else, we must begin by *formulating clear ideas* about our new subject matter. (Toulmin, 1971, pp. 28–29)

Even if the Baconian oversimplification were wholly correct, behavior analysis is no longer in the "begin-all" stage. It has now accumulated enough empirical facts to warrant more energetic activities in theory construction. An apt and promising place to focus these activities is in the domain of rule-governed behavior.

3. THE INFORMATION-PROCESSING APPROACH TO RULES

Anderson (1976) suggested that the aim of the information-processing approach, which is the cognitive approach emphasized herein, is ultimately "to improve human intelligence" (p. 16). Actually, however, this aim is not a consensus of the approach (Coulter, 1983, p. 5). Rather, the majority aim is to *understand* human intelligence. Utilitarian considerations have had little to do with the activity of scientists in any discipline, according to Laudan (1977), and most of the best scientific activity "is not directed at the solution of practical or socially redeeming problems" (p. 224). The information-processing approach has been applied to such practical tasks as learning to read, write, and calculate (Siegler, 1983b, pp. 181–193), but the interest has usually been more theoretical than practical.

3.1. Essence of the Approach

The basic question in the information-processing approach is: "What would an information-processing system require in order to exhibit the same behavior as the organism under study?" (paraphrased from Klahr & Wallace, 1976, p. 5). The answer in this approach is a model (i.e., a theory) described by a computer program, or a model that resembles a flow chart for a computer program, or a model that borrows loosely from programming language. However, as Klahr and Wallace (1976) noted, the number of possible models that could be formulated is unlimited, and therefore a proposed model should be accepted as plausible only if it meets certain criteria. The criteria are discussed later in the subsection entitled "Constraints on Models."

3.1.1. Fundamental Rationale

A fundamental rationale for the information-processing approach is provided by the Turing–Church thesis: "If a problem that could be presented to a Turing machine is not solvable by a Turing machine, then it is also not solvable by human thought" (Kurzweil, 1985, p. 260). Therefore, human thought can be modeled adequately by a machine. A Turing machine is an hypothetical machine that "can compute anything that any machine can compute, no matter how complex" (p. 260). Although this thesis is sometimes taken as a fact, it is actually only an hypothesis. A formal proof is impossible (Jones, 1973, p. 66), and therefore "the truth of the thesis is ultimately a matter of personal belief" (Kurzweil, 1985, p. 260).

This belief is reflected in the cognitive approach to research and explanation. In almost all cognitive research, a few variables are manipulated, and any correlated changes in behavior are attributed to cognitive activities assumed to be affected by the manipulations. Cognitivists think that ignoring these cognitive activities is acceptable for description but not for explanation. Alternatively, in almost all behavioristic research, a few variables are manipulated, and any correlated changes in behavior are attributed to the manipulations. Behaviorists think that referring to cognitive activities is unnecessary.

Both views are correct, for reasons that cannot be elaborated herein. Briefly, in cognitive theories, concepts are abstract; explanation means deduction of empirical relations from hypothetical relations among abstract concepts; and the goal is to understand the structure and functions of the mind. As Siegler (1983b, pp. 200–201) noted, the approach works—it has advanced cognitivists toward their goal. Alternatively, in behavior analytic theories, concepts are concrete in the sense of being induced directly from the manipulations and the data rather than being inferred from the manipulations and the data; explanation means description of empirical relations among concrete concepts; and the goal is prediction and control of behavior. As Skinner (1969, p. 86) noted, the approach works—it has advanced behavior analysts toward their goal.

Information-processing models are *competence* models in the sense that they deal with "normative" rules. A normative rule is a disposition, and as such, it is a kind of competence (for discussion, see the subsection, "Rules as Dispositions"). Information-processing models also deal with performance, but as discussed in the subsections "Turing's Test" and "Consistency with Behavior," performance is of interest primarily as a test of the hypothesized competence. (*Performance* and *competence* are sometimes used in other ways than used here. For example, Stone and Day referred to computer simulations as *performance* or *functional* models, as contrasted with *competence* models [1980, p. 338]; and in agreement with Pylyshyn [1972], they used *competence model* to refer to pure structural models.)

3.1.2. Characteristics of Cognitive Activities

Cognitivists distinguish between controlled or effortful cognitive processing and automatic cognitive processing. Effortful processing is the deliberate, consciously controlled use of rules; automatic processing is not deliberate and not consciously controlled. An incident reported by Baer (1982) can be interpreted to exemplify automatic use of a rule. He was discussing the algorithm for extracting square roots:

> I found that I could not recall the verbal algorithm sufficiently: What doubled? I was completely stalled, until I simply took up a pencil and applied it to paper as if I did recall the algorithm. My experience, as best I can report it, was that my hand still knew the algorithm, although "I" did not. I recovered the algorithm by watching my hand solve the problem; I induced what doubled from what my hand wrote in extracting the root. (Footnote 8, p. 305)

In cognitive terms, what happened can be described as follows. (The parenthetical numbers following some words indicate that explication is given later.) The algorithm was learned as a verbal rule and required conscious effort (1) for operation, but with extensive repetition it became automatic (2) and required no conscious effort for operation. After years of disuse (3), the context (the intention to extract a square root; the problem set up on the paper) was no longer an effective retrieval cue (4) for the verbal rule. The verbal rule may or may not have been still available (5) in long-term memory; but if still available, it had become inaccessible (5) by means of these contextual cues. However, when the hand-applying-the-pencil-to-the-paper was added to the context, the automatic version of the rule was activated (6) and the square-rooting behavior ran its course (7). Baer "knew" all along how to extract square roots, but he did not know that he knew until relevant procedural knowledge (8) was activated.

1. *Conscious effort.* Conscious effort is said to be required for performance when the performance cannot be done without awareness. Skinner (1969) defined "awareness" as follows: "We are aware of what we are doing when we describe the topography of our behavior" (p. 244). However, awareness of cognitive activities is different because one can "observe the results of 'cognitive processes' but not the processes themselves" (Skinner, 1977b, p. 10; p. 111 in 1978 reprint). Thus, being conscious (aware) of a cognitive activity means being conscious of what effect it has, not how it produces this effect. (The point has been debated: Galperin, 1957; Kellogg, 1982; Luria, 1973, pp. 91–93, 1980, pp. 292–293; Mandler, 1975; Miller, 1962, pp. 55–56, 1981; Nisbett & Wilson, 1977; Shiffrin & Schneider, 1977; White, 1980.)

Expert typists type words and phrases with conscious effort, but they type individual letters without conscious effort, that is, automatically (e.g., Swift, 1904—Steven Hayes called my attention to this study). When I type *psychology,* for example, I am conscious of typing it as a word, not as a sequence of letters. The typing of the word requires conscious effort, but the typing of the sequence of letters does not. (Grant, 1986, suggested that "the distinction between automatic and controlled processes is similar to the behavior analytic distinction between contingency-shaped and rule-governed behavior" [p. 159]. He did not give a rationale, but the idea seems worth exploring. For further discussion of issues about effortful and automatic processes, see Ahlum-Heath & Di Vesta, 1986; Hasher & Zacks, 1979; Hirst, Spelke, Reaves, Caharack, & Neisser, 1980; LaBerge & Samuels, 1974; Schneider & Shiffrin, 1977; Shiffrin & Schneider, 1977; Spelke, Hirst, & Neisser, 1976).

2. *Repetition and automatization.* Extensive repetition of a behavior that requires conscious effort eliminates the need for conscious effort, that is, extensive repetition makes performance of the behavior automatic. Obvious examples are riding a bicycle, driving a car, and—a research example (Bryan & Harter, 1897, 1899)—sending and receiving on the telegraph. These examples refer to motor activities; research examples referring to cognitive activities are reading (LaBerge & Samuels, 1974) and memorizing (Kliegl, Smith, & Baltes, in press).

The effects of repetition have been an enticement to theorizing about rules. Repetition with the same stimuli and the same reinforcement contingencies is readily interpreted as conditioning, and its effects are easily explained mechanically as habit formation (Hull), schedule control (Skinner), and so forth. Repetition of a skill, that is, repetition of the same task but with different stimuli in each repetition, is not so easily explained mechanically. The effects of this kind of repetition are seen dramatically in Harry Harlow's learning-set designs. (For discussion of learning set, see "Discrimination Learning Set" and "Other Learning Sets" in the subsection "Sets as Rules.")

3. *Effect of disuse.* In older theories, disuse—lack of use of a skill or of stored information—was assumed to result in decay of its memory trace, that is, a decline in availability of the representation (the concept of availability is explicated in Comment 5 below). The usual interpretation now is that disuse results in a decline in accessibility (also explicated in Comment 5). This interpretation is similar to the stimulus–response learning theory of forgetting: The habit connecting a stimulus and a response does not decline in strength through disuse, but other responses become conditioned to the stimulus and these newer habits compete with the excitatory potential of the old habit. In other words, the stimulus tends to elicit other responses, making the old response effectively inaccessible through this retrieval cue.

4. *Retrieval cue.* Retrieval is the cognitive activity of "getting at" information stored in memory (Klatzky, 1980, p. 236). (Incidentally, the word *information* is usually used in a general sense in cognitive approaches, referring to representations of both rules and facts.) Retrieval can be an effortful cognitive activity, as in mentally reciting the alphabet in an attempt to retrieve (remember) a person's name; or it can be automatic, as when a tune or other information "pops into" consciousness. In either case, theoretically, getting at the information is accomplished by means of a "retrieval cue." The retrieval cue functions like the stimulus item in a paired-associates list (Klatzky, 1980, pp. 254–255) or like the eliciting stimulus in any stimulus–response association or the discriminative stimulus in any three-term contingency.

5. *Availability and accessibility.* Most cognitive theorists agree that "declarative" knowledge ("knowing about things" or "knowing that," discussed in the subsection "Knowing Rules") is represented somehow in the mind, but they have various conceptions about the nature of the representation. For most of these conceptions, a distinction can be made between the availability and accessibility of the representation (Tulving, 1974). A representation is *available* for retrieval if it is in storage. If it is available for retrieval, it is *accessible* to retrieval if an appropriate retrieval cue is used. (The representation, or memory trace, is not assumed to have physical existence; hence, no physical locus of storage is postulated, and no physical retrieval is postulated.)

One reason for distinguishing between availability and accessibility is that, in general, free recall of information is inferior to cued recall of the same information, and cued recall of the information is inferior to recognition of the same information. Theoretically, these memory tests differ in the explicitness of the retrieval cue presented (e.g., "recall the list of items"; "recall the food names in the list"; "indicate whether or not each of the test items you will be shown was in the original list"). Correct recognition of an item that was not recalled in a free or cued recall test is interpreted to mean that the representation of the item was available in storage but was not accessible by means of the retrieval cues presented in the recall test or generated by the individual.

6. *Activation of a cognitive activity.* The activation of a cognitive activity is a complex problem, not yet solved by cognitive psychologists. It depends on both "declarative" and "procedural" knowledge and, often, on noncognitive variables such as motivation. (Declarative knowledge is characterized in Comment 5; procedural knowledge is characterized in Comment 8 below; and both are discussed in the subsection "Knowing Rules.")

7. *"The behavior ran its course."* If a rule, or cognitive activity, is automatic, then once activated it usually continues to operate until its function has been completed, just as the behaviors in a behavior chain are usually emitted in turn until the chain is completed.

For example, on hearing a recorded message, listeners normally encode (i.e., identify and remember) the sex of the speaker automatically (without conscious effort) if the meaning of the message is influenced by the sex of the speaker. This encoding process is activated when the message begins and normally continues to operate until the information has been recognized, encoded, and stored in memory. However, if the message denotes the sex of the speaker, then either the automatic encoding process is not initiated, or it is automatically terminated, and the information is not encoded separately from the encoding of the content of the message (Geiselman, 1979). Another example of early termination of automatic processing is found in research on shadowing (discussed briefly in "Other Problems" in the subsection "Awareness of Rule Use").

At least some automatic processes can be terminated deliberately as well as automatically. Conditions may activate automatic retrieval (recall) of certain information, but the retrieval can be terminated by deliberately attending to other events (or perhaps what is terminated is the automatic entry of the retrieved information into consciousness or "working memory").

8. *Procedural knowledge.* Procedural knowledge refers to cognitive activities, which are mental behaviors, operations, processes, rules, skills, strategies—they go by various names in various theories—for processing information. It includes processes for automatic and deliberate recognition, encoding, transformation, storage, retrieval, construction and reconstruction, planning, and execution in behavior. The concept is discussed further in the subsection "Knowing Rules." An incidental point here is that these cognitive activities, behaviors, and so forth, are conceptualized as *mental,* but the adjective *cognitive* is usually used instead of *mental*—often as an attempt to disguise the mentalism.

3.2. "Levels" of Cognitive Models

Kail and Bisanz (1982) characterized the information-processing approach as based on the computer metaphor; but Klahr (e.g., 1973; Klahr & Wallace, 1976, pp. 5–6) identified three "levels" of the computer metaphor: Level I is an actual computer simulation; Level II is the relatively strict use of computer-programming terminology; and Level III is the metaphorical use of computer-programming terminology. Level I is exemplified by actual programs that yield outcomes like the outcomes of human performance (e.g., Klahr & Siegler, 1978); Level II is exemplified by most of the theorizing in the information-processing approach (examples are Craik & Lockhart, 1972; Klahr & Wallace, 1976; Prytulak, 1971; Shiffrin & Schneider, 1977); and Level III is exemplified by Miller, Galanter, and Pribram's (1960) "TOTE" model, which Klahr (1973, p. 144) characterized as "the best example" of a Level-III model.

Klahr's three levels of models differ in scope and precision. The scope of a model is the range of phenomena it covers; precision is how closely the model approaches the ideal of generating one and only one explanation for each phenomenon in its scope. Information-processing models at Level I have the narrowest scope and greatest precision; those at Level III have the widest scope and least precision.

A fourth level of cognitive theories can be identified. Theories at this level have wider scope and less precision than Level-III models and do not include computer language. An example is Piaget's theory of cognitive development. Level-III and "Level-IV" theories are not considered further herein. (For background on the first two levels of information-processing theories, see Kail & Bisanz, 1982; Siegler, 1983a, b. For Piaget's theory, see, e.g., Piaget, 1970; or a survey such as Furth, 1969.)

3.2.1. Level-I Information-Processing Models

Level-I models in Klahr's (1973) typology are usually actual computer programs that can be run. However, a distinction is made between artificial-intelligence programs and computer-simulation programs. Artificial intelligence is not a model of human behavior (Kurzweil, 1985); it is a method for solving problems. Computer simulation is a model of human behavior.

Computer simulation of human behavior is an attempt to program the computer in such a way that it operates analogously to the human. If the human learns slowly, the computer must generate an output analogous to slow learning; if the human makes mistakes, the computer must generate analogous mistakes. An important point, however, is that *analogous* is a necessary modifier here. The computer *simulation* is only that—a model or an analogy. Failure to appreciate this point has sometimes led to the erroneous assertion that the organism *is* a machine (e.g., McCulloch, 1955) instead of the correctly worded assertion that the organism *functions like* a machine. (Although the latter assertion is correctly worded, it is not necessarily always correct.)

Hunt (1971) posed the question "What kind of computer is man?" The literal answer must be that man is no kind of computer, if "computer" means a machine of some kind. Contrary to Skinner's (1969) assertion that "man *is* a machine, but he is a very complex one" (p. 294), man is not literally any kind of machine, however complex. For that matter, neither is woman nor child a machine of any literal kind.

These quibbles aside, the answer Hunt gave is still problematic. Instead of answering with a computer program, he answered with flow charts. Computer programs are Level-I models in Klahr's (1973) typology, and flow charts are Level-II models. However, Level-II models do not refer literally to computers; they refer to computers only analogically. Therefore, Hunt begged his own question by answering the question, "What kind of analog to the computer is man?" In any case, the proper question is "What kind of computer—or better, computer program—is a useful model of human cognition or some other domain of human behavior?" However, the precision of this form of the question is bought at the expense of verve.

What kind of computer is the human being? No kind. Do any computer simulations of human behavior further the understanding of human behavior? Yes. Do other models of human behavior further the understanding of human behavior? Yes.

3.2.2. Level-II Information-Processing Models

Level-II (Klahr, 1973) information-processing models are couched in computer-programming terms, but they do not involve running programs. Such models have been developed to deal with many domains of human behavior. Two kinds are briefly discussed in the present subsection.

3.2.2a. Models of Memory. Hunt (1971) outlined a Level-II "Distributed Memory" model, but it has had less impact than the Level-II models developed by Shiffrin and his colleagues (e.g., Atkinson & Shiffrin, 1968; Schneider & Shiffrin, 1977; Shiffrin & Schneider, 1977). The essential features of models of this type are illustrated in Figure 1.

Another influential type of Level-II model of memory is Craik and Lockhart's (1972) "levels-of-processing" model. Instead of distinguishing between short- and long-term memory as kinds of memory, Craik and Lockhart attributed duration of memory to "depth" of processing. A problem with this type of model is to define *depth* of processing independently of duration of memory.

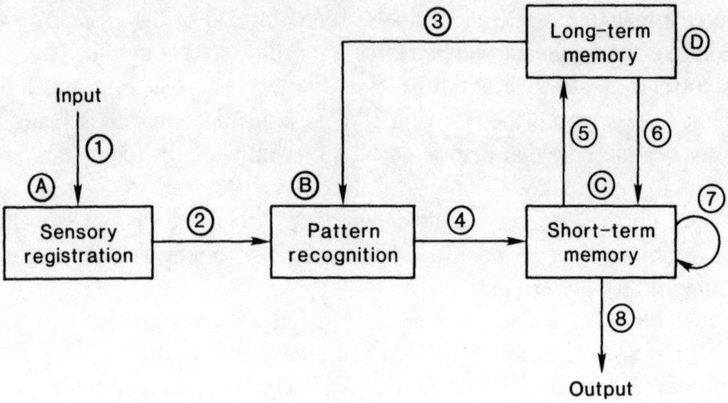

Figure 1. Essential features of information-processing models. Letters identify "structures," and numbers identify processes. The structures are metaphorical, not actually localized in the brain or elsewhere. *Structures:* A. Sensory registration is generally assumed to be modality-specific, that is, in visual, auditory, and so forth, sensory registers. The sensory registers are assumed to have enormous capacity (volume) but extremely brief duration of storage. B. Pattern recognition is generally not assumed to be any kind of structure except perhaps a temporal one. C. Short-term memory is the locus of conscious processes and information of which one is aware. In some models this structure is identified as "working memory," or "primary memory," and is distinguished from short-term memory as a locus of stored information. In the general sense, this structure has a limited capacity (about 7 units) and a short duration of storage (perhaps 30 sec, but see Process 7). D. Long-term memory is assumed to have a virtually unlimited capacity and long duration of storage. Storage may be permanent (depending, of course, on physiological intactness). *Processes:* 1. Reception of stimulation; transduction of external and internal environmental energy into neural or mental energy by sensory receptors. 2. Matching information from the sensory registers against known information. 3. Automatic retrieval of known information from long-term memory. 4. Attention. 5. A variety of processes for remembering, including repetition (rehearsal) and elaboration, for example. 6. Retrieval from long-term memory by a variety of processes; for example, scanning a list actually presented or present in short-term memory and trying to recognize the item sought. 7. Rehearsal or recirculation (maintains information in short-term memory). 8. Response selection and execution.

3.2.2b. Models of Text Comprehension. Comprehending and remembering a text are facilitated by activation of an appropriate *story schema*, *story grammar,* or *script* (Bower, Black, & Turner, 1979; Kintsch & van Dijk, 1978; Mandler & Johnson, 1977; Thorndyke, 1977). Deviation from the appropriate schema interferes with comprehending and remembering a text. For example, short stories and research reports have different schemata and therefore writing either one in the schema of the other would make comprehending and remembering more difficult. (The evidence thus vindicates strict requirements for preparing research reports, as specified, for example, in the *Publication Manual* of the American Psychological Association [1983].)

The theoretical and empirical issues are much too complex to be summarized here, much less explicated and criticized. To give a rough idea of what is meant by *story schema,* the story in Part A of Figure 2 is analyzed in parts B and C of the figure. The story schema used is a simplified version of a schema proposed by Thorndyke (1977).

3.3. Productions and Production Systems

One "Level-I" approach to human cognition is to model this domain by a *production system* computer simulation. This approach has been used by Klahr and his colleagues (e.g., 1973, 1984, 1985; Klahr & Wallace, 1972), among other cognitive psychologists (e.g., Anderson, 1982). The approach is described in the present subsection.

3.3.1. Characteristics

A production system is an ordered set of rules called productions (Simon, 1975). Each production contains a "condition" and an "action": (1) The *condition* is a collection of elements—representations of goals and knowledge—in "short-term memory." In behavior analytic terms, the *condition* is a collection of setting conditions and stimuli. (2) The *action* of a production is an output of some sort. It can be typing a message, for example, or transforming elements in short-term memory.

Given this conception of *action,* a production can be described as consisting of a condition, an action, and an outcome. The resemblance to the three-term contingency of discriminative stimulus, behavior, contingent stimulus is obvious; but the resemblance is superficial. (1) All the elements specified in the "condition" must be present for the action to occur; but as a result of generalization, the discriminative stimulus in behavior analysis can be partial. (2) The action in computer simulation is usually cognitive; the behavior in behavior analysis is usually overt. (3) The outcome in computer simulation is usually a transformation of information in short-term memory; the reinforcing stimulus in behavior analysis is usually a material stimulus.

The meanings of these terms are illustrated in the simple production system shown in Figure 3. The first production, P1, says if you have a circle and a plus, replace them with a triangle; P2 says if you have a triangle, replace it with a circle; and P3 says if you have two circles, replace them with a square and a plus (Klahr, 1984, p. 104). In the initial set of active elements (conditions) in Figure 3, the conditions for P1 and P3 are not satisfied (circle but no plus; circle but no second circle), and therefore P1 and P3 do not "fire." However, the condition for P2 (triangle) is satisfied, and therefore P2 fires, and its action yields the set of elements in the middle portion of the Data Base. Here, only the condition for P3 is satisfied, and therefore it fires, and its action

A

The Farmer Story

A farmer had a cow that he wanted to go into his barn. He tried to pull the cow, but it would not move. So the farmer asked his dog to bark and scare the cow into the barn. The dog refused to bark unless it had some food. So the farmer went to his house to get some food. He gave it to the dog. It barked and frightened the cow, which ran into the barn.

B

Story → Goal + Episode* + Resolution
Episode → Subgoal + Attempt* + Outcome
Attempt → Event* or Episode
Outcome → Event or State
Resolution → Event or State
Subgoal, Goal → Desired state

*means entity can be repeated any number of times

C

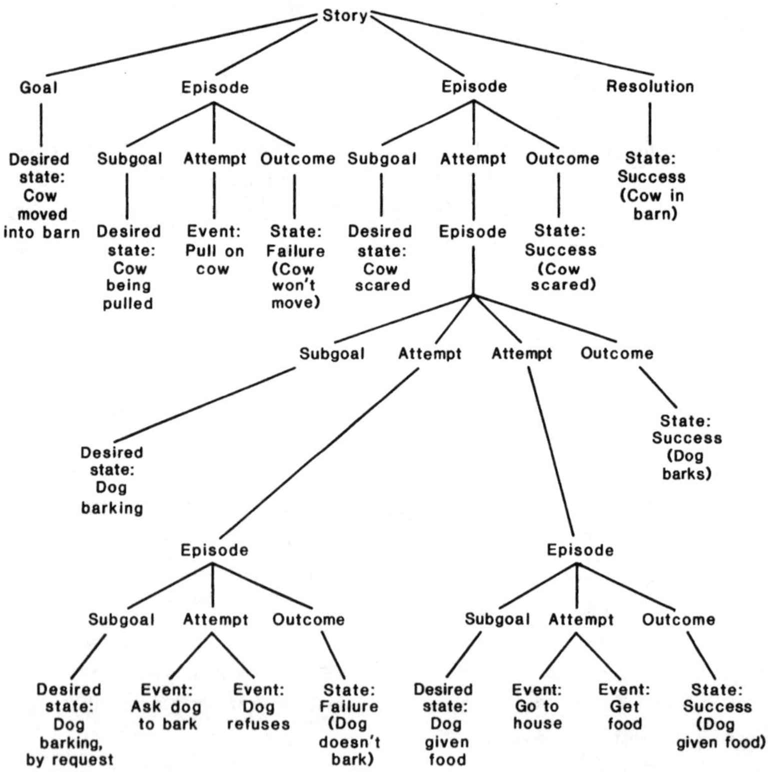

Figure 2. (A) The Farmer Story. (B) The rules in a simplified story schema. (C) Tree diagram showing use of these rules to analyze the structure of the Farmer Story. (Reprinted from *Human memory: Structures and processes* by Roberta L. Klatzky [Fig. 8.8, pp. 214–215]. W. H. Freeman and Company. Copyright (c) 1980. Reprinted by permission.)

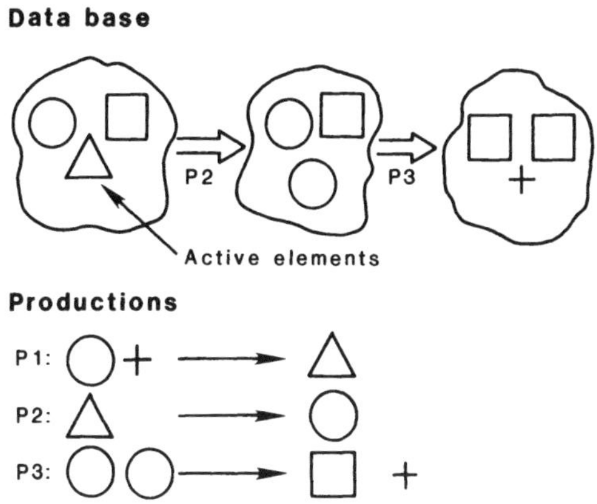

Figure 3. A simple production system. (Reprinted from "Transition processes in quantitative development," by David Klahr (Fig. 5–1, p. 105). In R. J. Sternberg [Ed.], *Mechanisms of cognitive development*. W. H. Freeman and Company. Copyright (c) 1984. Reprinted by permission.)

yields the right-most portion of the Data Base, in which no conditions are satisfied, and therefore information processing in this production system ceases.

Productions are rules. Evidently, then, the basic assumption for this kind of model is that behavior is *rule-governed* (Klahr's term, 1984, p. 106). The consensus among cognitive psychologists seems to be that productions (or their equivalent in other versions of the approach) are rules of the *normative* type that includes "normative dispositions." (Normative rules and normative dispositions are discussed in the subsection "Forms of Rules.") That is, the inferred rules are considered not to be mere mentalisms of the researcher; rather, they are considered to have "psychological reality"—to be real cognitive activities in real persons (e.g., Kail & Bisanz, 1982; Newell, 1972; Siegler, 1983a; Simon, 1972).

3.3.2. Reasons for Preferring the Approach

3.3.2a. Irrelevant Reasons. Advocates of an approach often try to advance the approach by arguing that alternative approaches are deficient. However, this argument is invalid because, as Pepper (1938) pointed out, the advocated approach is not demonstrated to be sufficient by a demonstration that the alternatives are deficient—the advocated approach could also be deficient.

Anderson (1980) used a variant of this argument—a variant that is actually a valid argument. He attributed four deficits to stimulus–response learning theories, showed that production systems have none of these deficits, and concluded that production systems are preferable to stimulus–response learning theories for the study of rules. However, although his argument was valid in the sense of correct logical deduction, his conclusion was unjustified because stimulus–response learning theories in fact have none of the deficits he attributed to them. Therefore, if production systems have greater utility than stimulus–response learning theories for the study of rules, the reasons must be otherwise.

The deficits Anderson attributed to stimulus–response learning theories are identified and criticized in the following paragraphs. In addition to showing that stimulus–response learning theories do not have these deficits, I also show that behavior analysis does not have them.

1. "Traditionally, stimulus–response theories have insisted that the controlling stimuli for behavior be external, perceivable conditions or events" (Anderson, 1980, p. 237). Quite the contrary, traditional stimulus–response learning theorists such as Hull and Spence distinguished between "external" *potential* stimuli and "internal" *actual* or *effective* stimuli (e.g., Hull, 1943, pp. 32–33; Spence, 1956, pp. 39–42). Furthermore, traditional stimulus–response learning theories include a number of hypothetical internal stimuli. Examples are:

a. The response-produced mediating stimulus s_m (e.g., Goss, 1961; Reese, 1962).
b. The stimulus s_g produced by the "fractional anticipatory goal response" r_g (Spence, 1960, p. 96).
c. The stimuli produced by frustration, s_f, and emotion, s_e (Amsel, 1958; Spence, 1956, pp. 49–51, 134–137, 1960, pp. 96–99).
d. Drive stimuli s_D (e.g., Brown, 1961, p. 75; Dollard & Miller, 1950, footnote 6, pp. 30–31; Hull, 1943, p. 71; Spence, 1956, p. 166).
e. Other "intraorganic stimuli" (Spence, 1956, p. 41).

Finally, although behavior analysis is not a stimulus–response learning theory in a strict sense, a noteworthy consideration here is that it includes conceptions of effective stimuli and internal stimuli (Skinner, 1953, Chapters 8, 17) that are similar to those of stimulus–response learning theories.

2. Traditional stimulus–response learning theories "cannot treat sequences of responses as a unit" (Anderson, 1980, p. 239). Admittedly, a sequence of behaviors was usually treated as formally a chain rather than as a unit. However, the identification of specific behaviors in the chain was recognized as somewhat arbitrary (Keller & Schoenfeld, 1950, pp. 197–205) because the chain is actually a continuous flux (Spence, 1956, p. 44).

Levine (1959) treated rules, or "hypotheses," as unitary: An hypothesis is "a pattern of responses to selected stimuli" (p. 365), and the "pattern as a whole is susceptible to the traditional effects of reinforcement operations, i.e., it is possible to reinforce some Hs [hypotheses] and to extinguish others" (p. 365). Similarly, Keller and Schoenfeld (1950) noted that a well-learned chain of behaviors functions as a unit (p. 202), and Skinner (1953) said, "Some chains have a functional unity" (p. 224).

3. "Although there are exceptions, traditionally stimulus–response theories treat organisms as responding to a single stimulus at a time" (Anderson, 1980, p. 238). On the contrary, the usual assumption was that behavior is conditioned to all effective stimuli present (e.g., Estes, 1950; Guthrie, 1960, pp. 23, 276; Hull, 1943, p. 71; Skinner, 1953, Chapter 8; Spence, 1937) and that behaviors can also be conditioned to stimulus patterns or compounds in certain tasks (Hull, 1943, pp. 395–398; Nissen, 1950, 1953; Spence, 1952).

4. Stimulus–response associations are very *specific* rather than *general* (Anderson, 1980, pp. 238–239). This assertion is correct, but it is so misleading that it must be challenged.

a. Behavior in these theories was traditionally treated as specific, but it was also treated as an *act* rather than as a sequence or pattern of muscular contractions, or *movements* (Spence, 1956, pp. 42–43). Acts "are specified in terms of what changes they produce in the immediate environment or in the relation of the organism to the immediate environment" (Spence, 1956, p. 42). Estes (1950) used the term *response-class* to label this concept: A response-class is "a class of behaviors which produce environmental effects within a specified range of values" (p. 95). Skinner (1953) used the term *operant* to refer to response classes of this kind (p. 65). An act, then, is defined in terms of an effect on the environment rather than patterns of movement or topography. As such, it is not "specific" in a way that precludes generality.
b. Regardless of the specificity of a stimulus–response association, stimulus and (perhaps) response generalization may occur and yield generality (e.g., Hull, 1943, Chapter 12; Skinner, 1953, pp. 93–95, 132–134; Spence, 1937). In behavior analysis, the concepts of stimulus class and response class provide additional sources of generality to the three-term contingency. (To be precise, the data rather than the *concepts* of stimulus and response class provide the generality. In all cases, the generality must be demonstrated empirically; for example, Barton and Ascione [1979] observed a limit on a response class in that they found generalization from training of verbal sharing in preschool children to physical sharing but not from training of physical sharing to verbal sharing. A final incidental comment is that I have argued elsewhere [Reese, 1986] that "behavior class" is a better designation than "response class" because "behavior" does not have the implicit reference to respondents.)
c. The concept of mediation provides perhaps the most important source of generality to stimulus–response associations. In behavior analysis, the concept of rule-governance provides the same source of generality.

3.3.2b. Relevant Reasons. The foregoing considerations indicate that for the study of rules, a preference for production systems (or computer simulations in general) rather than stimulus–response learning theories cannot be legitimately based on the argument that only productions can be controlled by internal mechanisms, can generate a behavior sequence as a unit, can be associated with multiple stimuli simultaneously, and can be generalized. Although productions have all these characteristics, so do stimulus–response associations. The preference is, I think, largely stylistic. Rules are the basic units of analysis in all information-processing theories (Siegler, 1983a). Productions are rules, and the basic premise for production systems (and other computer simulations) is that behavior is rule-governed. Given this premise, a search for underlying stimulus–response associations is unreasonable.

A substantive reason for preferring the computer-simulation approach for the study of rules is its great precision. This basis is developed in the following excursus.

3.3.2c. Excursus on Scope and Precision. Bever, Fodor, and Garrett (1968) tried to show that associationism is inadequate on its own ground rules. They based their argument on "the terminal metapostulate" of associationism:

> Associative principles are rules defined over the "terminal" vocabulary of a theory, i.e., over the vocabulary in which behavior is described. Any description of an n-tuple of elements between which an association can hold must be a possible description of the actual behavior. (p. 583)

This is a confused way of saying that the theoretical concepts of associationism must be defined in terms of stimuli and responses. The confusion is in the second sentence quoted.

In fact, the "description of the actual behavior" is part of the description of what is observed; the other parts are descriptions of observed stimuli and of the relation between these stimuli and the observed behavior. For example, the following statement is a description of what is observed: "Stimulus X in Setting Y was followed by Behavior Z." However, an *inferential* statement based on this observation might be: "The compound stimulus, X and Y, elicited an unobserved mediating response r_m, which produced a mediating stimulus s_m, which elicited Behavior Z." A corresponding *theoretical* statement might refer to various habit strengths of the hypothetical and observed responses, drive strength, and so forth. The point is that the inferential and theoretical statements contain concepts that are defined in terms of stimuli and responses but that are in no way a possible description of the behavior actually observed. They are not even *part of* the possible description of the behavior actually observed.

Bever *et al.* (1968) thought that the occurrence of reversals in serial order violates a corollary of the "terminal metapostulate"—"since behavior is organized in time, every associative relation is a relation between left and right elements of a sequence" (p. 583). (I assume they realized that "left" and "right" refer to temporal sequence only metaphorically. The point is of no consequence here.) They cited the typing of *Lalshey* for *Lashley* as an example. However, such reversals can be easily explained in the associationistic Hull–Spence theory on the basis of remote associations and oscillatory inhibition: The typing of *s* is directly associated with the typing of *a* in *Lashley*, and the typing of *l* is remotely associated with the typing of *a*. Normally when this name is typed, the habit strength for typing *s* after *a* is greater than the habit strength for typing *l* after *a*, but because of oscillatory inhibition, the excitatory potential for typing *l* after *a* can be momentarily greater than that for typing *s* after *a*.

This explanation does not violate any postulates underlying associationism, contrary to Bever *et al.*, and therefore the explanation cannot be rejected on philosophical grounds. Its merit, or lack of merit, is entirely an empirical issue. (Empirically, the concept of remote associations is questionable; for debate, see Bugelski, 1965; Dallett, 1965; Hakes & Young, 1966; Kausler, 1974, pp. 245–254; Slamecka, 1964, 1965).

Finally, Bever *et al.* believed that the recognition of mirror-image symmetry in figures without explicitly marked contours violates the terminal metapostulate. They felt that recognition of symmetry requires specifying a relation X (e.g., to represent the center around which the figure is symmetrical), and they noted that this X does not appear in the actual terminal behavior. I have already pointed out that if X is an inferred or theoretical concept, it is not expected to appear in the actual terminal behavior.

Bever *et al.* concluded that

> we have considered associationism to require certain constraints upon the formulation of learning principles. Theories that are more powerful than associationism are at least theories that have weaker constraints. Hence, any behavior that can be characterized by associationism can *ipso facto* be characterized by the more powerful models. (p. 585)

True; but the word *powerful* is seriously misleading. In this context, it refers to scope, but the increase in scope that results from weaker constraints is bought at the expense of precision. Those who prefer precision as the primary criterion will reject theories with the weaker constraints; those who prefer scope will embrace these theories.

3.3.3. Obtaining Precision

The rules (productions) in a running program are intended to generate a close approximation to the desired output. If the desired output is not generated, in principle the program is rejected as a theory of the modeled domain. In practice, the program is generally not rejected but rather is modified by the introduction of other variables. The reason is that in these cases the output of the initial program is generally at least a fair approximation of the desired output, thus demonstrating that the programmer–theorist is on the right track.

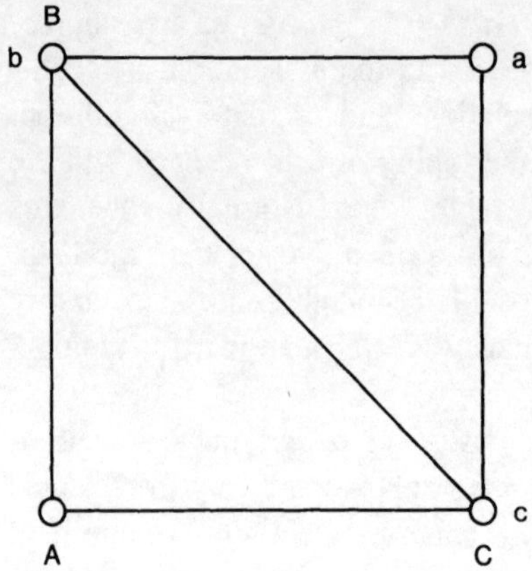

Figure 4. Symbolic representation of task used by Klahr (1985). The board contains four locations and five paths connecting pairs of locations. One location is empty, and the other three are occupied by different objects, here symbolized A, B, and C. The goal is to move the objects to a new configuration, here symbolized a, b, and c, in as few moves as possible, moving one object at a time along a path to a location (i.e., stopping in mid-path is not allowed), without having more than one object at any location at any time. The solution to the puzzle shown requires seven moves. (The number of moves required depends on the goal configuration. If a and b are interchanged in the figure, the solution requires only two moves.) In the actual puzzle used by Klahr, A, B, and C were toys—a dog, a cat, and a mouse—and the goal locations were marked by toy foods—a bone, a fish, and a piece of cheese. Klahr found that children as young as 4 years old exhibited systematic behavior rather than trial-and-error behavior.

An example is a study by Klahr (1985) of young children's performance on a tile-moving type of puzzle. The puzzle is symbolized in Figure 4. Klahr found that a production system with completely deterministic productions accounted for 49% of the variance in the children's performance. However, he observed that certain percentages of the time the children's performance was inconsistent with two of the productions in the system. He changed these two productions to a probabilistic form; the probabilistic productions were (1) to retrace a random 10% of the moves, and (2) on 69% of the occasions when alternative moves were possible, to select the move than yielded more objects in their end-state locations. The percentages used were derived from the data. With the probabilistic productions included, the system accounted for 71% of the variance in performance.

Klahr noted that the fit of the revised system worsened as the number of moves in the correct path increased, and he found that when the number of moves was included, the model accounted for 97% of the variance. Ideally, such adjustments would not be necessary; practically, they are needed because of the slippage between competence, definable as nonprobabilistic productions, and performance.

Stimulus–response learning theorists dealt with the slippage in a similar way—using part of the data to estimate the parameters needed to generate theoretical curves. As in the example of Klahr's study, the fit between the theoretical and obtained curves was often very impressive. (For examples, see Spence, 1956, Chapter 7; Spiker & Cantor, 1973; and references cited in these articles. The issue does not arise in behavior analysis, because this kind of curve fitting is not used.)

3.3.4. Ontogenesis

The basic strategy used for computer simulation of developmental domains, such as cognitive development, was formulated by Simon (1962):

> If we can construct an information-processing system with rules of behavior that lead it to behave like the dynamic system we are trying to describe, then this system is a theory of the child at one stage of development. Having described a particular stage by a program, we would then face the task of discovering what additional information-processing mechanisms are needed to simulate developmental change—the transition from one stage to the next. . . . Thus, a theory would have two parts—a program to describe performance at a particular stage and a learning program governing the transitions from stage to stage. (pp. 154–155)

The first part of the research program is to describe at least two stages of development, using computer programs; the second part is to write a computer program that will simulate the transition from one stage of development to the next. So far, researchers have not progressed to the second part. In other words, they have so far described developmental changes in production systems, but they have not yet explained (simulated) these changes.

Behaviorists do not have this problem because they reject the concept of *stages* of development except in various weak, nontechnical senses (Reese, 1970a, pp. 11–12). Their basic unit—the stimulus–response association or the three-term contingency—changes as a result of conditioning (among other processes such as extinction and generalization). In contrast, the basic unit in computer simulations—the production, for example—may change, as in self-modifying systems, but stagewise development is a change in production *systems*, not merely in the productions themselves.

Self-modifying production systems have been developed (Anderson, 1982; Klahr, 1984). Three of the several mechanisms of self-modification are *discrimination*, *generalization*, and *composition*.

Discrimination consists of adding more conditions to the condition side of a production. For example, the production

If RED and LARGE, then say YES

might be changed to

If RED and LARGE and TRIANGLE, then say YES

(from Klahr, 1984, p. 126).

Generalization is accomplished by either removing conditions from the condition side of a production or replacing a specific condition with a general condition. For example,

If RED and LARGE, then say YES

might be changed to

If ANY COLOR and LARGE, then say YES.

Composition means that productions that repeatedly fire in the same sequence are combined into a single production. Klahr's example was:

Production 1: If A and B, then C

and

Production 2: If C, then D and E

combined by the composition mechanism into

Production 3: If A and B, then D and E.

Evidently, a self-modifying production system is one that includes mechanisms that change productions, rather than ones that change the *system*, or structure, that integrates productions. The modifications are analogous to Piaget's concept of accommodation, which is a mechanism of change within a stage, rather than analogous to his concept of equilibration, which is the stage-to-stage transition mechanism (e.g., Piaget, 1970).

3.4. Evaluation of Cognitive Theories

Cognitive theories are subject to evaluation on the usual scientific criteria of scope, precision, and so on (Kuhn, 1977, Chapter 13; Pepper, 1942, Chapter 4). Another, less widely recognized criterion applicable to all sciences is progress (Lakatos, 1978, pp. 110–113; Laudan, 1977, Chapter 1). Progress is discussed in subsection 3.4.1. Cognitive theorists have specified additional criteria, including the so-called "Turing's test," which are discussed in the subsequent subsections.

3.4.1. *Progress*

A theory or an approach is progressing if its scope is being widened and/or if its precision is being increased. More specifically, progress is defined as increasing success in solving problems, not as discovering Truth or even as discovering closer approximations to the truth (Laudan, 1977, p. 125). Consequently:

> This approach . . . entails that we *may* find ourselves endorsing theories as progressive and rational which turn out, ultimately, to be false (assuming, of course, that we could ever definitely establish that any theory was false). But there is no reason for dismay at this conclusion. Most of the past theories of science are already suspected of being false; there is presumably every reason to anticipate that current theories of science will suffer a similar fate. But the presumptive falsity of scientific theories and research traditions does not render science either irrational or non-progressive. (Laudan, 1977, p. 126)

Increases in scope and precision usually result from modifications in the theory or approach. According to Toulmin (1971):

> The scientist's business is not simply that of "making predictions" which are to be either "verified" or "falsified"—that is, inferring particular *statements* about Nature, which experience will either bear out or show to be incorrect. Rather, his goal

> is to arrive at a better set of *terms*, or *concepts*, in which to describe, pose questions and think about Nature. Empirical enquiry then establishes not whether his predictions are true or false, but whether his concepts are applicable or inapplicable, relevant or irrelevant, operative or beside the point. (p. 38)

This conception is consistent with Laudan's relativistic analysis of progress (1977, Chapter 4) and with pragmatism (in the sense not of practicality or practicability but of the world view identified by Pepper, 1942, as contextualism).

The modification of theory reflects Mao Zedong's (1937/1965) practice–theory–practice dialectic. As Toulmin (1971) said, in discussing how conceptual (analytic) problems arise:

> We attempt to state what a concept entails, or to analyze its criteria of application; we then look and see how far this analysis squares with our actual practice; as a result, we recognize shortcomings, either in our verbal definitions, or in the criteria used in applying the concept to empirical situations; and, in the light of these discoveries, we refine our initial formulation and/or criteria so as to improve the match between our ideas and our experience. (p. 38)

(For an hypothetical example, see his p. 34.)

Laudan (1977) noted that such a procedure is used to deal with anomalous findings:

> Whenever a theory encounters a refuting instance, it is possible to modify the interpretative rules associated with the theory so as to disarm the "refuting" data. . . . [T]he modification of a theory arbitrarily in order to eliminate a refuting instance is open to criticism only if such a move would lead to a diminished problem-solving efficiency. That can generally be shown to happen only if the refuting instance is solved by some [other] theory in the domain. Hence, a refuting instance only counts as a serious anomaly when it has been solved by some [other] theory. (pp. 118–119)

The information-processing approach is strong on precision when the criteria for inferring rules are used carefully, as seems to be usually the case. It is also being applied to more and more tasks in the cognitive domain (e.g., Siegler, 1983a, mentioned using it for 13 different cognitive tasks), and in that sense the scope of the approach is increasing. Its scope is also increasing in the sense of being applied to more different domains (Siegler, 1983a). However, these applications have not been integrated with one another by any overarching model, and in that sense what has increased in not the *scope* of any one information-processing model but only the *range* of applications of the approach. Development of a precise, general model would be a major advance.

3.4.2. Turing's Test

Reynolds and Flagg (1983) said that Turing provided "one of the most widely accepted criteria for a definition of 'thinking' " (p. 257), and Howard

(1983) said that Turing "suggested the general form" for deciding whether a computer program "offers an accurate theory of human problem solving" (p. 14). However, what cognitive psychologists call *Turing's test* is different from the test Turing actually proposed.

Turing (1950) considered the question "Can machines think?"; but he rephrased it in terms of an "imitation game." In this game, an interrogator (C) attempts to determine which of two unknowns, X and Y, is A and which is B. The object of the game for A is to get C to make the wrong identifications; the object for B is to help C make the correct identifications. The question Turing (p. 434) asked is: If X and Y communicate with C via teletype, thereby removing all extraneous cues, will the interrogator decide wrongly as often when A is a machine and B is a person as when A is a man and B is a woman?

The test used in computer simulation of human performance is to observe the outcome of human performance and then to write a computer program that yields the same outcome (actually, the *analogous* outcome). Thus, the so-called "Turing's test" is based on a consistency criterion—agreement of computer output with human output. (This criterion is discussed later, in the subsection entitled "Consistency with Behavior.") The results of the test often indicate a reasonably good agreement that is improved by post hoc modifications of the program. The test can be applied analogically to "outputs" (i.e., predictions) of Level-II information-processing models, and again the agreement can be improved by post hoc modifications. Making such modifications is fully appropriate and justified—they are the essence of scientific progress—unless an alternative model provides agreement between prediction and observation without modifications.

In general, the information-processing approach is progressing according to this criterion. Post hoc modifications of a model have tended to accumulate until the model becomes top-heavy with patches and is replaced by an alternative model specifically developed to deal with the previous problems.

Pinsky (1951) commented that a better test than Turing's (1950) of whether a machine can think is to show that a machine can misuse its thinking powers as humans do. Such a "misuse" test might seem essential for evaluating computer simulation of human intelligence, but it is not practicable. The reason is that computers are not themselves rule-governed. Computers are problem-solving machines, but the apparent *purpose* in a computer's behavior is not really in the machine, its program, or its behavior. Rather, the purpose was in the programmer, or the programmer's behavior (Skinner, 1969, pp. 289–290). Skinner believed that computers follow rules (1969, pp. 149, 293), but a more defensible position is that computers are rule-governed devices only metaphorically. Literally, computers are program-governed devices; unlike persons, who on occasion may be said to have broken some rule, "for computers, there is no rule-*breaking*—only malfunctioning" (Coulter, 1983, p. 101). Therefore, the computer cannot misuse its powers; at best, its program can include an ''irrational'' routine that bypasses its ''rational'' routines, perhaps on a probabilistic basis.

3.4.3. Constraints on Models

At least seven criteria have been proposed for evaluating the plausibility of information-processing models. These criteria serve as constraints on assumptions about cognitive structures and activities. They are described and criticized in the present subsection, and the information-processing approach as a whole is evaluated on each criterion that seems useful. Evaluating the approach as a whole on these criteria is necessarily somewhat superficial, perhaps too much so to be important. More importantly, the criteria would be used to evaluate a specific information-processing theory of interest.

The first four criteria listed next were proposed by Simon (1972), but the wording given is from Klahr (1973, p. 143; Klahr & Wallace, 1976, p. 5). The fifth and sixth criteria were added by Klahr and Siegler (1978, p. 65), and the seventh was proposed by Overton and Newman (1982, pp. 218–219).

1. *Consistency with what we know of the physiology of the nervous system.* The usefulness of asking for consistency with neurophysiology is not obvious; too little is known about the neurophysiology of behavior and cognitive activity to make this constraint compelling. Inconsistency would probably be undesirable, but more for esthetic than practical reasons. Evaluation of the information-processing approach on this criterion therefore seems unnecessary.

2. *Consistency with what we know of behavior in tasks other than the one under consideration.* Asking for consistency with *all* we know of behavior would be unnecessarily restrictive, but asking for consistency with what we know of relevant or related behaviors is reasonable. For example, the condition side of a production should not require perceptual behavior that is known to be beyond human competence, but what we know of emotional behavior can often be ignored. This more lenient version of the constraint seems to be applied adequately in the information-processing approach, especially in applications to cognitive development. (Incidentally, the constraint is also used in other approaches. For example, Spiker and Cantor [1973] were implicitly using it when they tested predictions from an extension of Hull–Spence theory in several tasks. The constraint is also implicit in any multitest method.)

3. *Sufficiency to produce the behavior under consideration.* Asking for sufficiency to produce the target behavior is the crucial criterion; it is required for satisfaction of the so-called ''Turing's test'' as actually used. However, ''sufficiency'' is understood to mean *parsimonious* sufficiency, because otherwise the criterion imposes too little constraint. This point is essential but is often overlooked by critics of the information-processing approach. The information-processing approach meets this criterion well.

4. *Definiteness and concreteness.* Making definiteness and concreteness a major criterion may reflect a preference for computer simulation as a cognitive model. Klahr (1973) identified the three "levels" of information-processing models (described herein in the subsection "Levels of Cognitive Models") in specifying what this constraint means, and the models at the most definite and concrete level are "usually stated as running programs" (Klahr, 1973, p. 143; Klahr & Wallace, 1976, p. 5). The information-processing approach as a whole meets this criterion. Level-I models—actual running programs—are necessarily definite and concrete. Also, most if not all Level-II models are adequately definite and concrete in the sense that the explanations that are attributed to them are plausibly derivable from them. (A Level-II model can be represented by a flow chart, but the explanations attributed to the model are usually developed by narrative rather than by strict deduction. If the narrative is plausible, that is, persuasive, the model is adequate on the criterion of definiteness and concreteness.)

5. *Amenability to aggregation and disaggregation.* An information-processing model should be applicable to both group and individual data. This constraint is important because the model should have generality across persons, but agreement between the model and the data is most convincingly demonstrated on an individual basis. Siegler's (1981) "rule-assessment approach" requires individual analysis, but most Level-II models require only group analysis.

6. *Developmental tractability.* Developmental models need to include representations of early and later forms of competence that are easily interpretable as precursor and successor in a developmental sequence. Although Simon did not include this criterion in his primary list, he did not overlook it. In fact, he recognized that it is fundamental for an information-processing approach to human development (Simon, 1962).

7. *The "Kantian Question."* Overton and Newman presented another set of constraints for cognitive models in general. The major addition to the list is that the cognitivist should ask the "Kantian question": "What must one *necessarily* assume about the nature of the organism in order for it to have the behaviors which it does exhibit?" (Overton & Newman, 1982, pp. 218–219). (Or, "What conditions must be postulated in order that the admittedly given may be explained and accounted for?"—Smith, 1923, p. xxxviii.) Overton and Newman specified how this criterion can be satisfied:

> The method for answering this question is that of observing a sufficient subset of behaviors in the domain in question and constructing a competence model that best captures the universal features of the subset. If the model is valid and powerful, it will prove through further empirical demonstrations to be applicable to a much wider array of behaviors in the domain. The particular form of such a competence model is also guided by issues of parsimony, simplicity, internal coherence, and aesthetics. (p. 219)

4. MEANINGS OF "RULE"

The present section deals with the meanings and forms of rules and what is meant by "knowing rules." For the most part, the interpretations are my own.

4.1. Forms of Rules

Rule is a lexically complex word. The "lexical" meaning of a word is its *basic* meaning. For example, *plays, played,* and *playing* have different "grammatical" meanings but only one lexical meaning—*play* (*Webster's,* 1981, p. 1301). The greater the number of lexical meanings a word has, generally the more space it is given in a dictionary; therefore, the amount of space devoted to a word is at least a rough index of the complexity of its lexical meaning. In the *Oxford English Dictionary* (1933, Vol. 8), *rule* is given nine columns and related words, such as *rule of thumb* and *ruler,* are given four additional columns. (In contrast, *aardvark* is given about one-sixth of one column.)

Several taxonomies of rules have been proposed. For example, Argyle (1984) distinguished among norms, rules, and conventions: A norm is "modal behavior, i.e., what most people do" (p. 455). A rule is "behavior which members of a group believe should, or should not, [be] performed in some situations, or range of situations" (p. 455). A convention is an arbitrary custom: "It is a rule in cricket that the batsman should use a bat (rather than, say, a tennis racquet), but a convention that he should wear white trousers" (p. 455).

Distinguishing norms from rules and conventions seems useful, but distinguishing between rules and conventions seems much less useful. Both rules and conventions are to some extent arbitrary, both involve consequences that are at least implicit, and both can sometimes control behavior. Therefore, in the present subsection, I use a simpler distinction—between norms, or "normal" rules, and "normative" rules. The subsection also includes discussion of rules as guides and as dispositions.

4.1.1. Normal and Normative Rules

As a noun, *rule* has two general meanings that are relevant herein: a generality and a prescription. A generality is a *normal* rule, referring to what is; a prescription is a *normative* rule, referring to what should be (Reese & Fremouw, 1984).

A normative rule may be a prescription, specifying the way one ought to proceed, or it may be practical advice, specifying a way to succeed. In Skinner's (1957) terms, the former is a "mand" and the latter has the form of a "tact" but is actually a "mand." In Zettle and Hayes's (1982) terms, the former is a "ply" and the latter is a "track" (a ply specifies appropriate behavior and a track specifies "the way the world is arranged"—p. 81).

The following doggerel is an example of a practical normative rule (mand in tact form; track), referring to effective operation of a forge bellows.

> Up high, down low,
> Up quick, down slow—
> And that's the way to blow.
> (Skinner, 1969, p. 139)

Although this rule tacts effective operation of the bellows, it is an implicit mand when presented by a blacksmith to an apprentice.

A normative rule is *functional* if it sometimes affects behavior and *nonfunctional* if it does not affect behavior (Reese & Fremouw, 1984). According to this view, normative rules—prescriptions—are behaviors (or cognitive activities) of a speaker. When they affect the behavior of a listener (who may be the same person as the speaker), they are functional; otherwise, they are nonfunctional.

If a functional normative rule is always exhibited in behavior, it can be designated as a *normal rule.* A nonfunctional normative rule can be *normal* only as verbal behavior. (An important research question for behavior analysts is how a nonfunctional normative rule is maintained, and for cognitivists, why it is maintained; but these questions are not addressed in this chapter.) Hereinafter, I will ignore nonfunctional normative rules and use "normative rule" to refer only to functional ones.

4.1.2. Alternative Terms

As a generality, or norm, *rule* refers to a regularity. Calling a regularity a "rule" can be misleading, however, because as Bergmann (1957) said, " 'rule' carries some of the connotations that are also carried by 'arbitrary,' by 'convention,' by 'way to proceed,' and by 'man-made' " (p. 136). When a regularity is discovered, it can be described, and its description is also called a rule. This is, in fact, the usual textbook definition of *rule* (e.g., in Ault, 1983, p. 92; Bransford, 1979, p. 208; Dodd & White, 1980, p. 155; Gagné, 1970, Chapter 7; Horton & Turnage, 1976, p. 390; Reed, 1982, p. 173; Solso, 1979, p. 384; Wittig, 1981, p. 255).

Confusion might be avoided if the description of a regularity were called a *law* (Bergmann, 1957, p. 136), but *law* also has a juridical sense and therefore also connotes "arbitrary," "convention," "way to proceed," and "man-made." "Obeying" a natural law is a matter of fact; obeying a juridical law is a matter of choice, or at least it is often considered to be. Horton and Turnage (1976) used *concept* to refer to the regularity and *rule* to refer to the description of the regularity, but they noted that the two meanings are often hard to separate (p. 390). The point is that "normal rule" refers both to regularities in nature and to descriptions of regularities in nature.

4.1.3. Rules as Guides

In the sense of a regularity in nature, a normal rule is unproblematic. It occurs; it is exhibited. It is not a guide because behaving consistently with it is a matter of fact, not of choice. Persons and objects have no options with respect to rules defined as regularities of nature; these rules are followed inexorably.

A normal rule may be verbalized or unverbalized. In the verbal form, a normal rule is a description of a purported regularity in nature; in the nonverbal form, it *is* the regularity in nature. (The conception of nonverbal normative rules is developed in the next subsection.) Like the regularity itself, a verbal normal rule is not a guide; it is only a description of a regularity. The regularity as such will occur whether or not it is described accurately or is described at all. However, behavior can be controlled by a description, whether or not the description is accurate. When a description has this function, it has become a normative rule. Normative rules—moral, practical, and juridical—are guides that are optional in the sense that they can be followed or ignored (Skinner, 1969, p. 148). Why they are followed or ignored is therefore a problem (the problem is discussed later, in the subsection "Rules as Causes").

4.1.4. Rules as Dispositions

Dispositional concepts are defined by if-then statements (Bergmann, 1957, p. 60; Fodor, 1981). Examples are brittleness and irascibility:

> Brittleness means that if an object that has this property is hit, then the object shatters.
> Irascibility means that if a person who has this property is provoked even slightly, then the person becomes angry.

A brittle object does not express brittleness unless it is hit, that is, it does not shatter unless hit; and an irascible person does not express irascibility—become angry—unless provoked.

The distinction between disposition and action is the same as Aristotle's distinction between *hexis* and *energeia* (or *entelecheia*): *Hexis* is a potentiality that could be actualized but is not presently actualized, that is, not presently expressed in action; *energeia* is present actualization, or action (Aristotle, *Nichomachean Ethics*, Book 1, Chapter 8; 1926, pp. 38, 39). The distinction is also the same as that between competence and performance when competence means ability or capacity rather than effectiveness or fitness. A disposition, then, is competence to perform in a specified way; performance is the actualization or application of competence.

In "logical behaviorism," according to Fodor, cognitive causation is bypassed by if-then dispositions. For example, "Smith is thirsty" means "if there were water [or orange juice, etc.] available, then Smith would drink some" (Fodor, 1981, pp. 115–116). Such dispositions refer to potential regularities, that is, *normal* rules, and they can be labeled "normal" dispositions. Other dispositions refer to *normative* rules and can be labeled "normative" dispositions.

4.1.4a. "Normal" Dispositions. As a regularity in nature, a rule is the concatenation of two (or more) sets of events and their interrelation(s), for example, one set of events regularly antecedent to another set of events. Concretely, as a regularity in nature the law of falling bodies refers to the antecedent event of removing whatever has been holding a body in place and the subsequent event of the body's falling. The law $s = \frac{1}{2}gt^2$ is a description of this regularity; it is not the regularity. It can govern the behavior of persons but not the behavior of falling bodies (Moore, 1981; Skinner, 1969, p. 141).

A rule of this kind is "obeyed" inexorably; when the antecedent set is sufficiently complete, it is regularly followed by the subsequent set, and the rule can be said to be an actualization. When the antecedent set is not sufficiently complete, the subsequent set does not occur, and the rule can be said to be a disposition instead of an actualization. The connection between the rule as a disposition and the rule as an actualization depends entirely on the physical completeness of the antecedent set of events. For example, the rules relating patterns of key pecking to schedules of reinforcement are regularities. The scallop in the rate of behavior controlled by a fixed interval schedule and the high rate of behavior controlled by a variable ratio schedule are not caused by the respective rules; they are part of these rules. The actual key pecking—the actualization—is not *controlled* or *governed* by the rule; it is an *instantiation* of the rule.

4.1.4b. "Normative" Dispositions. Normative dispositions refer to normative rules—moral, practical, and juridical rules, and rules as competence. A normative rule is always a disposition because the rule itself cannot be actualized but can only *lead to* actual behavior. The actualization of the rule for operating a forge bellows, for example, is not part of this rule; it is caused or occasioned by the rule, in conjunction with other setting conditions. In cognitive psychology, a normative rule is a cognitive activity that can be utilized by a person to control his or her own behavior. In behavior analysis, a normative rule functions as a stimulus that elicits respondent behavior or that occasions operant behavior, given particular setting conditions. It could have the latter function as a discriminative stimulus or as an "establishing operation," an "establishing stimulus" (Chase & Hyten, 1985; Michael, 1982), an "augmental" (Zettle & Hayes, 1982), or a "precurrent stimulus" (e.g., Parsons, Taylor, & Joyce, 1981).

4.1.5. Normative Rules

The connection between a normative disposition, or competence, and an actualization, or performance, depends on variables that are not specified in the rule itself. A normative rule is one element in an antecedent set (and researchers have not yet identified all the other elements in this set).

An example is the normative rule, "If a speaker asks for something a listener can give, and the listener gives it, then the speaker will return the favor some time." If a speaker asks a listener for a glass of water, this request, or mand, together with the normative rule may occasion the listener's giving the speaker a glass of water. However, enormous complexities are involved in the actualization of this normative rule. The listener must have a glass and water available; the rule must not be superceded by a conflicting rule, such as the listener's own rule to hoard all the available water; perhaps the listener must believe the speaker is a person who can be expected to return the favor; and so forth.

In behavior analysis, a normative rule in its complete form specifies a three-term contingency: In the presence of a specified discriminative stimulus, occurrence of a specified behavior will be consequated in a specified way (Skinner, 1969, p. 160). Often, however, normative rules are incomplete in that the consequence is not specified explicitly, or neither the discriminative stimulus nor the consequence is specified explicitly (p. 158). In these cases, the discriminative and/or consequent stimuli are presumably implied or intended to be implied. An example is "Whatsoever ye would that men should do to you, do ye even so to them" (*Matt.* vii 12). This rule specifies neither the occasions nor the consequences for the doing and, as Skinner noted, it also leaves the doing pretty much unspecified. It is nevertheless a rule, and for all I know it governs some people's behavior some of the time.

At least implicitly, a normative rule states an antecedent and a consequent, and thus it is at least implicitly an if-then statement. The antecedent is a condition and an action that might be taken—the discriminative stimulus and the behavior. The consequent is the outcome that can be expected—the consequent stimulus. "If this action is taken in this situation, then this outcome should occur." Any of these components, however, may be implicit, and indeed the if-then form may be implicit. The rule for operating a forge bellows is an example: The action is specified, but the condition, the outcome, and the if-then form are all implicit. The Golden Rule is another example. These rules do not have the if-then structure on the surface, but one might say they have the deep structure of an if-then statement.

4.2. Knowing Rules

The concepts of *knowing* and *remembering* have posed problems for psychologists and philosophers, in part because of the felt need to postulate a trace of some kind and a locus for the trace in order to provide a physical basis for the knowledge or memory. The discussion herein is limited to one aspect of the problem, involving distinctions between "knowing that" and "knowing how."

4.2.1. Knowing That versus Knowing How

Consider the following two anecdotes:

1. I can describe how to drive a golf ball, in the sense that I can describe the component movements (and nonmovement with respect to my head) and how they are coordinated. However, the outcomes of my actual attempts to drive the ball are unpredictable.
2. I can transform any sentence from the active to the passive voice and vice versa. However, I cannot state a grammatical rule that covers all active/passive transformations—and evidently neither can the linguists (cf. Slobin, 1979, p. 5).

The distinction made in these two anecdotes is between knowing in a cognitive way and knowing in a behavioral way. The former is called *knowing that;* the latter is called *knowing how*. Alternatively: *knowing about things* versus *knowing how to do things* (Parrott, 1983) or *describing contingencies* versus *performing in accordance with them* (Matthews, Catania, & Shimoff, 1985, p. 155).

"Knowing that" refers to verbally expressed facts or information; "knowing how" refers to behavior. Hineline (1983) equated knowing that with tacting, in Skinner's (1957) sense, and knowing how with behaving. In cognitive psychology, "knowing that" refers to "declarative knowledge," and "knowing how" refers to "procedural knowledge," or "cognitive skill" (Anderson, 1980, p. 223, 1982; Cohen, 1984). These and other meanings of "knowing that" and "knowing how" are listed in Table 1. The postulation of a memory trace is strongly tempting in the case of "knowing that" but not in the case of "knowing how" (Coulter, 1983, p. 78; Skinner, 1969, p. 170).

Table 1
Knowing That and Knowing How

Knowing that	Knowing how
Cognitive knowing	Behavioral knowing
Knowing about things	Knowing how to do things
Describing contingencies	Performing in accordance with contingencies
Facts, information	Behavior
Tacting	Behaving
Declarative knowledge	Procedural knowledge, cognitive skill
Knowing a rule	Knowing a rule (behaving consistently with a rule)
Description of a regularity in performance	Regularity in performance
Stating a rule	Exhibiting know-how
Effects of discriminative stimuli (?)	Effects of contingencies
Symbolic representation of a learned capability	Learned capability
Information capability	Performance capability
Being able to state a rule	Behaving consistently with a rule
Normative disposition or rule	Normal disposition or rule
Not causal	Not causal

4.2.2. Rule Knowledge

In one sense, knowing a rule is "knowing that," and one can "know how" without "knowing that" (Miller, 1981, p. 3). That is, one can exhibit a regularity in performance (knowing how) without being able to describe the regularity (knowing that; knowing the rule).

In another sense, knowing a rule is "knowing how." A normal rule is a regularity in nature, as already noted. Knowing a rule can mean behaving consistently with the rule (Gagné, 1970, p. 57). However, in this case, behaving consistently with the rule is not a *result* of knowing the rule because "knowing the rule" in this sense is not itself any kind of behavior—it is only a descriptive phrase.

"Stating a rule" is also a descriptive phrase, but it is defined independently of behaving consistently with the rule. Stating a rule is verbal behavior, and it can affect other behavior. The stated rule is not the regularity in nature, however; it is a description of the regularity. As Skinner (1969) noted:

> Discriminative stimuli which improve the efficiency of behavior under given contingencies of reinforcement . . . must not be confused with the contingencies themselves, nor their effects with the effects of those contingencies. (p. 124)

The kind of confusion Skinner referred to is reflected in Chomsky's statement, "The child who learns a language has in some sense constructed the grammar for himself'' (quoted in Skinner, 1969, p. 124, from Chomsky, 1959, p. 57). Skinner commented that this statement ''is as misleading as to say that a dog which has learned to catch a ball has in some sense constructed the relevant part of the science of mechanics'' (p. 124).

According to Gagné (1974):

> The statement of a rule is merely the representation of it—the rule itself is a learned capability of an individual learner. We say that a learner has learned a rule when he can ''follow it'' in his performances. In other words, a rule is a learned capability which makes it possible for the individual to *do* something, using symbols (most commonly, the symbols of language and mathematics). The capability of doing something must be carefully distinguished from *stating* something, which is the information capability [i.e., a concept]. (p. 61)

In short, knowing a rule means either being able to state the rule (knowing that) or being able to behave consistently with the rule (knowing how). (''Being able'' is used here so that the statement refers to dispositions as well as actualizations. Cognitive abilities or capacities are not implied.)

Knowing a rule in the first sense (being able to state it) cannot by itself cause behavior; it can be at most only a normative disposition to behave. Likewise, knowing a rule in the second sense (behaving consistently with it) cannot cause behavior because knowing a rule in this sense is only an assertion that a normal disposition has been actualized. Nevertheless, rules can be legitimately conceptualized as causes: A normative rule (knowing that) can cause behavior by being applied, and a normal rule (knowing how) can cause behavior by being instantiated. However, conceptualizing rules as causes hides the need to understand how ''being applied'' and ''being instantiated'' are accomplished. These issues are beyond the scope of the present chapter.

4.2.3. *Rule Acquisition*

Some behaviorists point out that a rule is not a ''possession'' that can be ''acquired,'' but they are quibbling about words. ''Acquiring a rule'' has never, as far as I know, been used by psychologists to mean anything other than ''learning a rule.'' ''Forming a rule'' and ''developing a rule'' are also synonyms of ''learning a rule.'' The result of acquiring/learning/forming/developing a rule is either ''knowing that'' or ''knowing how.'' Nothing else is meant.

5. RULES AS CAUSES

The issues considered in the present section are whether any rules are optional, what they control, and how their effects differ from the effects of contingencies.

5.1. Why Obey Rules?

Most cognitive psychologists have ignored the question of why rules are followed; and most behaviorists who have considered the question have given the pat answer that rules are followed because following them is reinforced (without specifying the reinforcer) or because following rules has a history of reinforcement (without empirically demonstrating the reality of the purported history). The question is important and deserves empirical as well as theoretical attention. Work by Malott (e.g., 1982, 1986) illustrates what needs to be done. Work by Hayes and colleagues (e.g., Zettle & Hayes, 1982) on "pliance" may also be relevant. (However, the defining feature of pliance is that it is "under the control of apparent speaker-mediated consequences for following the rule" [Zettle & Hayes, 1982, p. 80]. Evidently, the consequence could be implicit in the rule rather than explicit.)

5.1.1. Role of Consequences

Skinner (1982) suggested that "most students study to avoid the consequences of not studying" (p. 4). However, Malott (1982) has argued that more immediate consequences are needed. Malott analyzed rules that appear to be "weak" because the specified consequence is far in the future. In addition to studying, examples include doing homework assignments and flossing teeth. Rules that specify the discriminative stimulus, the behavior, and the consequence may be more effective than our usual rules, which specify these components only vaguely; but the actual reinforcer for rule-following may not be the consequence that is specified in the rule. Malott suggested that rule-following is an escape procedure. An implication is that the functional consequence is not the one specified in the rule, such as the good grades that will result from studying and doing homework assignments or the sound teeth that will result from flossing, or the bad grades that will result from not studying and not doing homework assignments or the cavities and tooth loss that will result from not flossing. Rather, the functional consequences may be a negative reinforcer; rule-following terminates self-blame, guilt, anxiety, or some other private event and thereby is reinforced.

Riegler, Kohler, and Baer (1985) suggested that rules are obeyed because of "the development of a behavior class describable as *compliance with instructions*" (p. 3), which reflects generalization (1) from rules paired with reinforcement for compliance, to rules not previously paired with reinforcement for compliance; (2) from rule-staters and instruction givers who reinforce compliance, to rule-staters and instruction givers who have not previously reinforced compliance; and (3) from self-produced rules paired with reinforcement for compliance, to self-produced rules not previously paired with reinforcement for compliance. As Riegler *et al.* pointed out, this conceptualization suggests that the analysis of rule-governed behavior might be furthered by use of paradigms from the areas of compliance training, correspondence training (between saying and doing), and self-instruction training.

The question of interest to a behavior analyst is whether compliance, correspondence, and self-instruction training produce generalized compliance. If they do, the question of interest to a cognitive psychologist is *why* they do: What cognitive activities can plausibly be affected by the training and can plausibly lead to generalized compliance?

5.1.2. Are Any Rules Optional?

Skinner (1978) said that if human behavior is controlled by reinforcement and punishment rather than by free will, then it will be so controlled regardless of whether the human believes in the principles of reinforcement and punishment or believes in free will. Alternatively, however, if human behavior is controlled by free will rather than by reinforcement and punishment, then it will be so controlled whatever the human believes. The issue is about normative rules that are *sometimes* functional. Why is such a rule sometimes functional and sometimes nonfunctional? In every relevant scientific theory, the choice is assumed to be determined rather than a matter of free will. It is determined by the context in which the choice occurs, including the history of the individual and the present internal and external circumstances. A rule is optional only in the sense that present knowledge does not permit accurate prediction and effective control of when the rule if functional.

5.2. What Is Controlled?

As Skinner (1969) said, "The formula $s = \frac{1}{2}gt^2$ does not govern the behavior of falling bodies, it governs those who correctly predict the position of falling bodies at given times" (p. 141; see also Moore, 1981). In the terms used herein, the formula is a normal rule of the descriptive type when it is used to describe the rule-as-regularity of falling bodies; and when it governs those making predictions, it is a normative rule.

5.2.1. Locus of a Rule

Skinner (1977b) noted that the processes of association, abstraction, and the like are in the experiment, not in the research participant. Rules are also in the design of the experiment and may or may not be in the research participant. For example, Nissen (1953) discussed an "if-then" mechanism that could explain performance in conditional-discrimination and other stimulus-patterning tasks (e.g., if *red,* then choose *square;* if *green,* then choose *circle*). However, the if-then relation is in the task, not necessarily in the research participant.

In the conditional-discrimination task, two-dimensional stimuli are presented, and the correct choice is determined by the conjunction of two conditional rules:

(If A, then B) and (if a, then b)

where *A* and *a* refer to the *presence* of alternative values on one dimension and *B* and *b* refer to the *choice* of alternative values on another dimension. Children as young as 5 years of age can solve the conditional-discrimination task (e.g., Doan & Cooper, 1971), but children do not fully understand the verbal if-then rule until teen age (O'Brien & Overton, 1982), perhaps late teen age (Overton, Byrnes, & O'Brien, 1985). Evidently, young children can recognize a conditional regularity before they understand a verbal description of conditional regularities. The verbal if-then rule—"knowing that"—therefore seems to be not in the young child but in the experimenter.

5.2.2. Description or Control?

According to Searle (1976), "the rules of language are not like the laws of physics, for the rules must do more than describe what happens, they must play a role in guiding behavior" (p. 1120). Chomsky (1980) agreed: "The rules of grammar are mentally represented and used in thought and behavior" (p. 129). (However, Chomsky disagreed with Searle on some other points.)

Actually, the rules of language might be like the laws of physics, descriptions of regularities in nature—in this case regularities in language. Speakers exhibit regularities in language use, and linguists describe these regularities. The relevant rules are normal: Rules as regularities are exhibited in language use, and rules as descriptions are induced by linguists. The issue is whether the regularities are guided by normative rules (which presumably resemble the normal descriptive rules). Even mature speakers cannot state all the rules of grammar that linguists infer they use (Searle, 1976; Slobin, 1979, p. 5). Therefore, at least some of the rules are normal rather than normative; or put more weakly, at least some of the rules can be normal and need not be assumed to be normative.

Of course, once a normative rule has been formulated, it can control behavior. As Skinner (1969) said, "One may upon occasion speak grammatically by applying rules" (p. 162). Furthermore, even young children are amused by word play in which the rules of language are violated (Shultz & Robillard, 1980). If a rule is deliberately violated, it must be normative—a normal rule cannot be deliberately violated (otherwise, it would not be a *normal* rule). Therefore, even young children must understand some normative rules of language. However, their understanding may be vague or intuitive (Shultz & Robillard, 1980) rather than verbally formulated. Furthermore, their ordinary language may reflect normal rules rather than normative ones.

5.3. Are Rule-Governance and Contingency Shaping Different?

A distinction is made between rule-governance and contingency shaping, obviously, but the precise nature of the distinction has been unclear. In fact, Schnaitter (1977) suggested that rule-governance is really contingency shaping (see also Bentall, Lowe, & Beasty, 1985); and Brownstein and Shull (1985) argued that *rule-governed* is not a technical term and does not imply the existence of any behavior analytic principles different from those involved in contingency shaping. The distinction between the processes is discussed briefly and inconclusively below, then rule-governed and contingency-shaped behaviors are considered, and finally, "instructed" and "shaped" rules are discussed.

5.3.1. The Processes

Contingency shaping is operant behavior, but this behavior is by the shaper and not by the shapee. In the shapee, contingency shaping—or contingency governance (Catania, Matthews, & Shimoff, 1982)—is a function. It is a function of contingent stimuli. Rule-governance is also a function, but unlike contingency shaping, it is presumably not a *basic* function. That is, unlike contingency shaping, which according to Skinner works because it evolved through natural selection (1974, Chapter 3; 1984), rule-governance is an acquired function rather than a genetically determined function. How is the rule-governance function acquired?

One explanation of rule-governance is that "we tend to follow [rules] because previous behavior in response to similar verbal stimuli has been reinforced" (Skinner, 1969, p. 148; the bracketed word *rules* is substituted for Skinner's word *advice*). Or, without the unsupported assumption of stimulus similarity, "We tend to follow rules because we have been reinforced for following rules in the past." This explanation is very abstract because it requires defining "following rules" as an operant behavior. Such an operant can have no topography of its own (Baron & Galizio, 1983); it is a behavior class that includes all of a person's behaviors that have been or will be rule-governed. It is everything, and therefore it is nothing—it is all behaviors, not any one behavior.

The conception of rule-governance as an operant behavior, or as any other kind of behavior, is therefore unsatisfying. I do not have a better solution, or even an alternative one, and neither do the cognitivists. (In fact, Brainerd [1977] pointed out that cognitivists have ignored the possibility that cognitive development is contingency-shaped rather than rule-governed. In a commentary on Brainerd's article, Bickhard, Cooper, and Mace [1985] asserted that "a rule-governed learning model does not deny the facts of contingency-shaped learning. On the contrary, rule-governed learning models incorporate the facts of contingency-shaped learning as the learning of certain (rather simple) rules" [p. 252]. However, contrary to Bickhard *et al.* and in agreement with Brainerd, one could argue that contingency shaping underlies "discovery," which is the basis for cognitive development in Piaget's rule-governed learning model, and that cognitivists have overlooked this role of contingency shaping. Nevertheless, Bickhard *et al.* proposed a valuable refinement of the issues: Is contingency shaping involved in the development of complex as well as simple rules? Does contingency shaping have cognitive prerequisites? Are the cognitive prerequisites rules? Are the cognitive prerequisites organized as stages?)

The problem of whether rule-governance is behavior remains to be solved. It is a particularly intriguing problem because even though "following rules" is not an operant behavior, it is functionally like operant behavior in that it can be brought under schedule control—reinforcement, punishment, discrimination (Baron & Galizio, 1983).

5.3.2. Rule-Governed and Contingency-Shaped Behavior

All behaviors that are regular are rule-governed, either in the sense of control by a normative rule or in the sense of instantiation of a normal rule. To avoid this trivialization of the adjective, *rule-governed* is used herein to refer to the first sense and *contingency-shaped* is used to refer to the second sense. (I am ignoring innate behavior, which is rule-governed in the second sense but determined by genetic factors rather than by contingencies.)

Rule-governed behavior and contingency-shaped behavior are different operants:

> Rule-governed behavior is . . . never exactly like the behavior shaped by contingencies. . . . When operant experiments with human subjects are simplified by instructing the subjects in the operation of the equipment . . ., the resulting behavior may resemble that which follows exposure to the contingencies and may be studied in its stead for certain purposes, but the controlling variables are different, and the behaviors will not necessarily change in the same way in response to other variables. (Skinner, 1969, pp. 150–151)

(For further discussion of differences between rule-governed and contingency-shaped behavior, see Skinner, 1969, Chapter 6.)

Luria (1981) described a phenomenon that can be interpreted to reflect rule-governed versus contingency-shaped speech:

> For some people word meaning does not evolve on the basis of contextualized speech (i.e., in live communication), but consists of acquiring the dictionary meanings of

> individual words. In those instances, there may be considerable difficulty in comprehending the meanings of words in actual communication. Perhaps the most striking instance of this phenomenon is word comprehension by deaf-mute individuals for whom word meaning does not evolve as a result of participating in live communication. A deaf-mute child learns word meaning by acquiring individual words. . . . Similar phenomena occur in the learning of a foreign language, a process that begins not with contextual speech, but with the dictionary meaning of individual words. (p. 176)

Hineline (1983) made the same point: "A native speaker of German is not following the rules of a grammar book as is the language student who is following those rules" (p. 184). Speech acquired through "live communication" is contingency-shaped; speech acquired through the dictionary is rule-governed.

Baron and Galizio (1983) and Hayes, Brownstein, Haas, and Greenway (1985) made a similar point in noting that schedule sensitivity can be mimicked by following a rule but that the rule-governed behavior will generally be insensitive to changes in the schedule. (I can imagine, however, a complex rule that could produce behavior that mimicked sensitivity to schedule changes, provided the schedule changes are signaled in some way.)

Skinner (1977a) has argued:

> Behavior that consists of following rules is inferior to behavior shaped by the contingencies described by the rules. Thus, we may learn to operate a piece of equipment by following instructions, but we operate it skillfully only when our behavior has been shaped by its effect on the equipment. The instructions are soon forgotten. (p. 86; p. 12 in 1978 reprint; italics deleted)

This argument provides support for the familiar "learn-by-doing" dictum.

5.3.3. *Instructed and Shaped Rules*

In a learning situation, the relation between rules and performance should be interactive in the sense of Mao Zedong's (1937/1965) practice–theory–practice dialectic. Practice, in the sense of behaving, experimenting, and so on, leads to theory, in the sense of rules, knowledge, and so on, which in turn leads to changed behaving, experimenting, and so on, which leads to changed rules, knowledge, and so on—and on and on. In other words, rules are abstracted or induced from practice and then they change the practice, and the changed practice leads to changes in the rules, and so forth.

In the practice–theory–practice dialectic, the development of rules is contingency-shaped. The rule-governed behavior exhibited in the practice is not perfectly adaptive, and the feedback functions as a contingency that shapes modifications that improve the adaptiveness of the rule. Because rule-governed behavior is inferior to contingency-shaped behavior and because rules that govern behavior are themselves behaviors, one might expect rule-governed *rules* to be less effective than contingency-shaped rules. Catania *et al.* (1982) confirmed this expectation: Shaped verbal rules controlled nonverbal behavior more reliably than did instructed rules. Thus, the learn-by-doing dictum is supported with respect to rules as well as with respect to other behaviors.

A cognitivist might hypothesize that a person is more likely to believe shaped rules because they are discovered rather than taught. Discovery, according to cognitivists, yields understanding, and instruction yields mere information. Understanding is retained; information is forgotten. (This distinction was endorsed by St. Augustine [*De Diversis Quaestionibus,* Quaestio IX], St. Thomas Aquinas [*Summa Theologica,* Pt. 1, Question 84, Article 6], Piaget [e.g., Aebli, 1979; Furth & Wachs, 1974, Chapter 1; Pulaski, 1971, Chapter 18], and others.)

In addition to the general superiority of shaped rules over instructed rules, shaped rules in a psychological experiment might be superior because the research participants are suspicious of instructed rules. In the study by Catania *et al.* (1982), the participant might well have thought that the experimenter must have been using deception in saying, for example, "Write 'press fast' for the left button and write 'press slowly' for the right button." The participants might therefore have inferred that the schedules were the same for both buttons.

Any given instructed rule may or may not accord with reality, that is, it may or may not be an accurate description of natural contingencies. However, the received opinion among cognitivists is that the effectiveness of an instructed rule in controlling behavior depends less on its being accurate than on its being believed to be accurate. As Thomas and Thomas (1928) said, "If men define situations as real, they are real in their consequences" (p. 572). (Thomas's editor commented that this sentence is "one of the most quoted in the literature on social relations" [Thomas, 1951, footnote 14, p. 81]. The same point was made by Karl Marx, Sigmund Freud, and others, according to Merton [1968, p. 475], and also by Anaxagoras: "There is also recorded a saying of Anaxagoras to some of his disciples, that things would be for them as they judged them to be" [Aristotle, *Metaphysics,* Book 4, Chapter 5, 1009b 25–26; 1933, p. 187].)

6. INFERRING RULE USE

The question of concern in the present section is how an observer can know that another person is using a rule. The answer that is developed is that inference is required but that it is based on objective evidence. The first of three major subsections deals with the need for and nature of inference, the next explicates six criteria on which relevant inferences can be based, and the third summarizes evidence about spontaneously learned rules.

6.1. Inferences and Observations

The present subsection deals with objectively unobservable events and problems associated with making scientifically acceptable statements about them in the cognitive and behavioristic approaches. A major part deals with the nature of inference, which is the basis for all scientific statements about objectively unobservable events.

6.1.1. Objectively Unobservable Events

An event is said to be objectively observable if its occurrence can be verified by independent observers—Pepper's concept of "multiplicative corroboration" (1942, Chapter 3). Otherwise, it is an "objectively unobservable event." Objectively unobservable events are dealt with in both cognitive psychology and behaviorism; they are usually conceptualized as cognitive activities in cognitive psychology and as covert behaviors in behaviorism. However, cognitive "activities" are identified as *activities,* and covert "behaviors" are identified as *behaviors* by definition—by fiat—not as a consequence of objective observation in the sense of independent verification. Overt activities and behaviors are objectively observable in the sense of independent verifiability, but covert activities and behaviors are not objectively observable in this sense because only first-person observation is possible.

Covert activities/behaviors are therefore not at the same level of observation as overt activities/behaviors. They may not even have the same relationships to other variables, and they cannot be made to have the same relationships by fiat, such as the assertion by Morris, Higgins, and Bickel (1982), among similar assertions by many other behaviorists, that "covert activity is not qualitatively different from overt activity; it is only inaccessible" (p. 115). That is, covert activities/behaviors are necessarily subjective and no direct objective evidence can be marshaled to support their being qualitatively the same as overt activities or behaviors. However, indirect objective evidence is often available.

6.1.1a. Indirect Objective Evidence. Some objectively unobservable events have objectively observable concomitants. For example, different brain potentials are evoked by bright versus dim flashes of light, and when expectancies are manipulated such that research participants expect to see a bright or dim flash, the potential evoked by a middle-bright flash varies in agreement with the expected brightness. Furthermore, research participants report seeing the middle-bright flash as a bright or dim flash consistently with the expectation and with the evoked potential (Begleiter, Porjesz, Yerre, & Kissin, 1973). The evoked brain potentials and the verbal reports can be interpreted as concomitant evidence about perception, which is itself not objectively observable. Although the evoked potentials and the reports of seeing are objectively observable, the *seeing* is a private event and is not objectively observable. A verbal report about the seeing is said to be subjective because its referent is not objectively verifiable.

Because first-person reports about objectively unobservable events are subjective, their truth cannot be evaluated on the basis of the "truth-by-agreement" criterion (Pepper's criterion of "multiplicative corroboration"). Therefore, their truth must be evaluated on some other basis. Skinner (1945) adopted the pragmatic criterion of truth by successful working, in opposition to the criterion of truth by agreement:

> The ultimate criterion for the goodness of a concept is not whether two people are brought into agreement but whether the scientist who uses the concept can operate successfully upon his material—all by himself if need be. What matters to Robinson Crusoe is not whether he is agreeing with himself but whether he is getting anywhere with his control over nature. (p. 293)

Objectively unobservable events can be hypothesized to have particular overt behavioral concomitants or to generate particular observable products, and the relationships of these to other observable variables can be objectively analyzed. (Objectively unobservable events that are not hypothesized to have any overt concomitants or products would be of no interest to cognitive psychologists or behaviorists and consequently need not be considered.) If the observed relationships are expectable on the basis of hypothesized relationships to objectively unobservable events, then statements about these events have a truth value based on the pragmatic truth criterion (consistent with Pepper's "structural corroboration" [1942, Chapter 3] and Kaplan's "pattern model" of explanation [1964, p. 332]).

The fact that cognitive activities are not objectively observable is therefore no more a problem for cognitive psychologists than is the objective unobservability of covert behaviors for behaviorists. Incidentally, anyone who takes seriously the argument that first-person observation of cognitive activities or covert behaviors makes these events objective in a scientifically acceptable sense should read Freud and other literature on self-deception, misinterpretation, secondary elaboration, illusion, and so on, as well as the debate on the possibility of even first-person observation of cognitive activities (references for this debate were given earlier, in the discussion of "Conscious Effort" in the subsection "Characteristics of Cognitive Activities"). The appropriate interpretation of such first-person observation, including verbal self-report or introspective report, is that it may accompany objectively unobservable events.

6.1.1b. Ephemerality. Evidence about the concomitants and products of cognitive activities has led cognitive psychologists to conclude that these activities have very brief durations. However, being ephemeral is not a problem because they are hypothesized to have products that are sufficiently long-lived to permit leisurely observation. Similarly, Skinner (1969) commented that overt behaviors are ephemeral—and insubstantial (p. 160)—but that they yield records that can be studied.

A cognitive example is mentally scanning a short list of digits in short-term memory; the scanning can occur at a rate of 38 msec per digit or, after extensive experience, at a rate of around 8 to 9 msec per digit (Seamon, 1980, pp. 179–180). A behavioral example is a single key peck under control of a thin variable ratio schedule: Ferster and Skinner (1957) observed local rates as high as 10 pecks per sec (100 msec per peck) on VR 360, although around 4 pecks per sec (250 msec per peck) was more usual (pp. 393–397). One peck occurs too quickly to be observed directly with enough reliability to yield a useful analysis, but its usual product is an increment on a cumulative record that is reliably analyzable. A high-speed photographic record would also be reliably analyzable.

6.1.2. The Nature of Inference

The use of a rule is an objectively unobservable event, but if use of a rule is hypothesized to have a particular effect on behavior or to yield a particular product, then observing this effect is considered to justify the inference that the rule was used.

6.1.2a. Inference versus Induction. Inference is not the same as post hoc induction. An example of the latter is found in an article by Brewer (1974). Brewer concluded that the evidence on operant and classical conditioning of human adults was unconvincing. He was able to reach this conclusion partly because he invented built-in mechanisms (the workhorse of many cognitivists) to explain away any supporting evidence. (Also, as Dulaney [1974] noted, Brewer's coverage of the relevant literature was selective.) Thus: "In classical autonomic conditioning, once [the subject] has developed a hypothesis about the CS-UCS relationship, a built-in system is brought into operation, so that [the subject's] expectation of shock or food automatically produces the autonomic response" (p. 2). This induction is merely a reworded description of the observed phenomenon, and it has no cognitive value in the absence of independent evidence for the "built-in system."

Even without this kind of post hoc circularity, inferences are problematic—instead of being merely empty, they can be wrong. Nevertheless, they are necessary for making statements about the occurrence of objectively unobservable events—despite arguments by some behavior analysts (e.g., Moore, 1984; Skinner, 1945) against reliance on formal logic. (Schnaitter, 1985, commented that most behavior analysts do not reject mathematical principles, even though the same arguments are relevant.)

Table 2
Affirming the Consequent (Rows 1–2) and Denying the Consequent (Rows 3–4) in an "Hypothetical Syllogism"

1	2	3	4	5	6	7	8
Row	X	Y	If X then Y	Y	(If X then Y) and Y	A	If (6) then (A)
1	T	T	T	T	T	T	T
2	F	T	T	T	T	F	F
3	F	F	T	F	F	T	T
4	T	F	F	F	F	F	T

Note. For convenience, Column 5 repeats Column 3. In Column 7, "A" refers to X in Rows 1–2 and not-X in Rows 3–4; therefore, in Rows 1–2 the truth values of A are the same as for X in Column 2, and in Rows 3–4 they are the negations of those for X in Column 2. The statement symbolized in Column 8 is "If [(if X then Y) and Y] then A." The truth values in Columns 4 and 8 reflect the standard definition of the conditional ("if, then") relation; those in Column 6 reflect the standard definition of the conjunctive ("and") relation.

6.1.2b. The "Hypothetical Syllogism." The inference that a rule was or was not used has the form of an "hypothetical syllogism" (Werkmeister, 1948, pp. 346–352, 396). The hypothesis is the major premise, the observation is the minor premise, and the inference about rule use is the conclusion. For example:

Major premise	If Rule X is used, Performance Y will be observed.
Minor premise	Performance Y is observed.
Conclusion	Rule X was used.

This is the logical *fallacy of affirming the consequent;* it is a fallacy because the consequent (Y) in the major premise can be true whether the antecedent (X) is true or false. In the form of a statement, the hypothetical syllogism in the example is:

If [(If Rule X is used, then Performance Y will be observed) and (Performance Y is observed)], then Rule X was used.

Symbolically, the hypothetical syllogism in statement form is:

If [(If X then Y) and Y] then X.

As shown in Rows 1 and 2 in Table 2, the statement is true only if X is true. In other words, affirming the consequent is valid only if the antecedent (X) is already known to be true. However, the truth of the antecedent is exactly the issue in question.

In contrast, if the predicted performance does not occur (−Y), the inference that the rule was not used (−X) is logically justified. As shown in Rows 3 and 4 in Table 2, this statement is true under all conditions; therefore, the argument—called denying the consequent—is valid. However, the inference that the rule was not used is not necessarily justified *psychologically*. As can be seen in Row 4, the *argument* is valid even if in fact the rule was used. The argument is valid in this case because it is based on a false major premise (that is, "If X then Y" is false, as shown in Row 4, Column 4).

For example, in memory tasks, young children often perform as though they do not use mnemonic strategies (Kail, 1979, Chapter 2), that is, they often perform as though their behavior is not rule-governed. However, inferring that they do not use rules is not necessarily justified; they may use rules but use them so inconsistently or inefficiently that their performance is nothing like that predicted to result from use of rules (Miller, Haynes, DeMarie-Dreblow, & Woody-Ramsey, 1986; Siegler, 1981). (Actually, they do use a number of rules—Kail, 1979, pp. 29–32; Shultz, Fisher, Pratt, & Rulf, 1986.)

The flaw in the logically valid argument is that the major premise—the hypothesized effect of rule use—may be false. The following hypothetical syllogism illustrates the point.

Major premise	If rehearsal is used in a free-recall task, then a primacy effect will be obtained.
Minor premise	A primacy effect was not obtained.
Conclusion	Rehearsal was not used.

The major premise can be derived from many cognitive theories of memory—for example, rehearsed items are transferred to long-term storage, but the capacity of "working memory" is so limited that only the initial items can be rehearsed, and therefore only the initial items are stored in long-term memory. However, for young children the major premise may be false; they may use rehearsal so inefficiently that rehearsed items are not transferred to long-term storage; hence no primacy effect is produced even though they rehearsed.

Incidentally, this illustrative hypothetical syllogism can also be used to show why inferences based on affirming the consequent are problematic. Even if the major premise is true, it is not the only theoretically justified premise. For example, a primacy effect could reflect proactive interference: The learning of the early items is not facilitated, but rather this learning interferes with the learning of the later items. (For brief discussion of the primacy effect and the cognitive and learning explanations, see Kausler, 1974, pp. 392–397. I suspect that the primacy effect in animals [e.g., Buchanan, Gill, & Braggio, 1981; Sands & Wright, 1980; Wright, Santiago, Sands, Kendrick, & Cook, 1985] reflects the learning mechanism and that in humans it reflects the cognitive mechanism.)

Another example is speaking grammatically. As Skinner (1969) said:

> One may speak grammatically under the contingencies maintained by a verbal community without "knowing the rules of grammar" in any other sense, but once these contingencies have been discovered and grammatical rules formulated, one may upon occasion speak grammatically by applying rules. (p. 162)

This distinction implies two possible major premises and hence two possible inferences:

Major premise 1	If speaking grammatically is contingency-shaped, then normal children reared in a normal environment will speak grammatically (on some occasions).
Major premise 2	If speaking grammatically is rule-governed, then normal children reared in a normal environment will speak grammatically (on some occasions).
Minor premise	Normal children reared in a normal environment are observed to speak grammatically (on some occasions).

Given the first major premise and the minor premise, the reasonable inference (conclusion) is that speaking grammatically is contingency-shaped. According to this inference, speaking grammatically reflects a normal rule—a regularity in nature. In contrast, given the second major premise and the minor premise, the reasonable inference if that speaking grammatically is rule-governed. According to this inference, speaking grammatically reflects a normative rule.

Because of the possibility of these two inferences, some further evidence or argument is needed to justify inferring that the observed behavior or product reflects a normative rule. However, any relevant further evidence will be tentative because the further evidence will be relevant only if it implicates a rule, and the rule it implicates will also need to be inferred. Further *argument* may be more convincing than further *evidence*, if the further argument provides a theoretical basis for the major premise that is adopted (this point is discussed further later, in the section entitled "The Role of Theory").

6.1.2c. "Objective Inference." The foregoing discussion indicates that any conclusion about the use of a rule depends on inference, and in psychology the inference is always based on the argument of affirming the consequent or denying the consequent. However, the discussion showed that both of these arguments can yield false conclusions because affirming the consequent is logically fallacious and denying the consequent depends on knowing that the major premise is true.

Some psychologists seem to believe that "objective inference" avoids this subjectivity. However, even objective inference is fallible. Objective inference is based on syllogistic reasoning of the "hypothetical" form, with the stipulation that the premises refer to observed behavior. Mackenzie (1977) expressed the form as follows:

> If a particular capacity . . . is necessary for the performance of an action, and if the [agent] performs the action, then the capacity can be inferred. (p. 64; *agent* is substituted for Mackenzie's word, *animal*)

Mackenzie contrasted objective inference with "subjective inference," by which he meant inferring the mental life of animals by analogy to human mental life, specifically the mental life of the observer (pp. 56–63). Subjective inference would probably better be called subjective speculation; it seems to be the same as anthropomorphizing and the old sociological method of *Verstehen* (Abel, 1948/1953). It is not used in modern cognitive psychology.

However, the point is not that objective inference should not be used but that it should be used with full realization that it can yield false conclusions. In other words, inferences about rule use are always tentative.

6.1.2d. The Role of Theory. The inference that a rule was used is based on an hypothesis about how use of the rule affects performance. Such an hypothesis cannot be compelling, nor the subsequent inference persuasive, unless the hypothesis has a theoretical basis. Although the need for theory is seen as an impediment by some behavior analysts, Skinner himself has emphasized that much of his own work is theoretical (1969, pp. vii–xii).

In fact, inference always involves at least a simple, low-level theory (Reese, 1971, 1986). The reason is that scientists are seldom if ever interested in their literal manipulations and observations. These phenomena are part of the *methodological* domain, but the real interest is in phenomena in the *theoretical* domain (as Rychlak, 1976, distinguished between these domains). The methodological domain is the domain of independent and dependent variables; the theoretical domain is the domain of causes and effects. Such a distinction is reflected in Cook and Campbell's (1979, Chapter 2) distinction between internal validity and construct validity: Internal validity is established by showing that "extraneous" independent variables do not vary systematically with the independent variable of interest; construct validity is established by arguing persuasively that the theoretical interpretations of the independent and dependent variables are appropriate.

The following statement is illustrative:

> If a particular stimulus (S^D) precedes a particular behavior, and if given this behavior another particular stimulus (S^R) is now less probable, and if the rate of the behavior in the presence of S^D increases, then S^R is a negative reinforcer.

This is, of course, the behavior analytic definition of "negative reinforcer" (incidentally, most psychologists outside behavior analysis are evidently ignorant of this definition—Moore, 1984). The point is that the statement refers not to the methodological domain but to the theoretical domain, because "stimuli" and "behaviors" are not events in the real world, they are interpretations of events in the real world. Furthermore, the definition of "negative reinforcer" cannot be meaningfully isolated from its relations to other theoretical concepts such as *operant behavior* and *schedule control.*

6.1.3. Mentalism

According to the *Oxford English Dictionary,* the major meanings of *mental* are:

1. Of or pertaining to the mind.
2. Carried on or performed by the mind. Mental arithmetic.
3. Relating to the mind as an object of study; concerned with the phenomena of mind (*Oxford,* 1933, Vol. 6, p. 341).

Many behavior analysts reject these meanings and use *mentalistic* as a technical term. For example, Moore (1981) characterized mentalism as follows:

> (a) the bifurcation of human experience into a behavioral dimension and a pre-behavioral dimension, (b) the use of psychological terms to refer to organo-centric entities from the pre-behavioral dimension, and (c) the use of the organo-centric entities as causally effective antecedents in explaining the behavior. (p. 62)

More generally among behavior analysts, mentalism means making statements about any domain that is inferred to be related to observed behavior but that is different from the domain of observed behavior.

6.1.3a. Mentalistic Theories. The use of either of the foregoing technical senses has led some behavior analysts to identify some theories as mentalistic that are not mentalistic in the dictionary senses. Theories that include hypothetical constructs such as *mediating responses* are mentalistic in the technical sense but not in the dictionary senses. Piaget's theory is mentalistic in all these senses. The use of "mentalistic" to name the technical senses can be misleading, but this use is reasonable and clear if one keeps in mind that "mentalistic" in the technical senses refers to mental activity of observers and theorists (Skinner, 1969, pp. 237–238) and not necessarily to postulated mental activities in the theories they invent.

In the discussion in the rest of the present subsection, *mentalism* is used in the more general technical sense, referring to explanations that include causes from a domain other than the domain observed. The discussion is limited to "hard mentalism," that is, mentalistic statements that are "objective inferences."

6.1.3b. Inferred versus Observed Domains. Behavior analysts reject mentalism (in the sense described above) because, as Morris *et al.* (1982) put it:

> If behavior is the subject matter of the behavioral sciences, then the use of objective inference should be restricted to this domain. Inferences about supposed theoretical cognitive processes occurring at other levels [than the behavioral level], or in other dimensions, create problems for the logic of science. (p. 115)

Skinner and other behavior analysts have made the same point many times. However, the reference should be to the logic of *behavior analysis* instead of "the logic of science" because not all sciences have the same logic.

The logic of behavior analysis is pragmatism (Reese, 1986), in the technical philosophical sense rather than in the sense of practicality or practicability

(Pepper, 1942, Chapter 10). Nothing in this philosophy makes mentalism an *intrinsic* problem; rather, in this philosophy mentalism is a problem only if it turns out not to be useful for whatever purposes are under consideration. According to behavior analysts, mentalism has turned out not to be useful for their purposes—the prediction and control of behavior—but its not being useful is an empirical conclusion and not an *a priori* logical principle. The point is that rejecting mentalism is not a principle *within* the logic of behavior analysis; rather, it is a principle derived from application of that logic. It is a pragmatic principle and is firmly held, as "principles" must be in order to be so designated in this philosophy (Prosch, 1964, p. 337); but it is subject to change if its usefulness is found to change.

Cognitive psychology is mentalistic in the technical sense. Behavior is observed, and cognitive activities are inferred. The rationale is that behavior is caused by cognitive activities, and therefore behavior can be understood only if the cognitive activities are identified. How they are identified and how their identification is legitimized are major concerns in this chapter.

6.2. Criteria for Inferring Rule Use

A problem in research on rules is how to know what rules participants use or, expressed behavioristically, what rules govern participants' behavior. The issue here is not the criteria for evaluating theories about rules. Those criteria are discussed in the subsection entitled "Evaluation of Cognitive Theories." The issue here is what criteria to use in attributing rules to individuals; these criteria—six of which are discussed in the following subsections—range from weak to stringent as bases for inferring rule use (Slobin, 1979, pp. 97–99).

6.2.1. Regularity of Behavior

Regularity of behavior is sometimes used as evidence for rule-use, but it is weak evidence (Slobin, 1979, p. 98). Behavior that is rule-governed may be regular, but behavior may be regular without being rule-governed. Behavior may be regular because it is instinctive (unconditioned) or because it has been conditioned rather than because it is rule-governed. (Regularity as such is discussed further in Subsection 6.2.4, "Consistency with Behavior.")

6.2.2. Continuity versus Discontinuity

Continuous changes in performance are sometimes interpreted as contingency-shaped and discontinuous as rule-governed. (Discontinuous changes are also called "noncontinuous" and "saltatory" or "jumpwise.") These interpretations can be challenged, however. For example, Levinson and Reese (1967) showed that two-phase curves of Trial 2 performance in the discrimination learning set task can be interpreted to reflect rule-governance even if they are not discontinuous. Therefore, continuous changes in performance do not necessarily contradict cognitive theory. Conversely, as Spence (1956, pp. 108–110) showed, discontinuous "insight" curves do not necessarily contradict incremental learning theory.

In another guise, the continuity–discontinuity issue refers to whether prior experience influences present performance (continuity) or does not (discontinuity) (e.g., Overton & Reese, 1981). For example, Krechevsky (1938) found that in rats, reversals of reward contingencies in the "presolution" phase of a learning task did not affect the speed of learning. He cited the continuity–discontinuity issue (indeed, he seems to have coined the designations *continuity* and *non-continuity*—p. 111) and inferred from the evidence that rats exhibit discontinuity. He therefore concluded that rats exhibit rules, which he called *hypotheses*. ("Hypotheses" are discussed further under "Discrimination Learning Set" in the subsection "Sets as Rules.")

Bower and Trabasso (1963; Trabasso & Bower, 1964) used the same kind of evidence as a basis for inferring discontinuity in human research participants—in fact, like Krechevsky, they inferred that the behavior is rule-governed rather than shaped by incremental learning. Actually, although Spence (1940) acknowledged the existence of "systematic response tendencies or 'hypotheses' " in animals (p. 287; p. 323 in 1960 reprint), he argued that these response tendencies do not indicate intelligence or insight but rather differ from blind or slow learning only in degree. He was careful to note, however, that this interpretation did not refer to "certain higher forms of adjustment such as are mediated by the complex symbolic mechanisms of man" (Footnote 6, p. 288; p. 324 in 1960 reprint).

6.2.3. Awareness of Rule Use

Research participants who use a rule may be aware (conscious) of using it, whether or not they are aware of the relation between the rule and their behavior. Awareness of using a particular rule is therefore sometimes taken as evidence that the rule was actually used.

6.2.3a. A Problem with the Criterion. One problem with this criterion is that "awareness" cannot be assessed directly. The criterion should refer to *reported* awareness, but with this modification, it loses its force because of the well-known problems with verbal reports: They can reflect a research participant's honest beliefs about his or her covert activities/behaviors, but these beliefs may be erroneous because of self-deception, misinterpretation, secondary elaboration, illusion, and so on. Alternatively, they can reflect deliberate distortion resulting from attitudinizing or wishing to cooperate with the experimenter.

In his selective review of the conditioning literature, Brewer (1974) ignored these problems when he favored explicit questionnaires over nonleading questions for evidence of awareness. Awareness that conditioning had occurred could arise as a result of the explicit questioning. Brewer was also much impressed by findings indicating that some "aware" research participants exhibited effects of experimental conditions only if they were also "cooperative." But did they exhibit the effects because they were aware and cooperative, or were they aware and cooperative because they were affected?

The problem arises when verbal reports about awareness are treated as observations of awareness. The problem also arises with respect to verbal reports about other cognitive events. An article by Tranel and Damasio (1985) is subject to this problem. They reported physiological evidence that pattern recognition can occur without awareness. Specifically, they studied two patients with prosopagnosia—"the consistent failure to recognize the faces of familiar persons who continue to be normally recognized through other sensory channels," such as the voice (p. 1453). The patients exhibited larger and more frequent electrodermal skin conductance responses to familiar faces than to unfamiliar faces, yet experienced no feeling of familiarity and failed to recognize the target faces formally. The skin conductance of normal individuals is similar, but, of course, normal individuals are able to identify familiar faces. The problem is that in this description "awareness" should be "reported awareness," "experienced no feeling of familiarity" should be "reported no feeling of familiarity," and "failed to recognize the target faces formally" should be "gave no formal indication of recognizing the target faces."

The problem seems unlikely to lead to serious misunderstanding of the Tranel and Damasio report. However, the problem occurs in much of the cognitive literature and seems to have misled many cognitive researchers as to what they were actually observing. ("Seems to," because they may have been not misled but only careless with language.) I will not cite examples; cursory examination of the cognitive literature will provide many. The problem is treating inferences about rule use as observations of rule use.

6.2.3b. Other Problems. Other problems make awareness even more problematic as a criterion for inferring cognitive events. In selective-attention or "shadowing" tasks, two sets of material are presented simultaneously, with instructions to attend to ("shadow") one of the sets. For example, the sets may be presented by earphones to different ears, or on alternating lines of text printed in different colors. Research has shown that memory for the unattended material is poor, except that research participants recognize their own name presented in the "unattended" set (e.g., Wolford & Morrison, 1980; for review of relevant research and theories, see Howard, 1983, pp. 64–75). This phenomenon indicates semantic processing of a participant's own name, that is, processing of the meaning of this item. Evidently, semantic processing of each item in the "unattended" set is initiated, but this processing is completed only for important items such as one's own name. The processing is automatic: It does not require conscious control or effort, and it occurs without awareness.

Eich (1984) obtained further relevant evidence: Even though automatic semantic processing did not lead to identification of items in the unattended set when a recognition test was given, it influenced the way items were spelled. The items in the unattended set were presented auditorially; the critical items were homophones paired with words selected to "prime" their less common meanings (e.g., taxi-FARE; youngest-SON). In a later spelling test, the research participants were found to give spellings for the less common meanings of the primed words (e.g., "fare" rather than "fair"; "son" rather than "sun") more often than for homophones that had not been included in the unattended set, that is, unprimed homophones. Thus the automatic semantic processing, even if partial, led to long-term retention and influenced performance without the research participants' awareness.

Awareness is therefore not a strong criterion for inferring cognitive events. However, Eich found that the priming effect in this study was considerably weaker than in a study in which the paired items were presented as the attended set—actually the only initial set—with intentional memory instructions. Therefore, awareness is not an irrelevant criterion.

6.2.4. Consistency with Behavior

If observed behavior can be described by a rule or is consistent with a rule, then use of the rule can be inferred. As Kant said (according to Bennett, 1966, p. 96), the proof that an intellectual skill is possessed lies in its exercise. This criterion is often used by cognitivists (Hayes, 1986). It is being used whenever an inference that a process was operative is based on consistency of observed behavior with behavior expected to be generated by the process. Ideally, the criterion involves comparison of observed behavior with behavior expected from several alternative processes. For example, I used this criterion to infer mediational deficiency in young children and to infer processes underlying transposition (Reese, 1962, 1968); and Gholson and Beilin (1979) used it to infer processes underlying concept identification.

If a rule is not definite and specific, an inference that it was used cannot be compelling because the rule cannot be shown to be consistent with the behavior (or a product of the behavior) that is observed. That is, the inference cannot be compelling because the behavior (or product) that is observed cannot be shown to be consistent with the rule.

6.2.4a. A Negative Example. The following is an example of using the consistency criterion with an inadequately definite and specific rule. Nissen,

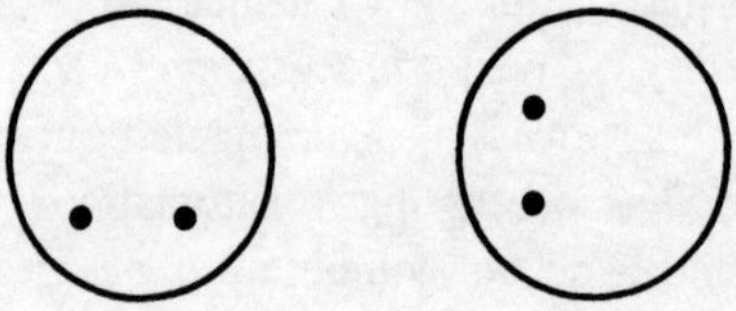

Figure 5. Goodnow asked children to finish each of these drawings that "someone else started." (Reprinted from Goodnow, 1972, Fig. 5.3, p. 94. Reprinted by permission.)

Levinson, and Nichols (1953) referred to "hypotheses" in chimpanzees (consistently and, I think, correctly putting the word in quotation marks). They used the word in a vague explanation of otherwise unexplainable behavior:

> The possibility that unknown experiences provided a basis for the preferences shown . . . cannot, of course, be completely excluded. For the present, however, we are left with the unsatisfactory conclusion that the results were a function either of individually variable innate determinants, or of arbitrary, unpredictable whims or "hypotheses" of the individual [subjects]. It is possible that variations in the "emphasis" or "attention" given by [the subject] to one or another stimulus was responsible for the uneven distribution of choices. The complete determination of such variations may be beyond experimental control. (p. 340)

This kind of speculation is unsatisfactory, as Nissen *et al.* themselves noted; it means nothing more than the following statement they made in their summary: "No satisfactory explanation of these preferences was found" (p. 340).

6.2.4b. A Positive Example. Research on children's drawings of human figures provides a positive example of using the consistency criterion. Young children often draw human figures upside down or sideways relative to the rest of the picture. Goodnow (1972) noted that one interpretation of this phenomenon has been that young children are indifferent to spatial orientation. However, she obtained evidence that the phenomenon is actually rule-governed. Children usually draw the head first, then the eyes, and then other facial and body features. Children sometimes do not put the eyes at the top of the head, perhaps because of carelessness or a lack of motor coordination (Goodnow, p. 94). Goodnow observed that "some of the upside down or sideways figures seemed to be determined by wherever the eyes were drawn" (p. 93). One could infer the use of a rule: Use the eyes to identify the top of the head and draw the body opposite the top of the head.

Goodnow obtained confirmatory evidence by asking children to complete the drawings shown in Figure 5. She found that 4-year-olds produced "a large number of upside down and sideways drawings" (p. 94). Thus, what earlier investigators interpreted as "error" in young children's drawings turned out to be interpretable as rule-governed behavior. The problem was to find the rule with which the behavior was consistent. Here, the primary evidence was obtained by observing children's spontaneous drawing behavior; the further evidence was obtained by controlling the initial portion of the drawings. In general, analysis of "errors" is useful for rule assessment if some one rule predicts the errors and other plausible rules do not (Siegler, 1983a).

This example also illustrates another feature of the cognitive research on rules: Most researchers have not attempted to determine whether the rules they infer were normal or normative. The rules inferred by Goodnow could be either; that is, the children's behavior could have been contingency-shaped or rule-governed.

6.2.4c. Another Positive Example. In research on concept identification, patterns of observed choices across trials provide a basis for inferring that certain rules were used. In some of this research, the inference has been bolstered by the further evidence of age-group differences of theoretically expectable sorts. The top part of Figure 6 shows a sequence of four trials in a relevant task. In this symbolized example, the stimuli are four-dimensional, the dimensions are represented by letters, and the attributes (values) on the dimensions are represented by upper and lower case letters (e.g., *A* and *a* might represent the attributes *large* and *small,* respectively, on the size dimension). Two stimuli are presented on each trial, and they differ on all four dimensions. Between trials, each stimulus is changed on two dimensions. The rule involved is that some one of the attributes is "relevant" (that is, selecting this attribute is rewarded). This is a *normal* rule because, although the relevant attribute is selected arbitrarily by the researcher, its being relevant (its relation to reward) is a regularity in the experiment. The research participants' problem is to "identify the attribute," or to "discover the rule," or to "identify the concept." If they verbally identify the relevant attribute, they are stating a normal rule, that is, describing the regularity. However, if the stated rule governs their behavior, then it is a normative rule.

The researcher's interest is not in the rule described in the preceding paragraph, that is, the problem-solution rule, but in the rules participants use in trying to discover the problem-solution rule. These rules could be called "discovery" rules, although this designation is seldom used in the relevant literature. Discovery rules may be normal or normative—regularities in the participants' behavior preceding their exhibiting the problem-solution rule or deliberate strategies for discovering problem-solution rules. Most researchers have made no attempt to distinguish between these two senses of discovery rules.

Three rules that participants have been inferred to use in attempting to solve the problem are *attribute testing, dimension testing,* and *focusing.* In *attribute testing,* the participant tests one attribute at a time; up to seven tests would be required to test all eight attributes (seven negative answers would leave one attribute untested, but this attribute would necessarily be the correct one). In *dimension testing,* the participant's first test eliminates half the attributes (one for each dimension); then the remaining attributes are tested one at a time. A maximum of four tests would be required to identify the correct

Trial	Stimulus 1	Stimulus 2
1	ABCD	abcd
2	ABcd	abCD
3	AbCd	aBcD
4	AbcD	aBCd

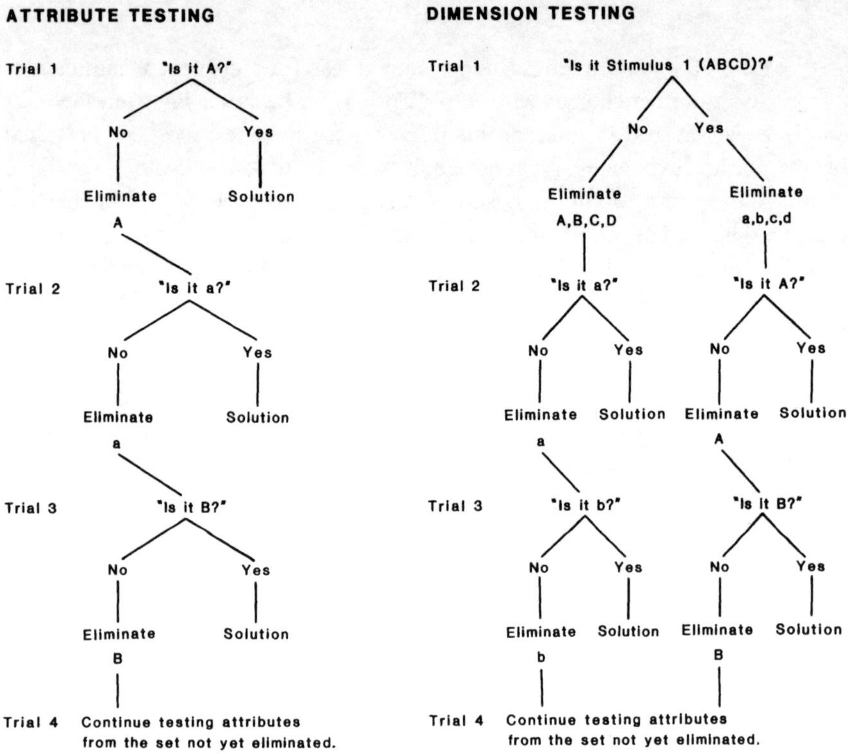

Figure 6. Example of a sequence of four trials on a concept-identification task and decision trees representing three of the rules participants use in such tasks.

attribute. In *focusing,* each of the participant's tests eliminates half the possibilities that have not already been eliminated. A maximum of three tests is required. (Less than the maximum is required for attribute testing and dimension testing if the correct attribute is fixed before the task begins and if the participant is lucky. In the usual procedure, the experimenter determines the correct attribute as the task proceeds, such that the participant is never lucky.)

The bottom part of Figure 6 shows these rules as "decision trees." In the procedure the decision trees refer to, the participants' tests are in the form of questions about the attributes, and the questions must be answerable with a *yes*

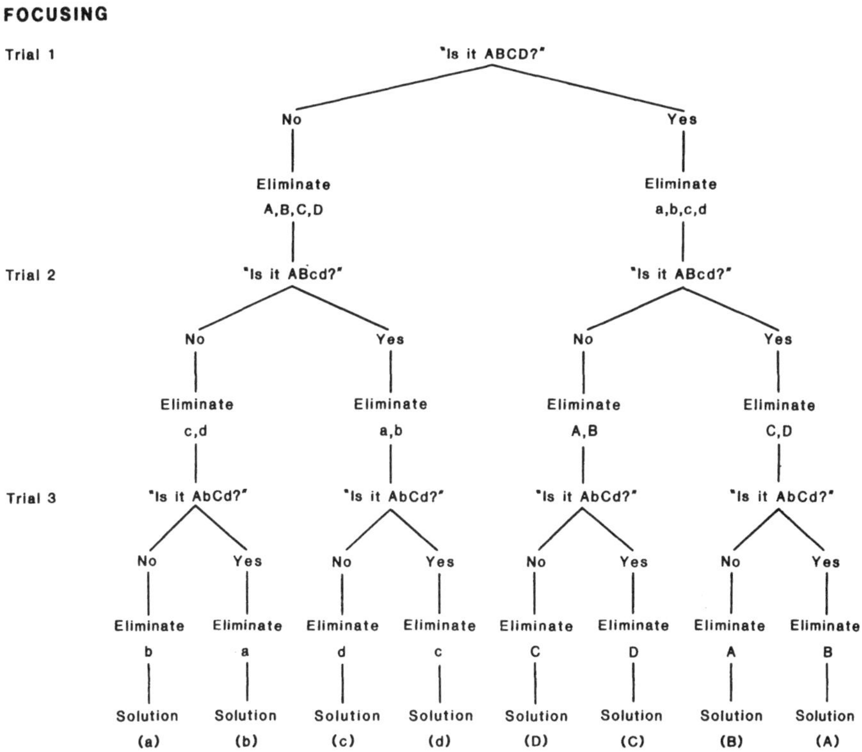

Figure 6 *(Continued)*

or a *no*. (This is not the usual procedure in the relevant research. For description of a more usual procedure, see Gholson & Beilin, 1979).

Figure 7 shows typical inferences based on consistency of behavior with the various rules: 5-year-olds tended to perform stereotypically, that is, disregarding feedback; 7-year-olds tended to exhibit attribute testing and, especially, dimension testing; and college students exhibited dimension testing and focusing. (For a theoretical rationale for expecting these age-group differences, see Gholson & Beilin, 1979.)

6.2.4d. Applying the Criterion. Siegler (1981) has described a "rule-assessment approach" in which the consistency criterion is used in studying cognitive development:

> The first step . . . is generating a series of alternative rules that children might use to solve a problem. Rational task analyses, general cognitive-developmental theories, and previous empirical work are the usual sources of the hypothesized rules. Next, a set of problem types is formulated that yields distinctive patterns of correct answers and errors for children following each of these rules. Finally, if there are

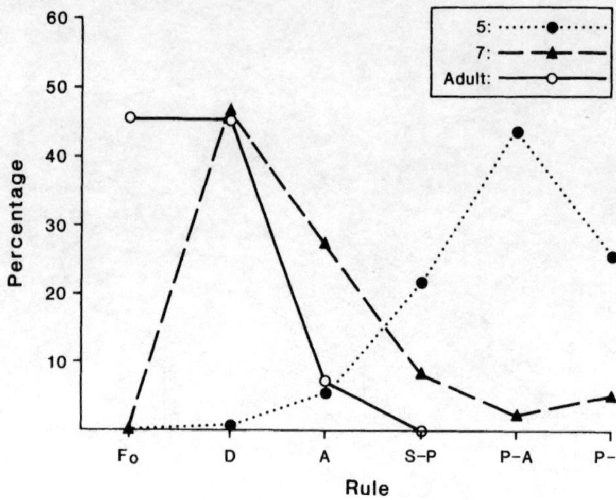

Figure 7. Percentages of children and adults exhibiting various rules in a concept-identification task. The rules are focusing (Fo); dimension testing (D); attribute testing (A); stimulus perseveration (S-P); position alternation (P-A); and position perseveration (P-P). (After Gholson, Levine, & Phillips, 1972, Figures 3 and 4. Adapted by permission.)

> two or more tasks for which comparable problem types can be formulated, and if there is a theoretical prediction either of developmental synchrony or of an invariant developmental ordering, the between-concept sequence may be studied. (pp. 3–4)

Klahr and Robinson (1981) characterized the approach as follows:

> The basic idea underlying the strategic analysis is that, given a set of plausible strategies, we can compare each subject's . . . profile [of performance] with the profiles generated by each strategy over the same problem set. For each subject, the strategy producing the best matching profile is then taken as the strategy used by that subject. (p. 132)

In short, the approach involves describing possible rules, developing tasks on which the rules lead to different performance, administering the tasks to appropriate research participants, and determining which rule best fits the observed performance. One method for determining the best fit is to require some minimum percentage agreement between the rule and individual performance across tasks, with the minimally acceptable percentage selected to be unlikely to be attained at random. Siegler (1976, Exp. 1), for example, used this criterion in a study of children's performance on 30 different balance scale problems and applied it to each child's predictions (balance, tip left, or tip right) and explanations (referring to weight alone, distance alone, or both). Other methods for determining the best fit are mentioned in Subsection 6.2.4i.

Siegler has used this approach to identify children's rules on 13 tasks, such as the balance scale, various conservation tasks, counting, and the Tower of Hanoi (Siegler, 1983a, summarized some of this research). The approach has also been used extensively by other cognitive developmentalists (such as Ferretti & Butterfield, 1986; Klahr & Robinson, 1981).

The approach might be especially interesting to behavior analysts because it requires task analysis and examination of individual performance—both familiar procedures in behavior analytic research. (However, the task analyses deal with cognitive activities rather than overt behaviors; and the individual performance is usually examined without within-organism manipulation of experimental conditions.)

Siegler discussed problems with this approach (1981, pp. 67–69; 1983). The major problem, perhaps, is that the observed behavior often does not fit any of the preselected rules, and therefore the investigator often needs to propose additional rules post hoc to fit the observed behavior.

6.2.4e. Persuasiveness of the Criterion. Actually, consistency between a rule and behavior is not strong evidence of rule-governance regardless of the specificity of the rule. Coulter (1983) said:

> I think that it is possible to specify rules with which persons' conduct is in non-trivial accord . . . , even though . . . one cannot claim to have discovered the rule which he was *following* or by which his conduct was actually *guided*. (Note 10, p. 70)

Furthermore:

> Children are not baby scientists or theoretical linguists/logicians/mathematicians, making and testing hypotheses and working out formal analytic rules for what they hear, see, say and do, even though their successful achievements in adding, counting and speaking *may accord with* the propositionally statable prescriptions of Peano's axioms or generative-grammatical syntax rules. [The fault is] confusing the fact of being *in accord with a rule* with the fact of being *guided by a known rule*. (p. 24)

In short, the occurrence of behavior that is consistent with a rule does not necessarily indicate that the behavior was governed by the rule.

For example, Holborn (1982) studied the performance of children on fixed interval schedules. One child, who exhibited a low rate, said "the slower you go the faster the light [the reinforcer] goes on." Another child, who exhibited a high rate, said "the faster you go the faster the light goes on." If the rates were contingency-shaped, they would be expected to be low and scalloped. They were not and therefore they may have been rule-governed. However, although the behavior may have followed the rule that was stated, the rule may have followed the behavior. (Other investigators have obtained results of a similar nature; for example, Bentall *et al.*, 1985; Catania *et al.*, 1982.)

Behaviors that seem to be rule-governed may actually be contingency-shaped. I believe that the behavior of rats and other animals fairly low on the phylogenetic scale can be contingency-shaped but cannot be rule-governed because such animals cannot learn normative rules. If so, then whenever the behavior of animals and human beings is responsive to contingencies in the same way, the behavior of the human beings can be parsimoniously interpreted as contingency-shaped rather than rule-governed.

Weiner (1969a, b) demonstrated that a person's history of experience with reinforcement schedules affects the pattern of performance under other schedules. For example, under fixed interval schedules, humans often exhibit high constant performance rates rather than scalloping. The former pattern is typical of persons who have been given laboratory experience with ratio schedules, and the latter is typical of persons given experience with differential reinforcement for low rates (DRL schedules).

Rats exhibit the same kind of phenomenon: In a study by Urbain, Poling, Millam, and Thompson (1978), rats were trained for 50 sessions on either a fixed ratio schedule (FR 40), which typically produces a high rate of responding, or a DRL schedule (DRL 11 s), which typically produces a low rate of responding. The rats were then given 93 sessions on a fixed interval schedule (FI 15 s), which typically produces scalloping. The results showed that throughout the sessions with the fixed interval schedule, the rats in the fixed ratio group exhibited a high rate of responding and the rats in the DRL group exhibited a low rate of responding. (The number of fixed interval sessions was specified as 93 in the abstract of the Urbain *et al.* report, but the numbers of sessions specified in the body of the report sum to 73. In either case, the number is large enough to demonstrate a very long-lasting effect of the initial schedule.)

6.2.4f. Inconsistency with Behavior. The argument against the consistency criterion can be extended: The occurrence of behavior that is *not* consistent with a rule does not necessarily indicate that the behavior was *not* governed by the rule. Why should rule-governed behavior be consistent with behavior specified in the rule? Rule-governed behavior is called "rule-governed" because it has been inferred to be under control of a rule, not because its topography resembles the topography specified in a rule. Thus, once a behavior has been identified as rule-governed, the problems of explaining its occurrence and its topography remain.

For example, why does the flossing rule—"Use dental floss after every meal"—result in flossing instead of brushing or some other behavior? (In the real world, it usually does not result in flossing, but that is a different problem.) If flossing has a history of being reinforced on occasions when the rule was presented, then the flossing could be contingency-shaped rather than rule-governed.

Parrott (1982) argued that rule-governed behavior resembles the behavior specified in the rule because the rule has real-world reference. The issue seems trivial, perhaps, in the case of the flossing rule and other rules that refer to specific behaviors; surely, anyone who knows how to use dental floss and whose behavior is governed by the rule will floss instead of brush. However, in the case of more general rules the issue is clearly not trivial. For example, no behavior is specified in "whatsoever ye would that men should do to you, do ye even so to them." The problem is similar to the problem of explaining imitation, which is not itself a behavior (for the argument, see Baron & Galizio, 1983; Reese, 1986).

6.2.4g. Another Kind of Inconsistency with Behavior. Ericsson and Simon (1984) argued that if research participants are required to give verbal reports of their concurrent cognitive activities, then the cognitive activities can be inferred to be rule-governed if the reporting does not interfere with the cognitive activities. That is, as Hayes (1986) put it, "rules are implicated only when task-relevant verbalization does not alter performance" (p. 358). The argument is too complex to be summarized here, other than to note that it involves consistency versus inconsistency between the verbal behavior and the cognitive activities. (Hayes, 1986, summarized the argument and discussed implications for behavior analytic research.)

6.2.4h. Variability of Behavior. Even if a rule is definite and specific, perfect consistency between the rule and the behavior is not expected because of behavioral variability. Given behavioral variability, one way to show consistency is by means of analysis of variance. Wilkening and Anderson (1982) argued, if I read them right, that the use of analysis of variance or any other statistical test of the goodness of fit of behavior to a rule requires that the rule theory include an error theory "to handle response variability" (p. 225) or to allow for "unreliability or variability in the response" (p. 228).

Actually, the possibility of performance errors is already at least implicit in all psychological theories, and therefore the consistency criterion needs to be interpreted as probabilistic regardless of the theory being used. For example, Skinner gave chance and accident a role in creativity (1974, p. 114; 1984, p. 22); in doing so, he introduced a source of error undermining the predictability and controllability of behavior. The Hull–Spence theory also included an unpredictable source of moment-to-moment fluctuation in excitatory potential ("behavioral oscillation": Hull, 1943, Chapter 17; "oscillatory inhibition": Spence, 1956, pp. 95–101). Excitatory potential is based on habit (and drive) strength, and the effect of the fluctuation is to yield levels of performance below the level predictable from habit (and drive) strength alone, that is, below the "competence" level. Finally, cognitive developmentalists have assumed that performance may be below the competence or "metacognitive" level whenever the relevant strategy has not yet been completely mastered (Flavell, 1977; Reese, 1976b; Siegler, 1981). For example, Flavell (1977) said:

> The target strategy may not yet be well enough mastered—qua cognitive activity, as an end in itself—to be brought into service as a means to a . . . goal. (p. 217)

Furthermore, the limits on acceptable error are already set by existing data-analytic methods. Unreliability and variability in performance are expected; they are also tolerated when not extreme. The meaning of "extreme" is given by the method used. In the best-designed group research, the number of observations collected (per group or per participant) is predetermined to yield the amount of power wanted in the statistical test. Variability of performance contributes to the error term in the statistical analysis, and the number of (independent) observations moderates this contribution by serving as a divisor. In the best-designed single-organism research, observations continue until a trend is obvious in spite of performance variability. Therefore, the variability of behavior is not really a problem for application of the consistency criterion.

6.2.4i. Example. A study by Leon (1984) provides an example of the use of analysis of variance to define consistency between rules and behaviors. (Another example is a study by Levin, Wilkening, and Dembo [1984], not discussed herein. Consistency has also been evaluated in other ways: For example, in a study not discussed herein, Klahr and Robinson [1981] used a criterion of significantly better than chance fit between individual data and rules, and Ravn and Gelman [1984] used inspection of individual data. Klahr [1985] used multiple regression in a study described in the subsection entitled "Obtaining Precision.")

Leon studied the rules of punishment approved by mothers and their 6- to 7-year-old sons. (Leon said he was studying the rules these individuals *used,* but he assessed the amounts of punishment they *said* were appropriate rather than the amounts of punishment they actually used.) He presented nine scenarios varying factorially in three levels of intent (accident, displaced anger, malice) and three levels of damage (none, moderate, severe), with three repetitions of each scenario to permit analysis of variance of each participant's performance. He found that all 32 of the mothers tested could be classified as exhibiting one or another of three rules:

- *Intent plus damage linear rule.* In the "linear" rule, intent and damage are weighted equally and additively. The evidence is a significant main effect of both intent and damage, with increasing punishment for increasing maliciousness and damage, and no significant interaction between intent and damage. The pattern of significant and nonsignificant results for this rule—and the others—is shown in Table 3.
- *Nonlinear accident-configural rule.* The "nonlinear" rule is the same as the linear rule except that no punishment is assigned for accidents. The evidence is a significant main effect of both intent and damage, as in the linear rule, and a significant interaction reflecting increased punishment for increased damage only when damage was intended.
- *Damage-only rule.* In the "damage-only" rule, punishment depends only

Table 3
Analysis-of-Variance Evidence for Four Rules in Leon's (1984) Study

Rule	Intent main effect	Damage main effect	Intent × damage interaction
Linear	Significant	Significant	Nonsignificant
Nonlinear	Significant	Significant	Significant
Damage only	Nonsignificant	Significant	Nonsignificant
Intent only	Significant	Nonsignificant	Nonsignificant

Note. Evidence for a rule was not only the specified pattern of significant and nonsignificant effects but also, for significant effects, a specified variation among the means. The variations are specified in the text.

on the amount of damage, regardless of intent. The evidence is a nonsignificant main effect of intent, a significant main effect of damage, with increasing punishment for increasing damage, and a nonsignificant interaction.

The analyses of the data for the individual mothers revealed no other rules, although other rules are, of course, possible. An example is:

- *Intent only.* In the "intent-only" rule, punishment depends only on the maliciousness of intent, regardless of amount of damage. The evidence is a significant main effect of intent, with increasing punishment for increasing maliciousness, no significant main effect of damage, and no significant interaction.

Four of the sons exhibited the intent-only pattern of performance.

Table 4 shows the classifications of the mothers and their sons. The fact that the sons tended to exhibit the same rules as their mothers is important to developmental theory, but the point that is important here is the way the rules

Table 4
Rules Endorsed by Mothers and Their Sons in Leon's (1984) Study

Sons' rules	Mothers' rules: Linear	Nonlinear	Damage only
Linear	12	1	2
Nonlinear	3	6	0
Other[a]	3	3	2

Note. Numbers in table are frequencies of participants.
[a]Leon did not report separate data for sons classified as endorsing damage only ($N=3$), intent only ($N=4$), and no evident rule ($N=1$).

were identified. What was observed was the administration of several combinations of stimulus conditions and several patterns of performance. The use of analysis of variance disentangled the effects of the individual stimulus conditions and their combined effects, which in turn permitted classification of the participants into different groups. The use of theory permitted interpretation of how these groups differed. Saying that the persons in one group used a linear rule is the same as saying that this group exhibited certain main effects of both intent and damage and no interaction. This statement is entirely descriptive. However, cognitivists tend—strongly—to go beyond this kind of descriptive statement and to make assertions such as that the group exhibited the main effects of both intent and damage and no interaction *because* they used a linear rule. (This point is also discussed briefly in the subsection entitled "The Ontogenetic Approach to Rules.")

6.2.5. *Concomitant Behavior*

A very important criterion for inferring rule use is the observation of concomitant behavior, that is, behavior that can be expected to accompany rule use but that is not the behavior expected to be directly affected by rule use. The criterion is so widely used that it need not be elaborated here. (A refinement may be to distinguish between concomitant behavior that is "adjunctive" versus "collateral," but this distinction cannot be elaborated here other than to note that moving the lips while thinking is adjunctive behavior in young children, and scratching the head and frowning while thinking are collateral behaviors.)

Flavell, Beach, and Chinsky (1966) implicitly used the concomitant-behavior criterion, inferring from observed lip movements that young children rehearsed; the behavior that should be directly affected by rehearsal is memory performance rather than lip movements. A behavior analytic example is Lamarre and Holland's (1985) argument that certain behavior they observed was not rule-governed because they observed "no tell-tale autoclitics and no public fragments of private instructional behavior" (p. 17).

6.2.6. *Rule Generalization*

Overton and Newman (1982) specified generalization as a criterion for the validity and power of models, through empirical demonstration that they are applicable to new behaviors in the domain covered. Generalization is also a powerful and frequently used criterion for rule learning. Toulmin attributed the criterion to Wittgenstein, specifically as a criterion of knowledge or understanding of a concept (Toulmin, 1971, Footnote 2, p. 41; no specific citation of Wittgenstein). The criterion is that spontaneous performance in novel situations or with new stimuli or new behaviors can be inferred to reflect the rule about which an inference is desired.

Berlyne (1965) suggested that if behavior is rule-governed (not his term), the behavior that represents the rule should be performed "with equal mastery" in all relevant situations, but if the behavior reflects "the acquisition of certain stimulus-response associations by direct learning and the emergence of other stimulus-response associations by stimulus-response generalization, then we should expect a generalization decrement, such as is found with stimulus generalization and with response generalization" (pp. 172–173).

Along the same line, Gagné (1970) said that a rule "enables the individual to respond to a class of stimulus situations with a class of performances" (p. 191; italics deleted). "Rule-governed behavior exhibits the learner's capability of responding to entire *classes* of stimuli with *classes* of response. . . . [M]aking classes of response to classes of stimuli is . . . regular and, therefore, is called rule-governed" (p. 211).

In a study by Rosser and Brody (1981), the criterion for rule learning was that a trained group should outperform an untrained group on a training task and on two generalization tasks that were given. In each task, dowels of different lengths were presented in a disordered array. The training task required rearranging the dowels into the correct seriation of lengths; the generalization tasks required either multiple-choice selection of a drawing that showed the dowels correctly seriated or drawing a picture of the dowels correctly seriated. Thus all the tasks involved the same stimuli and the same rule (seriation of lengths), but they had different performance requirements. The participants were 3½ to 6 years old. Significant effects of seriation training were found in all tasks; consequently, the trained group was inferred to have learned and used the seriation rule.

Pratt, McLaren, and Wickens (1984) also used generalization as a criterion for rule learning. The task involved "referential communication": A speaker selects a stimulus from an array and verbally describes this stimulus so that a listener can identify it without having witnessed the selection. The speakers were 6-year-old children, and the listener was the examiner. In the training task, the child selected one of several multidimensional stimuli and described it so that the examiner could identify it. In one of two generalization tasks, the child built a block tower and described it to allow the examiner to build a duplicate tower; in the other generalization task, the child placed one of six chess pieces on a modified chess board and described the piece selected and its location on the board. Trained groups outperformed an untrained group, satisfying the generalization criterion for rule use.

The generalization criterion is the most stringent basis for inferring rule use. First, it requires a prior inference of rule learning by application of some other criterion. The generalization criterion is used most often in studies in which training is given in an attempt to generate rule learning, and the consistency criterion can be used as a basis for inferring that the training was effective. An implicit example is Baer's (1982) discussion of the algorithm for extracting square roots (Baer's discussion is summarized later in the discussion, "Application to Cognitive Activities," in the subsection "The Ontogenetic Approach to Rules"). Second, if rule learning is inferred, then performance on generalization tests is used as evidence as to whether the consistency between the inferred rule and the observed behavior reflects rule use or reflects only rote learning of appropriate performance with respect to specific stimuli. Of course, inferences are always more compelling when they are based on more than one criterion, but the generalization criterion automatically involves more than one criterion, and it is the only criterion that involves tests with novel situations or new stimuli or behaviors.

6.3. Spontaneously Learned Rules

The spontaneous development of rules can be inferred to be a usual outcome in studies of concept identification and sets. These kinds of studies are discussed in the next two subsections; an interpretation of the phenomenon is discussed in the subsection entitled "The Ontogenetic Approach to Rules."

6.3.1. *Concept Identification*

According to the usual textbook definition, rules in concept identification indicate how stimulus attributes are to be combined or related so as to classify the stimuli into mutually exclusive categories (Ellis, 1978, p. 138; Howard, 1983, p. 485; Matlin, 1983, pp. 179, 181; Mayer, 1983, p. 84; Navarick, 1979, p. 240).

Bourne (1970) studied the learning of rules relevant to two-dimensional stimuli. The rules studied are illustrated in Figure 8. Descriptively, they are:

- *Conjunctive.* All stimuli that are red and square are positive instances (implying that all other stimuli are negative instances).
- *Disjunctive.* All stimuli that are red and/or square are positive instances.
- *Conditional.* If a stimulus is red, then it must be square to be a positive instance (implying that if a stimulus is not red, then it is also a positive instance).
- *Biconditional.* If a stimulus is red, then it is a positive instance if it is square; and if a stimulus is square, then it is a positive instance if it is red (implying that if a stimulus is not red and not square, then it is also a positive instance).

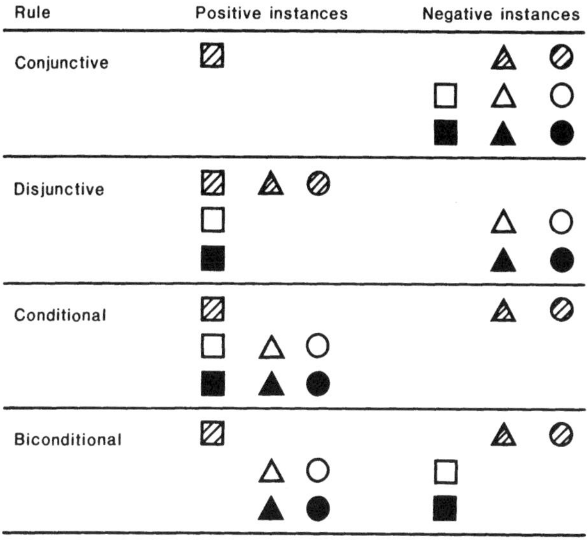

Figure 8. Positive and negative instances of stimuli for four concept-identification rules. The stimuli differ in color (symbolized by black, white, and cross-hatched) and form. (Adapted from L. E. Bourne, Jr. [1970]. "Knowing and using concepts." *Psychological Review, 77,* 546–556 [Fig. 1, p. 548]. Copyright 1970 by the American Psychological Association. Adapted by permission of the author.)

Bourne found that in the process of learning a number of these rules, college students also learned a superordinate rule—"Construct a truth table."

The truth tables for the rules Bourne studied are shown in Table 5. Constructing and using such tables should have two effects: The research participant can easily induce the rule from the pattern of Ts and Fs and can easily

Table 5
Truth Tables for Four Concept-Identification Rules

		Conjunctive	Disjunctive	Conditional	Biconditional
X	Y	X and Y	X and/or Y	If X, then Y	X iff Y[a]
T	T	T	T	T	T
F	T	F	T	T	F
T	F	F	T	F	F
F	F	F	F	T	T

Note. X and Y are stimulus attributes. Positive instances of a rule (concept) are those stimuli in which X and Y have the values (shown in Columns 1 and 2) in any row marked T (true) in the column for that rule; negative instances are those in rows marked F (false) in the column for that rule.
[a]That is, "Y if and only if X," or "X is equivalent to Y."

classify stimuli according to a rule by finding the row in which each stimulus falls. For example, let X and Y (in the table) symbolize red and square, respectively. The truth table for the *conjunctive* rule indicates that a stimulus is a positive instance only if it is both red and square (both X and Y are true). The truth table for the *disjunctive* rule indicates that if a stimulus is not red and not square (both X and Y are false) it is a negative instance and that otherwise it is a positive instance. The truth table for the *conditional* rule indicates that a stimulus is a positive instance unless it is red and not square (X is true and Y is false); and the truth table for the *biconditional* rule indicates that a stimulus must be both red and square or neither red nor square (X and Y are either both true or both false) to be a positive instance.

6.3.2. Sets as Rules

The spontaneous development of rules can be seen in the development of perceptual set (e.g., Bugelski & Alampay, 1961; Reese & Ford, 1962), cognitive set (e.g., Luchins, 1942), discrimination learning set (e.g., Reese, 1963, 1964), and other learning sets. These kinds of sets are discussed in the present subsection.

6.3.2a. Perceptual Set. When preceded by drawings of animals, the drawing in Figure 9 is usually seen as a rat; and when preceded by drawings of human faces, it is usually seen as a baldheaded man wearing glasses. The phenomenon has been demonstrated in children (e.g., Reese & Ford, 1962) and adults (Bugelski & Alampay, 1961) and is an example of perceptual set. A cognitive theory of the phenomenon is that during the presentation of the unambiguous animals (or faces), the research participant spontaneously learns a set—an expectation or a rule—that animals (or faces) are being presented, and this set leads the research participant to encode the ambiguous input as an animal, specifically, a rat (or as a human face). Stimulus–response learning theory explanations have also been proposed (for discussion, see Reese, 1970b).

6.3.2b. Cognitive Set. The Luchins (1942) jars task provides an example of cognitive set. The task consists of a series of problems, each requiring the research participant to obtain a designated quantity of water using three jars of different capacities. An example is given in Table 6. The first three problems can be solved only by filling Jar B and pouring once into Jar A and twice into Jar C. In equation form, the solution is:

$$D = B - A - 2C \qquad \text{(Equation 1)}$$

Problems 4 and 5 can be solved by using this equation or a simpler equation:

$$D = A - C \qquad \text{(Equation 2)}$$

Problem 6 can be solved only by using Equation 2.

Research participants spontaneously induce Equation 1 and use it on

Figure 9. An ambiguous figure used in perceptual-set research. (After Bugelski & Alampay, 1961, Figure 1, p. 206. Copyright (1961), The Canadian Psychological Association. Reprinted by permission.)

the remaining problems—even though it does not generate a solution for Problem 6.

6.3.2c. Discrimination Learning Set. In the most intensively studied learning-set design, two-stimulus discrimination-learning tasks are presented, with different stimuli in each task and usually with a small, fixed number of trials in each task. The choice on Trial 1 of a task, that is, on the first presentation of a new pair of stimuli, can be correct only by chance; but after the learning set has developed, the choices on all subsequent trials of the task are always correct. In other words, after the learning set has developed, the organism exhibits one-trial learning.

The performance on Trial 2 in blocks of problems is a good index of the development of the discrimination learning set. In the early problems, perfor-

Table 6
Examples of Luchins Jars Problems

Problem	Capacity			Amount required (D)
	Jar A	Jar B	Jar C	
1	14	163	25	99
2	18	43	10	5
3	9	42	6	21
4	23	49	3	20
5	14	36	8	6
6	28	76	3	25

Note. Adapted from Luchins, 1942, unnumbered table, p. 1. Reprinted from *Basic learning processes in childhood* by Hayne W. Reese (Table 7.3, p. 154). Copyright © 1976a by Holt, Rinehart & Winston. Reprinted by permission of CBS College Publishing.

mance on Trial 2 is little if any better than the chance level; after the learning set has developed, Trial 2 performance is always correct (or nearly so, allowing for "random" errors).

The most popular way to explain a discrimination learning set—and the effects of repetition in the other learning-set designs—has been to assume that the behaviors are rule-governed. Harlow (e.g., 1959) assumed that organisms have a hierarchy of rules and that the generalized solution of tasks of the kind being presented in dominated by incorrect rules, which he called "error factors." He attributed the final level of performance—the one-trial learning—to elimination of all the error factors during the course of training. The theory was incomplete, however, because the origins of the error factors and their dominance over the generalized solution were not explained.

Learning sets have also been attributed to rules called "strategies" (Bowman, 1963; Levinson & Reese, 1967) or, more often, "hypotheses" (Barker & Gholson, 1984; Levine, 1959; Levinson & Reese, 1967; Reese, 1963, 1970b). The concept of *hypotheses* was derived from Krechevsky's use of this term to refer to the presolution performance of rats in discrimination learning tasks. Krechevsky (1932a) referred to the concept as *descriptive*—he said it is defined in "purely behavioral and objective terms" (p. 529); it is merely a name for a relationship between variables (Tolman & Krechevsky, 1933, p. 63)—but he also said that the concept correctly connotes the notion of "purposive, 'if-then' behavior" (1932a, p. 529). Also, he clearly used it as explanatory in referring to hypotheses as "attempted solutions" and " 'attempts' at solution" (examples: 1932a, p. 526; 1932b, p. 43; 1932c, p. 63; 1938, p. 107). When *hypothesis* is used as a descriptive concept, the rat is said to have a leftward position hypothesis, for example, because the rat consistently turns leftward; when it is used in explanations, the rat is said to turn consistently leftward because it has a leftward position hypothesis.

Levine (1959) defined hypotheses entirely on the basis of performance, and he explicitly identified them as dependent variables (p. 365). However, they have also come to be used as explanatory. For example, the discrimination learning set has come to be attributed to the learning of the hypothesis "win-stay-object, lost-shift-object": If the Trial 1 choice is correct ("win"), choose the same stimulus on the subsequent trials (stay with the same object); and if the Trial 1 choice is incorrect ("lose"), choose the other stimulus on the subsequent trials (shift to the other object).

Descriptively, "win-stay-object, lose-shift-object" means only that the research participant exhibits one-trial learning. However, this hypothesis is given an explanatory status when the one-trial learning is attributed to the hypothesis, and the theory has the same problem as Harlow's error-factor theory: The origins of hypotheses are not explained. An alternative approach is described later, in the subsection "The Ontogenetic Approach to Rules."

6.3.2d. Other Learning Sets. Just as discrimination learning set develops during training on a series of discrimination learning tasks, so other learning sets develop during training on other series of tasks. Examples are sets for relational responding (Reese, 1968, pp. 67–80), matching to sample, oddity matching, imitating, and following instructions (e.g., Baron & Galizio, 1983). In the sets—rules, actually—for relational responding, matching to sample, and oddity matching, as in discrimination learning set, the behavior is specified, but the stimulus is specified only abstractly as "the middlesized stimulus" (for example), "the sample," or "the odd stimulus." (One might argue that "the middlesized stimulus" is not abstract because stimulus relations are as concrete as abstract attributes. This issue is not important here; the point here is that training on certain tasks induces a set to respond to stimulus relations.) In the rules for imitating and following instructions, both the behavior and the stimulus are abstract: The behavior is "whatever is modeled or named," and the stimulus is "whatever is modeled or named." Such topography-free behaviors and dimensionless stimuli are characteristic of widely generalizable rules and make these rules especially intriguing.

6.3.3. The Ontogenetic Approach to Rules

Focusing on a rule that has already been learned can obscure its nature. The rule—the end result—may be less illuminating than how it was learned. Focusing on how a rule (or other behavior) is learned is the *ontogenetic approach.* This approach has been recommended by Watson (1926), Toulmin (1971), Vygotsky (1978, Chapter 5), and others (e.g., Baron & Galizio, 1983; Bijou, 1984). Toulmin said, "The concept of *knowledge* can be analyzed adequately only as the product of—and as correlative with—the process of *coming-to-know*" (p. 37).

6.3.3a. Application to Learning Set. Consistently with the ontogenetic approach, Bugelski (1956) suggested that focusing on the one-trial learning in discrimination learning set is misleading:

> The fact of the easy late learning gets in the way of an understanding by misdirecting attention. The place to look for an explanation is at the other end, the time of difficulty for the monkey [Bugelski was referring to Harlow's learning-set research with monkeys]. The first problems are difficult to solve and it is this difficulty that calls for explanation. Why cannot the monkey solve the first problem easily? (p. 401)

In other words, the theoretical problem is not why the later learning is rapid but why the early learning is slow.

Bugelski proposed a stimulus–response learning theory explanation of the difficulty of the early tasks in learning-set designs. He noted that position habits are initially strong and that in the standard procedure they are intermittently reinforced (by chance any position habit will be reinforced on a random half of the trials) and therefore are hard to extinguish. In addition, the stimuli used in the standard procedure are multidimensional, and therefore the effects of reinforcement generalize from the positive object to negative objects, further delaying learning. In short, Bugelski attributed the development of learning sets to habit formation, extinction, and generalization.

Reese reviewed the literature on discrimination learning set in rhesus monkeys (1964) and children (1963)—which were by far the usual research participants—and showed that in monkeys the variables that affect performance on a single discrimination learning task have the same effects on performance in the learning-set design. This result is exactly what would be expected from Bugelski's theory, and Reese (1964) extended the theory by proposing detailed explanations of the effects of the relevant variables and of the error factors identified by Harlow. The results for children, in contrast, were not consistent with this kind of theory (Reese, 1963, 1970b). One very important difference is that monkeys require several hundred problems to develop the learning set, but preschool children can develop it in solving a single discrimination-learning task (Reese, 1965). Reese therefore concluded that in children the learning set—the one-trial learning—is rule-governed. The ontogenetic approach yielded the critical premises.

6.3.3b. Application to Cognitive Activities. Baer (1982) argued for the ontogenetic approach to understanding unobservable events, specifically the use of the rule for extracting square roots:

> Teachers . . . do not need to *infer* what unobservable processes their secondary-school students are possessed of that enable them to extract square roots across an infinite class of stimuli; the teachers *know* what they are using because the teachers gave it to them, knowing also that it would become unobservable rather quickly. . . . How do teachers know that it hasn't changed, now that it is unobservable? It

> may very well have changed; the point is whether or not a student's ability to extract accurate square roots has changed too. If it has not, then the teacher still knows that the advent of square-rooting behaviors in this student was accomplished by the teaching of the algorithm; whatever transformations it may have undergone within the unobservable privacy of the student are not necessary to an understanding of its continuing function, or to an understanding of the student's continuing ability. (p. 305)

Similarly, Berlyne (1965) said:

> When we say that an organism learns a rule, which expresses itself in the performance of different responses in different stimulus situations, we are obscuring the fact that the rule is acquired as a result of specific learning experiences in specific stimulus situations and that these learning experiences cause other specific responses to be performed in other, equally specific stimulus situations. (p. 172)

(Berlyne noted that rules can be acquired in the way described, that is, through experience with exemplars, or through instruction. For discussion herein, see the subsection entitled "Instructed and Shaped Rules.")

How does a well-trained and well-rehearsed person extract square roots? By having learned the rule, according to Baer and Berlyne. But from the cognitive viewpoint, this is the answer to the question of how the person learned the skill, not how the skill operates. The latter question is answered, in the case of unobservable skills, by inferring what the unobserved activities are like. The inference is based on observation of overt behavior or concrete products that theoretically would be produced by the inferred activities. Knowing how the activities were learned is useful if this knowledge provides premises for the inference.

7. SUMMARY

A distinction is made between "normal" and "normative" rules. A normal rule is a regularity in nature; a normative rule is a prescription—moral, practical, or juridical. A normal rule is not causal; it can be instantiated, but it does not cause the instantiation. For example, the law of falling bodies as a regularity can be distinguished from the formula $s = \frac{1}{2} gt^2$, which is not the law but only a description of the law. The law as such does not cause bodies to fall; mutual attraction is the cause. A normative rule is causal if it controls behavior (in conjunction with other variables). The present chapter deals with approaches to normative rules.

The cognitive approaches to rules include information-processing theories, of which the most precise but narrowest in scope are computer simulations of human behavior. In one version of computer simulation, rules are represented as "productions" consisting of an antecedent condition, an action, and a consequent output. The resemblance to the behavior analytic concept of the three-term contingency is superficial.

In another kind of information-processing theory, computer programming language is used metaphorically; the theory is represented by a flow chart, but the program is not actually written. These theories and computer simulations are evaluated on some seven criteria. The most important is "Turing's test," or sufficiency to produce the behavior under consideration, but in order to satisfy this criterion, the theoretical specification of purported cognitive activities and their relations to behavior must be sufficiently definite and precise to permit assessment of the consistency between observed and expected behavior.

Perhaps the best way to understand rules and rule-governance—whether the approach is cognitive or behavioristic—is to study their ontogenesis. A distinction is made in both approaches between spontaneously generated and imposed rules: In the cognitive approach, this distinction is referred to as *discovery* versus *instruction;* in the behavior analytic approach it is *shaping* versus *instructing*.

Rules and rule-governance are not susceptible to direct third-person observation, and in this sense they are not objectively observable. Indeed, they may not even be susceptible to reliable first-person observation. However, rules that are postulated to have objectively observable concomitants or consequences can be studied inferentially through study of their postulated concomitants or consequences. The reasoning involved is syllogistic: The postulate serves as a major premise, the observed correlate serves as a minor premise, and the inference about the rule is the conclusion deduced. Showing that the postulate is consistent with a theory of some scope adds significantly to the persuasiveness of the inference.

Cognitivists have used at least six kinds of observed correlates on which to base inferences about rule use. The least persuasive observations are that the target behavior is regular, that the development of the target behavior is discontinuous, and that research participants evidence awareness of rule use. Consistency of observed behavior with expected behavior is considerably more persuasive; but it is not a definitive criterion because of behavioral variability, among other problems. It becomes much more persuasive when more than one kind of behavior is expected and is observed, and when the inferred rule is further inferred to have generalized to other behaviors or tasks.

8. REFERENCES

Abel, T. (1953). The operation called *Verstehen*. In H. Feigl & M. Brodbeck (Eds.), *Readings in the philosophy of science* (pp. 677–687). New York: Appleton-Century-Crofts. (Reprinted from *American Journal of Sociology*, 1948, *54*, 211–218)

Aebli, H. (1979, June). Continuity-discontinuity from the perspective of Piagetian and post-Piagetian theory. In H. W. Reese & W. F. Overton (Chair), *Continuity-discontinuity as metatheoretical and theoretical issues*. Symposium presented at the meeting of the International Society for the Study of Behavioral Development, Lund, Sweden.

Ahlum-Heath, M. E., & Di Vesta. F. J. (1986). The effect of conscious controlled verbalization of a cognitive strategy on transfer in problem solving. *Memory & Cognition, 14,* 281–285.

American Psychological Association. (1983). *Publication manual of the American Psychological Association* (3rd ed.). Washington, DC: Author.

Amsel, A. (1958). The role of frustrative nonreward in noncontinuous reward situations. *Psychological Bulletin, 55,* 102–119.

Anderson, J. R. (1976). *Language, memory, and thought.* Hillsdale, NJ: Lawrence Erlbaum Associates. (Cited from Coulter, 1983, p. 5)

Anderson, J. R. (1980). *Cognitive psychology and its implications.* San Francisco: Freeman.

Anderson, J. R. (1982). Acquisition of cognitive skill. *Psychological Review, 89,* 369–406.

Argyle, M. (1984). The components of long-term relationships. In K. M. J. Lagerspetz & P. Niemi (Eds.), *Psychology in the 1990's* (pp. 453–481). Amsterdam: North-Holland.

Aristotle. (1926). *The Nichomachean ethics* (Trans. H. Rackham). London: William Heinemann.

Aristotle. (1933). *The metaphysics: Books I–IX* (Trans. H. Tredennick). London: William Heinemann.

Atkinson, R. C., & Shiffrin, R. M. (1968). Human memory: A proposed system and its control processes. In K. W. Spence & J. T. Spence (Eds.), *The psychology of learning and motivation: Advances in theory and research* (Vol. 2, pp. 89–195). New York: Academic Press.

Ault, R. L. (1983). *Children's cognitive development* (2nd ed.). New York: Oxford University Press.

Baer, D. M. (1982). Applied behavior analysis. In G. T. Wilson & C. M. Franks (Eds.), *Contemporary behavior therapy* (pp. 277–309). New York: Guilford.

Barker, P., & Gholson, B. (1984). The history of the psychology of learning as a rational process: Lakatos versus Kuhn. In H. W. Reese (Ed.), *Advances in child development and behavior* (Vol. 18, pp. 227–244). New York: Academic Press.

Baron, A., & Galizio, M. (1983). Instructional control of human operant behavior. *Psychological Record, 33,* 495–520.

Barton, E. J., & Ascione, F. R. (1979). Sharing in preschool children: Facilitation, stimulus generalization, response generalization, and maintenance. *Journal of Applied Behavior Analysis, 12,* 417–430.

Begleiter, H., Porjesz, B., Yerre, C., & Kissin, B. (1973). Evoked potential correlates of expected stimulus intensity. *Science, 179,* 814–816.

Bennett, J. (1966). *Kant's analytic.* Cambridge: Cambridge University Press.

Bentall, R. P., Lowe, C. F., & Beasty, A. (1985). The role of verbal behavior in human learning: II. Developmental differences. *Journal of the Experimental Analysis of Behavior, 43,* 165–181.

Bergmann, G. (1957). *Philosophy of science.* Madison: University of Wisconsin Press.

Berlyne, D. E. (1965). *Structure and direction in thinking.* New York: Wiley.

Bever, T. G., Fodor, J. A., & Garrett, M. (1968). A formal limitation of associationism. In T. R. Dixon & D. L. Horton (Eds.), *Verbal behavior and general behavior theory* (pp. 582–585). Englewood Cliffs, NJ: Prentice-Hall.

Bickhard, M. H., Cooper, R. G., & Mace, P. E. (1985). Vestiges of logical positivism: Critiques of stage explanations. *Human Development, 28,* 240–258.

Bijou, S. W. (1984). Cross-sectional and longitudinal analysis of development: The interbehavioral perspective. *Psychological Record, 34,* 525–535.

Bourne, L. E., Jr. (1970). Knowing and using concepts. *Psychological Review, 77,* 546–556.

Bower, G. H., Black, J. B., & Turner, T. J. (1979). Scripts in memory for text. *Cognitive Psychology, 11,* 177–220.

Bower, G. [H.], & Trabasso, T. (1963). Reversals prior to solution in concept identification. *Journal of Experimental Psychology, 66,* 409–418.

Bowman, R. E. (1963). Discrimination learning-set performance under intermittent and secondary reinforcement. *Journal of Comparative and Physiological Psychology, 56,* 429–434.

Brainerd, C. J. (1977). Cognitive development and concept learning: An interpretative review. *Psychological Bulletin, 84,* 919–939.

Bransford, J. D. (1979). *Human cognition: Learning, understanding and remembering.* Belmont, CA: Wadsworth.

Brewer, W. F. (1974). There is no convincing evidence for operant or classical conditioning in adult humans. In W. B. Weimer & D. S. Palermo (Eds.), *Cognition and the symbolic processes* (pp. 1–42). Hillsdale, NJ: Lawrence Erlbaum Associates.

Brown, J. S. (1961). *The motivation of behavior.* New York: McGraw-Hill.

Brownstein, A. J., & Shull, R. L. (1985). A rule for the use of the term, "rule-governed behavior." *Behavior Analyst, 8,* 265–267.

Bryan, W. L., & Harter, N. (1897). Studies in the physiology and psychology of the telegraphic language. *Psychological Review, 4,* 27–53.

Bryan, W. L., & Harter, N. (1899). Studies on the telegraphic language. The acquisition of a hierarchy of habits. *Psychological Review, 6,* 345–375.

Buchanan, J. P., Gill, T. V., & Braggio, J. T. (1981). Serial position and clustering effects in a chimpanzee's "free recall." *Memory & Cognition, 9,* 651–660.

Bugelski, B. R. (1956). *The psychology of learning.* New York: Holt.

Bugelski, B. R. (1965). In defense of remote associations. *Psychological Review, 72,* 169–174.

Bugelski, B. R., & Alampay, D. A. (1961). The role of frequency in developing perceptual sets. *Canadian Journal of Psychology, 15,* 205–211.

Catania, A. C., Matthews, B. A., & Shimoff, E. (1982). Instructed versus shaped human verbal behavior: Interactions with nonverbal responding. *Journal of the Experimental Analysis of Behavior, 38,* 233–248.

Chase, P. N., & Hyten, C. (1985). A historical and pedagogical note on establishing operations. *Behavior Analyst, 8,* 121–122.

Chomsky, N. (1959). Review of *Verbal behavior,* by B. F. Skinner. *Language, 25,* 26–58.

Chomsky, N. (1980). *Rules and representations.* New York: Columbia University Press.

Cohen, N. J. (1984). Preserved learning capacity in amnesia: Evidence for multiple memory systems. In L. R. Squire & N. Butters (Eds.), *Neuropsychology of memory* (pp. 83–103). New York: Guilford.

Cook, T. D., & Campbell, D. T. (1979). *Quasi-experimentation: Design and analysis issues for field settings.* Boston: Houghton Mifflin.

Coulter, J. (1983). *Rethinking cognitive theory.* New York: St. Martin's Press.

Craik, F. I. M., & Lockhart, R. S. (1972). Levels of processing: A framework for memory research. *Journal of Verbal Learning and Verbal Behavior, 11,* 671–684.

Dallett, K. M. (1965). In defense of remote associations. *Psychological Review, 72,* 164–168.

Doan, H. McK., & Cooper, D. L. (1971). Conditional discrimination learning in children: Two relevant factors. *Child Development, 42,* 209–220.

Dodd, D. H., & White, R. M., Jr. (1980). *Cognition: Mental structures and processes.* Boston: Allyn & Bacon.

Dollard, D., & Miller, N. E. (1950). *Personality and psychotherapy: An analysis in terms of learning, thinking, and culture.* New York: McGraw-Hill.

Dulany, D. E. (1974). On the support of cognitive theory in opposition to behavior theory: A methodological problem. In W. B. Weimer & D. S. Palermo (Eds.), *Cognition and the symbolic processes* (pp. 43–56). Hillsdale, NJ: Lawrence Erlbaum Associates.

Eich, E. (1984). Memory for unattended events: Remembering with and without awareness. *Memory & Cognition, 12,* 105–111.

Ellis, H. C. (1978). *Fundamentals of human learning, memory, and cognition* (2nd ed.). Dubuque, IA: Brown.

Ericsson, A. K., & Simon, H. A. (1984). *Protocol analysis: Verbal reports as data*. Cambridge, MA: MIT Press.

Estes, W. K. (1950). Toward a statistical theory of learning. *Psychological Review, 57*, 94–107.

Ferretti, R. P., & Butterfield, E. C. (1986). Are children's rule-assessment classifications invariant across instances of problem types? *Child Development, 57*, 1419–1428.

Ferster, C. B., & Skinner, B. F. (1957). *Schedules of reinforcement*. New York: Appleton-Century-Crofts.

Flavell, J. H. (1977). *Cognitive development*. Englewood Cliffs, NJ: Prentice-Hall.

Flavell, J. H., Beach, D. R., & Chinsky, J. M. (1966). Spontaneous verbal rehearsal in a memory task as a function of age. *Child Development, 37*, 283–299.

Fodor, J. A. (1981). The mind-body problem. *Scientific American, 244*(1), 114–123.

Furth, H. G. (1969). *Piaget and knowledge: Theoretical foundations*. Englewood Cliffs, NJ: Prentice-Hall.

Furth, H. G., & Wachs, H. (1974). *Thinking goes to school: Piaget's theory in practice*. New York: Oxford University Press.

Gagné, R. M. (1970). *The conditions of learning* (2nd ed.). New York: Holt, Rinehart & Winston.

Gagné, R. M. (1974). *Essentials of learning for instruction*. Hinsdale, IL: Dryden.

Galperin, P. Ya. (1957). An experimental study in the formation of mental actions (Trans. N. Parsons). In B. Simon (Ed.), *Psychology in the Soviet Union* (pp. 213–225). Stanford, CA: Stanford University Press.

Geiselman, R. E. (1979). Inhibition of the automatic storage of speaker's voice. *Memory & Cognition, 7*, 201–204.

Gholson, B., & Beilin, H. (1979). A developmental model of human learning. In H. W. Reese & L. P. Lipsitt (Eds.), *Advances in child development and behavior* (Vol. 13, pp. 47–81). New York: Academic Press.

Gholson, B., Levine, M., & Phillips, S. (1972). Hypotheses, strategies, and stereotypes in discrimination learning. *Journal of Experimental Child Psychology, 13*, 423–446.

Goodnow, J. J. (1972). Rules and repertoires, rituals and tricks of the trade: Social and informational aspects to cognitive and representational development. In S. Farnham-Diggory (Ed.), *Information processing in children* (pp. 83–102). New York: Academic Press.

Goss, A. E. (1961). Verbal mediating responses and concept formation. *Psychological Review, 68*, 248–274.

Grant, L. (1986). Categorizing and concept learning. In H. W. Reese & L. J. Parrott (Eds.), *Behavior science: Philosophical, methodological, and empirical advances* (pp. 139–162). Hillsdale, NJ: Lawrence Erlbaum Associates.

Guthrie, E. R. (1960). *The psychology of learning* (Rev. ed.). Gloucester, MA: P. Smith.

Hakes, D. T., & Young, R. K. (1966). On remote associations and the interpretation of derived-list experiments. *Psychological Review, 73*, 248–251.

Harlow, H. F. (1959). Learning set and error factor theory. In S. Koch (Ed.), *Psychology: A study of a science* (Vol. 2, pp. 492–537). New York: McGraw-Hill.

Hasher, L., & Zacks, R. T. (1979). Automatic and effortful processes in memory. *Journal of Experimental Psychology: General, 108*, 356–388.

Hayes, S. C. (1986). The case of the silent dog—verbal reports and the analysis of rules: A review of Ericsson and Simon's *Protocol analysis: Verbal reports as data. Journal of the Experimental Analysis of Behavior, 45*, 351–363.

Hayes, S. C., Brownstein, A. J., Haas, J. R., & Greenway, D. E. (1985). *Rules, multiple schedules, and extinction: Distinguishing differential responding from schedule sensitivity when rules are present*. Unpublished manuscript, University of North Carolina at Greensboro.

Hineline, P. N. (1983). When we speak of knowing. *Behavior Analyst, 6*, 183–186.

Hirst, W., Spelke, E. S., Reaves, C. C., Caharack, G., & Neisser, U. (1980). Dividing attention without alternation or automaticity. *Journal of Experimental Psychology: General, 109,* 98–117.

Holborn, S. W. (1982, April). *The effect of reinforcement schedules on exercise in obese and nonobese boys.* Paper presented at colloquium, Department of Psychology, West Virginia University, Morgantown.

Horton, D. L., & Turnage, T. W. (1976). *Human learning.* Englewood Cliffs, NJ: Prentice-Hall.

Howard, D. V. (1983). *Cognitive psychology: Memory, language, and thought.* New York: Macmillan.

Hull, C. L. (1943). *Principles of behavior: An introduction to behavior theory.* New York: Appleton-Century-Crofts.

Hunt, E. (1971). What kind of computer is man? *Cognitive Psychology, 2,* 57–98.

Jones, N. D. (1973). *Computability theory: An introduction.* New York: Academic Press.

Kail, R. (1979). *The development of memory in children.* San Francisco: Freeman.

Kail, R., & Bisanz, J. (1982). Information processing and cognitive development. In H. W. Reese (Ed.), *Advances in child development and behavior* (Vol. 17, pp. 45–81). New York: Academic Press.

Kaplan, A. (1964). *The conduct of inquiry.* San Francisco: Chandler.

Kausler, D. H. (1974). *Psychology of verbal learning and memory.* New York: Academic Press.

Keller, F. S., & Schoenfeld, W. N. (1950). *Principles of psychology: A systematic text in the science of behavior.* New York: Appleton-Century-Crofts.

Kellogg, R. T. (1982). When can we introspect accurately about mental processes? *Memory & Cognition, 10,* 141–144.

Kintsch, W., & van Dijk, T. A. (1978). Toward a model of text comprehension and production. *Psychological Review, 85,* 363–394.

Klahr, D. (1973). An information-processing approach to the study of cognitive development. In A. D. Pick (Ed.), *Minnesota Symposia on Child Psychology* (Vol. 7, pp. 141–177). Minneapolis: University of Minnesota Press.

Klahr, D. (1984). Transition processes in quantitative development. In R. J. Sternberg (Ed.), *Mechanisms of cognitive development* (pp. 101–139). New York: Freeman.

Klahr, D. (1985). Solving problems with ambiguous subgoal ordering: Preschoolers' performance. *Child Development, 56,* 940–952.

Klahr, D., & Robinson, M. (1981). Formal assessment of problem-solving and planning processes in preschool children. *Cognitive Psychology, 13,* 113–148.

Klahr, D., & Siegler, R. S. (1978). The representation of children's knowledge. In H. W. Reese & L. P. Lipsitt (Eds.), *Advances in child development and behavior* (Vol. 12, pp. 61–116). New York: Academic Press.

Klahr, D., & Wallace, J. G. (1972). Class inclusion processes. In S. Farnham-Diggory (Ed.), *Information processing in children* (pp. 143–172). New York: Academic Press.

Klahr, D., & Wallace, J. G. (1976). *Cognitive development: An information-processing view.* Hillsdale, NJ: Lawrence Erlbaum Associates.

Klatzky, R. L. (1980). *Human memory: Structure and processes* (2nd ed.). San Francisco: Freeman.

Kliegl, R., Smith, J., & Baltes, P. B. (in press). Testing-the-limits, expertise, and memory in adulthood and old age. In F. Klix & H. Hagendorf (Eds.), *Proceedings of symposium in memoriam Hermann Ebbinghaus.* Amsterdam: North-Holland.

Krechevsky, I. (1932a). "Hypotheses" in rats. *Psychological Review, 39,* 516–532.

Krechevsky, I. (1932b). "Hypotheses" versus "chance" in the pre-solution period in sensory discrimination-learning. *University of California Publications in Psychology, 6*(3), 27–44.

Krechevsky, I. (1932c). The genesis of "hypotheses" in rats. *University of California Publications in Psychology, 6*(4), 45–64.

Krechevsky, I. (1938). A study of the continuity of the problem-solving process. *Psychological Review, 45,* 107–133.

Kuhn, T. S. (1977). *The essential tension: Selected studies in scientific tradition and change.* Chicago: University of Chicago Press.

Kurzweil, R. (1985). What is artificial intelligence anyway? *American Scientist, 73,* 258–264.

LaBerge, D., & Samuels, S. J. (1974). Toward a theory of automatic information processing in reading. *Cognitive Psychology, 6,* 293–323.

Lakatos, I. (1978). *Philosophical papers. Vol. 1: The methodololgy of scientific research programmes* (J. Worrall & G. Currie, Eds.). Cambridge: Cambridge University Press.

Lamarre, J., & Holland, J. G. (1985). The functional independence of mands and tacts. *Journal of the Experimental Analysis of Behavior, 43,* 5–19.

Laudan, L. (1977). *Progress and its problems: Toward a theory of scientific growth.* Berkeley: University of California Press.

Leon, M. (1984). Rules mothers and sons use to integrate intent and damage information in their moral judgments. *Child Development, 55,* 2106–2113.

Levin, I., Wilkening, F., & Dembo, Y. (1984). Development of time quantification: Integration and nonintegration of beginnings and endings in comparing durations. *Child Development, 55,* 2160–2172.

Levine, M. (1959). A model of hypothesis behavior in discrimination learning set. *Psychological Review, 66,* 353–366.

Levinson, B., & Reese, H. W. (1967). Patterns of discrimination learning set in preschool children, fifth-graders, college freshmen, and the aged. *Monographs of the Society for Research in Child Development, 32*(7, Serial No. 115).

Luchins, A. S. (1942). Mechanization in problem solving: The effect of *Einstellung. Psychological Monographs, 54*(6, Whole No. 248).

Luria, A. R. (1973). *The working brain: An introduction to neuropsychology* (Trans. B. Haigh). New York: Basic Books.

Luria, A. R. (1980). *Higher cortical functions in man* (2nd ed., rev. & expanded; Trans. B. Haigh). New York: Basic Books.

Luria, A. R. (1981). *Language and cognition* (J. V. Wertsch, Ed.). New York: Wiley.

Mackenzie, B. D. (1977). *Behaviourism and the limits of scientific method.* Atlantic Highlands, NJ: Humanities Press.

Malott, R. W. (1982, May). *Some theoretical considerations about rule-governed behavior.* Paper presented in H. W. Reese (Chair), Rule-governed behavior. Symposium presented at the meeting of the Association for Behavior Analysis, Milwaukee, WI.

Malott, R. W. (1986). Self-management, rule-governed behavior, and everyday life. In H. W. Reese & L. J. Parrott (Eds.), *Behavior science: Philosophical, methodological, and empirical advances* (pp. 207–228). Hillsdale, NJ: Lawrence Erlbaum Associates.

Mandler, G. (1975). Consciousness: Respectable, useful, and probably necessary. In R. L. Solso (Ed.), *Information processing and cognition: The Loyola symposium* (pp. 229–254). Hillsdale, NJ: Lawrence Erlbaum Associates.

Mandler, J. M., & Johnson, N. S. (1977). Remembrance of things parsed: Story structure and recall. *Cognitive Psychology, 9,* 111–151.

Mao Zedong. (1965). On practice. In *Selected works of . . .* (Vol. 1, pp. 295–309; trans. of 2nd Chinese ed.). Peking: Foreign Languages Press. (Original work dated 1937)

Matlin, M. (1983). *Cognition.* New York: Holt, Rinehart & Winston.

Matthews, B. A., Catania, A. C., & Shimoff, E. (1985). Effects of uninstructed verbal behavior on nonverbal responding: Contingency descriptions versus performance descriptions. *Journal of the Experimental Analysis of Behavior, 43,* 155–164.

Mayer, R. E. (1983). *Thinking, problem solving, cognition.* New York: Freeman.

McCulloch, W. S. (1955). Mysterium iniquitatis—of sinful man aspiring into the place of God.

Scientific Monthly, 80, 35–39. Reprinted in P. G. Frank (Ed.), *The validation of scientific theories* (pp. 148–156). New York: Collier, 1961.

Merton, R. K. (1968). *Social theory and social structure: 1968 enlarged edition.* New York: Free Press.

Michael, J. (1982). Distinguishing between discriminative and motivational functions of stimuli. *Journal of the Experimental Analysis of Behavior, 37,* 149–155.

Miller, G. A. (1962). *Psychology: The science of mental life.* New York: Harper & Row.

Miller, G. A. (1981). *Language and speech.* San Francisco: Freeman.

Miller, G. A., Galanter, E., & Pribram, K. H. (1960). *Plans and the structure of behavior.* New York: Holt.

Miller, P. H., Haynes, V. F., DeMarie-Dreblow, D., & Woody-Ramsey, J. (1986). Children's strategies for gathering information in three tasks. *Child Development, 57,* 1429–1439.

Moore, J. (1981). On mentalism, methodological behaviorism, and radical behaviorism. *Behaviorism, 9,* 55–77.

Moore, J. (1984). On the tactful specification of meaning: A review of Harre and Lamb's *The Encyclopedic Dictionary of Psychology. Journal of the Experimental Analysis of Behavior, 41,* 387–395.

Morris, E. K., Higgins, S. T., & Bickel, W. K. (1982). Comments on cognitive science in the experimental analysis of behavior. *Behavior Analyst, 5,* 109–125.

Navarick, D. J. (1979). *Principles of learning: From laboratory to field.* Reading, MA: Addison-Wesley.

Newell, A. (1972). A note on process-structure distinctions in developmental psychology. In S. Farnham-Diggory (Ed.), *Information processing in children* (pp. 125–139). New York: Academic Press.

Nisbett, R. E., & Wilson, T. DeC. (1977). Telling more than we can know: Verbal reports on mental processes. *Psychological Review, 84,* 231–259.

Nissen, H. W. (1950). Description of the learned response in discrimination behavior. *Psychological Review, 57,* 121–131.

Nissen, H. W. (1953). Sensory patterning versus central organization. *Journal of Psychology, 36,* 271–287.

Nissen, H. W., Levinson, B., & Nichols, J. W. (1953). Reinforcement and "hypothesis" in the discrimination behavior of chimpanzees. *Journal of Experimental Psychology, 45,* 334–340.

O'Brien, D. P., & Overton, W. F. (1982). Conditional reasoning and the competence-performance issue: A developmental analysis of a training task. *Journal of Experimental Child Psychology, 34,* 274–290.

Overton, W. [F.], Byrnes, J. P., & O'Brien, D. P. (1985). Developmental and individual differences in conditional reasoning: The role of contradiction training and cognitive style. *Developmental Psychology, 21,* 692–701.

Overton, W. F., & Newman, J. L. (1982). Cognitive development: A competence-activation/utilization approach. In T. M. Field, A. Huston, H. C. Quay, L. Troll, & G. E. Finley (Eds.), *Review of human development* (pp. 217–241). New York: Wiley.

Overton, W. F., & Reese, H. W. (1981). Conceptual prerequisites for an understanding of stability-change and continuity-discontinuity. *International Journal of Behavioral Development, 4,* 99–123.

Oxford English dictionary (13 vols.). (1933). Oxford: Clarendon Press.

Parrott, L. J. (1982, May). *Rule-governed behavior: An implicit analysis of reference.* Paper presented in H. W. Reese (Chair), Rule-governed behavior. Symposium presented at the meeting of the Association for Behavior Analysis, Milwaukee, WI.

Parrott, L. J. (1983). Perspectives on knowing and knowledge. *Psychological Record, 33,* 171–184.

Parsons, J. A., Taylor, D. C., & Joyce, T. M. (1981). Precurrent self-prompting operants in children: "Remembering." *Journal of the Experimental Analysis of Behavior, 36*, 253–266.

Pepper, S. C. (1942). *World hypotheses: A study in evidence.* Berkeley: University of California Press.

Piaget, J. (1970). Piaget's theory. In P. H. Mussen (Ed.), *Carmichael's manual of child psychology* (3rd ed.; Vol. 1, pp. 703–732). New York: Wiley. (Reprinted in P. H. Mussen [Ed.], *Handbook of child psychology* [4th ed.], Vol. 1, *History, theory, and methods* [W. Kessen, Ed.; pp. 103–128]. New York: Wiley, 1983)

Pinsky, L. (1951). Do machines think about machines thinking? *Mind, 60*, 397–398.

Pratt, M. W., McLaren, J., & Wickens, G. (1984). Rules as tools: Effective generalization of verbal self-regulative communication training by first-grade speakers. *Developmental Psychology, 20*, 893–902.

Prosch, H. (1964). *The genesis of twentieth century philosophy: The evolution of thought from Copernicus to the present.* Garden City, NY: Doubleday.

Prytulak, L. S. (1971). Natural language mediation. *Cognitive Psychology, 2*, 1–56.

Pulaski, M. A. S. (1971). *Understanding Piaget: An introduction to children's cognitive development.* New York: Harper & Row.

Pylyshyn, Z. W. (1972). Competence and psychological reality. *American Psychologist, 27*, 546–552.

Ravn, K. E., & Gelman, S. A. (1984). Rule usage in children's understanding of "big" and "little." *Child Development, 55*, 2141–2150.

Reed, S. K. (1982). *Cognition: Theory and applications.* Monterey, CA: Brooks/Cole.

Reese, H. W. (1962). Verbal mediation as a function of age level. *Psychological Bulletin, 59*, 502–509.

Reese, H. W. (1963). Discrimination learning set in children. In L. P. Lipsitt & C. C. Spiker (Eds.), *Advances in child development and behavior* (Vol. 1, pp. 115–145). New York: Academic Press.

Reese, H. W. (1964). Discrimination learning set in rhesus monkeys. *Psychological Bulletin, 61*, 321–340.

Reese, H. W. (1965). Discrimination learning set and perceptual set in young children. *Child Development, 36*, 153–161.

Reese, H. W. (1968). *The perception of stimulus relations: Discrimination learning and transposition.* New York: Academic Press.

Reese, H. W. (1970a). The scope of experimental child psychology. In H. W. Reese & L. P. Lipsitt (Eds.), *Experimental child psychology* (pp. 1–12). New York: Academic Press.

Reese, H. W. (1970b). Set. In H. W. Reese & L. P. Lipsitt (Eds.), *Experimental child psychology* (pp. 263–278). New York: Academic Press.

Reese, H. W. (1971). The study of covert verbal and nonverbal mediation. In. A. Jacobs & L. B. Sachs (Eds.), *The psychology of private events: Perspectives on covert response systems* (pp. 17–38). New York: Academic Press.

Reese, H. W. (1976a). *Basic learning processes in childhood.* New York: Holt, Rinehart & Winston.

Reese, H. W. (1976b). The development of memory: Life-span perspectives. In H. W. Reese (Ed.), *Advances in child development and behavior* (Vol. 11, pp. 189–212). New York: Academic Press.

Reese, H. W. (1986). On the theory and practice of behavior analysis. In H. W. Reese & L. J. Parrott (Eds.), *Behavior science: Philosophical, methodological, and empirical advances* (pp. 1–33). Hillsdale, NJ: Lawrence Erlbaum Associates.

Reese, H. W., & Ford, L. H., Jr. (1962). Expectancy and perception of an ambiguous figure in preschool children. *Journal of Verbal Learning and Verbal Behavior, 1*, 188–191.

Reese, H. W., & Fremouw, W. J. (1984). Normal and normative ethics in behavioral sciences. *American Psychologist, 39,* 863–876.

Reynolds, A. G., & Flagg, P. W. (1983). *Cognitive psychology* (2nd ed.). Boston: Little Brown.

Riegler, H. C., Kohler, F. W., & Baer, D. M. (1985, May). *Rule-governed behavior: A discussion of its origins, functions, and maintenance.* Paper presented at the meeting of the Association for Behavior Analysis, Columbus, OH.

Rosser, R. A., & Brody, G. H. (1981). Acquisition of a concrete operational rule through observational learning: How abstract is the acquired abstraction. *Merrill-Palmer Quarterly, 27,* 3–13.

Rychlak, J. F. (1976). Psychological science as a humanist sees it. In W. J. Arnold (Ed.), *Nebraska Symposium on Motivation. Vol. 23: 1975* (pp. 205–279). Lincoln: University of Nebraska Press.

Sands, S. F., & Wright, A. A. (1980). Primate memory: Retention of serial list items by a rhesus monkey. *Science, 209,* 938–940.

Schnaitter, R. (1977). Behaviorism and ethical responsibility. In J. E. Krapfl & E. A. Vargas (Eds.), *Behaviorism and ethics* (pp. 29–42). Kalamazoo, MI: Behaviordelia.

Schnaitter, R. (1985). The haunted clockwork: Reflections on Gilbert Ryle's *The Concept of Mind. Journal of the Experimental Analysis of Behavior, 43,* 145–153.

Schneider, W., & Shiffrin, R. M. (1977). Controlled and automatic human information processing: I. Detection, search, and attention. *Psychological Review, 84,* 1–66.

Seamon, J. G. (1980). *Memory and cognition: An introduction.* New York: Oxford University Press.

Searle, J. (1976). The rules of the language game [review of N. Chomsky, *Reflections on language*]. *Times Literary Supplement,* September 10, pp. 1118–1120.

Shiffrin, R. M., & Schneider, W. (1977). Controlled and automatic human information processing: II. Perceptual learning, automatic attending, and a general theory. *Psychological Review, 84,* 127–190.

Shultz, T. R., & Robillard, J. (1980). The development of linguistic humour in children: Incongruity through rule violation. In P. E. McGhee & A. J. Chapman (Eds.), *Children's humour* (pp. 59–90). Chichester: Wiley.

Shultz, T. R., Fisher, G. W., Pratt, C. C., & Rulf, S. (1986). Selection of causal rules. *Child Development, 57,* 143–152.

Siegler, R. S. (1976). Three aspects of cognitive development. *Cognitive Psychology, 8,* 481–520.

Siegler, R. S. (1981). Developmental sequences within and between concepts. *Monographs of the Society for Research in Child Development, 46*(2, Serial No. 189).

Siegler, R. S. (1983a). Five generalizations about cognitive development. *American Psychologist, 38,* 263–277.

Siegler, R. S. (1983b). Information processing approaches to development. In P. H. Mussen (Ed.), *Handbook of child psychology* (4th ed.). Vol. 1: *History, theory, and methods* (W. Kessen, Ed.; pp. 129–211). New York: Wiley.

Simon, H. A. (1962). An information processing theory of intellectual development. In W. Kessen & C. Kuhlman (Eds.), *Thought in the young child: Report of a conference on intellective development with particular attention to the work of Jean Piaget* (pp. 150–155). *Monographs of the Society for Research in Child Development, 27*(2, Serial No. 83).

Simon, H. A. (1972). On the development of the processor. In S. Farnham-Diggory (Ed.), *Information processing in children* (pp. 3–22). New York: Academic Press.

Simon, H. A. (1975). The functional equivalence of problem solving skills. *Cognitive Psychology, 7,* 268–288.

Skinner, B. F. (1945). The operational analysis of psychological terms. *Psychological Review, 52,* 270–277.

Skinner, B. F. (1953). *Science and human behavior*. New York: Free Press.

Skinner, B. F. (1957). *Verbal behavior*. New York: Appleton-Century-Crofts.

Skinner, B. F. (1969). *Contingencies of reinforcement: A theoretical analysis*. New York: Appleton-Century-Crofts.

Skinner, B. F. (1974). *About behaviorism*. New York: Knopf.

Skinner, B. F. (1977a, September). Between freedom and despotism. *Psychology Today*, pp. 80–91. Reprinted as "Human behavior and democracy" in B. F. Skinner (1978), *Reflections on behaviorism and society* (pp. 3–15), Englewood Cliffs, NJ: Prentice-Hall.

Skinner, B. F. (1977b). Why I am not a cognitive psychologist. *Behaviorism, 5*(2), 1–10. Reprinted in B. F. Skinner (1978), *Reflections on behaviorism and society* (pp. 97–112). Englewood Cliffs, NJ: Prentice-Hall.

Skinner, B. F. (1978). Are we free to have a future? In B. F. Skinner, *Reflections on behaviorism and society* (pp. 16–32). Englewood Cliffs, NJ: Prentice-Hall.

Skinner, B. F. (1982). Contrived reinforcement. *Behavior Analyst, 5*, 3–8.

Skinner, B. F. (1984). The evolution of behavior. *Journal of the Experimental Analysis of Behavior, 41*, 217–221.

Slamecka, N. J. (1964). An inquiry into the doctrine of remote associations. *Psychological Review, 71*, 61–76.

Slamecka, N. J. (1965). In defense of a new approach to old phenomena. *Psychological Review, 72*, 242–246.

Slobin, D. I. (1979). *Psycholinguistics* (2nd ed.). Glenview, IL: Scott, Foresman.

Smith, N. K. (1923). *A commentary to Kant's 'Critique of pure reason'* (2nd ed, rev. & enlarged). New York: Humanities Press. (1962 reprint)

Solso, R. L. (1979). *Cognitive psychology*. New York: Harcourt Brace Jovanovich.

Spelke, E., Hirst, W., & Neisser, U. (1976). Skills of divided attention. *Cognition, 4*, 215–230.

Spence, K. W. (1937). The differential response in animals to stimuli varying within a single dimension. *Psychological Review, 44*, 430–444. Reprinted in K. W. Spence (1960), *Behavior theory and learning: Selected papers* (pp. 292–307). Englewood Cliffs, NJ: Prentice-Hall.

Spence, K. W. (1940). Continuous versus non-continuous interpretations of discrimination learning. *Psychological Review, 47*, 271–288. Reprinted in K. W. Spence (1960), *Behavior theory and learning: Selected papers* (pp. 308–325). Englewood Cliffs, NJ: Prentice-Hall.

Spence, K. W. (1952). The nature of the response in discrimination learning. *Psychological Review, 59*, 89–93. Reprinted in K. W. Spence (1960), *Behavior theory and learning: Selected papers* (pp. 359–365). Englewood Cliffs, NJ: Prentice-Hall.

Spence, K. W. (1956). *Behavior theory and conditioning*. New Haven: Yale University Press.

Spence, K. W. (1960). The roles of reinforcement and non-reinforcement in simple learning. In K. W. Spence (1960), *Behavior theory and learning: Selected papers* (pp. 91–112). Englewood Cliffs, NJ: Prentice-Hall.

Spiker, C. C., & Cantor, J. H. (1973). Applications of Hull-Spence theory to the transfer of discrimination learning in children. In H. W. Reese (Ed.), *Advances in child development and behavior* (Vol. 8, pp. 223–288). New York: Academic Press.

Stone, C. A., & Day, M. C. (1980). Competence and performance models and the characterization of formal operational skills. *Human Development, 23*, 323–353.

Swift, E. J. (1904). The acquisition of skill in type-writing; a contribution to the psychology of learning. *Psychological Bulletin, 1*, 295–305.

Thomas, W. I. (1951). *Social behavior and personality: Contributions of W. I. Thomas to theory and social research* (Ed. E. H. Vokart). New York: Social Science Research Council.

Thomas, W. I., & Thomas, D. S. (1928). *The child in America: Behavior problems and programs*. New York: Knopf.

Thorndyke, P. W. (1977). Cognitive structures in comprehension and memory of narrative discourse. *Cognitive Psychology, 9*, 77–110.

Tolman, E. C., & Krechevsky, I. (1933). Means-end-readiness and hypothesis—A contribution to comparative psychology. *Psychological Review, 40,* 60–70.

Toulmin, S. (1971). The concept of ''stages'' in psychological development. In T. Mischel (Ed.), *Cognitive development and epistemology* (pp. 25–60). New York: Academic Press.

Trabasso, T., & Bower, G. [H.] (1964). Presolution reversal and dimensional shifts in concept identification. *Journal of Experimental Psychology, 67,* 398–399.

Tranel, D., & Damasio, A. R. (1985). Knowledge without awareness: An autonomic index of facial recognition by prosopagnosics. *Science, 228,* 1453–1454.

Tulving, E. (1974). Cue-dependent forgetting. *American Scientist, 62,* 74–82.

Turing, A. M. (1950). Computing machinery and intelligence. *Mind, 59,* 433–460.

Urbain, C., Poling, A., Millam, J., & Thompson, T. (1978). *d*-Amphetamine and fixed-interval performance: Effects of operant history. *Journal of the Experimental Analysis of Behavior, 29,* 385–392.

Vygotsky, L. S. (1978). *Mind in society: The development of higher psychological processes* (Eds. M. Cole, V. John-Steiner, S. Scribner, E. Souberman). Cambridge, MA: Harvard University Press.

Waston, J. B. (1926). What the nursery has to say about instincts. In M. Bentley, K. Dunlap, W. S. Hunter, K. Koffka, W. Kohler, W. McDougall, M. Prince, J. B. Watson, & R. S. Woodworth, *Psychologies of 1925: Powell Lectures in Psychological Theory* (pp. 1–35). Worcester, MA: Clark University Press.

Webster's third new international dictionary of the English language (Unabridged). (1981). Springfield, MA: Merriam.

Weiner, H. (1969a). Conditioning history and the control of human avoidance and escape responding. *Journal of the Experimental Analysis of Behavior, 12,* 1039–1043.

Weiner, H. (1969b). Controlling human fixed-interval performance. *Journal of the Experimental Analysis of Behavior, 12,* 349–373.

Werkmeister, W. H. (1948). *An introduction to critical thinking: A beginner's text in logic.* Lincoln, NB: Johnsen.

White, P. (1980). Limitations on verbal reports of internal events: A refutation of Nisbett and Wilson and of Bem. *Psychological Review, 87,* 105–112.

Wilkening, F., & Anderson, N. H. (1982). Comparison of two rule-assessment methodologies for studying cognitive development and knowledge structure. *Psychological Bulletin, 92,* 215–237.

Wittig, A. F. (1981). *Schaum's outline of theory and problems of psychology of learning.* New York: McGraw-Hill.

Wolford, G., & Morrison, F. (1980). Processing of unattended visual information. *Memory & Cognition, 8,* 521–527.

Wright, A. A., Santiago, H. C., Sands, S. F., Kendrick, D. F., & Cook, R. G. (1985). Memory processing of serial lists by pigeons, monkeys, and people. *Science, 229,* 287–289.

Zettle, R. D., & Hayes, S. C. (1982). Rule-governed behavior: A potential framework for cognitive-behavioral therapy. In P. C. Kendall (Ed.), *Advances in cognitive-behavioral research and therapy* (Vol. 1, pp. 73–118). New York: Academic Press.

CHAPTER 2

The Behavior of the Listener

B. F. SKINNER

1. INTRODUCTION

In the traditional view of a speech episode, held by philosophers for thousands of years, the speaker perceives some part of the world in the literal sense of capturing or taking it in (or rather, because there is no room for the world itself, taking in a copy or representation) and then puts the copy into words, the meanings of which correspond in some way with what the speaker perceived. The listener takes the meanings out of the words and composes another copy or representation. The listener thus *receives* or *conceives* what the speaker has *perceived.* Something has been communicated in the sense of made common to both speaker and listener. A message has been sent, the content of which is sometimes called information. Information theory, however, was invented to deal only with the structural features of a message (how many bits or bytes could be sent through a telephone line or stored in a computer?). The content of a message is more appropriately called knowledge, from a root that gave the Greek word *gnomein,* the Latin *gnoscere,* the late-Latin *co-gnitio,* and at last our own *cognition.*

In a behavioral account, the direction of action is exactly reversed. Speakers do not take in the world and put it into words; they respond to it in ways that have been shaped and maintained by special contingencies of reinforcement. Listeners do not extract information or knowledge from words and compose second-hand copies of the world; they respond to verbal stimuli in ways that have been shaped and maintained by other contingencies of reinforcement. Both contingencies are maintained by an evolved verbal environment or culture.

That is a very great difference, as great, perhaps, as the difference be-

B. F. SKINNER • Department of Psychology, Harvard University, Cambridge, Massachusetts 02138.

tween creation and natural selection in evolutionary theory. The origin of behavior raises quite as many problems as the origin of species. A minor problem will be illustrated in what follows. In using modern English, you find yourself implying the traditional view in the very act of challenging it. Only at special times can you be technical and correct. The rest of the time everyday English must suffice, and one must expect to be accused of inconsistency.

The problem is especially hard to solve when the behavior is verbal. Speakers are not initiators. Neither in the evolution of a verbal environment nor in the conditioning of speakers and listeners does speaking come first. There must be a listener before there can be a speaker. That seems to be true of the signaling behavior of nonverbal species. Something one animal does (making a noise, moving in a given way, leaving a trace) becomes a signal only when another animal responds to it.

Most of my book, *Verbal Behavior* (1957), was about the speaker. It contained a few diagrams showing interactions between speakers and listeners but little direct discussion of listening. I could justify that because, except when the listener was also to some extent speaking, listening was not verbal in the sense of being "effective only through the mediation of other persons" (Skinner, 1957). But if listeners are responsible for the behavior of speakers, we need to look more closely at when they do.

2. THE VERBAL OPERANT

When we say that behavior is controlled by the environment, we mean two very different things. The environment shapes and maintains repertoires of behavior, but it also serves as the occasion upon which behavior occurs. The concept of the operant makes this distinction. We say that we reinforce a response when we make a reinforcer contingent upon it, but we do not change that particular response. What we reinforce in the sense of strengthen is the operant, the probability that similar responses will occur in the future. That is more than the distinction between class and member of a class. My paper "The Generic Nature of Stimulus and Response" (1935) was about classes. Responses are never exactly alike, but orderly changes appear if we count only those instances that have a defining property. An operant is a class of responses, not an instance, but it is also a probability.

When that distinction is ignored, references to behavior are often ambiguous. Nest building, for example, can mean (1) a *kind* of behavior (something birds characteristically do), (2) a *probability* of behaving ("Nest building appears shortly after mating"), and (3) an *instance* ("The bird is building a nest"). Similarly, pressing a lever can mean (1) a *kind* of behavior (something operant conditioners often study), (2) a *probability* (pressing is strengthened when a response is followed by a reinforcer), and (3) an instance ("The rat is pressing the lever.'') Something of the sort may be said of cultural practices. Plowing is (1) a *kind* of behavior (''Plowing first appeared in ancient Mesopotamia and Egypt), (2) a *probability* (plowing depends upon the weather), and (3) an instance (''The farmer is plowing his field.'')

Similar distinctions are crucial in speaking of verbal behavior. (1) A *language* is a *kind* of behavior (English, Arabic, and so on). It exists even though no one is speaking it. (No one need speak it at all if it is a dead language.) Its practices are recorded in dictionaries (which give meanings only as words having the same meanings) and in grammars (rules describing conventional arrangements of words). (2) A verbal *operant* is a probability. Five kinds of operants—mand, tact, intraverbal, echoic, and textural—are distinguished by their respective contingencies of reinforcement. They are maintained by verbal environments or cultures—that is, by listeners. (3) The verbal behavior we observe and study is composed of instances, with respect to which listeners play their second role as part of the occasion upon which behavior occurs. We call a verbal response a *mand* or a *tact* but only to indicate the kind of reinforcing history responsible for its occurrence. It would be more precise, but less convenient, to say mand response or tact response, using *mand* and *tact* as nouns to refer to operants and as adjectives to identify kinds of instances. Intraverbal, echoic, and textual are already adjectives, and we convert them into nouns to refer to operants. (Incidentally, the difference between an operant and a response is not the differences between competence and performance. A performance is a response, but a probability of responding is more than merely being *able* to respond. The difference between probability and instance is also not the difference between a verbal operant and an assertion.)

There is no very good word for the occurrence of a verbal response. *Utter* simply means to *outer* or *bring behavior out,* not to have any effect on a listener. *Speak* first meant merely to make a noise; a gun can speak. *Say* and *tell,* however, imply effects on listeners. We say or tell something to someone. When we ask what someone has said, we may be given either the same words (the utterance) or other words having the same effect on the listener and hence ''saying the same thing.'' Let us look at some of the major effects on the listener that shape and maintain the behavior of the speaker.

3. EFFECTS ON THE LISTENER

3.1. The Listener Is Told

In one type of speech episode, speaker and listener compose what would otherwise be one person. If there is no doorman at a hotel, we go to the curb and hail a taxi. To a doorman, however, we say *Taxi, please. Taxi* is a mand, and the doorman hails a taxi. (The *please* is an autoclitic. It identifies *taxi,* not only as a mand, but as the particular kind called a request.) If, on the other hand, we have ordered a taxi and are waiting for it in the lobby, and the doorman comes and says *taxi* when it arrives, that is a tact, and we respond as if we had seen the taxi ourselves. The mand frees us from making a response. The tact replaces a discriminative stimulus controlling a response.

Verbal behavior usually occurs in larger samples called sentences. Whole sentences may be operants, but most are put together or "composed" on the spot. (Because a sentence may never have occurred before if the conditions responsible for its parts have never occurred before, the number of potential sentences is therefore infinite. They are presumably realizable only in infinite time, however.)

Traditionally, a sentence is said to "express" something, again in the sense of "bring it out." Until it has been expressed, the something is presumably accessible only through introspection and is usually called a thought. A sentence is also said to express a feeling. (The word *sentence* is etymologically close to *sentiment*.) What is felt is often called an intention. (We use *mean* as a synonym of *intend* when we say *I mean to go*.) The wrong meaning has been drawn from what is said if the listener does not do what the speaker "intended."

Because introspective evidence of feelings and states of mind still resists systematic analysis, cognitive psychologists have turned to other evidence of what is happening when a person behaves verbally. Their basic formulation is close to that of the old stimulus–response formula. People do not respond to the world about them; they "process" it as information. What that means must be inferred from what they do, however. The data consist of input and output. What is seen is processed and stored as a representation, which can be retrieved and described upon a given occasion. When the something done has been reinforced, the contingencies are "processed" and stored as rules, to be retrieved and put to use. The behavior itself can be analyzed in a much simpler way by looking directly at the contingencies of reinforcement, but that is something cognitive psychologists almost never do.

The contingencies easily account for another problem that seems to be out of reach of introspection. Listeners are said to respond to what speakers say if they *trust* or *believe* them. It is simpler to say that trust and belief are simply bodily states resulting from histories of reinforcement. We use the same words for nonverbal behavior. I "believe" a small object on my desk is my pen, in the sense that I tend to pick it up when I am about to write something. I do so because when I have picked up similar objects in the past they have proved to be pens. I "trust" my chair will hold me because it has always done so.

In the long run, we believe or trust those who most often qualify what they say with appropriate autoclitics. Perhaps we are more likely to respond to a speaker who says, "The door *is* unlocked" than one who says "*I think* the door is unlocked," or "The door *may be* unlocked," but in the long run we shall believe or trust those who have added the qualifying autoclitics to tell us something about the strength of their behavior and have therefore less often misled us.

In the simplest case, then, a speaker tells a listener what to do or what has happened because listeners have reinforced similar behavior in similar situations, and the listeners have done so because in similar situations certain reinforcing consequences have followed for them.

3.2. The Listener Is Taught

Teaching is more than telling. When the doorman said *taxi,* we "learned" that a taxi was waiting, but we were not taught. When we were first told *that's a taxi,* we "learned what a taxi looks like," but again we were not taught. Teaching occurs when a response is primed, in the sense of being evoked for the first time, and then reinforced. For example, a teacher models a verbal response and reinforces our repetition of it. If we cannot repeat all of it, we may need to be prompted, but eventually the behavior occurs without help.

The same two steps can be seen when we teach ourselves. We read a passage in a book (thus priming the behavior), turn away and say as much of it as we can, and turn back to the book for prompts if needed. Success in saying the passage without help is the reinforcing consequence.

Instructional contingencies in schools and colleges are designed to prepare students for contingencies of reinforcement that they will encounter at some later time. Few, if any, natural reinforcers are therefore available, and reinforcers must be contrived. Something like a spoken "Right!" or "Good!" or confirmation by a teaching machine must be made contingent on the behavior. Grades are almost always deferred, and the prevailing contingencies are therefore usually aversive. When we correct someone in the course of a conversation we are also teaching. We are priming the kind of response that will not be corrected. Unfortunately, that too is usually aversive.

3.3. The Listener Is Advised

Different effects on the listener distinguish telling and teaching from advising or warning. *Look out!* is a warning; the listener looks and avoids harm—escapes being struck by a car, perhaps. *Look!* is advice; the listener looks and sees something—an interesting person passing in a car, perhaps. Those are not contrived consequences. Advice and warning bring uncontrived consequences into play.

Not all advice has the form of a mand, of course. To a friend who has expressed an interest in seafood, you may say *The Harborside Restaurant serves excellent seafood.* To someone who is merely learning about the city as a place to live, that is only telling. To someone who is preparing to be a guide to the city, it is one step in teaching. Only to a listener who is looking for a particular kind of restaurant is it advice. The instructions that come with complex equipment *tell* us what the equipment will do. They *advise* us how to use it for the first time. They *teach* us to use it if it functions in a reinforcing way.

Two familiar autoclitics, *ought* and *should,* are used in advice. *Ought* means *owed. You ought to go to the Harborside Restaurant* means you owe it to yourself to go there. *You ought to serve your country* means you owe it to your country, for reasons we shall consider in a moment. *Should* is the past tense of *shall,* which has a remote etymological connection with commitment or inevitability. In other words, *ought* and *should* allude, if only indirectly, to the contingencies that reinforce taking advice.

Because we define *advice* by its effect on the listener, it cannot be advice when it is first given. Advice is taken first because the behavior it specifies has been reinforced in some other way. *Look out!* is perhaps first a simple mand, effective because of earlier aversive consequences. When other consequences follow, it becomes advice.

Proverbs and maxims are public advice. Etymologically, a proverb is a saying "put forth": a maxim is a "great saying." Transmitted by books or word of mouth, they have lives of their own. They are seldom specific to the situations in which they occur and are often simply metaphors. Only a blacksmith can "strike while the iron is hot," but the expression is easily remembered and may help in advising people to act while the probability of reinforcement is high.

3.4. The Listener Is Rule-Directed

There are many reasons why groups of people observe "norms," or why their members behave in "normal" ways. Some of the ways are traceable to the natural selection of the species and others to the common reinforcing environments of the members of a group. Members imitate each other and serve as models. They reinforce conformity and punish deviance. At some point in the history of a group, however, a new reason for behaving as others have behaved appears in the form of a rule. Like proverbs and maxims, rules have a life of their own apart from particular speakers or listeners. They help members of a group behave in ways most likely to be commended and least likely to be censured, and they help the group commend and censure consistently. Rules may be mands *(Don't smoke here)* or tacts *(Smoking is forbidden here).* A posted *No smoking* identifies a kind of behavior and a punitive consequence. *Black tie* on an invitation specifies the clothing to be worn to avoid criticism. The clothing worn by the military is "regulation," from the Latin *regula* or *rule*. Organizations conduct orderly meetings when their members observe rules of order. The rules tell us what we ought to do in the sense of what we owe the group. That is rather different from what we ought to do to please ourselves. The autoclitic *ought* takes on the ethical sense of what is right or normal for the group.

We "discover the meaning" of a rule when we engage in the behavior it specifies and are affected by the consequences. That is hard to do with proverbs or maxims. Having learned that procrastination is the a thief of time, we are probably no less likely to put off unpleasant tasks. Much later, when the contingencies themselves have shaped a readier completion of required work, we may discover what the maxim means—the effect it was intended to have on us.

Cognitive psychologists confuse matters by arguing that rules are *in* the contingencies and must be extracted from them. Presumably they do so because they need something to be stored according to their theories. A hungry rat presses a lever, receives food, and then begins to press more rapidly. We ourselves do something rather like that when, exploring an unfamiliar coffee machine, we press a lever, fill our cup, and subsequently press the lever whenever a full cup is reinforcing. Neither of us has discovered a rule; a bit of behavior has simply been reinforced. We differ from the rat, however, because we can report what has happened ("pressing the lever produced coffee.") We can also advise others how to use the machine for the first time. We can post a rule (*press lever to get coffee*). Only when we behave verbally in some such way, however, is a rule involved.

The rules of games describe invented contingencies of reinforcement. There are natural contingencies in which running faster than another person is reinforced, but the contingencies in a marathon are contrived. Fighting with one's fists has natural consequences in the street but additional contrived consequences in the ring. Games like baseball or basketball are played according to rules. The play is nonverbal, but the rules are maintained by umpires and referees whose behavior is decidedly verbal. The moves of go and chess are themselves verbal in the sense that they are reinforced only by their effects on the other player. The games suggest genuine conflicts—the conquest of territory in go and a war between royal houses in chess, but the pieces are moved only in rule-governed ways, and winning is a conventional outcome.

Although those who play games begin by following the rules, they may discover ways of playing that are not explicitly covered—new strategies in baseball and basketball, for example, or new openings and replies in go and chess. Advanced players sometimes described these strategies in additional rules. When they do not, we call them intuitive.

Logic and mathematics presumably arose from simple contingencies of reinforcement. The distinction between *is* and *is not* and the relation of *if* to *then* are features of the physical world, and numbers must have appeared first when people started to count things. When rules were once formulated at that level, however, new rules began to be derived from them, and the practical contingencies were soon left far behind. Many mathematicians have said that what they do has no reference whatsoever to the real world, in spite of the uses made of it.

Are logic and mathematics then games? There is a distinction between "play" and "game" that is worth preserving. Games are competitive. The move made by the go or chess player who is at the moment "speaking" is reinforced by any sign that it strengthens a position against the current "listener." Skillful repertoires are shaped and maintained by such consequences. The "moves" of logicians and mathematicians are reinforced primarily by progress toward the solution of a problem. Small animals are said to play when they are behaving in ways that are not yet having any serious consequences, and logicians and mathematicians are perhaps playing in much the same sense. "Game," however, too strongly suggests a winner and a loser.

3.5. The Listener Is Law Governed

Rules work to the mutual advantage of those who maintain the contingencies and those who are affected by them. Rules are, in short, a form of group self-management. That can be said of the laws of governments when the governments are chosen by the governed, but that is not always the case. The so-called parliamentary laws are rules of order; they govern parliaments. The laws passed by parliaments govern nations. Special branches of a government, the police and the military, maintain the contingencies, and throughout history the contingencies have usually worked to the advantage of those who maintained them. Religious laws seem to have begun as statements about norms, but they became more than rules when supernatural sanctions were invoked in their support. What were presumably certain norms of the Jewish people, for example, became laws when formulated as the Ten Commandments.

Goods and services were presumably first exchanged according to evolved norms. One thing was "worth" another if it was equally reinforcing. Money as a conditioned reinforcer made it easy to compare reinforcing effects. The price posted on a loaf of bread is a rule. It describes a contingency of reinforcement: "Pay this much, and take it with you". The rules of business and industry usually become laws only when the sanctions of governments and religions are invoked. It is *illegal* or *sinful,* not unbusinesslike, to steal goods, lie about them, fail to keep promises, and so on.

3.6. The Listener Is Governed by the Laws of Science

The laws of nations and religions had been in existence for many centuries, and what it meant to be well governed must have been debated for almost as long a time before Francis Bacon suggested that the natural world might also be governed. Its laws were, we should say now, the contingencies of reinforcement maintained by the environment. The laws of science describe those contingencies as the laws of governments or religions describe some of the norms or rules of societies. We discover the laws of nature from experience—not, as the phenomenologists would have it, from the *appearances* of things in consciousness, but in the original sense of the word *experience*, from what has happened. Scientists improve upon experience by experimenting—by doing things in order to watch what happens. From both *exper*ience and *exper*iment come *exper*ts, those who either behave in ways that have been shaped and maintained by the contingencies or can describe them.

Science means knowledge, and that is almost always thought of as a personal possession; those who possess it know what to do. Behaviorally speaking, it is a possession in the sense of a bodily state. The state results either from reinforcement (when the behavior is contingency shaped) or from responding to a particular kind of verbal stimulus (when the behavior is rule-governed). If cognitive psychologists were correct that rules were *in* the contingencies, it would not matter whether we learned from the contingencies or from the rule—in other words, from acquaintance or description. The results, however, are obviously different. Those who have been directly exposed to contingencies behave in much more subtle and effective ways than those who have merely been told, taught, or advised to behave, or who follow rules. It is in part a difference due to the fact that rules never fully describe the contingencies they are designed to replace. It is also, of course, a difference in the states of the body felt.

The latter difference has created a problem for certain philosophers of science, such as Michael Polanyi and P. W. Bridgman, who insisted that the knowledge we call science must be personal. True, everything scientists now do must at least once have been contingency shaped in someone, but most of the time scientists begin by following rules. Science is a vast verbal environment or culture.

New sciences come only from contingencies, and that was Bacon's point in his attack on the scholastics. The scholastics were the cognitivists of the Middle Ages. For them knowledge was rule-governed. One learned by reading books—Aristotle, Galen, and so on. Bacon, an early experimental analyst, insisted that books follow science. Hypotheses and theories follow data. The contingencies always come first.

3.7. The Listener as Reader

The contingencies we have been reviewing are often clearest when the speaker is a writer and the listener a reader. If architecture is frozen music, then books are frozen verbal behavior. Writing leaves durable marks, and as readers we respond to durable stimuli. What is transmitted or communicated is pinned down for study. Books of travel quite obviously *tell* us what their authors have seen, heard, or read about, and books of adventure what they have done. Textbooks *teach* us, but only if, like programmed texts, they provide contingencies of reinforcement. A cookbook could be said to tell us something about what people eat if we are interested in the practices of a culture. It *advises* us how to make a cherry pie if we are interested in doing so. It *teaches* us to make one if the pie proves reinforcing. Games are played according to Hoyle, an early codifier of rules. Logic and mathematics are scarcely possible except in written form, and law books are no less essential to lawyers and legislators than are the tablets and bibles of religion to religious leaders. Among the tablets of science are the so-called tables of constants.

3.8. The Listener Agrees

We have been considering a kind of superorganism, the first half of which gains when the second half acts upon the world, and the second half gains when the first half makes contact with that world. Those were probably the advantages that played a selective role in the evolution of verbal behavior. But when you meet someone and start to talk, you do not always tell, teach, advise, or invoke rules or laws to be followed. You converse. You talk about things both of you are familiar with. There is little to be told, taught, advised, put in order, or regulated. Speaking is reinforced when the listener tends to say more or less what the speaker says, and listening is reinforced when the speaker says more or less what the listener tends to say. Conversing is not reinforced by the consequences we have been considering but by agreement. (It may be the kind of exchange called an *argument,* but the point of that is to reach agreement.) To put it another way, as speakers, we look for listeners and as listeners, for speakers who think as we think, where what we think is simply what we do, often covertly and verbally.

The importance of agreement is shown by the frequency with which we use autoclitics to ask about it. We say, "A lovely day," and then add "isn't it?," or "Don't you think?," or "N'est-ce pas," or "*Nicht wahr?.*" We also mand agreement, as in saying "Believe me, it was a lovely day."

As listeners or readers, we look for speakers or writers who say what we are on the point of saying. Speakers who say what we are already strongly inclined to say contribute little or nothing, and we call them boring. We listen as little as possible to speakers who say what we are not at all inclined to say (about things in which we are not interested, for example, or in terms we seldom or never use). The speakers we like are those who help us say things we have not been quite able to say—about the situation in Europe, for example. What we hear or read is what we should have said ourselves if we had had more time. Unless we like to argue, we do not listen to or read those who have said things with which we have strongly disagreed.

Classical rhetoric was the art of inducing the listener to say what the speaker was saying, but often for irrelevant reasons. Many of its devices appealed to intraverbal or echoic support. Poetry does that, too. A line seems just right, not because of what it says, but because it scans or rhymes. Fiction with lots of conversation and drama, which is all conversation, reinforce the reader or listener by slowly building strong operants and then offering textual or echoic stimuli to which responses can be made. You most enjoyed *Gone with the Wind* if, along with Clark Gable as Rhett Butler, you were just ready to say, "Quite frankly, my dear, I don't give a damn." If you were not ready and wondered why Gable said it, or if you thought the remark was long since overdue and were inclined to say "Well, it's about time!", you were less likely to see the movie again sometime or recommend it to others.

3.9. The Listener and Speaker Think

All this takes on a much greater significance when the speaker and listener reside within the same skin. If that meant that they were the same person, there would be no need for verbal behavior. The listener told would know as much, in the sense of having the same history, as the teller; the listener taught would know as much as the teacher, and so on. But there are many persons or selves within one skin. We imply as much when we speak of self-observation, in which one self observes another, or self-management, in which one self manages another. When we say that we talk to ourselves, we mean that one self talks to another. Different repertoires have been shaped and maintained by different verbal environments.

The selves may be identical except for time. We tell the same self to do something later by leaving a note. We teach a single self by rehearsing and checking our performance. We advise the same self when, for example, after an unpleasant evening, we say, "Never go there again!" We memorize maxims, rules, and laws for later use. We play solitaire or take alternating sides in a solitary game of chess. We doublecheck our solutions in logic and mathematics. In all this, our role as listener is the important thing. We are better listeners than speakers. We were listeners before we became speakers, and we continue to listen to and read much more than we ever say or write.

Internal dialogues of this sort are most often called *thinking,* but all behavior is thinking, as I argue in the last chapter in *Verbal Behavior*. There are many reasons why we talk to ourselves covertly. Occasions for overt behavior may be lacking, aversive consequences may follow if we are overheard, and so on. We also use *I think* as an autoclitic to indicate that our behavior is barely strong enough to reach the overt level. But accessibility to others is not the important distinction. When repertoires of speaker and listener come together in the same skin, things happen that are much less likely to happen when they are in separate skins. We converse with ourselves, arguing perhaps, but looking for agreement. The selves who converse have different histories (or silent verbal behavior would be useless), but they are not as different as the histories in a group discussion. Variety makes a contribution, but uniformity of background has its advantages, too. Speaker and listener speak the same language, borrow from the same sources, and so on.

Not all silent speech is of that sort. We do not always need listeners if our verbal behavior has been strongly reinforced or reinforced on an intermittent schedule. The witty response at a cocktail party occurs again and again before we go to sleep that night, and we need not ask who the listener is, any more than we need ask what the reinforcer is for every response in a scheduled performance.

Not all thinking is vocal, of course. Artists "speak" by putting paint on canvas and, as "listeners," they leave it on or take it off. They may do both covertly. Composers are both speakers and listeners, even when there are no instruments or sounds. Inventors put things together and watch how they work, either in a shop or covertly in a comfortable chair. Very little of that is likely to happen when the two repertoires are in separate skins.

This is not, of course, anything like an adequate analysis of thinking, but it moves in a promising direction. The evolution of cultures and of cultural practices has vastly extended the scope of individual behavior. The practices of the culture we call the verbal environment, or language, are the greatest achievement of the human species, and verbal environments are composed of listeners.

4. REFERENCES

Skinner, B. F. (1957). *Verbal behavior*. New York: Appleton-Century-Crofts.

Skinner, B. F. (1935). The generic nature of the concept of stimulus and response. *Journal of General Psychology, 12,* 40–65.

CHAPTER 3

Rule-Governed Behavior in Behavior Analysis

A Theoretical and Experimental History

MARGARET VAUGHAN

1. INTRODUCTION

The field of behavior analysis,[1] committed to a basic science of human behavior, has never had an easy time of it. Two different but related criticisms have plagued the field. First, it has been argued that the rich workings of mental life stand in the way of a science attempting to explain all human behavior in terms of physical laws. This presumed paradox has led various philosophers, psychologists, educators, and layman to assert that there can never be such a science. Nonetheless, there were those who, resisting such a proposition, proceeded to demonstrate powerful functional relations between behavior and environmental events (e.g., Azrin & Holz, 1966; Ferster & Skinner, 1957; Skinner, 1938). Within the last 75 years, a science of human behavior has emerged, and it appears that what has been traditionally called mental life is subject to the same laws that govern observable behavior. Unfortunately, for most of those 75 years, behavior analysts could only speculate as to whether a relation existed between simple responses observed in the laboratory and more elaborate sequences of human behavior found in daily life.

The second and more intimidating criticism directed at behavior analysts, however, has come most recently from other basic researchers who are confident that such a science is possible but not as a function of studying rats and

[1]The field of behavior analysis is the area of philosophy, research, and application that encompasses the experimental analysis of behavior, applied behavior analysis, operant psychology, operant conditioning, behaviorism, and Skinnerian psychology.

MARGARET VAUGHAN • Department of Psychology, Salem State College, Salem, Massachusetts 01970.

pigeons within a stimulus–response–reinforcement paradigm. Cognitive psychologists accept the fact that behavior can be shaped by its consequences, but they find such behavior, by definition, uninteresting. That is, the real difference between humans and nonhumans, they argue, is in the area of cognition, which must be studied in its own right (e.g., Lachman, Lachman, & Butterfield, 1979).

Behavior analysts have not been immune to this criticism. Nor have they relinquished to cognitive psychology the investigation of this essential feature of complex human behavior. Indeed, cognition, or the various kinds of behaviors often subsumed under this general term (e.g., thinking, problem solving, knowing, perceiving, imaging) has been written about by behavior analysts for more than 30 years (e.g., Bijou & Baer, 1961; Keller & Schoenfeld, 1950; Skinner, 1953). Despite the early theoretical attention paid to these concepts, however, much of the early behavior analytic research using humans as subjects systematically isolated and eliminated any effects of these so-called higher cognitive processes. It was not until the mid-1970s that human operant researchers began to study the functional aspects of these phenomena directly. As a result, a distinction was gradually drawn between behavior shaped directly by its consequences and behavior under the control of a rule. It was a distinction that not only breathed new life into the field, it unequivocally linked behavior analytic research and cognitive processes.

Obviously, it was no coincidence that this shift within human operant research appeared at a time when cognitive psychology emerged as a dominant force in psychology. The research on rule-governed behavior was meant to provide an analysis, in physical terms, of at least some of the activities that preoccupy the behavior of cognitive psychologists.

But the current interest in rule-governed behavior by behavior analysts was also a function of the developments in basic nonhuman research. It was the natural result of a maturing science of behavior. With the advent of more sophisticated laboratory equipment and methods of data analysis, basic nonhuman research advanced at an unprecedented rate in uncovering the variables of which behavior is a function. As a result, the interest in relations between responses and reinforcement soon expanded to include an interest in the relations between responses and the context in which they occurred. As Sidman (1978) noted:

> Terms like *cognition* or *knowledge* refer to the control of behavior by its environmental context, by events which, unlike consequences, precede or accompany the behavior. (p. 265)

The current interest in rule-governed behavior is not solely academic, though. Often behavior analysts have been characterized as having an obsession with the practical implications of their research. Indeed, because of their practical concerns, it has been suggested that the field "risks" becoming nothing more than a technology (Meazzini & Ricci, 1986, p. 26). But a more attractive view is that behavior analysts, as scientists, are concerned about the world in which they live. It is this concern that has drawn some to the concept of rule-governed behavior. Anyone who has read a newspaper or watched the evening news over the last decade could not help but be affected by the gloomy predictions of the endangered species mankind. Nuclear war, overpopulation, shortage of food, pollution of our air, soil, and water, and a collapse of the world economy have all been proposed as likely future scenarios and, for some countries (e.g., China, Ethiopia), the future has already arrived. It seems only reasonable that if anyone can stop this spinning out of control it will be experts in the science and technology of human behavior. Unfortunately, behavior analysts are not so sanguine. As they have learned more about the power of consequences in shaping behavior, they also have learned, regrettably, about some of its limitations in dealing with problems of such magnitude. How does one shape the individual behavior of 5 billion people? It is this problem that has led many culturally conscientious behavior analysts to seek a clearer understanding of rule-governed behavior.

Ironically, as more attention has been focused on the concept and how it is distinguished from contingency-shaped behavior, behavior analysts have become increasingly aware of confusions as to the precise nature of this distinction. As Mark Twain might say: "There are some discrepancies."

There have been attempts by some behavior analysts to change the name of the concept, arguing that *rule-governed* implies too much control by the rule and not enough control by the underlying contingencies (e.g., Skinner, 1982). Others seem less concerned about what it is called and more concerned in emphasizing the fact that the term should not be viewed as a technical one (Brownstein & Shull, 1985), even though others have implied that the behavioral process that underlies the concept, by its very nature, requires a technical term (Hayes, 1986).

But if rule-governed behavior is to be a technical term, then it is fitting for behavior analysts to argue that a functional definition is needed (Vaughan, 1987; Zettlel & Hayes, 1982), even though others seem content with a descriptive one (Brownstein *et al.*, 1985). But more fundamental is the disagreement in terms of the concept's defining features. Is rule-governed behavior nothing more than behavior under the control of a verbal stimulus (Parrott, 1987)? If this is the case, what is to be made of various kinds of verbal behavior cataloged by Skinner, in *Verbal Behavior* (e.g., echoic or intraverbal), which are defined as behavior under the control of verbal stimuli but are not considered rule-governed? In attempting to resolve this difficulty, some behavior analysts have drawn a distinction between verbal stimuli that function as discriminative stimuli and those verbal stimuli that are relation-altering (Vaughan, 1987) or function-altering (Schlinger & Blakely, 1987).

Ultimately, these disagreements will be resolved through research, and it is research that fills many of the pages of this volume. But to adequately evaluate current debate and research, it is often useful to know something about what has been thought, said, and studied in the past. Thus, the purpose of this chapter is to examine the origin of the concept and chart its history first through the theoretical literature and then the experimental literature of behavior analysis. In doing so, the conditions under which the concept has been used and the kinds of behavior it is meant to explain will be highlighted. With this as an objective, it is hoped that if the defining features of rule-governed behavior do not easily emerge to assuage the confusions and disagreements, we may at least find agreement in terms of the predicament we face.

2. A THEORETICAL HISTORY OF RULE-GOVERNED BEHAVIOR

That people talk to themselves and to others and are changed by these interactions is not a new insight into the human condition. Nor are behavior analysts the first to distinguished between this kind of learning, or rule-governed behavior, and learning through direct contingency shaping. As Marr (1986) pointed out, Ernst Mach drew attention to this distinction in 1893. But it also echoes Bertrand Russell's (1912/1961) knowledge by description and knowledge by acquaintance, and Gilbert Ryle's (1949) *knowing that* and *knowing how*. In fact, this may have been what Demacritus had in mind when, during the fifth century B.C., he distinguished between ''obscure knowledge, resting on sensation alone, and genuine, which is the result of inquiry by reason.'' (*Encyclopedia Britannica, Inc.*, 1940, *7*, p. 188). Within the science of behavior analysis, however, we need only reach back to the 1940s where we find some of Skinner's earliest writings.

2.1. Rule-Governed Behavior: Its Roots in the Analysis of Verbal Behavior

During the early years of behavior analysis, very little research was conducted with human subjects. Behavior analysts' main interest was in formulating an objective natural science of behavior, starting with the most fundamental laws of behavior. Nonhuman subjects served their purpose well: Rats and pigeons were inexpensive; they were relatively small and thus well suited for laboratory research; and most important, their phylogenic and ontogenic histories were known and could be controlled. But it was not long before researchers began to speculate about the extrapolation of these laws to human behavior. Ironically, as Skinner wrote in 1938 that perhaps the only difficulty in this extrapolation would be in the area of verbal behavior, he was already working on an extensive analysis of verbal behavior in terms of the basic laws of behavior coming out of the nonhuman research laboratory. It was nearly 10 years later, however, before Skinner publicly presented in a systematic fashion his analysis of verbal behavior.

In 1947, Skinner was asked to give the distinguished William James Lectures at Harvard University. His topic was verbal behavior, and his yet unfinished manuscript (*Verbal Behavior,* 1957) became the material for the lectures. It is here where Skinner first makes reference to the effects of a description of a contingency as opposed to being directly exposed to it. It occurs in the section called "Conditioning the behavior of the listener."

The James Lectures (Skinner, 1947) and *Verbal Behavior* (1957) emphasized the behavior of the individual speaker, outlining the variables that lead someone to emit a particular response. Verbal behavior was defined as behavior reinforced through the mediation of another person (1957, p. 2). The behavior of "another person," or the listener, was discussed only in terms of explaining the behavior of the speaker. As Skinner (1957) noted: "The behavior of the listener is not necessarily verbal in any special sense. It cannot, in fact, be distinguished from behavior in general, and an adequate account of verbal behavior need cover only as much of the behavior of the listener as is needed to explain the behavior of the speaker" (p. 2). Thus, in both sources Skinner devotes only a brief section to conditioning the behavior of the listener. In part it reads (from the James Lectures):

> The behavior of the listener is not essentially verbal at all. When the listener is also behaving as a speaker, his behavior is verbal because it has consequences which bring it within the scope of our original definition [of verbal behavior], but listening, as such, is not covered by the definition and differs in no important way from responses to non-verbal stimuli. The behavior of listening is, however, always conditioned, and it is conditioned under circumstances which involve the behavior of a speaker. The listener comes to react to the behavior of the speaker as a stimulus which has in the past accompanied other stimuli, verbal or otherwise. (p. 115)

To explain such a conditioning process, Skinner begins with a simple example involving respondent behavior:

> We condition a glandular response, say, the sweating of the palms of the hand by repeatedly presenting the sound of a bell and a shock at about the same time. The previously neutral sound of the bell begins to elicit the response which was under the control of the shock. We can make this case verbal with the trivial substitution of the verbal stimulus "shock" for the bell. In a somewhat amplified case we might say: "When I say 'shock' you will feel this"—and then administer the shock. The listener's behavior with respect to future occurrences of the verbal stimulus "shock" would be changed. And when "shock" becomes effective in this way it may be paired with another verbal stimulus to yield a case which is wholly verbal: "When I say 'three' you will receive a shock." The effect upon the listener is a change in his future behavior with respect to the stimulus "three." In another variation on this theme, the pairing of verbal stimuli may make a non-verbal stimulus subsequently effective. "When you hear the bell you will feel a shock." The future response to the bell is as non-verbal as the original example, but it has been set up without using either the bell or the shock at the time of conditioning.

He then moves to examples involving operant behavior:

> Close parallels are available in which the later behavior of the listener is a discriminated operant. "When I say 'three', go," might be called a discriminated operant. It has no immediate effect which can be classified as a response, but the subsequent behavior of the listener with respect to "Go" is changed. In another variation the stimulus which is later in control is non-verbal. "When the fire burns out, close the damper" leads to subsequent behavior under the control of a non-verbal stimulus arising from the fire. "When I say 'come and get it,' dinner will be ready," the verbal stimulus "come and get it" will have the same discriminative function as "dinner is ready." Examples comparable to the last two in which the listener's subsequent behavior is verbal call for only a trivial modification of the formulae. (pp. 123–124)

Skinner then elaborates on the process:

> It is commonly objected that the change in the listener cannot be conditioned because the process is too fast. A single verbal stimulus—say, "Germany has invaded Poland"—may have subsequent effects which could be duplicated only with weeks or months, or years of experimentation. But the full effect of such a stimulus, also requires years, as may be seen by examining the effects upon children at different ages. Some of the exceptional speed in verbal instruction is due to the autoclitic frame[2] which carries the primary paired terms. When we bring a naive subject into the laboratory and present pairings of the sound of a bell and shock, it may take some time to learn the connection, as we say. We can shortcut most or all of this by simply telling him "Whenever you hear the bell you will receive a shock." The greater speed must be attributed to the difference between the cases, and this difference is simply the autoclitic frame: "When you hear ———, you will receive a ———." This is effective because many similar patterns have been conditioned upon past occasions. The effect upon the listener (in these examples) may properly be called instruction. We have altered the future probability of some responses. (pp. 124–125)

Two points need to be made regarding the preceding quotes. First, Skinner is clearly distinguishing between two types of operant behavior: behavior that is directly shaped by the contingencies and behavior that is altered by a description of contingencies. But the distinction is of a practical nature—and this is the second point. Behavior under the control of a description involves no new process: It is the result of an extensive reinforcement history involving both verbal and nonverbal behavior. And it is an intricate fusion of repertoires, if not fragile, as Skinner implies when considering the variables that influence the strength of the listener's resulting future behavior (pp. 121–122).

For example, having heard the aphorism "If you wish to be a good writer, then you must become an effective reader,"[3] what is the probability that a freshman in college will now become a good writer? It appears that at least

[2]The autoclitic frame can be described as secondary verbal behavior, which alters the listener's behavior with respect to the primary terms included in the frame.

[3]This point was made by Don Murray in *Read to Write* (1986).

five variables must be taken into account: (1) the extent to which the autoclitic frame "if . . . , then . . ." already shows some control over the student's behavior; (2) the kinds of behavior that are brought to strength when the second term is added to the autoclitic frame; (3) the extent of change required in bringing the behavior of the second term under the control of the first term in the autoclitic frame; (4) the conditioning history of the student with respect to receiving and taking advice; and (5) the student's motivation. (Given this analysis, it should come as no surprise to teachers or parents that their advice is seldom heeded.)

Obviously, such a process is extremely important for the individual as well as the culture at large. It is these practical implications that Skinner addresses next.

2.2. Rule-Governed Behavior: An Elaboration of Its Practical Significance

Skinner again discusses conditioning the behavior of the listener and the process of instruction in his book *Science and Human Behavior* (1953). His treatment here, however, is of particular importance because he gradually shifts from talking exclusively about the conditioning process to an analysis of the various classes of behavior that can be evoked given this conditioning history. In fact, all subsequent references to rule-governed behavior (*Verbal Behavior* being an exception) are in terms of evoking behavior under the control of rules. This change in emphasis gave new meaning to the concept: The behavior of the listener was now being considered in its own right, no longer as solely the third term (the mediated reinforcement) in the analysis of the speaker's behavior. As a result, the practical implications of the conditioning process were brought into focus.

For example, in *Science and Human Behavior,* Skinner outlined the various controlling agencies within the culture that rely extensively on this conditioning process. Governments, religions, therapists, educators, businesses, and science establish certain rules of conduct (or laws) as techniques of control. These agencies then exercise certain control over individuals by "specifying the consequences of certain actions which in turn 'rule' behavior" (p. 339).

Such techniques of control, however, are just as real or unrelenting as forms of coercion as Skinner passionately states in *Freedom and the Control of Men* (1955–1956). In arguing for a reexamination of the literature on freedom, Skinner points out that the procedures encouraged by such literature—education, moral discourse, persuasion—as opposed to the direct control of behavior—coercive forms of control called: "wrong," "illegal," or "sinful" by the culture—have been misrepresented. That is, the literature implies "that these procedures do not involve the control of behavior; at most, they are simply ways of 'getting someone to change his mind' " (p. 54). In fact, Skinner argues that an analysis of such techniques "reveals the presence of well-defined behavioral processes, it demonstrates a kind of control no less inexorable, though in some ways more acceptable, than the bully's threat of force" (p. 54). By resorting to "verbal mediating devices [issuing a command, supplying information, pointing out logical relationships, appealing to reason, etc.], which emphasize and support certain 'contingencies of reinforcement'—that is, certain relations between behavior and its consequences—" (p. 55), we strengthen the behavior of interest. "The same consequences would possibly set up the behavior without our help, and they eventually take control no matter which form of help we give. But if we have worked a change in his behavior at all, it is because we have altered relevant environmental conditions . . ." (p. 55).

Skinner's unparalleled concern for the practical implications of a science of behavior are well known. Perhaps equally well known are his concerns with the current status of cognitive psychology within the general field of psychology. As it turns out, it was this latter concern that eventually led Skinner to elaborate more fully on the behavior called rule-governed. For in so doing, he was able to analyze in physical terms many of processes studied by cognitive psychologists.

2.3. Rule-Governed Behavior: A Further Elaboration in Light of the Emerging Psychology of Cognition

Skinner's next several references to so-called rule-governed behavior occur in the context of defining the activities of other researchers, namely cognitive psychologists. In his paper "Operant Behavior" (1963, p. 509) Skinner suggests that because of the "complex arrangements of interrelated operants" in an analysis of human behavior, techniques have evolved which circumvent an operant analysis:

> The manipulation of independent variables appears to be circumvented when, instead of exposing an organism to a set of contingencies, the contingencies are simply described in "instruction." Instead of shaping a response, the subject is told to respond in a given way. A history of reinforcement or punishment is replaced by a promise or threat: "Movement of the lever will sometimes operate a coin dispenser" or "deliver a shock to your leg." (p. 509)

Descriptions of contingencies are often valuable, Skinner states, but only when "the resulting behavior is not the primary object of interest" (p. 510). The fact is that the two approaches—explicitly arranging contingencies versus offering a description of those contingencies—generate quite different effects. If descriptions of contingencies are used rather than exposing the subject to the contingencies, the verbal contingencies themselves must be considered in a complete account. "Instructions must in some way promise or threaten consequences not germane to the experiment if the subject is to follow them" (p. 510). The contingencies operating between experimenter and subject are obviously important features to consider for successful research.

It should be noted that Skinner's treatment of behavior under the control of rules, up to this point, was always imbedded in analyses of other topics. It was not until his article, "An Operant Analysis of Problem Solving" was given in 1965 (and later published in *Contingencies of Reinforcement,* 1969) that this behavior was dealt with independently. It was also the first time this behavior was referred to as rule-governed.

It was no coincidence that only a few years earlier George Miller and Jerome Bruner established the Center for Cognitive Studies at Harvard University to study such cognitive processes as problem solving and rule following. But this was not an isolated event. Indeed, it was the culmination of many activities taking place during the preceding decade, which heralded the new science of cognition.[4] One of the first books foreshadowing this development was written by a mathematician, Norbert Wiener. His book *Cybernetics* (1948) applied Shannon and Weaver's theory of information to animals and machines. It was a theory obviously based upon the new form of communication, the computer. Noam Chomsky's *Syntactic Structures* (1957), and later "A Review of B. F. Skinner's *Verbal Behavior*" (1959), reoriented the field of linguistics toward a cognitive approach, which indirectly, but profoundly, affected the field of psychology. But perhaps the most influential book in psychology during this time was written by George Miller, Eugene Galanter, and Karl Pribram, entitled *Plans and the Structure of Behavior* (1960). It is here where an alternative to the behavioral approach was articulated to explain complex human behavior. In their attempt to bridge the gap between knowledge and action, they proposed the notion of a "plan," which "describe[s] how actions are controlled by an organism's internal representation of the universe" (p. 12).

Skinner was obviously well aware of what was in the air at Harvard during those years. As he reports in his autobiography, *A Matter of Consequences* (1983):

> A different issue was taking the center of the cognitive stage, and I heard a good deal about it from our graduate students. Behavior was not always shaped and maintained by contingencies of reinforcement, it could be rule-governed. Cognitive psychologists were arguing that even the behavior of the rat in the box was rule-governed: The rat pressed a lever, received food, and was then more likely to press again when hungry, not because it had been conditioned, but because "it had learned (and now knew) that pressing the lever produces food." The phrase "pressing the lever produces food" was a description of the contingencies in the apparatus; somehow or other it was said to move into the head of the rat in the form of knowledge.
>
> Human subjects did not need to be exposed to contingencies of reinforcement;

[4]See Knapp (1986) for a very readable history of cognitive psychology.

> they could be told what to do and thus "given the necessary knowledge." . . . I extended the analysis in a paper at a symposium on problem-solving at the Carnegie Institute of Technology in April 1965. Israel Goldiamond and I represented the experimental analysis of behavior, and the other speakers were specialists in information-processing and computers. I brought the issue I wanted to talk about under the rubric of problem-solving by defining a problem as a set of contingencies for which there is no immediate effective response. It can be solved either by emitting available behavior until a response appears which satisfies the contingencies (trial and error) or by analyzing the contingencies. In the second case, the problem is solved by manipulating rules. The solution is a rule constructed on the spot. Individuals also profit from rules constructed by others—for example, by taking advice, heeding warnings, observing maxims, and obeying governmental and religious laws and the laws of science. (pp. 283–284)

The paper Skinner presented at this symposium was published a year later. The elegant analysis found within is lengthy but remarkable in its lucidity. Skinner had laid out the nuts and bolts of problem solving and, as a result, rule-governed behavior. A rule was defined as a contingency-specifying stimulus—an object in the environment. He then asked, "How does it govern behavior?"

> As a discriminative stimulus, a rule is effective as part of a set of contingencies of reinforcement. We tend to follow a rule because previous behavior in response to similar verbal stimuli has been reinforced. (*Contingencies of Reinforcement*, 1969, p. 148)

He noted, however, that rules only control the topography of behavior. Whether a person follows a rule can only be determined by the person's history with respect to rule-following and the context in which the current rule is stated. He also spent much time analyzing the value of formulating rules. When discussing the practical advantages of rule-governed behavior, Skinner compared it to contingency-shaped behavior. A similar but compressed analysis occurs in *About Behaviorism* (1974). There he specifies several important issues, three of which follow:

1. Rules can be learned more quickly than the behavior shaped by the contingencies that the rules describe.
2. Rules make it easier to profit from similarities between contingencies.
3. Rules are particularly valuable when contingencies are complex or unclear. (p. 125)

It is interesting to note that despite Skinner's lengthy treatment of rule-governed behavior in "An Operant Analysis of Problem-Solving," the distinction between rule-governed and contingency-shaped behavior did not become a dominant theme for behavior analysts until the publication of *About Behaviorism*. The book was written as a refutation of the criticisms leveled against behaviorism by cognitive psychologists. Althought its influence on those outside the field of behavior analysis is hard to assess, for those within the field the impact was great. By sharpening the general issues dividing behavior analysts and cognitive psychologists, it outlined a sweeping agenda for researchers. In particular, it made clear that behavior analysts needed to come to grips with the activities of cognitive psychologists.

But perhaps the real importance of Skinner's book, *About Behaviorism,* was that he firmly established that behavior analysts had the tools to analyze and study so-called higher mental processes. And they could do so by studying descriptions of contingencies and noting the effect on behavior directly. There was no need to hypothesize internal events, plans, or representations that would explain how knowledge was transformed into action.

In sum, it appears that Skinner's distinction between contingency-shaped and rule-governed behavior is that the former involves a discriminative stimulus, verbal or nonverbal, which sets the occasion for some response, where as the latter involves two stimuli, one of which is verbal that describes a relation between some other stimulus, a response and consequence. Thus, a rule can be defined as a function-altering stimulus in that it alters the probability of some response at another time in the presence of a different stimulus. Thus some kinds of behavior under the control of verbal stimuli—for example, echoic and intraverbal—do not qualify as rule-governed behavior because the verbal stimuli evoking such behavior do not meet the definition of a rule. This distinction, then, maintains the integrity of Skinner's analysis of verbal behavior while making a practical dichotomy between two types of behavior. Eventually, however, such an analysis must be subjected to experimental validation. Happily, the process has begun, and the evidence thus far encouraging.

3. AN EXPERIMENTAL HISTORY OF RULE-GOVERNED BEHAVIOR

Skinner's theoretical treatment of rule-governed behavior evolved over a period of 40 years. But it has been only in the last 10 years that behavior analysts began talking about it technically and studying it directly (e.g., Galizio, 1979). The concern for such behavior, however, extends back to the early literature on human operant research.

As a popular subfield in behavior analysis, human operant research emerged in the 1950s. Although some researchers were interested in showing the direct role of consequences in modifying socially significant human behavior (e.g., Ayllon & Michael, 1959), others were more concerned with confirming experimentally and systematically the generality of the principles of behavior discovered in the nonhuman laboratory. Thus the human operant area emerged as a means of assessing whether humans emitted similar patterns of behavior under circumstances resembling research with rats and pigeons (cf. Long, Hammack, May, & Campbell, 1958).

Although sometimes effective in their attempts (e.g., Holland, 1958a), all too often researchers were unable to generate similar patterns of behavior. Many theories were proposed in explaining the discrepancies and a flurry of research followed. Eventually, orderly data were found with human subjects but only through sometimes elaborate modifications of standard procedures. For example, by changing the force requirement of the dependent variable (Azrin, 1958) by instituting a response-cost procedure (Weiner, 1962), by controlling subjects' conditioning histories (Weiner, 1964) by adding a response-produced digital clock to the intelligence panel (Lowe, Harzem, & Bagshaw, 1978), by providing verbal instructions (Ayllon & Azrin, 1964; Baron & Kaufman, 1966; Baron, Kaufman, & Stauber, 1969), or by removing all verbal instructions (Matthews, Shimhoff, Cantania, & Sagvolden, 1977).

In retrospect, such practices apparently were to serve two purposes: (1) to override the subject's conditioning history prior to the experimental situation, and (2) to attenuate the effects of what a subject might say to him- or herself during the experimental task, about the task, that could then influence subsequent performance.

To be sure, researchers were always well aware of these confounding variables. In fact, the human operant methodology was specifically designed to circumvent individual subjects' conditioning history prior to the experimental situation by establishing the dependent variable as an arbitrary response (pushing buttons, displacing levers, or any other kind of response) that was unique to the experimental situation. Moreover, the fact that subjects talked to themselves during the experimental task, which in turn influenced their performance was also acknowledged early on (see Bijou, 1958; Dews & Morse, 1958; Holland, 1958b; Laties & Weiss, 1963), but it did not inspire a great deal of research (although see Ayllon & Azrin, 1964; Bem, 1967). Why researchers preferred to alleviate its effects rather than study it directly was undoubtedly due to philosophical and methodological bents that related to the spirit of the time. But with the rising tide of cognitive processes dominating the field of psychology, the *Zeitgeist* changed—and so did many behavior analysts.

By the mid-1970s the role of instructions, experimenter-generated or self-generated by the subject, became a major independent variable in the human operant literature. And it was during this time that instructions and instruction following began to be equated with rules and rule-governed behavior, respectively.

3.1. Rule-Governed Behavior: Schedule-Sensitivity Research

Ayllon and Azrin (1964) were the first to investigate instruction within a behavior analytic methodology. They demonstrated in a very straightforward manner that instructions, if supported by consequences for instruction following, could bring about rapid change on the part of hospital patients. Under laboratory conditions Kaufman, Baron, and Kopp (1966) also found that instructions facilitated responding but that this responding was insensitive then to the actual programmed contingencies. That instructions facilitate appropriate responding to the experimental contingencies but produce insensitivity to changes in these contingencies generated more than a little research.

One of the first to tease apart the suspect variables was Galizio (1979) who found that general insensitivity persisted when there was no cost to the subject for following the inaccurate instructions, but when penalties were imposed, reduction in instruction following occurred rather abruptly. That is, only when subjects were in direct contact with the penalty contingency did they show sensitivity to the experimental conditions. Instructional control occurred when there were consequences that supported it.

Matthews *et al.* (1977) and Shimoff, Catania, and Matthews (1981), who were more concerned about the specific pattern of responding that occurred as a function of accurate instructions, found insensitivity to different experimental contingencies when subjects were instructed, but when subjects' responses were shaped, sensitivity to different scheduled contingencies developed. But they also found that instructed subjects continued to show insensitivity despite contact with the contingencies. In fact, Shimoff *et al.* argued that "such insensitivity is a defining property of instructional control" (p. 207) and that their results were consistent with Skinner's distinction between contingency-shaped and rule-governed behavior.

In a clever extension of their basic findings, Catania, Matthews, and Shimoff (1982) showed that the distinction between contingency-shaped and rule-governed behavior was relevant to verbal as well as nonverbal behavior. That is, when these researchers shaped subjects' verbal statements during the experiment regarding the required performance, rather than instructing them on what they should do, subjects showed a great deal more sensitivity to the programmed contingencies.

As it turned out, their subjects were not the only ones being shaped. Going one step farther, Matthews, Catania, and Shimoff (1985) began to analyze the various critical features of a description. Is one kind of description better than another in generating sensitivity to the programmed contingencies? In the end, they found that "performance" descriptions had consistent effects on nonverbal responding but that "contingency" descriptions generated a great deal of variability. When subjects where shaped to provide performance descriptions (e.g., "push rapidly on the right button"), rather than contingency descriptions (e.g., "# of presses for green light to go on."), a consistent correspondence was found between what they described and what they did. This same consistency was lacking when contingency descriptions were shaped.

In a more recent study, Shimoff, Matthews, and Catania (1986) completed the circle. They concluded that even when subjects' shaped performance shows sensitivity to changes in the experimental contingencies, this sensitivity may be illusory. That is, such sensitivity has implied that the responding was contingency shaped but under closer scrutiny the responding may in fact be rule-governed. Although these two kinds of behavior may appear topographically the same, the similarity ends there; the responses are functionally different. Hayes, Brownstein, Haas, and Greenway (1986) came to a similar conclusion but rightly point out in addition that many different kinds of rules (e.g., general, specific, paradoxic, precursor, or rules that encourage the testing of other rules) undoubtedly will generate varying degrees of sensitivity to the experimental conditions.

A synthesis of schedule-sensitivity research seems to be this: Experimenter instructions facilitate stimulus control but are likely to establish insensitivity to changes in contingencies unless there are conspicuous consequences (i.e., punishment) for following outdated or inaccurate instructions. Moreover, if subjects are shaped to respond in a certain way rather than instructed, they show greater sensitivity to changes in the experimental contingencies. Subjects' verbal behavior can also be shaped regarding experimental contingencies and this, too, seems to generate more sensitivity but only if this shaped verbal behavior is performance-specific. But such performance may be in reality rule-governed behavior despite the apparent contingency-shaping procedure.

The intriguing implication of this line of research is that self-talk may underlie and influence much of human adult responding. This is not to overlook the fact that self-talk is itself a function of something and most likely a function of the circumstances in which the speaker finds him- or herself. But what is important here is the fact that self-talk does at least sometimes determine the form of the response as well as its probability of occurrence. We can no longer ignore this additional controlling variable. At the same time, we need to determine exactly when self-talk is and is not a controlling variable. (Just as we do not always follow the advice of others, we sometimes do not follow our own.) Obviously, instructions or rules have varying degrees of control over nonverbal behavior because of all the reasons Skinner listed in the William James Lectures. Discovering the conditions that produce correspondence between saying and doing may be the most profound contribution behavior analysts make in advancing a science of human behavior. The question is what is the best way to do it?

Some behavior analysts (e.g., Poppen, 1982) have argued that we may need to reconsider our approach. That is, some researchers have opined that adult humans come to the laboratory setting with an already extensive repertoire of formulating rules and reacting to them. Because such a repertoire is a function of the individual's own unique history, any general laws emerging from such research may be highly suspect. Thus, some researchers have begun to study the origins of rule-governed behavior. How does rule-stating and rule-following develop and when?

3.2. Rule-Governed Behavior: Developmental Research

It has been reported for some time in the child development literature that a fundamental change in learning occurs around the age of 5 years. For example, White (1965) states:

> Before this age [5], the pattern of findings obtained with children resembles those obtained when animals are used in like procedures. After this age, the pattern of findings approximates that found for human adults. The transition is from animal-like to human-like learning. This transition is associated with an increased apparent influence of language upon learning. (pp. 195–196)

This point has not gone unnoticed. For example Lowe, Beasty, and Bentell (1983), using infants as subjects, found performances resembling those performances of rats and pigeons. They hypothesized that as long as human subjects are young enough so that they are still incapable of formulating rules about the experimental contingencies, sensitivity to changing contingencies occurs much as they do with other organisms in the laboratory. In a follow-up, developmental study, Bentell, Lowe, and Beasty (1985) found that preverbal children, up to about age 2½ years, produced patterns of behavior similar to nonhumans (i.e., showing sensitivity); from 5 years on, children produced patterns similar to adult humans (i.e., showing insensitivity), and children between the ages of 2½ to 5 years showed variations in performance, some responding like preverbal children and some responding like adults.

The present author (Vaughan, 1985) showed that when young children, ages 2½ to 5 years, are taught to generate their own rules about the experimental contingencies, they perform much more proficiently on a task then children who are not taught to verbalize the contingencies.

The general analysis usually offered for this kind of research has been simply that once children learn to be speakers and listeners they can speak to themselves and react to what they say just as if someone else had said it. But again we are confronted with the question: Is all behavior, or only some behavior, influenced by what one says to oneself?

The work by Parsons, Taylor, and Joyce (1981) leads one to be hesitant about the ubiquity of self-talk as a necessary variable. They found that by training collateral nonverbal responding (i.e., preccurent behavior) on a delayed matching-to-sample task, subjects were far more likely to emit the reinforced response (i.e., current behavior) than if they had not been taught specific precurrent behavior. That is, subjects who were taught to engage in "sample-specific," nonverbal mediated behavior during a 5- and 10-sec delay consistently responded more accurately—they remembered—than those children who where not taught specific precurrent behavior. This relatively new line of research may prove to be an interesting link in the development of verbal/nonverbal relations.

In sum, this line of "developmental" research has supported the notion that if changes do take place in the learning process, these changes are highly susceptible to environmental manipulations. But is it solely an issue of expanding repertoires or are other behavioral processes at work? More to the point: Can the relation between verbal and nonverbal behavior eventually be explained by the minimal list of technical terms and concepts within the field of behavior analysis? Rules are typically defined as contingency-specifying stimuli. But what does it mean to "specify"? Does the concept of a "referent" or "representation" or some other process need to be included in our technical vocabulary? A relatively new line of research in the field of behavior analysis implies the answer is *yes*.

3.3. Rule-Governed Behavior: Stimulus-Equivalence Research

Recently, Devaney, Hayes, and Nelson (1986) have proposed a relation between rule-governed behavior and stimulus equivalence. In very general terms, stimulus-equivalence research involves teaching subjects to match comparison stimuli to sample stimuli. The stimuli are said to be equivalent if three relations between these stimuli can be shown: reflexivity, symmetry, and transitivity (Sidman & Tailby, 1982). For a relation to be reflexive, each stimulus must be matched to itself, for example, if "A" is the sample stimulus, then the subject matches it to the comparison stimulus "A." For a relation to be symmetrical, stimulus "A," for example, must be matched to "B," and then "B" must be matched to "A" (A=B). Finally, for a relation to be transitive, a subject is taught to match "A" to "B," and then "B" to "C," and, as a result, without further training, the subject matches "A" to "C."

Devaney *et al.* found that children who were verbal readily learned equivalence classes but that verbal-deficient, retarded children did not show equivalence formation. They argue that although the nature of the relation between verbal behavior and stimulus equivalence is yet to be defined, their results support the notion that stimulus equivalence is very relevant to verbal behavior. In fact Hayes (1986) implies that stimulus equivalence is an instance of a more general phenomenon whereby humans come to respond to "symbolic" stimuli that indicate a relation between stimuli. This occurs because subjects learn a relational frame that allows them to respond to symbolic stimuli, stimuli that are arbitrarily associated with other stimuli but whose choice is the basis for reinforced responding. Given the symbolic nature of language, Hayes asserts that the relational-frame repertoire in all likelihood facilitates language acquisition. Thus behavior under the control of a rule may characterize a fundamentally different process than behavior under the control of nonverbal discriminative stimuli. Under these conditions, instructional control, or rule-governed behavior, is only one of the results of a relational-frame repertoire. Rules work because they enter into a relational frame with some other aspect of the verbal or nonverbal world. And thus, as Sidman and Tailby (1982) assert: "By definition, the existence of a class of equivalent stimuli permits any variable that affects one member of the class to affect all members" (p. 20). The nature of the relational frame (or of what stuff it is made) remains unclear, but what is becoming clearer is that the stimulus equivalence research must be considered relevant to the experimental study of why and how verbal stimuli come to evoke behavior.

Unfortunately, such a view breaks with the traditional behavior-analytic arsenal of terms and concepts. Although Hayes attempts to analyze this research in terms of the three-term contingency, as opposed to Sidman's (1986) recent analysis where he argues that stimulus equivalence requires four and five terms, problems remain. By referring to the stimuli that enter into equivalence formation as "symbolic" and by suggesting that the behavior generated by such stimuli is "fundamentally" different from behavior under the control of discriminative stimuli, Hayes implies that our present data language is insufficient to accommodate this basic process.

That behavior analysts are hesitant to incorporate new concepts and processes into the existing technical vocabulary of their field is not unreasonable. There is wisdom in protecting a system that has worked in the past. Thus, although not attempting to diminish the value of stimulus-equivalence research, some behavior analysts (e.g., Bentall & Lowe, 1987) have argued that stimulus equivalence may in fact be a function of verbal behavior, rather than the other way around or the product of some additional behavioral process (e.g., a relational-frame repertoire). That is, given rudimentary verbal skills, subjects are able to show stimulus equivalence because they talk to themselves about the relations between stimuli and thus are able to show reflexivity, symmetry, transitivity. If verbal behavior does play a critical role in stimulus equivalence research, Lowe argues, then it should not be surprising to find that stimulus equivalence does not occur easily with nonhuman subjects.

Others, too, (Schlinger & Blakely, 1987; Vaughan, 1987) have attempted a more systematic analysis of rule-governed behavior using the existing vocabulary of behavior analysts. And there is evidence to suppose that these terms and concepts (e.g., response classes, stimulus classes, discriminative stimuli) are adequate in describing rule-governed behavior and the history necessary for rules to evoke it.

But, of course, the proof lies in the pudding. Which is the best way of talking about such behavior must eventually be determined by the greatest degree of effectiveness found in predicting and controlling it.

4. CONCLUSION

Skinner first distinguished between rule-governed and contingency-shaped behavior when analyzing verbal behavior. In the last paragraph of his book dealing with the topic, he states:

> There is nothing exclusively or essentially verbal in the material analyzed in this book. It is all part of a broader field—of the behavior of a most complex creature in contact with a world of endless variety. For practical purposes a special field has been set apart in terms of characteristics imparted to it by special controlling variables. It is in terms of these variables—of the contingencies arranged by the verbal community—that verbal behavior can be defined and analyzed. (p. 452)

Skinner's general approach to the study of verbal behavior was of a practical nature. So, too, was the distinction he drew between rule-governed and contingency-shaped behavior. The terms used to describe and analyze both verbal behavior and rule-governed behavior were used as a means of categorizing for practical purposes the larger field of behavior. They were not meant to reveal the essence of anything; they only pointed to the origin or history responsible for bringing about certain kinds of behavior. Unfortunately, this approach has proven to be difficult for some.

In attempting to pin these terms and concepts down to specific defining features and functional definitions—so as to give them equal status with the other terms and concepts making up the technical vocabulary of behavior analysts—problems have arisen. Although Skinner's categorization of this subfield of behavior was not meant for such scrutiny (they were not meant as technical terms), if compelling evidence is provided that some additional behavioral process is at work, then the present analysis must be suspended. It is with much interest that behavior analysts review current research in the field.

But whether rule-governed behavior is or is not of the same stuff as contingency-shaped behavior, there are many things still to be learned while the issue remains unresolved. What are the conditions that engender rule-following when the rule is stated by others? And what are the conditions that lead to rule-following when the rule is stated by oneself? Most of the research to date involves situations where immediate consequences (e.g., approval, praise, points, removal of a threat) follow the relevant (or irrelevant) behavior. All too little attention has been paid to cases of rule-following where the consequences are either weak, delayed, nonexistent, or worse, punishing. Unfortunately, the obvious methodological problems in researching such activity has inspired few to tackle it experimentally. Nonetheless, some people have begun to speculate about such a process (Malott, Chapter 8 this volume), and still others have begun to use the basic framework in clinical settings (e.g., Zettle & Hayes, 1982).

In sum, behavior analysts have begun to analyze complicated behavior often referred to as higher mental activity and have done so within the language of an experimental science of behavior. It is becoming clearer that one need not refer to internal representations or processes or some other internal surrogate as that which mediates information and action. Instead, behavior analysts have begun to describe in physical terms the necessary history that leads to such behavior. The significance of this accomplishment was emphasized a long time ago by Bertrand Russell (1912/1961):

> The chief importance of knowledge by description is that it enables us to pass beyond the limits of our private experience. In spite of the fact that we can only know truths which are wholly composed of terms which we have experienced in acquaintance, we can yet have knowledge by description of things which we have never experienced. In view of the very range of our immediate experience, this result is vital, and until it is understood, much of our knowledge must remain mysterious and therefore doubtful. (p. 224)

We hear you.

Acknowledgment

I thank Jack Michael, teacher and friend, for his instructive comments on an earlier draft of this chapter.

5. REFERENCES

Ayllon, T., & Azrin, N. H. (1964). Reinforcement and instructions with mental patients. *Journal of the Experimental Analysis of Behavior, 7*, 327–331.

Ayllon, T., & Michael, J. (1959). The psychiatric nurse as a behavioral engineer. *Journal of the Experimental Analysis of Behavior, 2*, 323–334.

Azrin, N. H. (1958). Some effects of noise on human behavior. *Journal of the Experimental Analysis of Behavior, 1*, 183–200.

Azrin, N. H., & Holz, W. C. (1966). Punishment. In W. K. Honig (Ed.), *Operant behavior: Areas of research and application* (pp. 380–447). New York: Appleton-Century-Crofts.

Baron, A., & Kaufman, A. (1966). Human, free-operant avoidance of "time out" from monetary reinforcement. *Journal of the Experimental Analysis of Behavior, 9*, 557–565.

Baron, A., Kaufman. A., & Stauber, K. (1969). Effects of instructions and reinforcement-feedback on human operant behavior maintained by fixed-interval reinforcement. *Journal of the Experimental Analysis of Behavior, 12*, 701–712.

Bem, S. L. (1967). Verbal self-control: The establishment of effective self-instruction. *Journal of Experimental Psychology, 64*, 485–491.

Bentall, R. P., & Lowe, C. F. (1987). The role of verbal behavior in human learning: III. Instructional effects in children. *Journal of the Experimental Analysis of Behavior, 47*, 177–190.

Bentall, R. P., Lowe, C. F., & Beasty, A. (1985). The role of verbal behavior in human learning: II. Developmental differences. *Journal of the Experimental Analysis of Behavior, 43*, 165–181.

Bijou, S. W. (1958). Operant extinction after fixed-interval schedules with young children. *Journal of the Experimental Analysis of Behavior, 1*, 25–29.

Bijou, S. W., & Baer, D. M. (1961). *Child development I: A systematic and empirical theory.* New York: Appleton-Century-Crofts.

Browstein, A. J., & Shull, R. L. (1985). A rule for the use of the term, "rule-governed behavior." *The Behavior Analyst, 8,* 265–267.

Catania, A. C., Matthews, B. A., & Shimoff, E. (1982). Instructed versus shaped human verbal behavior: Interactions with nonverbal responding. *Journal of the Experimental Analysis of Behavior, 38,* 233–248.

Chomsky, N. (1957). *Syntactic structures.* The Hauge: Mouton.

Chomsky, N. (1959). A Review of B. F. Skinner's *Verbal behavior. Language, 35,* 26–58.

Devaney, J. M., Hayes, S. C., & Nelson, R. O. (1986). Equivalence class formation in language-able and language-delayed children. *Journal of the Experimental Analysis of Behavior, 46,* 243–257.

Dews, P. B., & Morse, W. H. (1958). Some observations on an operant in human subjects and its modification by dextro amphetamine. *Journal of the Experimental Analysis of Behavior, 1,* 359–364.

Ferster, C. B., & Skinner, B. F. (1957). *Schedules of reinforcement.* Englewood Cliffs, NJ: Prentice-Hall.

Galizio, M. (1979). Contingency-shaped and rule-governed behavior: Instructional control of human loss avoidance. *Journal of the Experimental Analysis of Behavior, 31,* 53–70.

Harzem, P., Lowe, C. F., & Bagshaw, M. (1978). Verbal control in human operant behavior. *Psychological Record, 28,* 405–423.

Hayes, S. C. (1986). The case of the silent dog—verbal reports and the analysis of rules: A review of Ericsson and Simon's *protocol analysis: Verbal reports as data. Journal of the Experimental Analysis of Behavior, 45,* 351–363.

Hayes, S. C., Brownstein, A. J., Haas, J. R., & Greenway, D. E. (1986). Instructions, multiple schedules, and extinction: Distinguishing rule-governed from schedule-controlled behavior. *Journal of the Experimental Analysis of Behavior, 46,* 137–147.

Holland, J. G. (1958a). Human vigilance. *Science, 128,* 61–67.

Holland, J. G. (1958b). Counting by humans on a fixed-ratio schedules *[sic]* of reinforcement. *Journal of the Experimental Analysis of Behavior, 1,* 179–181.

Kaufman, A., baron, A., & Kopp, R. E. (1966). Some effects of instructions on human operant behavior. *Psychonomic Monograph Supplements, 11,* 243–350.

Knapp, T. J. (1986). The emergence of cognitive psychology in the latter half of the twentieth century. In T. J. Knapp & L. C. Robertson (Eds.), *Approaches to cognition: Contrasts and controversies* (pp. 13–35). Hillsdale, NJ: Lawrence Erlbaum Associates.

Keller, F. S., & Schoenfeld, W. N. (1950). *Principles of psychology.* New York: Appleton-Century-Crofts.

Lachman, R., Lachman, J., & Butterfield, E. C. (1979). *Cognitive psychology and information processing.* Hillsdale, NJ: Lawrence Erlbaum Associates.

Laties, V. G., & Weiss, B. (1963). Effects of a concurrent task on fixed-interval responding in humans. *Journal of the Experimental Analysis of Behavior, 6,* 431–436.

Long, E. R., Hammack, J. T., May, F., & Campbell, B. J. (1958). Intermittent reinforcement of operant behavior in children. *Journal of the Experimental Analysis of Behavior, 1,* 315–339.

Lowe, C. F., Beasty, A., & Bentall, R. P. (1983). The role of verbal behavior in human learning: Infant performance on fixed-interval schedules. *Journal of the Experimental Analysis of Behavior, 39,* 157–164.

Lowe, C. F., Harzem, P., & Bagshaw, M. (1978). Species differences in temporal control of behavior II: Human performance. *Journal of the Experimental Analysis of Behavior, 29,* 351–361.

Malott, R. W. (1989). The achievement of evasive goals: Control by rules describing contingencies that are not direct acting. In S. C. Hayes (Ed.) *Rule-governed behavior: Cognition, contingencies, and instructional control*. New York: Plenum.

Marr, M. J. (1986). Mathematics and verbal behavior. In T. Thompson & M. D. Zeiler (Eds.), *Analysis and integration of behavioral units* (pp. 161–183). Hillsdale, NJ: Lawrence Erlbaum Associates.

Matthews, B. A., Shimoff, E., Catania, A. C., & Sagvolden, T. (1977). Uninstructed human responding: Sensitivity to ratio and interval contingencies. *Journal of the Experimental Analysis of Behavior, 27*, 453–467.

Matthews, B. A., Catania, A. C., & Shimoff, E. (1985). Effects of uninstructed verbal behavior on nonverbal responding: Contingency descriptions versus performance descriptions. *Journal of the Experimental Analysis of Behavior, 43*, 155–164.

Meazzini, P., & Ricci, C. (1986). Molar vs. molecular units of behavior. In T. Thompson & M. D. Zeiler (Eds.), *Analysis and integration of behavioral units* (pp. 19–43). Hillsdale, NJ: Lawrence Erlbaum Associates.

Miller, G. A., Galanter, E., & Pribram, K. H. (1960). *Plans and the structure of behavior*. New York: Holt, Rinehart & Winston.

Murray, D. M. (1986). *Read to write*. New York: Holt, Rinehart and Winston.

Parrott, L. (1987). Rule-governed behavior: An implicit analysis of reference. In S. Modgil & C. Modgil (Eds.), *B. F. Skinner: Consensus and controversy* (pp. 265–276). London: Falmer Press.

Parsons, J. A., Taylor, D. C., & Joyce, T. M. (1981). Precurrent self-prompting operants in children: "Remembering." *Journal of the Experimental Analysis of Behavior, 36*, 253–266.

Poppen, R. (1982). Human fixed-interval performance with concurrently programmed schedules: A parametric analysis. *Journal of the Experimental Analysis of Behavior, 37*, 251–266.

Russell, B. (1961). Knowledge by acquaintance and knowledge by description. In R. E. Egner & L. E. Denonn (Eds.), *The basic writings of Bertrand Russell: 1903–1959* (pp. 217–224). New York: Simon and Schuster. (Original work published 1912)

Ryle, G. (1949). *The concept of mind*. New York: Barnes and Noble Books.

Schlinger, H., & Blakely, E. (1987). Function-altering effects of contingency-specifying stimuli. *The Behavior Analyst, 10*, 41–45.

Shimoff, E., Catania, A. C., & Matthews, B. A. (1981). Uninstructed human responding: Sensitivity of low-rate performance to schedule contingencies. *Journal of the Experimental Analysis of Behavior, 36*, 207–220.

Shimoff, E., Matthews, B. A., & Catania, A. C. (1986). Human operant performance: Sensitivity and pseudosensitivity to contingencies. *Journal of the Experimental Analysis of Behavior, 46*, 149–157.

Sidman, M. (1978). Remarks. *Behaviorism, 6*, 265–268.

Sidman, M. (1986). Functional analysis of emergent verbal classes. In T. Thompson & M. E. Zeiler (Eds.), *Analysis and integration of behavioral units* (pp. 213–245). Hillsdale, NJ: Larence Erlbaum Associates.

Sidman, M., & Tailby, W. (1982). Conditional discrimination vs. matching to sample: An expansion of the testing paradigm. *Journal of the Experimental Analysis of Behavior, 37*, 5–22.

Skinner, B. F. (1938). *The behavior of organisms*. New York: Appleton-Century-Crofts.

Skinner, B. F. (1947). *The William James Lectures*. (Available from the Association for Behavior Analysis, Verbal Behavior Special Interest Group, Department of Psychology, Western Michigan University, Kalamazoo, MI 49008.)

Skinner, B. F. (1953). *Science and human behavior*. New York: The Free Press.

Skinner, B. F. (1955–1956). Freedom and the control of men. *The American Scholar, 25*(1), 47–65.

Skinner, B. F. (1957). *Verbal behavior*. New York: Appleton-Century-Crofts.

Skinner, B. F. (1963). Operant behavior. *American Psychologist, 18*, 503–515.

Skinner, B. F. (1969). *Contingencies of reinforcement: A theoretical analysis.* New York: Appleton-Century-Crofts.

Skinner, B. F. (1974). *About behaviorism.* New York: Knopf.

Skinner, B. F. (1982, May). *Some unusual instances.* Paper presented at the annual meeting of the Association for Behavior Analysis, Milwaukee, WI.

Skinner, B. F. (1983). *A matter of consequences.* New York: Alfred A. Knopf.

Vaughan, M. E. (1985). Repeated acquisition in the analysis of rule-governed behavior. *Journal of the Experimental Analysis of Behavior, 44,* 175–184.

Vaughan, M. E. (1987). Rule-governed behavior and higher mental processes. In S. Modgil & C. Modgil (Eds.), *B. F. Skinner: Consensus and controversy* (pp. 257–264). London: Falmer Press.

Weiner, H. (1962). Some effects of response cost upon human operant behavior. *Journal of the Experimental Analysis of Behavior, 5,* 201–208.

Weiner, H. (1964). Conditioning history and human fixed-interval performance. *Journal of the Experimental Analysis of Behavior, 7,* 383–385.

Wiener, N. (1948). *Cybernetics: Or control and communication in the animal and the machine.* Cambridge: MIT Press.

White, S. H. (1965). Evidence for a hierarchical arrangement of learning processes. In L. P. Lipsitt & C. C. Spiker (Eds.), *Advances in child development and behavior: Vol. 2* (pp. 187–220). New York: Academic Press.

Zettle, R. D., & Hayes, S. C. (1982). Rule-governed behavior: A potential theoretical framework for cognitive-behavior therapy. In P. C. Kendall (Ed.), *Advances in cognitive-behavioral research and therapy* (pp. 73–118). New York: Academic Press.

CHAPTER 4

An Experimental Analysis of Rule-Governed Behavior

A. CHARLES CATANIA, ELIOT SHIMOFF,
and BYRON A. MATTHEWS

1. INTRODUCTION

Contingency-shaped behavior is behavior directly controlled by the relations between responses and their consequences. But behavior may also come under the control of antecedent stimuli, stimuli in the presence of which responses produce their consequences. We find important examples of such stimuli in human verbal communities, which arrange contingencies that bring behavior under the control of antecedent verbal stimuli called commands, instructions, or rules.

These contingencies are presumably effective because they make consequences depend on correspondences between the behavior specified by the verbal antecedents and the behavior that occurs. Thus they may establish and maintain rule-following as a response class. Once such a class is established, the consequences involved in maintaining it are likely to differ from those involved in specific instances of behavior. For example, consider a child told to put on boots before going out to play in the snow. We must distinguish the social consequences of obeying or disobeying the parents from the natural consequences of shod or unshod feet.

Behavior controlled by verbal antecedents rather than more directly by its particular consequences is characterized by its membership in the higher-order class of rule-following and may be called rule-governed. In this usage, rules

A. CHARLES CATANIA and ELIOT SHIMOFF • Department of Psychology, University of Maryland Baltimore County, Catonsville, Maryland 21228. BYRON A. MATTHEWS • Department of Sociology, University of Maryland Baltimore County, Catonsville, Maryland 21228.

are defined functionally, in terms of their roles as antecedent verbal stimuli, rather than structurally, by topographic or syntactic criteria. Thus commands or instructions may function as rules, but to the extent that they generate relevant verbal or nonverbal behavior, so also may definitions or statements of fact.

We will emphasize rule-following that is already established rather than the conditions under which it develops. Thus, unless otherwise specified, our references to contingencies will imply the direct consequences that operate for specific responses rather than the indirect consequences that establish and maintain the rule-governed behavior; the latter must eventually become the subject of further analysis, but in the present account those indirect consequences will typically remain implicit.

Contingency-shaped behavior, which is by definition under the control of its consequences, will necessarily be sensitive to those consequences. Rule-governed behavior, on the other hand, will be sensitive to those consequences only to the extent that the rules are consistent with the contingencies. When this is not the case, the contingencies that maintain rule-following, even though often remote, may override the other consequences of the behavior. To that extent, rule-governed behavior may be said to be insensitive to its consequences.

We may reasonably assume that nonhuman performances in general are contingency-shaped. In human performances, however, verbal behavior is pervasive, and both verbal and nonverbal behavior may be either contingency-shaped or rule-governed. It follows that a primary task of experimental analyses of human performances is to determine how contingencies and rules respectively contribute to establishing and maintaining behavior.

2. CONTINGENCIES AND RULES

Let us begin with a college student pressing a button that occasionally produces points exchangeable for money. There are at least two possible sources of control. First, button pressing may be maintained by the contingent relation between presses and point deliveries; in this case, we characterize the points as reinforcers and the button pressing as the operant class. Second, the student may be following instructions; under these circumstances, the performance depends upon the student's history of reinforced compliance with instructions and the operant class is rule-compliance rather than button pressing. Either type of control may operate alone, or both may enter into intermediate cases in which performance is jointly controlled by contingencies and by rules.

The distinction between the two forms of button pressing is in terms of the sources of their control and not in terms of their topographies. To the extent that button pressing is contingency-shaped, or controlled by the contingent relation between presses and point deliveries, it will be independent of instructions; to the extent that it is rule-governed, or controlled by instructions, it may be insensitive to changes in the contingencies.

To characterize a performance as rule-governed is to say that a response (e.g., a button press or a chain pull) or one of its properties (e.g., rate or force) is determined by the rule. A problem, however, is that the rule may not be easily accessible. The ease with which we can identify a rule as a part of a particular controlling environment depends on who generated it, on whether it is overt or covert, and on which properties of behavior it specifies. In an experimental setting, for example, a rule that has been overtly provided by the experimenter in a set of instructions may be easier to identify than one covertly generated by the subject, and one that specifies a recorded property of behavior may be easier to identify than one that specifies a property the experimenter has not chosen to measure.

Rules may or may not be consistent with contingencies. When they are consistent with contingencies, the rule-governed performances they occasion may change with contingencies accordingly. But rule-governed behavior, though sometimes sensitive to contingencies in this sense, cannot be sensitive to contingencies in the same way as behavior that is contingency-shaped. In fact, we can only be certain that behavior is controlled by rules when rules and contingencies are pitted against each other. If we studied rules and contingencies that produced comparable performances, we would have no basis for deciding whether the rules or the contingencies were in control.

Consider again the student whose button presses produce points. If we provided a rule specifying high-rate button pressing while contingencies operated that would generate low-rate pressing without the rule, we could then distinguish between rule-governed and contingency-shaped performances on the basis of the different rates. Another strategy would be to determine whether performances changed with changes in rules or with changes in contingencies. Regardless of which experimental strategy we adopted, the conclusion that a performance was rule-governed would be based on its insensitivity to contingencies.

Rule-governed behavior may be established by verbal communities precisely because such behavior is insensitive to contingencies (Skinner, 1966; see also 1969, pp. 133–171). We often resort to instructions when natural consequences are weak (as when we tell children to study) or when natural consequences are likely to maintain undesirable behavior (as when we warn against drug abuse). It is not necessary to tell people to do what they would do even if not told.

Experimental analyses of human behavior have often concentrated on the finding that human performances maintained by various reinforcement schedules differ in significant ways from the performances of nonhuman organisms (e.g., Weiner, 1969). In retrospect, those differences can be interpreted as arising from human rule-governed responding. Such responding is likely to differ from the uninstructed performances of rats, pigeons, or monkeys because rule-governed behavior in such settings is often insensitive to contingencies (Matthews, Shimoff, Catania, & Sagvolden, 1977; Shimoff, Catania, & Matthews, 1981).

But to account for species differences in schedule performances on the basis of the distinction between rule-governed and contingency-shaped responding raises another issue. Humans are verbal organisms. Even if an experimenter does not directly instruct a response, humans are likely to talk to themselves and thus to generate their own rules (Lowe, 1979, 1983). The frequency with which people talk to themselves about what they are doing suggests that contingency-shaped human behavior may be relatively uncommon. What if human behavior is typically rule-governed? How and when does it come under the control of its consequences? How can behavior that is insensitive to contingencies adapt to a changing environment?

One possibility is that the verbal behavior that constitutes a rule is itself typically shaped by the contingencies that would otherwise operate on the nonverbal behavior: Rules that work remain effective as rules, whereas those that do not lose their power to govern behavior. Such contingencies have made the generation of rules and the shaping of compliance with them a standard part of the practices of human verbal communities (cf. Zettle & Hayes, 1982). If this is the case, the important experimental issues are not just those of distinguishing between rule-governed and contingency-shaped behavior. We must also examine the conditions under which effective rules are established and maintained, and the interactions that may occur between the rules and the consequences of the behavior governed by them.

2.1. Descriptions of Performances and of Contingencies

Our experimental studies of the functions of verbal behavior began with procedures in which nonverbal behavior was observed while verbal behavior was either shaped or instructed. College students' button presses produced points according to multiple random-ratio (RR) random-interval (RI) schedules, with different buttons for each 1.5-min schedule component; the RR schedule was typically assigned to the left button and the RI schedule to the right button. In nonhuman performances, RR schedules, which arrange consequences for a response after varying numbers of responses, consistently produce higher response rates than RI schedules, which arrange consequences for a response at the end of varying intervals of time (Ferster & Skinner, 1957). Sensitivity of human behavior to these schedule contingencies can therefore be assessed on the basis of whether RR and RI rate differences emerge and, if they do, whether they change appropriately when the schedules assigned to the two buttons are reversed.

The contribution of verbal responding to the maintenance of other behavior has been examined by manipulating instructions (e.g., Kaufman, Baron, & Kopp, 1966), by using preverbal subjects (e.g., Lowe, Beasty, & Bentall, 1983; Bentall, Lowe, & Beasty, 1985), by "tying up" verbal responding (e.g., Lowe's [1979] use of shadowing), and by using responses unlikely to be accompanied by relevant verbal behavior (e.g., Hefferline & Keenan's [1961] conditioning of an invisibly small thumb twitch). In our studies, we monitored and manipulated verbal responding by requiring our subjects to respond to questions in writing after every pair of schedule components; awarding points for these "guesses" allowed us to shape verbal behavior (the shaping of verbal behavior, once controversial, is now a standard experimental procedure; cf. Greenspoon, 1955).

We first compared the effects of instructed and shaped guesses (Catania, Matthews, & Shimoff, 1982). Button pressing produced points according to multiple RR 20 RI 10-s schedules, with 1.5-min component durations; one RR and one RI component constituted a cycle (in multiple schedules, two component schedules alternate, each in the presence of a different stimulus). Between cycles, students completed sentences of the form "The way to earn points with the left [or right] button is to . . ."; thus the required verbal report was a description of performance. Instructed guesses, established by telling students to write "press fast" for one button and "press slow" for the other, had inconsistent effects on button pressing. For some students, pressing rates corresponded to the verbal reports, but for others they did not. When performance descriptions were shaped, however, by differentially awarding points for successive approximations to "press fast" for one button and to "press slow" for the other, pressing rates were consistent with the verbal reports rather than with the schedules. For example, "press slow" was accompanied by slow rates of pressing on a button even with the RR instead of the RI schedule arranged for that button. Thus by shaping performance descriptions we had created performances that were insensitive to contingencies.

But verbal responses may describe contingencies as well as performances. People often tell others about the contingencies operating in some environment, assuming that a description of the contingencies will somehow produce behavior appropriate to them. A description of contingencies that has implications for performance, however, is not equivalent to an explicit description of that performance.

Our concern with the difference between performance descriptions (e.g., "The way to earn points is by pressing fast") and contingency descriptions (e.g., "The computer makes points available for a press after a random number of presses") began when, in attempting to shape performance descriptions, we inadvertently shaped contingency descriptions and found no differences in corresponding button-pressing rates. A more systematic investigation (Matthews, Catania, & Shimoff, 1985) confirmed that pressing rates, typically consistent with shaped *performance* descriptions (as in Catania *et al.*, 1982), are often inconsistent with shaped *contingency* descriptions. Three different types of outcomes were obtained: correspondences between verbal reports of contingencies and the rates appropriate to those contingencies (regardless of the actual contingencies for pressing); equal response rates unrelated to contingency descriptions; and rates sensitive to contingencies but independent of contingency descriptions.

These findings set the stage for the experiments reported here. We were interested first in whether we could account for the inconsistent effects of contingency descriptions on pressing rates in terms of different verbal repertoires brought into the experimental setting by different subjects. We then became concerned with specifying the necessary and sufficient conditions for synthesizing behavior sensitive to contingencies in humans.

3. EXPERIMENT 1: SAMPLING PERFORMANCE HYPOTHESES

Matthews *et al.* (1985) found individual differences in the effects of shaped contingency descriptions on button-pressing rates. It seemed appropriate to attribute some of the variability in outcomes to differences in the students' verbal repertoires. One student, correctly identifying two schedules as RR and RI, might go on to say that point earnings increase with higher RR rates but not with higher RI rates. Another student, also correctly identifying the two schedules, might instead go on to say that, because point deliveries in both are unpredictable, point deliveries are unaffected by pressing rates. We might expect the first student but not the second to show rate differences appropriate to the schedules.

To determine whether button-pressing rates depended on the students' verbal formulation of how to respond under given contingencies, we sampled "performance hypotheses" at the beginning and again at the end of each session. Performance hypotheses were sampled by having students read descriptions of three schedules, then asking them to write their "best guess about the way to earn the most points" on each. The schedules described were RR, RI, and DRL (differential reinforcement of low rate, which arranges consequences for a response only after some minimum period without responding). During sessions, accurate contingency descriptions (or identifications) were shaped using procedures similar to those reported in Matthews, Catania, and Shimoff (1985). If RR and RI pressing rates did not diverge, performance descriptions were then shaped, to see if they would control pressing rates as in Catania *et al.* (1982) and Matthews *et al.* (1985). But if RR and RI rate differences did accompany accurate identification of the contingencies, we next shaped reversed contingency descriptions, so that the respective left and right schedules were incorrectly identified as RI and RR. If rates did not reverse with the reversed contingency descriptions, the schedules themselves were reversed to assess sensitivity to contingencies.

3.1. Method

3.1.1. Subjects

Ten UMBC undergraduates participated in sessions at 2- to 4-day intervals as an option in satisfying introductory psychology course requirements. Introductory psychology sections were taught by different instructors who covered operant behavior and related topics at different times and gave varying emphasis to them. No attempt was made to assess students' familiarity with reinforcement schedules, however, because our previous work suggested that simply administering a questionnaire about schedules affected the verbal behavior with which the students entered the experiment.

3.1.2. Apparatus

During each session, the student sat at a console in a sound-attenuating cubicle. The upper portion of the console contained a point counter, two green lamps, and a small black button. Whenever the two green lamps were lit, a press on the black button turned them off and added a point to the counter. The lower portion of the console contained two 2.4-cm diameter red buttons, each beneath a blue lamp and operable by a minimum force of 15 N. White noise presented through headphones masked sounds from an adjacent control room. When the blue lamp above either red button was lit, presses on that button briefly interrupted the masking noise. A stack of "guess sheets" and a pencil were provided on the table beside the console.

3.1.3. Procedure

Except for the addition of the sampling of performance hypotheses, the procedures described here are identical to those for shaped contingency descriptions in Matthews *et al.* (1985).

Performance Hypotheses. Immediately before and after each session, students were seated at a table in a room adjacent to that containing the response console and were provided a sheet of paper with the following text:

> Imagine that you can earn points by pressing a button. For each of the following, write your best guess about the way to earn the most points. (Do not use more than the space provided; do not take more than 2 minutes.)
>
> If the button works only after a random number of presses, you should:

If the button works only after a random time without any presses, you should:

If the button works only at random time intervals, you should:

No feedback for the accuracy of these performance hypotheses for RR, DRL, and RI contingencies was provided. Performance hypotheses were collected before each session began and again after the completion of each session. Following the presession collection of performance hypotheses, the student was immediately escorted to the cubicle containing the response console, and the session began.

Button Presses. Presses on the red buttons occasionally initiated the nominal reinforcement period (the lighting of the green lamps, during which a press on the black button produced a point). Presses on one red button became eligible to do so according to a random-ratio schedule that selected responses with a probability of .05 (RR 20). Presses on the other became eligible after a random interval determined by selecting pulses generated at the rate of 1 per sec with a probability of .1 (RI 10-sec with $t = 1.0$ and $p = .1$). The RR schedule was normally arranged for left-button presses and the RI schedule for right-button presses.

The left-button and right-button lamps lit alternately (multiple RR RI) for 1.5 min each (excluding reinforcement periods), and sessions always began with the left-button (RR) schedule. The two lamps were never lit simultaneously, and presses on the button beneath an unlit lamp had no scheduled consequences. After 1.5 min of each schedule (3-min schedule cycle), both blue lamps were turned off, and a buzz replaced the white noise in the headphones; this marked the beginning of the guess period.

Guesses. An ample supply of guess sheets was available next to the console. Each guess sheet had six sentences to be completed. For guess sheets requiring descriptions of contingencies, the sentences were "the computer will let your press turn on the green lights depending on:"; the first three followed the heading "left button:" and the last three the heading "right button:". Guess sheets requiring descriptions of performance (used for two students) were identical to those in Catania *et al.* (1982) and Matthews *et al.* (1985), with sentences for each button of the form "the way to turn the green lights on with the left [right] button is to:". Students were instructed to pass each completed guess sheet through an 8-cm hole in the wall next to the console.

To shape guesses, an experimenter assigned each guess 0, 1, 2, or 3 points, writing point values next to each guess and passing the sheet to the student through the hole in the wall; the guess period ended when the student returned the graded guess sheet. During shaping, both the ratio-interval distinction and the variability of outcomes were taken into account in awarding points to guesses, but no distinction was made between technical and colloquial vocabularies. For example, both "variable ratios" and "a changing number of presses" were typically awarded the maximum of three points in the shaping of RR contingency descriptions. The decision to shape a particular schedule description for a particular button was always made in advance of the shaping session. In all cases, RR guesses were initially shaped for the left button and RI guesses for the right button, corresponding to actual contingencies.

At the end of the guess period, the buzz was replaced by white noise, and the light above the left button was again lit. Points earned by guessing did not appear on the point counter, but at the end of each session students were given a card showing total session earnings; they were paid at the end of their final sessions. Each session lasted about 50 min; sessions varied with time spent writing guesses but usually included 8 to 12 schedule cycles and guess periods.

Instructions. During all sessions, the following instructions were mounted on the wall above the console:

> Each point you earn is worth 1 cent. For example, if you earn 300 points, you will be paid $3.00.
>
> You have two ways to earn points: (1) by pressing the RED BUTTONS, and (2) by GUESSING.
>
> RED BUTTONS. At the lower center of the console are two red push buttons. At any time, only one of the two red buttons will work (the blue lights above the buttons will tell you which one is working).
>
> If you press in the right way: (1) The GREEN LIGHTS next to the counter will light up, and (2) when the green lights come on, you can add 1 point to your total by pressing the small BLACK BUTTON next to the counter.
>
> *Guessing.* Every few minutes, the console will shut off for about 2 minutes. During this time, you may fill in as many blanks as you wish on the GUESS SHEET.
>
> When you have written as many guesses as you wish (don't take longer than about 2 minutes altogether), roll up the guess sheet and SLIDE IT THROUGH THE HOLE IN THE WALL just to the left of the console.
>
> The sheet will come back with your point earnings written in red. Each guess can earn 0, 1, 2, or 3 points.
>
> After you have seen your points for guessing, PASS THE SHEET BACK AGAIN, and the console will come on.
>
> Do not remove your headphones once the experiment is under way.

3.2. Results

For 2 of the 10 students, performance hypotheses about the "way to earn the most points" failed to describe different rates. Data for one of these (1A) are presented in Figure 1. Before the first session, this student's performance hypotheses for RR and RI schedules were "press it a lot of times" and "press it constantly"; at the end of the first session, the student wrote "press it a lot of times" for both schedules. Shaping of contingency descriptions was com-

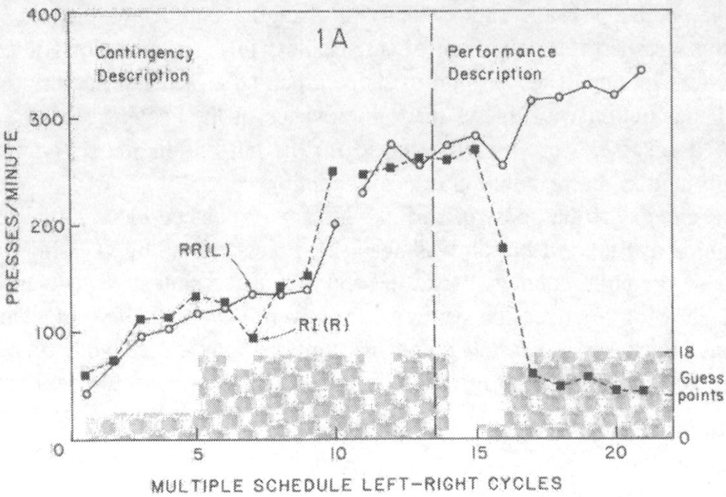

Figure 1. Left (L) and right (R) response rates of Student 1A over cycles of multiple random-ratio (RR), random-interval (RI) schedules of point delivery for button presses. The shaded areas show point deliveries for verbal behavior (guesses) during the shaping of contingency and performance descriptions. Connected points were obtained within a single session; unconnected points indicate the interruption between sessions.

pleted by the fifth guess period, after which Student 1A consistently identified the RR contingency as depending on "# of presses" and the RI contingency as depending on "time intervals"; during most cycles, RR rates were slightly lower than RI rates. The contingency descriptions were accurate, but they were not accompanied by substantial and consistent differences in RR and RI response rates.

Shaping of performance descriptions began in the guess period of the fourth cycle of the second session; response rates diverged at about the time Student 1A began describing the appropriate performance as "fast" for the RR (left) and "slow" for the RI (right) button. When performance hypotheses were obtained at the end of the second session, Student 1A wrote "press it fast" and "slowly" for the RR and RI schedules respectively. (The other student whose performance hypotheses did not include rate differences gave "number of presses" and "random intervals" as the respective contingency descriptions for the RR and RI schedules, with no consistent differences in pressing rates; we were unable to shape performance descriptions over 17 cycles in two sessions.)

Performance hypotheses written by the other eight students specified different rates for the RR and RI contingencies. Typical hypotheses included "push the button as fast as you can" versus "press it a lot once in a while," "press as often as possible'' versus ''determine when those times are,'' or ''keep pressing the button'' versus ''wait and press the button.''

Figure 2 presents data for one of these students (1B), whose initial hypotheses were ''press as many times as possible fast'' for the RR schedule and ''press and wait randomly'' for the RI schedule. By the end of the first session, contingency descriptions had been shaped, with the left button (RR), depending on ''random no. of pushes,'' and the right (RI), depending on ''random intervals,'' and left (RR) rates were systematically higher than right (RI) rates.

Was the rate difference controlled by the interval and ratio contingencies or by the student's contingency descriptions? To find out, we shaped reversed contingency descriptions in the second session (after cycle 12) by awarding points for descriptions of the respective left and right contingencies as RI and RR. On the left button, still producing points according to the RR schedule but now described as RI, rates decreased, whereas on the right button, still an RI schedule but now described as RR, rates increased. For Student 1B and for two others not shown, this reversal of the verbal reports demonstrated that the contingency descriptions rather than the contingencies themselves controlled response rates. For one other student with rate hypotheses and different RR and RI response rates, the reversal of guesses inconsistently affected pressing rates, but the reversal of the RR and RI schedules produced a corresponding reversal of response rates, demonstrating sensitivity to contingencies. For the four remaining students, we did not attempt shaping of reversed contingency descriptions because of constraints on student availability over extended sessions.

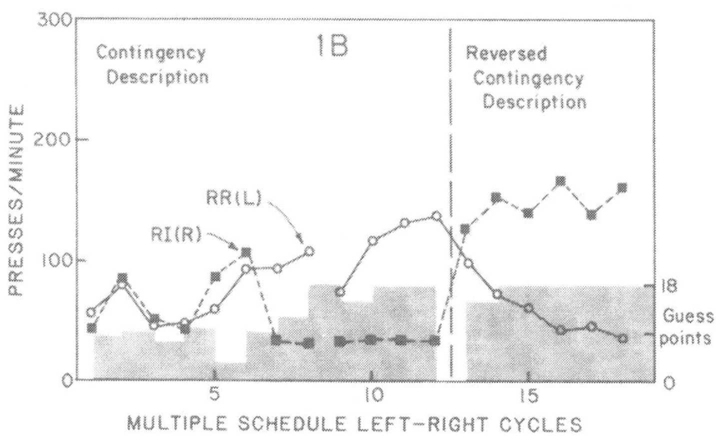

Figure 2. Left (L) and right (R) response rates of Student 1B over cycles of multiple random-ratio (RR), random-interval (RI) schedules, with shaded areas showing point deliveries for verbal behavior (guesses) during the shaping and reversal of contingency descriptions.

3.3. Discussion

Ten students read descriptions of RR and RI contingencies and were then exposed to actual RR and RI schedules. Two of the 10 did not include different rates in their hypotheses about RR and RI performances, and differences in their RR and RI rates did not accompany the subsequent shaping of their accurate identifications of the RR and RI contingencies.

Eight of the 10, however, had generated performance hypotheses in which RR rates were higher than RI rates. In each case, the subsequent shaping of appropriate descriptions of these contingencies was accompanied by corresponding RR and RI rate differences. With four students for whom reversed contingency descriptions were later shaped, the corresponding reversal of pressing rates in three cases showed that these rates were under the control of verbal behavior; in the remaining case, the reversal of rates only with the reversal of schedules showed the rates to be under the control of contingencies.

These findings are consistent with the assumption (Matthews *et al.*, 1985) that the variable effects of identifying contingencies depend on variations in the correlated verbal repertoires with which the students enter an experimental setting. Shaped contingency descriptions control different RR and RI rates only if the student can also report that different rates of responding are appropriate to RR and RI contingencies. The paradox is that the RR and RI rate difference emerges reliably in the behavior of nonverbal organisms. Why then does it seem to emerge in verbal humans only if it is incorporated into a verbal repertoire? We may characterize this indifference of human nonverbal behavior to ratio versus interval contingencies in the absence of appropriate verbal behavior as insensitivity to contingencies.

4. EXPERIMENT 2: INSTRUCTING ACCURATE PERFORMANCE HYPOTHESES

Experiment 1 was a first step in the experimental analysis of the variable effects of contingency descriptions on pressing; it confirmed that contingency descriptions controlled pressing rates only when correlated performance hypotheses (verbal descriptions of rates appropriate to schedules) specified high-rate RR and low-rate RI responding. If that analysis is correct, it should be possible to create reliably schedule-appropriate performances by providing students with accurate hypotheses about how best to respond on RR and RI schedules and then shaping descriptions of those contingencies. The second experiment examined that possibility. Students were given presession lessons describing RR and RI contingencies and specifying rates appropriate for each schedule; experimental sessions were similar to those in Experiment 1, and in some cases included reversals of either contingencies or contingency guesses. In addition, we examined the performance of one subject who was highly sophisticated in the language and findings of the experimental analysis of behavior.

4.1. Method

Seven UMBC undergraduates served. One other participant, a visitor to the laboratory, had extensive formal experience with schedules and verbal descriptions of contingencies; at the time of his participation, he was serving as the editor of a journal for the "original publication of experiments relevant to the behavior of individual organisms."

Apparatus, instructions, and procedures were identical to those of Experiment 1, except that before each session subjects read a sheet containing the following "lesson," which described RR, RI, and DRL contingencies along with response rates appropriate to each:

> Imagine that you can earn points by pressing a button. A computer decides whether a press earns a point according to one of three rules:
>
> 1. The computer lets your press earn a point after a random number of presses. The more presses you make, the more points you earn. The best thing to do is to press fast.
> 2. The computer lets your press earn a point after a random time interval. The number of presses does not matter, so there is no reason to press fast. The best thing to do is to press at a moderate rate.
> 3. The computer lets your press earn a point only after a random time without any presses. There should be long intervals between presses; you should wait and then press. The best thing to do is to press slowly.

After reading the lesson, students filled out the following "schedules quiz" to test their ability to describe RR, RI, and DRL contingencies:

> Imagine that you can earn points by pressing a button. A computer decides whether a press earns a point according to one of three rules. These rules are [the following sentence repeated three times]:
> The computer lets your press earn a point after a random ______.

If the quiz sheet was filled out incorrectly, students were required to reread the lesson and take the schedules quiz again. Once the quiz was completed correctly, a "performance quiz" designed to test students' ability to describe performances appropriate to each schedule was presented:

> If the button works only after a random number of presses, you should press:
> If the button works only after a random time interval, you should press:
> If the button works only after a random time without presses, you should press:

The performance quiz was presented three times, with the sentences given in three different orders. If there were errors, students were required to reread

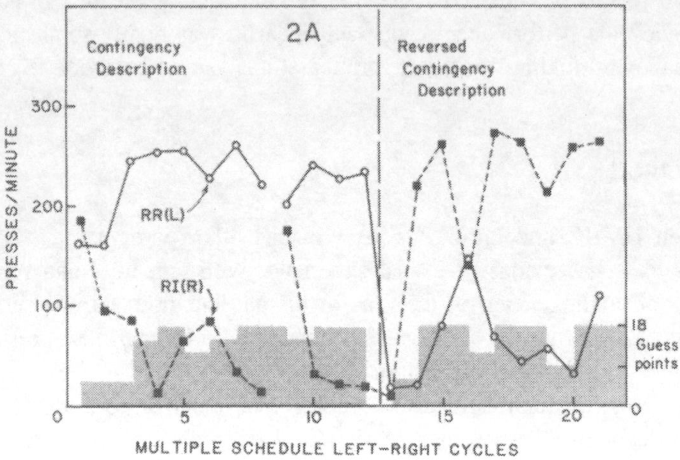

Figure 3. Left (L) and right (R) response rates of Student 2A over cycles of multiple random-ratio (RR), random-interval (RI) schedules, with shaded areas showing point deliveries for verbal behavior (guesses) during the shaping and reversal of contingency descriptions.

the lesson and take the quizzes again until they could answer all items correctly.

4.2. Results

Substantial rate differences were apparent in all eight subjects. For 2A (Figure 3), as well as for three other students, the contingency guesses controlled pressing rates; when reversed contingency descriptions were shaped, rates conformed to the description rather than to the contingency between presses and points, despite a substantial decrease in earnings due to the reduced RR rates.

Figure 4 presents data for 2B, one of two students whose button-pressing rates were controlled by the contingencies and were independent of the shaped contingency guesses. In the first session, as well as the first three cycles of the second session, rates were higher on the left button, which was correctly described as producing points according to an RR schedule. To determine whether the rate difference reflected control by the schedules or by the contingency descriptions, reversed contingency descriptions were shaped; rates on the left button (RR schedule, now identified by the student as RI) remained high. When contingencies were reversed (cycles 18 to 20) and again reversed (cycles 21 to 23), pressing rates conformed to contingencies and were independent of the contingency guesses.

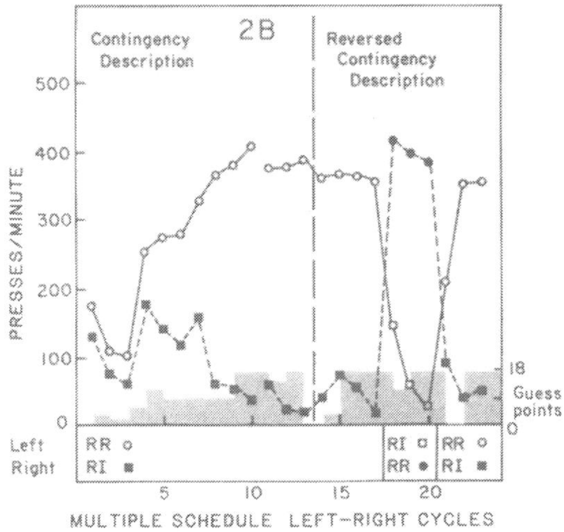

Figure 4. Left (L) and right (R) response rates of Student 2B over cycles of multiple random-ratio (RR), random-interval (RI) schedules, with shaded areas showing point deliveries for verbal behavior (guesses) during the shaping of contingency descriptions, the reversal of contingency descriptions, and two reversals of the multiple RR RI schedules. The key to the schedule reversals is provided in the bottom panel.

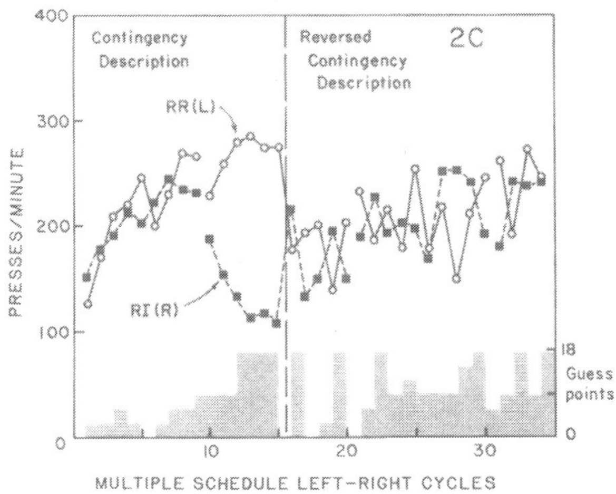

Figure 5. Left (L) and right (R) response rates of Student 2C over cycles of multiple random-ratio (RR), random-interval (RI) schedules, with shaded areas showing point deliveries for verbal behavior (guesses) during the shaping and reversal of contingency descriptions.

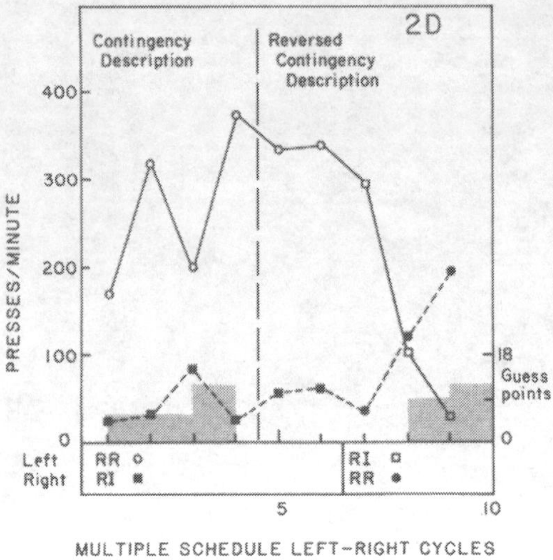

Figure 6. Left (L) and right (R) response rates of Laboratory Visitor 2D, the editor of a behavior-analytic journal, over cycles of multiple random-ratio (RR), random-interval (RI) schedules, with shaded areas showing point deliveries for verbal behavior (guesses) during the shaping and reversal of contingency descriptions and a reversal of the multiple RR RI schedules.

The performance of 2C (Figure 5) was controlled both by contingencies and by the shaped contingency descriptions. Contingency descriptions were well established by the beginning of the second session, and rates were substantially higher on the left (RR) button. After Cycle 15, points were awarded for reversed contingency descriptions (i.e., for identifying the RR left button as RI and vice versa). In this instance, however, pressing conformed neither to the contingency descriptions (cf. Figure 3) nor to the contingencies (cf. Figure 4). Contingency guesses became variable, guesses that earned full points in one guess period were not repeated in the following guess period, and rate differences became inconsistent. Contingencies and contingency guesses appeared to be competing sources of control over this performance, as in a tug-of-war.

Figure 6 presents the data from our sophisticated participant, 2D. Differences in pressing rates were evident within the first cycle, and contingency guesses were correct in the first guess period. (The full 18 points were not always earned only because the subject did not consistently write guesses for all the blanks available on the guess sheet.) Our attempts to shape reversed contingency descriptions had no effects either on pressing rates or on the contingency guesses themselves; this subject continued to respond at high rates on the RR button and at low rates on the RI button but never wrote reversed contingency descriptions. When contingencies were reversed, pressing rates changed appropriately. Contingency guesses remained accurate throughout the session, regardless of our criteria for awarding points for guesses. For this sophisticated subject, therefore, contingency descriptions were strictly determined by the contingencies, and pressing rates were therefore always consistent with those contingencies.

4.3. Discussion

When accurate performance hypotheses were established by a presession lesson, shaped contingency descriptions were invariably associated with differences in pressing rates appropriate to schedules. Rates of pressing were subsequently found to be controlled by students' contingency descriptions in four cases, sensitive to contingencies and independent of contingency descriptions in two cases, and apparently under competing verbal and contingency control in one case. For our participant with an extensive history of correctly identifying contingencies, contingency descriptions were controlled by the contingencies, and pressing rates were appropriate to those contingencies. It was reassuring to find such sensitivity to both verbal and nonverbal contingencies in the behavior of a journal editor.

5. EXPERIMENT 3: INSTRUCTING INACCURATE PERFORMANCE HYPOTHESES

Experiment 2 showed that shaping descriptions of RR and RI contingencies invariably resulted in appropriate rate differences when students were provided with performance hypotheses appropriate to the two classes of schedules. If accurate descriptions of contingencies always result in performances appropriate to contingencies when accompanied by appropriate performance hypotheses, can inappropriate performances be produced by instructing incorrect performance hypotheses? This was the focus of the third experiment.

5.1. Method

Six UMBC undergraduates served in Experiment 3. Apparatus, instructions, and procedures were identical to those used in Experiment 2, except that the presession lesson described only RR and RI schedules and the performance hypotheses provided to the student specified high-rate pressing as appropriate for both schedules:

> Imagine that you can earn points by pressing a button. A computer decides whether a press earns a point according to one of two rules:

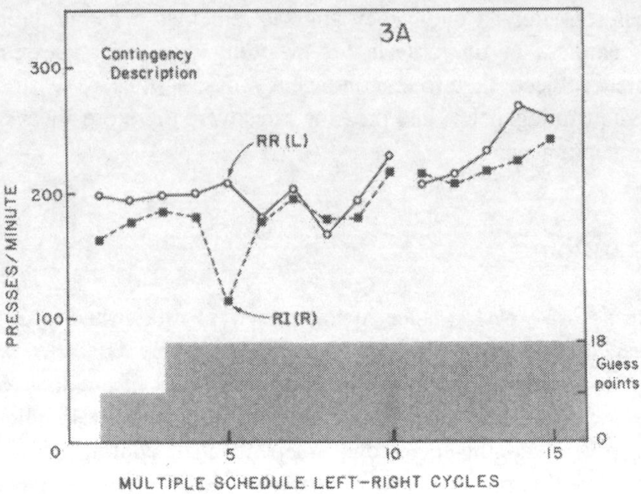

Figure 7. Left (L) and right (R) response rates of Student 3A over cycles of multiple random-ratio (RR), random-interval (RI) schedules, with shaded areas showing point deliveries for verbal behavior (guesses) during the shaping of contingency descriptions.

1. The computer lets your press earn a point after a random number of presses. There is no way of knowing which press will earn a point. To earn as many points as possible, the best thing to do is press fast.
2. The computer lets your press earn a point after random time intervals. There is no way to know when the time intervals are up. To earn every point as soon as it becomes available (and thus to earn as many points as possible), the best thing to do is press fast.

5.2. Results

For three of six students (represented by student 3A, Figure 7), accurate contingency descriptions shaped after our misleading lesson were not associated with systematic differences between RR and RI pressing rates; these students responded at high rates on both buttons, consistent with the performance hypotheses provided in the lesson.

For the other three students (represented by 3B, Figure 8), rate differences appeared despite our lesson. But 3B's performance was not sensitive to the difference between the RR and RI contingencies; when contingencies were reversed in the second session, rates on the left button (which was shifted from RR to RI) remained high. The same pattern characterized the performance of one of the other two students, whereas the remaining student's rates on both buttons became high and about equal after the contingency reversal.

5.3. Discussion

Instructing a high-rate performance hypothesis for RI contingencies produced high-rate responding inappropriate to this schedule in three of six cases; rates maintained by an RI schedule correctly identified as RI were approximately equal to those maintained in the RR component. For the three other students in Experiment 3, low RI rates did appear, but when contingencies were subsequently reversed, pressing was insensitive to the difference between interval and ratio contingencies.

The failure in three cases to produce high RI rates by instructing a high-rate RI performance hypothesis suggests that our lessons were not sufficiently plausible and convincing to generate consistent and enduring verbal behavior with respect to high-rate RI pressing. It seems likely that these lessons, which described contingencies and relations between response rates and point earnings, sometimes occasioned other covert verbal behavior relevant to appropriate performance. Despite our best efforts to mislead them, three of our students presumably formulated more accurate performance hypotheses on how best to respond given RI contingencies, and these hypotheses in turn produced lower rates on the schedule that was identified as RI in their shaped verbal reports.

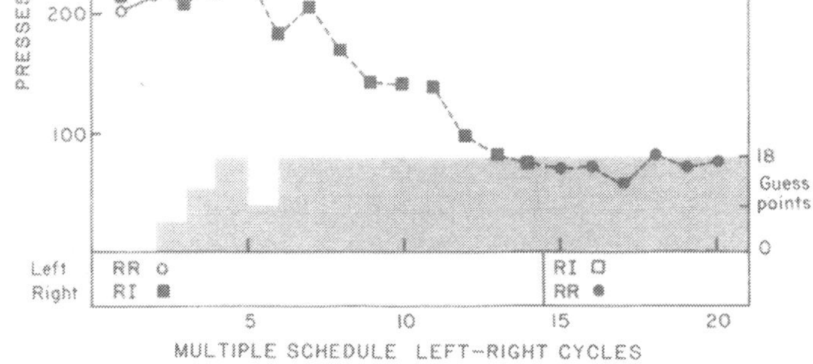

Figure 8. Left (L) and right (R) response rates of Student 3B over cycles of multiple random-ratio (RR), random-interval (RI) schedules, with shaded areas showing point deliveries for verbal behavior (guesses) during the shaping of contingency descriptions and the reversal of the multiple RR RI schedules.

6. EXPERIMENT 4: INSTRUCTING SCHEDULE DISCRIMINATIONS

Taken together, the results of the first three experiments are generally consistent with an account in which verbal behavior that identifies contingencies reliably controls responding appropriate to those contingencies only when accompanied by other verbal behavior (i.e., a performance hypothesis) accurately specifying performances appropriate to those contingencies. But those experiments also found that such verbally controlled responding was typically not sensitive to changes in the contingencies. The key to making human nonverbal behavior sensitive to contingencies may be to make verbal behavior sensitive to those contingencies.

Experiment 4 attempted to establish behavior that would be sensitive to contingencies by providing instructions about how to discriminate between RR and RI schedules. Experiment 4 also began to explore the possible limitations of such instructed sensitivity to contingencies by observing students' performances when the RR component of the multiple schedule was replaced by a tandem RI DRL schedule. (In a tandem schedule, two contingencies operate in succession. In tandem RI DRL, for example, a response must first satisfy the RI contingency, and then the DRL contingency comes into effect; the response that satisfies the DRL contingency then produces a consequence [Ferster & Skinner, 1957].)

6.1. Method

6.1.1. Subjects

Six UMBC undergraduates completed Experiment 4; four other students were dropped from the experiment because the RR and RI contingencies did not maintain different response rates after the schedule discrimination lessons described next.

6.1.2. General Procedures

Procedures in Experiment 4 differed from those of Experiments 2 and 3 in four respects. First, to increase the likelihood that pressing would become sensitive to contingencies, we did not shape or sample students' descriptions of contingencies, which might otherwise have constituted a competing source of control. Second, to make the difference between schedule components more discriminable, multiple RR 40 RI 10-s schedules were used instead of multiple

RR 20 RI 10-s, with responses eligible for reinforcement producing two points instead of one point in both schedule components; in three cases, the schedules were RR 20 and RI 5-s, with eligible responses earning one point. These schedule combinations made average rates of point delivery lower in RR than in RI components given typical response rates, unlike the original schedules, which usually generated more similar rates of point delivery. Third, we provided a schedule discrimination lesson that described a method for discriminating between RR and RI schedules by "testing the contingencies." Fourth, a test for the generality of contingency sensitivity was introduced; once performance appeared sensitive to the difference between RR and RI contingencies, a multiple RI tandem RI DRL schedule was imposed. The tandem RI DRL contingency made responses eligible for point delivery only if they first met the RI requirement and then terminated an interresponse time greater than 1 s. With pigeons (Ferster & Skinner, 1957), adding such a DRL contingency to an interval schedule consistently reduces the rate of responding. For convenience, we will sometimes refer to the tandem RI DRL schedule simply as DRL.

6.1.3. Sequence of Procedures

Before each session, students were seated in a room adjacent to that containing the response console, where they read the following lesson describing RR and RI contingencies and response rates appropriate to each:

> Imagine that you can earn points by pressing a button. A computer decides whether a press earns a point according to one of two rules:
>
> 1. The computer lets your press earn a point after a RANDOM NUMBER OF PRESSES. The more presses you make, the more points you earn. The best thing to do is to press fast.
> 2. The computer lets your press earn a point after a RANDOM TIME INTERVAL. The number of presses does not matter, so there is no reason to press fast. The best thing to do is to press slowly.

Students next were required correctly to fill out two quiz sheets, like those used in Experiment 2. One quiz asked for sentence completions describing RR and RI contingencies and the other for pressing rates appropriate for each. If there were errors, students were required to reread the lesson until both quizzes were correctly answered.

Students were then seated at the console; printed instructions about how to operate the console were mounted on the wall. The instructions were identical to those used in the first three experiments, except that all references to guessing were eliminated; between schedule cycles, a brief "rest period" replaced the guess period.

If the RR and RI schedule components did not maintain different response rates by the midway point (5 to 7 cycles) of the first session, the session was interrupted and students were given a sheet containing the following lesson about how to discriminate between RR and RI contingencies:

> TO FIND OUT WHICH RULE THE COMPUTER IS USING
>
> To tell which rule the computer is using, you should WAIT FOR A WHILE WITHOUT PRESSING.
> If your next press makes the green lights come on, the button is probably working after RANDOM TIME INTERVALS, and there is no reason to press fast.
> If your next press does not make the green lights come on, the button is probably working after RANDOM NUMBERS OF PRESSES, and the faster you press the more you will earn.

After they had read the lesson, students were given the following schedule discrimination quiz:

> Sometimes the computer lets your press turn on the green lights after a random number of presses and sometimes after a random time interval.
> What can you do to find out which way the computer is working?

The lesson and quiz were repeated until the student was able to describe the "wait-and-press" strategy given in the lesson; the session then continued. If, as occurred in four cases, the RR and RI schedules still did not maintain different pressing rates, the student was dropped from the experiment. If rate differences did appear, the contingencies were reversed between the two buttons to test for contingency sensitivity. If contingency reversals produced appropriate changes in pressing rates, a multiple RI tandem RI DRL 1-s schedule was introduced as a further test of contingency sensitivity. As in the previous experiments, all lessons and quizzes were repeated before the start of every subsequent session.

6.2. Results

For all 10 students, pressing during the first five to seven cycles of the first session was insensitive to contingencies; both the RR and the RI schedules maintained high and approximately equal pressing rates. Thus, in the absence of shaped contingency descriptions instructions describing contingencies and appropriate rates were not sufficient to generate performances appropriate to schedules. In four cases, pressing rates still did not diverge after the schedule discrimination lesson was given midway through the first session, and those students were dropped. For the 6 other students, performances on the multiple RR RI schedule became sensitive to contingencies after the lesson; rates changed appropriately when contingencies were reversed between the two buttons.

Data for a typical student, 4A (whose button presses produced points according to a multiple RR 40 RI 10-s schedule), are presented in Figure 9. After initial lessons describing the schedules and appropriate performances, RR and

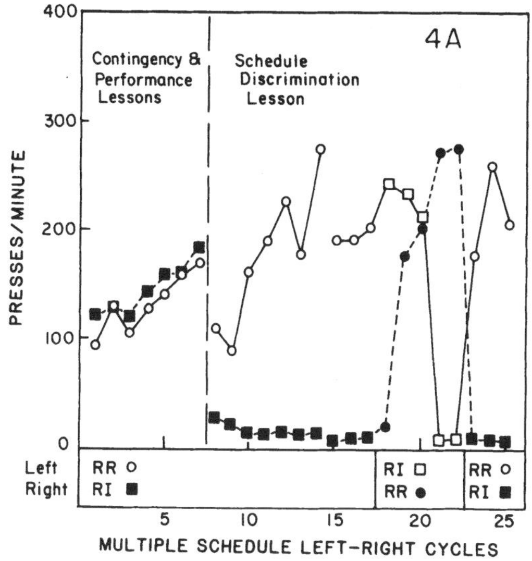

Figure 9. Left (L) and right (R) response rates of Student 4A over cycles of multiple random-ratio (RR), random-interval (RI) schedules given contingency and performance lessons, a lesson on discriminating schedules, and two reversals of the multiple RR RI schedules.

RI rates were approximately equal. Appropriate rate differences appeared after the schedule discrimination lesson was given, following Cycle 7. Rate differences were maintained in the second session. When contingencies were reversed between the two buttons (after Cycle 17), and then again reversed (after Cycle 22), rates changed quickly and appropriately. Thus pressing was highly sensitive to the difference between RR and RI contingencies.

When the multiple RI tandem RI DRL schedule was later imposed (not shown), 4A's rates on both buttons became low and about equal to those for the RI component of the multiple RR RI schedule. This pattern of low and equal rates maintained by the multiple RI tandem RI DRL schedule was characteristic of four other students. Although data from pigeons show that an added DRL contingency reduces rates, our students' button pressing appeared insensitive to such a change in contingencies.

Data from 4B (Figure 10) provide additional information about the limitations of the kind of contingency sensitivity established by our schedule discrimination lesson. The figure presents data only from the third and fourth sessions, which began with a multiple RR 20 RI 5-s schedule. At the start of the third session, the RR schedule was assigned to the right button and maintained higher rates than the RI schedule. When schedule assignments were reversed (after Cycle 33), rates changed appropriately.

Observation of this student's performance during the session suggested

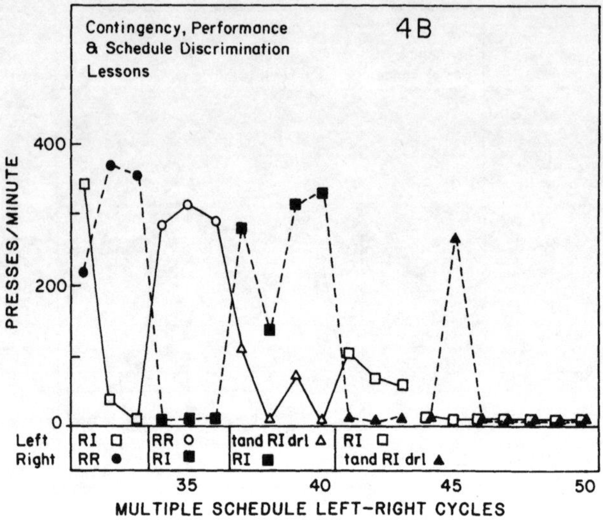

Figure 10. Left (L) and right (R) response rates of Student 4B over cycles of multiple random-ratio (RR), random-interval (RI) schedules, multiple random-interval low-rate (tandem RI DRL) schedules, and their reversals.

that this sensitivity to the difference between ratio and interval contingencies was strongly rule-governed. In each cycle, this student always "tested" only the first schedule component by waiting several seconds before pressing. If the first press after the wait produced a point, rates were low in the first component and high in the second, which was never tested. If the first press did not produce a point, rates were high in the first component and low in the second. Following the shift to a multiple RI 5-s tandem RI 5-s DRL 1-s schedule (after Cycle 38), rates on the left button (for which contingencies were changed from RR to DRL) quickly decreased. But rates on the right button, which continued to produce points according to the RI schedule, increased to the level previously maintained by the RR. When contingencies were subsequently reversed (Cycles 41 to 50), rates on the right button (which was changed from RI to DRL) decreased; left-button rates also decreased, so that rates on both buttons were low by the end of the experiment.

6.3. Discussion

In Experiment 4, the experimental strategy was to instruct all of the verbal repertoire necessary to produce sensitivity to the difference between RR and RI contingencies: descriptions of the contingencies themselves, descriptions of the performances appropriate to those contingencies, and a method for determining which contingencies were in effect. For six students, these instructions reliably generated performances that were highly sensitive to the difference between RR and RI contingencies; contingency reversals quickly produced corresponding changes in performance. But when the RR component of the multiple schedule was subsequently replaced by a DRL schedule, the rule-governed nature of that contingency sensitivity became apparent.

Although our students' button pressing was highly sensitive to the difference between RR and RI contingencies, it was clearly not sensitive in the same way that a pigeon's behavior is sensitive. The behavior of the pigeon is contingency sensitive because it is contingency governed. That is, the pigeon's behavior is under the control of the relations between responding and its consequences; when those relations change, the pigeon's behavior changes also. Our students' pressing, on the other hand, was sensitive to the difference between RR and RI contingencies because it was controlled by verbal behavior that described how to respond once a contingency had been identified and how to identify the contingency. The limitations of such rule-governed sensitivity to contingencies became apparent, however, when contingencies were altered in a way that rendered the rule for discriminating between RR and RI schedules less useful or even misleading; the most extreme case was student 4B, for whom the substitution of DRL for the RR component of the multiple schedule resulted in high-rate ratiolike responding in the unchanged RI component.

7. EXPERIMENT 5: ASSESSING SENSITIVITY TO CONTINGENCIES

Experiment 4 showed that responding could be made sensitive to contingencies through instructions. But our results also suggested that such responding remained rule-governed and that its sensitivity was unlike that of contingency-shaped behavior. Experiment 5 continued the investigation of instructed sensitivity to contingencies. As in Experiment 4, sensitivity to the difference between RR and RI contingencies was established through lessons describing the contingencies, appropriate performances, and a way to determine which schedule was in effect. To explore the characteristics of such instructed sensitivity further, the schedule was changed from multiple RR 20 RI 5-s to multiple RI 5-s RI 10-s, and a brief extinction period was sometimes introduced at the beginning of one component of the schedule.

7.1. Method

Three UMBC undergraduates served. Apparatus, instructions, and procedures were those of Experiment 4 with the following differences. First, the

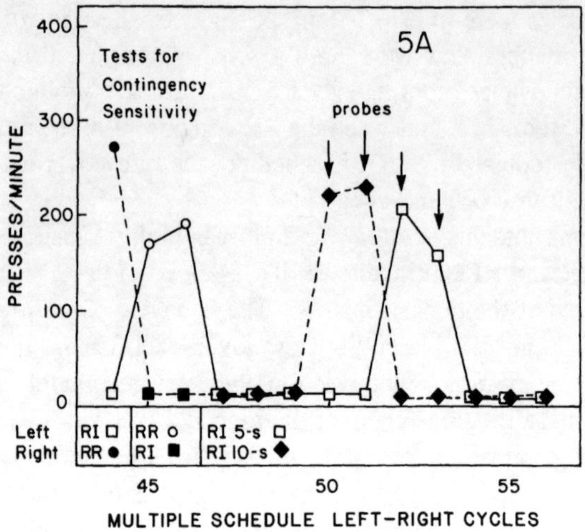

Figure 11. Left (L) and right (R) response rates of Student 5A over cycles of multiple random-ratio (RR) random-interval (RI) schedules, their reversal, multiple RI 5-s RI 10-s schedules, and probes (at arrows) of the student's sampling of contingencies at the beginning of multiple-schedule components.

basic schedule was multiple RR 20 RI 5-s, with 1-min instead of 1.5-min components; presses eligible for reinforcement earned one point. The shorter component durations were used so that more contingency reversals could be included in a session. Second, once sensitivity to the difference between RR and RI contingencies had been demonstrated, the schedule was changed to multiple RI 5-s RI 10-s; these RI values provided rates of point delivery in the two components roughly equal to those in the corresponding components of the multiple RR RI schedule. Finally, for two students, a brief extinction period was sometimes imposed at the beginning of one component of the multiple RI RI schedule.

7.2. Results

Data for 5A are presented in Figure 11. By Cycle 44, rate differences were well-established, and rate changes following contingency reversals (Cycles 45 and 46) demonstrated that the performance was sensitive to contingencies. When multiple RR RI was replaced by multiple RI 5-s RI 10-s, rates on both buttons became low and approximately equal, also indicating contingency sensitivity. Had performance come under control of the changing schedules, or did it remain rule-governed? Informal observation of the performance suggested that the rate changes accompanying contingency reversals reflected a rule like "Check each component by waiting before the first press; if the first press produces a point, press slowly for the rest of the component; otherwise press fast."

A simple way to test that possibility was to add a new contingency, based on our observation that response rate within a component generally did not change after the fourth or fifth response. The added contingency made the first five or six responses of a component ineligible for reinforcement. (Technologically, the intervention was crude; rather than revise the computer program, we manually disconnected the student's button from the interface to the computer.) The results of this probe were dramatic: Response rates were high for any component (identified in the figure as "probes") in which the first five or six responses did not produce a point. Data for a second student were similar to those for 5A.

Data for the remaining student, 5B, are presented in Figure 12. As with 5A, rates changed appropriately when contingencies were reversed (cf. Cycles 33 to 38 and 39 to 40). Informal observation of the performance suggested that the student was testing only the first component of each cycle, by waiting before the first press; if the first press after a wait produced a point, rates were low in the first component and high in the second; otherwise, rates were high in the first component and low in the second. Our informal observation was confirmed when the multiple RI 5-s RI 10-s schedule was imposed. Rates decreased on the left button, for which the schedule had been changed from RR to RI 5-s. But rates increased on the right button, which had been changed

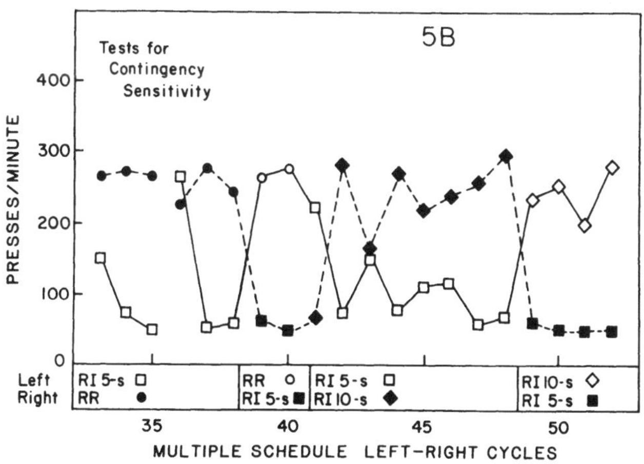

Figure 12. Left (L) and right (R) response rates of Student 5B over cycles of multiple random-ratio (RR), random-interval (RI) schedules, multiple RI 5-s RI 10-s schedules, and their reversals.

from RI 5-s to RI 10-s, to levels approximating those maintained when the RR schedule was in effect. Rates reversed when contingencies were reversed (Cycles 49 to 52).

Whatever else might be said of the performances of these students, their sensitivity to contingencies was not like that of nonverbal organisms.

8. GENERAL DISCUSSION

Our data are relevant to several issues. One is whether the behavior of verbal humans is in general rule-governed rather than contingency-shaped. To the extent that behavior is rule-governed, contingencies have their effects on performance only by altering verbal behavior with respect to the performance and its relation to events in the environment. In that case, the contingency sensitivity of a nonverbal performance would depend on the sensitivity of the controlling verbal behavior.

Another issue involves the variables that control verbal behavior relevant to nonverbal performance. Specifically, it may be that instructed verbal behavior will be less sensitive to contingencies than verbal behavior shaped by contact with contingencies. Perhaps the kind of human behavior most likely to be contingency-shaped is verbal behavior (one reason might be that only a little of our language with respect to verbal behavior is effective language: cf. Skinner, 1975).

Still another issue arises because some behavior that began as rule-governed eventually seems to occur without verbal accompaniment, as when performance is well practiced and contingencies are stable. For example, for a person learning to drive, verbal rules provided by a teacher are important sources of control over the complex performances involved, but experienced drivers rarely seem to talk to themselves about what they are doing. How and why is verbal control superseded, and by what? Does rule-governed behavior drop out at some level of expertise (cf. Dreyfus & Dreyfus, 1986)? If the performance of the experienced driver has become contingency-shaped, why does a change in contingencies trigger the reappearance of relevant verbal behavior? (Some of these questions have been concerns of the literatures of awareness and of incidental learning: e.g., Brewer, 1975; Chaiklin, 1984; Dulany, Carlson, & Dewey, 1984, 1985; Reber, Allen, & Regan, 1985.)

Our explorations of rule-governed and contingency-shaped human behavior began with the finding that although shaped descriptions of appropriate performances reliably controlled responses rates within multiple RR RI schedules, shaped descriptions of ratio and interval contingencies did not. Experiments 1, 2, and 3 demonstrated that the identification of a contingency produces responding appropriate to that contingency only when the identification is accompanied by verbal behavior describing appropriate performance, that is, by an accurate performance hypothesis. In Experiments 4 and 5, we attempted to establish contingency-sensitive responding more reliably by providing subjects with descriptions of schedules and schedule-appropriate response rates and with methods for discriminating between RR and RI contingencies. Such instructions usually succeeded in establishing performances that were highly sensitive to transitions between the RR and RI schedules but not to other schedule transitions. We concluded that rule-governed contingency sensitivity is unlike the contingency-shaped sensitivity observed in nonverbal organisms, because in the former behavior remains under the control of verbal antecedents rather than the relations between responding and consequences.

How shall we describe the multiple RR RI performances observed in Experiments 4 and 5? Clearly they were rule-governed, and yet they appeared sensitive to the differences between the RR and RI contingencies. But we cannot characterize the performances as sensitive to contingencies in any general sense; how should we characterize button pressing that is sensitive to the difference between ratio and interval contingencies but is insensitive to the difference between RI 5-s and RI 10-s schedules? We must recognize that the terminology of rule-governed and contingency-shaped behaviors identifies rules or contingencies as controlling variables; placing particular instances of behavior in one or the other class is a matter of experimental analysis (cf. the discussion of pseudosensitivity in Shimoff, Matthews, & Catania, 1986).

By definition, contingency-shaped responding is never insensitive to contingencies. Rule-governed responding, however, is often so. But such insensitivity is precisely what makes verbal rules so useful; we establish responding with rules when the contingencies alone are too weak or too remote to shape performances effectively (as when we tell students to review the text each night), or when contact with the contingencies might be dangerous (as when we tell drivers to wear seatbelts), or when we are trying to overpower competing natural contingencies (as when we ask authors to complete manuscripts by a deadline), or when the contingencies are too complex (as when we teach students how to do research). Early in training, it is sometimes obvious that performance is rule-governed; we may see awkward topographies (e.g., in complex motor skills such as writing or operating an automotive manual shift), or we may observe students overtly repeating or rereading instructions.

But the insensitivity of rule-governed performances is unlikely to persist indefinitely against the inexorable power of contingencies; eventually, behavior is shaped by its consequences. This shaping might come about in one of two ways: Control by rules may drop out, or, as in Experiments 4 and 5, the rules may become consistent with the contingencies (in which case we sometimes speak of correspondences between verbal and nonverbal behaviors, as in correspondences between saying and doing: cf. Catania, Shimoff, & Matthews, 1987; Matthews, Shimoff, & Catania, 1987; Risley & Hart, 1968).

Under many circumstances, we might be indifferent to which course behavior followed. But when contingencies change suddenly (as they did in the shift from multiple VR VI to multiple VI VI and as they might in a complex and dynamically changing environment), the distinction becomes important. What are the conditions under which rule-governed behavior can revert to contingency-shaped behavior?

Whenever verbal instruction is effective, performances must be insensitive to the contingencies and thoroughly controlled by the rules. How can such performances ever make contact with contingencies? Presumably, only through controlling verbal behavior. With extended exposure to the contingencies, the rules may come to conform to those contingencies, and performances controlled by these rules then follow. The verbal rules may gradually become less prominent (for example, as repetitions of the rules become covert). But if contingencies change, the verbal rules may reappear and may continue to function until the rules (and their correlated performances) conform to the new contingencies. If this is so, human contingency-shaped behavior might best be sought in relatively unimportant incidental acts such as drumming one's fingers or doodling and in well-practiced skills such as playing a musical instrument or visually exploring one's environment.

It may be relevant that another factor in the effectiveness of rules in controlling behavior is how the rules themselves were established. Rule-governed behavior presumably was a crucial feature of the origin and evolution of human language (Catania, 1986). Sensitivity of behavior to contingencies is, in effect, determined by the sensitivity of the rules to contingencies. This may in part be why rule-governed rules (i.e., instructed verbal behavior) have a less consistent effect on nonverbal behavior than do contingency-shaped rules (Catania *et al.*, 1982).

If this analysis is accurate, it follows that a substantial part of human nonverbal behavior is almost always rule-governed and that its sensitivity to contingencies is likely to be mediated by rules. Only verbal behavior is directly sensitive to contingencies, and it remains to be seen whether that sensitivity should be characterized as contingency-shaped or as something else. In any case, the long-term effectiveness of instructions must then depend on the extent to which those instructions foster rule-governed sensitivity.

For example, formal statistical procedures are often described as "cookbook," and the analogy can be carried further. One distinction between a mundane cook and a great chef is in the extent to which either can deviate from the recipe when appropriate (e.g., as demanded by changes in the availability of ingredients); the same point can be made with respect to a scientist's deviation from experimental design "recipes." Good cooking and good science have in common such sensitivity, albeit the sensitivity is to different kinds of contingencies. In training laboratory researchers, some instructors emphasize formal statistical designs (e.g., Winer, 1962), whereas others describe how the experimenter's behavior interacts with the natural contingencies in the laboratory (e.g., Skinner, 1956). Both forms of instructions result in rule-governed experimenting, but the experimental behavior generated by the latter is more likely to come to correspond with the contingencies of the research environment.

Let us close with some rules. When we speak of human nonverbal behavior, we should call it rule-governed. When we speak of human verbal behavior, we should call it contingency-shaped. But, as with all rules, we should allow these to be shaped by contingencies. Our third rule is a corollary of a familiar one: Always be alert for exceptions. We may hope to prove rules, but it is more important to think of them as subject to experimental analysis. That is how we make our scientific rules answerable to the contingencies of our subject matter.

9. REFERENCES

Bentall, R. P., Lowe, C. F., & Beasty, A. (1985). The role of verbal behavior in human learning: II. Developmental differences. *Journal of the Experimental Analysis of Behavior, 43,* 165–181.

Brewer, W. F. (1975). There is no convincing evidence for operant or classical conditioning in adult humans. In W. B. Weimer & D. S. Palermo (Eds.), *Cognition and the symbolic processes* (pp. 1–42). Hillsdale, NJ: Erlbaum.

Catania, A. C. (1986). Rule-governed behavior and the origins of language. In C. F. Lowe, M. Richelle, D. E. Blackman, & C. Bradshaw (Eds.), *Behavior analysis and contemporary psychology* (pp. 135–156). Hillsdale, NJ: Erlbaum.

Catania, A. C., Matthews, B. A., & Shimoff, E. (1982). Instructed versus shaped human verbal behavior: Interactions with nonverbal responding. *Journal of the Experimental Analysis of Behavior, 38,* 233–248.

Catania, A. C., Shimoff, E., and Matthews, B. A. (1987). Correspondences between definitions and procedures: A reply to Stokes, Osnes, and Guevremont. *Journal of Applied Behavior Analysis, 20,* 401–404.

Chaiklin, S. (1984). On the nature of verbal rules and their role in problem solving. *Cognitive Science, 8,* 131–155.

Dreyfus, H. L., & Dreyfus, S. E. (1986). *Mind over machine.* New York: Free Press.

Dulany, D. E., Carlson, R. A., & Dewey, G. I. (1984). A case of syntactical learning and judgment: How conscious and how abstract? *Journal of Experimental Psychology: General, 113,* 541–555.

Dulany, D. E., Carlson, R. A., & Dewey, G. I. (1985). On consciousness in syntactic learning and judgment: A reply to Reber, Allen, and Regan. *Journal of Experimental Psychology: General, 114,* 25–32.

Ferster, C. B., & Skinner, B. F. (1957). *Schedules of reinforcement.* New York: Appleton-Century-Crofts.

Greenspoon, J. (1955). The reinforcing effect of two spoken sounds on the frequency of two responses. *American Journal of Psychology, 68,* 409–416.

Hefferline, R. F., & Keenan, B. (1961). Amplitude-induction gradient of a small human operant in an escape-avoidance situation. *Journal of the Experimental Analysis of Behavior, 6,* 41–43.

Kaufman, A., Baron, A., & Kopp, R. E. (1966). Some effects of instructions on human operant behavior. *Psychonomic Monograph Supplements, 1*(11), 243–250.

Lowe, C. F. (1979). Determinants of human operant behaviour. In M. D. Zeiler & P. Harzem (Eds.), *Advances in analysis of behaviour: Vol. 1. Reinforcement and the organization of behaviour* (pp. 159–192). Chichester, England: Wiley.

Lowe, C. F. (1983). Radical behaviorism and human psychology. In G. C. L. Davey (Ed.), *Animal models of human behavior: Conceptual, evolutionary and neurobiological perspectives* (pp. 71–93). Chichester, England: Wiley.

Lowe, C. F., Beasty, A., & Bentall, R. P. (1983). The role of verbal behavior in human learning: Infant performance on fixed-interval schedules. *Journal of the Experimental Analysis of Behavior, 39,* 157–164.

Matthews, B. A., Shimoff, E., Catania, A. C., & Sagvolden, T. (1977). Uninstructed human responding: Sensitivity to ratio and interval contingencies. *Journal of the Experimental Analysis of Behavior, 27,* 453–467.

Matthews, B. A., Catania, A. C., & Shimoff, E. (1985). Effects of uninstructed verbal behavior on nonverbal responding: Contingency descriptions versus performance descriptions. *Journal of the Experimental Analysis of Behavior, 43,* 155–164.

Matthews, B. A., Shimoff, E., & Catania, A. C. (1987). Saying and doing: A contingency-space analysis. *Journal of Applied Behavior Analysis, 20,* 69–74.

Reber, A. S., Allen, R., & Regan, S. (1985). Syntactic learning and judgment, still unconscious and still abstract: Comment on Dulany, Carlson, and Dewey. *Journal of Experimental Psychology: General, 114,* 17–24.

Risley, T. R., & Hart, B. (1968). Developing correspondence between the non-verbal and verbal behavior of pre-school children. *Journal of Applied Behavior Analysis, 1,* 267–281.

Shimoff, E., Catania, A. C., & Matthews, B. A. (1981). Uninstructed human responding: Sensitivity of low-rate performance to schedule contingencies. *Journal of the Experimental Analysis of Behavior, 36,* 207–220.

Shimoff, E., Matthews, B. A., & Catania, A. C. (1986). Human operant performance: Sensitivity and pseudosensitivity to contingencies. *Journal of the Experimental Analysis of Behavior, 46,* 149–157.

Skinner, B. F. (1956). A case history in scientific method. *American Psychologist, 11,* 221–233.

Skinner, B. F. (1957). *Verbal behavior.* New York: Appleton-Century-Crofts.

Skinner, B. F. (1966). An operant analysis of problem solving. In B. Kleinmuntz (Ed.), *Problem solving: Research, method, and theory.* New York: Wiley.

Skinner, B. F. (1969). *Contingencies of reinforcement: A theoretical analysis.* New York: Appleton-Century-Crofts.

Weiner, H. (1969). Controlling human fixed-interval performance. *Journal of the Experimental Analysis of Behavior, 12,* 349–373.

Winer, B. J. (1962). *Statistical principles in experimental design* (2nd ed.). New York: McGraw-Hill.

Zettle, R. D., & Hayes, S. C. (1982). Rule-governed behavior: A potential theoretical framework for cognitive-behavioral therapy. In *Advances in cognitive behavioral research and therapy. Volume 1* (pp. 73–118). New York: Academic Press.

PART II

THE NEW DIRECTIONS IN THE ANALYSIS OF RULE-GOVERNED BEHAVIOR

CHAPTER 5

The Verbal Action of the Listener as a Basis for Rule-Governance

STEVEN C. HAYES and LINDA J. HAYES

1. INTRODUCTION

In the traditional behavior-analytic account, most psychologically significant behavior (i.e., that of whole organisms in and with a context) is thought ultimately to be contingency shaped. An important subset of this behavior is rule-governed (Skinner, 1966, 1969, Chapter 6). Skinner (1969, p. 146) provides a worthwhile example. An outfielder moves to catch a ball. Following its trajectory, he moves under it and grasps it with his glove. Skinner views this event as contingency shaped. The outfielder is simply responding, as he has done hundreds of times before, based on the effects his behavior has on moving toward the ball. Skinner contrasts this with the ship captain moving to "catch" a descending satellite. The trajectory of the satellite is analyzed in detail. Mathematical models are consulted that take into account a host of factors such as wind speed and drag coefficients. Its place of impact is predicted and approached. This behavior is not controlled directly by the past consequences of the captain trying to catch satellites. The behavior has not had an opportunity to be shaped by such consequences—it is controlled by rules.

The term *rule* has been used by a variety of psychological theorists and means different things to each (see Reese, Chapter 1 in this volume). Part of the confusion about "rules" occurs because of the multiple meanings of the word in normal usage. *Rule* comes from the Latin *"regula."* Regula originally meant a straight stick, and then a straight stick used for measuring. Some of the current uses of rule in the culture at large are related to these earliest meanings as in a wooden ruler or ruled paper.

STEVEN C. HAYES and LINDA J. HAYES • Department of Psychology, University of Nevada—Reno, Reno, Nevada 89557.

A later sense of "rule" is that of consistency or regularity. Indeed, the English word regular comes from the same root as "rule." This sense is still current. A person might say, for example, "I take this route to school as a rule" and mean simply that this is the regular route taken.

The most etymologically recent sense of the word rule is "to govern." By extension, a "ruler" is one who governs, such as a king. To rule in this sense is to lay down the line or to proscribe what is regular.

Behavior analysts have emphasized rules in the sense of governing events. To some degree, this means that "rule-governed behavior" is a tautology but not completely because the event that *governs* in *rule-governed behavior* is an event that relates to the etymologically earlier sense of the term *rule*. The most popular behavioral definition of rules is Skinner's (1966, 1969): "contingency-specifying stimuli." To specify a contingency presumably involves constructing a regularity. Thus, *rule-governed behavior* is an amalgam of various senses of the term *rule*.

What kind of regularity is a rule? Is it a *verbal* construction of a regularity? If so, what is a verbal construction?

The more general question underlying these is the relation between rule-governed behavior and verbal behavior. The behavior-analytic study of rule-governed behavior was at first not thought to be a study of verbal behavior. From Skinner's perspective in the book *Verbal Behavior,* only the behavior of the speaker was thought to be verbal in any important sense. To construct a rule was to engage in verbal behavior. To follow it was not. This has caused notable problems for a behavioral approach to language, problems that are only now being solved. They are being solved by abandoning the idea that only the behavior of the speaker is verbal.

2. EXPERIMENTAL PROBLEMS CAUSED BY THE DEEMPHASIS OF THE LISTENER

Skinner chose to formulate his analysis of verbal behavior from the point of view of the speaker rather than the listener in a speaker–listener interchange. He defended this action on three primary grounds. First, he pointed out that a speaker speaks because a listener listens and vice versa. Thus, a complete account of the behavior of the speaker necessarily implies an account of the listener. No separate account is then required of listener behavior. Second, the analysis of the listener is unlikely to be productive. Third, he suggested that "the behavior of a man as listener is not to be distinguished from other forms of his behavior" (Skinner, 1957, p. 34). That is, the behavior of the listener is not verbal and requires no special account. It is just ordinary behavior under the discriminative control of speech.

This perspective has caused both theoretical and empirical difficulties. By emphasizing the speaker, a theory of verbal behavior could be constructed that ignored such issues as meaning, understanding, and reference. Whether or not these terms are the proper ones, they point to important issues that were largely ignored by behavior analysts (Parrott, 1984). They cannot be ignored when the behavior of the listener is seriously studied, however, and it is this fact that is changing the behavior-analytic approach to verbal behavior. Behaviorists were slow to this realization because Skinner's arguments discouraged an actual study of the listener.

Rather than leap directly into an analysis of the behavior of the listener, we will first take Skinner's argument on its own terms. Did it really make sense?

Skinner's first point—that understanding the speaker–listener interchange can *start* from either side—seems plausible enough. Because psychology, as psychology, can deal effectively only with the individual organism, it is necessary to focus on one side of the interchange at a time. Understanding each actor does not comprise an understanding of the interchange as a whole. The interchange never disappears from sight, however, because when the speaker is examined, psychologically speaking, the listener becomes context and vice versa. In short, to understand the speaker or listener fully, we must understand the context of the act, and there we are, back to the interchange.

Even if we agree that to understand the interchange we must begin with one or the other side of it, whether it would be more useful to make an initial analysis of the speaker or the listener is still at issue. The concentration on the speaker, then, is justified by Skinner's second two points: that the analysis of the listener as a primary emphasis is unlikely to be productive and that the behavior of the listener is not really verbal anyway.

2.1. Is the Analysis of the Listener More Difficult?

It is not clear from his writings that Skinner was referring to what he implied that the attempt to analyze the behavior of the listener as a starting point was likely to lead to unproductive analyses. It could be that he understood, as we are arguing here, that the behavior of the listener would raise the hoary issues of meaning, understanding, and reference. Skinner several times criticized reference, or meaning-based theories of verbal behavior (e.g., 1957, p. 87) and seemed at times to link these difficulties to an analysis of the listener as a verbal actor.

Unfortunately, the primary emphasis on the speaker creates several difficulties. There are several methodological and strategic problems with an empirical analysis based on the behavior of the speaker, and in each case the problems are less severe when we focus on the behavior of the listener.

2.1.1. Functional Units of Analysis

First, a functional analysis of verbal behavior implies functional units of analysis. Skinner's verbal operants—tacts, mands, and so on—are functional units for this reason. (We believe that the *kind* of functional units Skinner's verbal operants represent is problematic, but that is a topic for another paper.)

A functional account of language presents notable difficulties. Although it is easy to classify verbal events structuralistically (e.g., into words, phrases, nouns, verbs, and the like), it is extraordinarily difficult to do so functionally. The categorization of verbal events into functional classes requires understanding a person's past history and the current source of control over the behavior, both of which are typically unknown or inaccessible. Consequently, we are left with plausible guesses, often based on formal characteristics of the events in question, as the only readily available means of functional classification.

In this area, looking at the behavior of the listener offers certain advantages. We can look, for example, to see if a rule is followed or not followed. We can analyze the effects of rules on ongoing overt behavior. We can give novel stimulus events functions in a manner that fits with our theoretical interpretation of verbal stimuli and then see how these novel events participate in behavioral control. Identifying at least some functional categories of behavior is easier in the case of listener as compared to speaker behavior.

2.1.2. Measurements of Strength

There are no unambiguous measures of the strength of functional units of speaker activity. The problem is of two types. First, some functional categories are too gross for measurement purposes. We might agree, for example, that classical conditioning is a functional process, but we would be unlikely to count instances of, say, "CS-controlled behavior." As psychologists, we are interested in particular instances of this process, not the prevalence of the process in general. A person might count the number of times a phobic retreats in the presence of a particular CS associated with fear-producing stimuli, for example. Likewise, there is no categorization of functional units of speaker behavior adequate to such a task. It makes little sense to attempt to measure the strength of "manding" or "tacting," for example. What we would have to measure are particular subclasses. How we would identify these subcategories then becomes the issue.

The second problem is that even if it were possible to identify sufficiently fine-grained functional units of speaker behavior, there is no well-agreed-upon metric for measuring their strength. Response frequency is clearly inadequate because infrequent responses may be at high strength (e.g., as in the case when a stern parent says to a child, "I will say this once . . .") and repeated verbal responses may be weak (e.g., when a person repeats a newly met person's name several times in order to remember it). This, of course, is exactly the problem Skinner labored over in *Verbal Behavior*. He pointed out many other dimensions that could be used (e.g., loudness), but for every dimension you can name, there is a counterargument to be made. Skinner's resolution (measuring the "probability" of single instances of verbal actions) has never led to an empirical method of measurement.

In contrast, measuring the response strength of listener behavior presents less severe measurement problems. We can present a rule and assess whether the rule is followed. We can construct rules out of experimental languages, in which the subjects' history is relatively controlled, and assess rule-understanding. More will be said about this problem later in the chapter, but for our present purposes, it is sufficient to note that conventional measures of response strength provide useful vehicles for assessing the strength of some listener behavior.

2.1.3. Controlling the Context

It is difficult to limit the relevant context when analyzing the behavior of a speaker. The subtlety and multiplicity of variables that control the behavior of the speaker make an experimental analysis extremely difficult. The importance of history means that many of the most important variables are difficult to reach. A history could be constructed, as in the case of artificial languages, but even then the current situational context for speech must be controlled for the phenomena of interest to be observed and understood. When the current situation *is* controlled (e.g., if a person is deprived of food to see if food will be requested), the resulting behavioral phenomena are not those of primary interest to language researchers. No one doubts that speakers can be made to say particular things. The question is, what is the speaker doing when something is said. Control of the contexts relevant to this question is difficult to achieve.

The variables controlling the behavior of the listener are no less complex, but the relevant context is more manipulable. In particular, the primary (though not the only) context for the behavior of the listener is something to listen to, and the experimenter can present such events at will. The response of listening is not a solely a function of such events and is still historically based. Still, the experimenter has certain advantages in this situation as compared to the case of the speaker. The degree to which the relevant history and situational context can be manipulated, restricted, and specified is greater.

2.1.4. The Lure of Structure

There is a final problem with empirical research on the speaker. One of the most salient characteristics of language is that there is an inherent structuralism it promotes. The speaker produces words, signs, or other outputs that can be transcribed, recorded, or listened to. These words or signs are not behavior—they are products of behavior. A person reading these very sentences may be said to "understand what we have said," but he or she will not understand the contextualized act of our saying this.

A concern over the behavior of the speaker leads fairly directly to an interest in the structure of language. There is nothing wrong with such an interest, but behavior analysis has little to add to it, and, in any case, no amount of research on the structure of language can substitute for a functional analysis of language.

The lure of structuralism is much less of a problem when it is the behavior of a listener that is at issue. There is less of a tendency to fit the behavior of the listener into a structure. To the contrary, the lack of apparent structure has tended to mask the verbal nature of the behavior of the listener, as will be discussed shortly. We can study the behavior of the listener with the assurance that behavior analysts and their students, with only moderate preparation against it, will not be snared by structuralism in the attempt to conduct a behavioral analysis.

2.1.5. *The Answer Is No*

A functional account of the behavior of the listener is *not* more difficult than a functional account of the behavior of the speaker. Empirically, an analysis of the listener seems more readily mounted. Although the behavior of the listener is presumably equally complex, there are clear strategic advantages to beginning there.

Why, then, was a behavioral analysis of the listener ignored for so long? The most important reason seems to have been Skinner's final objection: The behavior of the listener is not verbal. The listener was not studied because there was no reason to do so. Most behavior analysts of the period came to believe that the listener was just behaving in accordance with normal processes of stimulus control. Although, as an applied matter, the study of human listeners was acknowledged to be useful, stimulus control itself could be better studied with organisms in controlled contexts—pigeons, for example. Behavior-analytic scientists interested in fundamental knowledge about behavioral processes directed their research programs elsewhere.

3. THE LISTENER AT THE BACK DOOR

We have so far not engaged the issue of the behavior of the listener *per se*. We have simply argued that the only *real* reason for not dealing with the listener is the conviction that the behavior of the listener is not verbal anyway.

We are still not quite ready to take on the problem of the listener directly. Instead, we will note how the problem arose historically. How did behavior analysis—with its conviction that the problem of the listener was not of fundamental importance—come over the last several years to have such a focus on the behavior of the listener?

This was possible because the problem of the listener arrived at the back door. It did not arrive under the label of *verbal behavior*. The rubric was, instead, *rule-governed behavior* or more generally, *instructional control*. As we will note in the next chapter, the analysis of rule-governed behavior was at first driven by practical and political concerns: It was an attempt to show that behavior analysis could indeed deal with complex human behavior. And at first behavior analysts did not appreciate that their interest in these topics provided an avenue to the empirical and theoretical analysis of verbal interactions.

Vaughan (Chapter 3 in this volume) shows how a theoretical interest in rule-governed behavior within behavior analysis emerged separately from an interest in verbal behavior. Behavior controlled by "contingency-specifying stimuli" was taken to be a particular type of behavior under stimulus control. It was not by accident, however, that Skinner never specified what it means to "specify" a contingency. To do so would require distinguishing functionally between verbal stimuli and other kinds of stimuli. That he has not done. For good reason, it turns out, because the distinction fundamentally revises a behavioral view of language itself.

Many behavior analysts act as if *specify* meant *specify verbally,* but Skinner himself did not say this at first. Skinner did not in fact distinguish between verbal rules and regularities observed in other complex antecedents such as modeling stimuli (e.g., see Skinner, 1969, p. 163). In a previous paper (Zettle & Hayes, 1982), we defined rule-governed behavior as behavior controlled by a verbal antecedent. Recently, Skinner took the same line when he suggested that rule-governed behavior might also be called *verbal stimulus controlled behavior* (Skinner, unpublished manuscipt). This solves one problem, but it presents another. What is a verbal stimulus?

In nontechnical terms, a verbal stimulus in the form of a rule is something that tells us what to do, when to do it, and what will happen when we do it. Doing what a verbal rule tells us to do is following the rule. And both of these together make up what is meant by rule governance. In technical terms, the concept of rule-governance, as traditionally articulated by behaviorists, means little more than this. Without knowing what "specifies" means in technical terms we are left with "rules tell us what to do, when to do it, and what will happen when we do it." And although we say things like rule-following is observed when "behavior comes under the control of a rule," we do not say in technical terms how the behavior specified in the rule comes to take place under the circumstances specified in the rule, so we are left with rule-following is "doing what a rule tells us to do." The purpose of the present chapter is to make some progress on these issues.

4. WHAT IS A VERBAL STIMULUS?

This question poses severe difficulties for a Skinnerian perspective on language. If the action of a listener is not itself verbal in any important sense, then the "verbal-ness" of a stimulus cannot be found in the actions of organisms making contact with it. Such an analysis allows no room for a functional concept of "verbal stimuli."

4.1. Verbal Stimuli as Products of Verbal Behavior

One superficially congenial solution is to suppose that a verbal stimulus is the stimulus product of verbal behavior (e.g., see Skinner, 1957, p. 34). This analysis confuses stimulus objects with stimulus functions. In behavior-analytic accounts, categories of stimuli are usually drawn on the grounds of the functional relations they sustain with behaviors, not on the nature of their sources. A light might be a discriminative stimulus for a bird, for example, but it is so based on the bird's behavior coordinated with it, not on how the light as an object was produced by others. As a psychological matter, it would be silly to call the light an "Edison stimulus" for the bird or claim that the bird was engaging in "Edison-produced behavior." The means by which a stimulus object was produced is beside the point—it is the nature of its psychological function that is at issue.

Viewing stimuli as verbal by virtue of their source leads to a variety of absurd conclusions. Suppose a dog responds appropriately to its master's request, "go get my slippers." Now imagine the same dog getting the slippers in response to the sound of its master's car in the driveway. It would be bizarre to call the former "rule-governed behavior" and the latter "contingency-shaped behavior" based on the means by which the stimulus objects occasioning the action were produced. Similarly, suppose a person hears her name being called and goes to the door. In one case, she finds a friend there calling her name. In another case, she finds that it was the murmur of the wind she heard. It would be absurd to argue that because the wind is not a product of verbal behavior, it operated in a fundamentally different manner than the friend's voice. It obviously did not.

The concept of a "verbal stimulus" (or, indeed, any kind of *stimulus* as a psychologist uses the term) only makes sense if we are talking about a particular kind of stimulus *function*. Thus the concept of a verbal stimulus only makes sense if there are verbal stimulus functions and the listener qua listener is therefore behaving verbally. But again, what is a verbal stimulus?

Nonbehavioral therorists have grappled with this issue, emphasizing the symbolic nature of verbal stimuli. As constituted, these analyses are not of much direct help in achieving behavior-analytic goals of prediction and control. They typically assume too much and consequently fail to specify, in naturalistic terms, the process that leads to the observed outcome. For example, we may be told that humans "manipulate symbols" (Clark & Clark, 1978) or "map words onto internal concepts" (Nelson, 1974). We all have a general familiarity with the kinds of behaviors being described, but more basic questions remain. How do humans come to manipulate symbols? What is a human doing when words are "mapped onto" concepts? How did the person learn to do these things? How did symbols come to function as symbols? And precisely what *is* a symbol anyway? It is of no use (when evaluated against behavior-analytic goals for science: prediction and control) to explain verbal stimuli on the basis of complex human actions (e.g., mapping words onto concepts) without then explaining those actions in terms of potentially manipulable events (see Hayes & Brownstein, 1986, for a detailed defense of this point). The need for naturalistic, environmentally based explanations arises when control is one of the goals of science. Symbols must not be explained just on the basis of complex human acts because situated actions, by definition, are not *directly* manipulable but are manipulable only through the manipulation of context.

Behavioral perspectives should be well positioned philosophically to address the nature of verbal stimulation in a naturalistic manner, but a Skinnerian perspective has limited the nature and scope of its investigation. Skinner views the functions of verbal events with respect to listeners as synonymous with normal processes of stimulus control, particularly discriminative control. This position is based on an attempt to derive explanations for complex human action from principles developed with infrahumans; not on a consideration of the complex behavior of listeners *per se*. It makes sense behaviorally to restrict definitions of stimuli to particular kinds of stimulus control, but there are good reasons to think that verbal stimuli are not just discriminative stimuli in the usual sense.

4.2. Verbal Stimulus Functions

Our strategy in considering the nature of verbal stimuli will be as follows. We will start with what seems obvious; with a commonsense understanding of language. The qualities we find there we will take as a starting point. We will deliberately suspend belief or disbelief in the commonsense understanding and "act as if" these obvious qualities *may* be important. We will then attempt to apply known behavioral principles to an understanding of the identified qualities. If the attempt is successful, we will consider whether these principles facilitate progress toward a scientific understanding of verbal behavior, as measured against the usefulness of the resulting account.

Verbal behavior is conventional in form. It is only by agreement that a given word refers to a given thing, there being no relation betwen word and referent based on similarity of form or other natural property.

Verbal behavior is ineffectual. It does not operate on the world directly.

The relation between a word and a referent is bidirectional. A word "stands for" the referent only if the referent "is called" the word.

Of these qualities, we will start with the issue of bidirectionality and see where this issue takes us. Most psychological processes are unidirectional. A conditioned stimulus (CS) reliably proceeds an unconditioned stimulus (UCS), and the CS comes to have some of the functions of the UCS. This does not mean that the UCS comes thereby to have some of the functions of the CS. The relation is unidirectional. Similarly, in the presence of a conditional Stimulus A, Stimulus B has a discriminative function. This does not mean that in the presence of conditional Stimulus B, Stimulus A has a discriminative function. The relation between conditional and discriminative stimuli is unidirectional.

There is one behavioral process, stimulus equivalence, that appears to resemble the kind of bidirectionality observed of word-referent relations (Sidman & Tailby, 1982). Our strategy will be to take this process as a starting point for an analysis of verbal stimulation. That is, we will start from the possibility that verbal stimulus functions, operating in word-referent relations, represent a different psychological process; and that although perhaps not synonymous with it, stimulus equivalence is part of this process.

When humans are taught a series of related conditional discriminations, the stimuli involved in these discriminations may become connected to each other in ways not explicitly taught. The phenomena involved are typically investigated in a matching to sample format. For example, suppose a person is taught, given the presence of a particular unfamiliar visual form (the sample), to choose another particular unfamiliar visual form from an array of three or four such forms (the comparisons). We could say that the person learns "given A1, pick B1" where "A1" and "B1" represent different visual forms. The person is then taught to select another unfamiliar visual form from another array of forms, given the same sample, or "given A1, pick C1." To control for a history of reinforcement for selecting particular stimuli, the incorrect comparison forms will be correct in the presence of other samples. With this kind of training, it is likely that, given the opportunity, the person will, without additional training, select A1 from an array of comparisons, given B1 or given C1 as samples. The person is also likely to select B1 given C1 as a sample and C1 given B1 as a sample (e.g., Sidman, 1971; Sidman, Cresson, & Willson-Morris, 1974). This set of phenomena is called *stimulus equivalence*.

An equivalence class is said to exist if the stimuli in the class show the three defining relations of reflexivity, symmetry, and transitivity (Sidman & Tailby, 1982). This definition has some notable difficulties, but we will adopt it as a point of departure. In matching-to-sample procedures, reflexivity is identity matching. For example, given A1, the person picks A1 from an array. Symmetry refers to the functional reversibility of the conditional discrimination: The trained discrimination "given A1, pick B1" leads to the derived discrimination "given B1, pick A1." This reversibility must be demonstrated in the absence of direct reinforcement to be considered symmetry (Sidman, Rauzin, Lazar, Cunningham, Tailby, & Carrigan, 1982). To demonstrate transitivity, at least three stimuli are required. If, after the discriminations "given A1, pick B1" and "given B1, pick C1" have been taught, "given A1, pick C1" emerges without additional training, transitivity has been demonstrated.

One reason stimulus equivalence has captured the imagination of behavioral researchers is the apparent similarity between the stimulus equivalence phenomenon and language phenomena. If a child of sufficient verbal abilities is taught to point to a particular object given a particular written word, the child may point to a word given the object without specific training to do so. In naming tasks, symmetry and transitivity between written words, spoken words, pictures, and objects is commonplace. Several studies on stimulus equivalence have used naminglike preparations involving auditory and visual stimuli (e.g., Dixon & Spradlin, 1976; Sidman, 1971; Sidman & Tailby, 1982; Sidman, Kirk, & Willson-Morris, 1985; Spradlin & Dixon, 1976). Behaviorists are excited at the possiblity that the equivalence phenomenon may provide a new avenue for the empirical investigation of language.

If stimulus equivalence is a preliminary model of verbal stimulation, one would expect to see it emerge readily in humans but not so readily or perhaps not at all in nonhumans. This expectation assumes only that humans have a relative facility with language and thus, if equivalence is in some way a model of verbal stimulation, humans should also have a facility with equivalence. This turns out to be the case. Stimulus equivalence has been shown with a wide variety of human subjects using a wide variety of stimulus materials (Dixon, 1976; Dixon & Spradlin, 1976; Gast, VanBiervlet, & Spradlin, 1979; Hayes, Tilley, & Hayes, 1988; Mackay & Sidman, 1984; Sidman, 1971; Sidman *et al.*, 1974; Sidman & Tailby, 1982; Spradlin, Cotter, & Baxley, 1973; Spradlin & Dixon, 1976; VanBiervlet, 1977; Wulfert & Hayes, 1988). Even children as young as 2 years old will display such performances without explicit experimental training (Devany, Hayes, & Nelson, 1986).

The interchangability of functiions characteristic of stimulus equivalence has not been shown with nonhuman organisms, however. Although conditional relationships have been demonstrated in a large variety of animals, including dolphins (e.g., Herman & Thompson, 1982), rats (e.g., Lashley, 1938), and monkeys (e.g., Nissen, 1951), these do not result in stimulus equivalence. To date, not a single unequivocal demonstration of stimulus equivalence in nonhumans has been shown (D'Amato, Salmon, Loukas, & Tomie, 1985; Kendall, 1983; Lipkens, Kop, & Matthijs, 1988; Sidman *et al.*, 1982. As for McIntire, Cleary, & Thompson, 1987, and Vaughan, 1988, see Hayes, S. C., in press b). Furthermore, children without spontaneous productive use of signs or speech also do not show equivalence (Devany *et al.*, 1986).

Can stimulus equivalence provide an adequate model of verbal stimulation? An answer depends on ones view of stimulus equivalence itself.

4.3. Explanations for Stimulus Equivalence

What is interesting about these findings—and what accounts for much of the excitement about equivalence phenomena in the behavioral field at present—is the fact that the findings are not fully nor readily explained by appeal to the history constructed solely in the experimental situation.

4.3.1. Operant Conditioning

Stimulus equivalence is not readily predicted from a three-term contingency formulation, at least not in any direct and obvious way. If an organism learns to pick B1, given A1, we can think of this as a conditional discrimination. The probability of reinforcement for selecting B1 is greater in the presence of A1 than in the presence of, say, A2. We would say that A1 is functioning as a conditional discriminative stimulus in the presence of which B1 is functioning as a discriminative stimulus for a selection response.

This does not mean, however, that the probability of reinforcement for selecting A1 is greater in the presence of B1 than in its absence. Consider a natural example. A primate may learn to hide in a thicket given the presence of a lion. We could think of this as a conditional discrimination: Given lion, select a thicket over open savanna. The lion is a conditional discriminative stimulus, in the presence of which the thicket is a discriminative stimulus for selection. Such a contingency arrangement provides no grounds to suppose that reversing the functions of the stimuli involved will be reinforced. The value of selecting a thicket given a lion does not imply the value of selecting a lion given a thicket. "Given thicket select lion" makes little sense.

A variety of examples could be generated. A frog may see flies, given a pool of water, but not water, given flies. A hyena may look for a carcass, given circling vultures, but not vultures, given a carcass. A monkey may look for and find a snake, given a rustling sound, but not listen for a rustling sound, given a snake.

We are not arguing that symmetrical contingencies do not exist in the natural environment, nor even that animals cannot show some degree of backward association. Our point is that in the natural environment, the functions of a conditional stimulus and discriminative stimulus, established in a given context, cannot be assumed to reverse. Most commonly, if the functions *were* reversed, the consequences would be neutral. Often they would be punishing. Only rarely would they be reinforcing. Thus derived bidirectional relations among events, such as that seen in stimulus equivalence, must be under conditional control and brought into the situation by something other than the relatae themselves.

4.3.2. Respondent Conditioning

Bidirectional relations among stimuli may be learned by respondent conditioning in the natural environment. In such cases, members of one class of stimuli sometimes precede and sometimes follow those of another class of stimuli, whereby members of each stimulus class may be expected to acquire some of the functions of the other class. For example, if sometimes a cat hears a bird before it sees a bird and sometimes the other way around—we may assume that by simple processes of respondent conditioning, the cat may be able to see the bird upon hearing it and hear the bird upon seeing it. In other words, the transfer of stimulus functions may be completed in both directions in a large number of natural circumstances.

There are problems in conceptualizing stimulus equivalence in terms of this process, however. First, we might suppose that stimulus equivalence emerges when subjects repeatedly pair samples and comparisons unidirectionally. Subjects may look first at the sample and then at the comparison and vice versa—producing two unidirectionally trained stimulus–stimulus relations (sample-comparison; comparison-sample). But equivalence emerges even in delayed matching-to-sample procedures in which the sample disappears before the comparisons are presented. In these cases, comparison-sample relations (as opposed to sample-comparison relations) must be indirectly acquired.

Second, even in the natural environment, the extent to which bidirectionality among stimulus events could occur is exhausted in the direct experiences giving rise to such occurrences for a given animal. In other words, all "bidirectional" relations must be unidirectionally trained. This does not seem to be what happens in human linguistic situations. For example, a child who sees an object and then hears the name for that object may orient toward that object upon hearing the name without prior explicit exposure to a reversal in the order of their presentation. The bidirectionality observed between words and objects appears to occur without explicit training—the bidirectionality seems to emerge for new sets of stimuli without explicit training on those sets.

Third, although it is conceivable that relations of symmetry could occur as a product of the immediate experimental history, this would not explain transitivity. Let us assume that A is the sample, B is the correct comparison, and the training procedure is such that the sample always precedes the comparison. By virtue of this training we may assume that A acquires stimulus functions of B but not vice versa. In the testing situation, B becomes the sample, A the correct comparison. If A has previously acquired stimulus functions of B such that some of the responses previously occurring with respect to B may now occur with respect to A, selecting A during the test may amount to a type of identity matching based on indirect stimulus functions.

The transitive relations are not possible to explain by this process, however. In these cases, the comaparisons B and C must be assumed to have acquired functions of the A sample in order to account for the correct selection of B given C or C given B. This result assumes that stimulus function transfer occurs *automatically* in both directions however.

Fourth, upon further consideration of equivalence findings, the plausibility of a respondent conditioning explanation, even for the finding of symmetry, cannot be sustained. Specifically, humans show both transitivity and symmetry, whereas animals show neither. If it is reasonable to interpret symmetry as indirect reflexivity, as attempted before, then there is no reason to suppose that animals would not show these same results. Animals show stimulus function transfers by way of respondent conditioning processes in the natural environment, and they have been observed to show reflexivity in the laboratory. Consequently, the failure to observe symmetry in animal performance under these circumstances suggests that equivalence findings are due to processes other than stimulus function transfer by way of respondent conditioning.

There are any number of possible explanations for the differences observed between animal and human findings in equivalence situations, but the most obvious is a difference in their learning histories. Elsewhere we have attempted to account for equivalence as a special kind of relational response (Hayes, S. C., in press a). In the present chapter we will extend that analysis to the issue of rule governance. First, we will summarize the argument.

4.4. A Relational Account of Verbal Stimulation

Both humans and infrahumans can repond to relations between stimuli. This was considered to be a crucial finding in the middle part of this century, in part because traditional S–R learning theory seemed to have a difficult time explaining these findings. Responding in terms of relations is clearly shown, for example, in the transposition literature (Reese, 1968). Although the methods involved differ in detail, a typical transposition problem is as follows: Subjects are given a history of selecting among stimuli that differ along some physical dimension (e.g., a long and short line, a large and small square, a light and a dark chamber, etc.). After a history of this sort, subjects are presented with a choice between a stimulus that had previously been correct. (e.g., a long line) and a new stimulus that is now correct (e.g., an even longer line) from the standpoint of responding in terms of the historical relation. In a wide variety of organisms, including humans (e.g., Reese, 1961), birds (e.g., Towe, 1954), nonhuman mammals (e.g., Hebb, 1937), and fish (e.g., Perkins, 1931), subjects will choose the stimulus that is correct in terms of the trained relation (e.g., the even longer line) over specific stimuli that have a history of reinforcement for their selection.

This finding shows that organisms can learn to respond to relations between events, such as "darker," "longer," and so on. In short, a relation between specific stimuli can function as a stimulus in and of itself. Note, however, that relations of this type are based on formal characteristics of the stimuli involved. That is, the relations are nonarbitrary. A darker chamber, for example, is actually a darker chamber (discounting the special case of sensory illusions). Thus it is fair to say that a wide variety of organisms can learn to respond to relations among stimuli based on nonarbitrary properties.

The human's history includes training of a sort that might permit other types of relational responding to emerge. Take the case of a young child learning the name of an object. A learning experience of this sort usually includes such elements as the following. The child is oriented toward the object and asked, "What's that?" Correct responses are rewarded, and incorrect responses result in additonal prompting of the name in the presence of the object. If the child shows any sign of acknowledgment (e.g., a smile when the name is given), the child is fussed over. The child is also asked, "Where is (name)" and moved so that a variety of objects are in view. Orientation toward the named object is rewarded with tickles, play, or verbal consequences ("That's right! That's the [name]"). Even before the child can speak, parents can to some degree assess whether actions with respect to objects are available upon contact with their names and vice versa by observing the orientation of the child as the names of objects in the presence of those objects are mentioned. The child, in other words, is taught to respond differentially to certain sounds (and later to produce them) in the presence of specific objects and vice versa.

We can think of the training history this way:

Trained in Context Z

Object A→Name A; Name A→Object A
Object B→Name B; Name B→Object B
Object C→Name C; Name C→Object C
Object D→Name D; Name D→Object D

. . . .

. . . .

. . . .

Derived in Context Z (derived results emboldened)

Object X→Name X; *Name X→Object X*

Training in this kind of symmetrical responding occurs only in certain contexts (''Z''). The example here is the context of naming. There are a variety of cues to indicate that this is a naming context, including the use of phrases such as *what's that?''* and the juxtaposition of objects and words. In short, with enough instances of directly trained symmetrical responding, symmetrical responding may emerge with respect to novel stimuli in that context. That is, the extensive training history may be brought to bear by a given context and provide a basis for generalized symmetrical responding.

Responding of this kind is relational, but the relation is not defined by the formal properties of the relatae. There is nothing about the form of a word that requires that it stand in relation to a particular referent. On the contrary, the stimuli placed in relation as well as the nature of that relation are determined by the social community without regard for the formal properties of the stimuli involved. The relation, in other words, is an *arbitrary* one, and as such, may be applied to any stimuli encountered in a naming context. Arbitrarily applicable relational responding of this sort must have three characteristics (Hayes, S. C., in press a):

4.4.1. Mutual Entailment

In the abstract, a relation between two events involves responding to the one event in terms of the other and vice versa. If A is related to B, then B is related to A. The specific relations need not be literally identical. If A is better than B, then B is worse than A. The second relation is entailed by the first—it is not possible to have a relation of better without one of worse. This quality is a defining characteristic of an arbitrarily applicable relation.

In arbitrarily applicable relational responding, a relational response must, by definition, be brought to bear on the situation by stimuli other than the relatae themselves. Thus, it must be contextually controlled. We may term this quality of relation *mutual entailment* and represent it this way:

$$C_{\text{rel}}\,\{A\ r_x\ B\ |||\ B\ r_y\ A\}$$

where C_{rel} symbolizes a context in which a history of a particular kind of relational responding is brought to bear in the current situation, r stands for a relation brought to bear, the subscripts x and y stand for the specific types of relations involved, A and B stand for the events in the relation, and $|||$ is a symbol for entailment.

Mutual entailment means that if a person is responding relationally to A and B in a given context, then the person is also responding relationally to B and A. If a response to one stimulus is an aspect of such relational responding, a response to the other stimulus must be another aspect. In terms of the diagram here, if a response to B is part of an r_x response, then a response to A must be available as part of a r_y response.

For example, a person is told that "this is a computer" in the presence of a computer. A relation is specified between the computer and the word *computer*. The form of the sentence, tone of voice, the words involved (e.g., "is"), the specification of a particular object, and so on, are a context (C_{rel}) in which a history of a particular type of relational responding is brought to bear. In this case the specific relation (r_x) is a synonymic relation (what we will later call a "frame of coordination"). Given that relation, if a computer is "a computer," then "a computer" is a computer.

4.4.2. Combinatorial Mutual Entailment

Relational responding is sensitive not only to a single instanciation but to combinations of relations. If A is related in a particular way to B and B is also related to C, then some kind of relation must be entailed betwen A and C. We will term this property "combinatorial mutual entailment" (or simply "combinatorial entailment") and will represent it in this manner:

$$C_{\mathrm{rel}}\ \{A\ r_x\ B \text{ and } B\ r_x\ C\ |||\ A\ r_p\ C \text{ and } C\ r_q\ A\}$$

This type of entailment is mutual. In the stimulus equivalence area, conceptual difficulties have been caused by viewing transitivity in a linear fashion (A-B, B-C leads to A-C) rather than emphasizing the mutuality emphasized here. In addition, the principle is not limited to any particular combination of relations. The nature of the relational network is irrelevant to the principle. Thus, for example, $A\ r_x\ B$ and $A\ r_x\ C$ entails relations between B and C.

Combinatorial entailment differs from simple mutual entailment in more than mere complexity. In mutual entailment, the specified relation A and B entails a relation between B and A at the same level of precision. That is, however precise the defined relation between A and B is known to be, the derived relation between B and A must be equally precise. In the formula given before, however, the A-C and C-A relations (r_p and r_q) may not be specified, or not to the same degree, as that between A and B, and B and C (r_x). For example, if A is different than B and B is different than C, we cannot say what the relation is between A and C and between C and A. This lack of precision, however, is *specified* by the nature of the relation of "difference" that applies to A and B and to B and C.

The most common form of specified imprecision of relation occurs when the two or more relations involved exist along different dimensions. In that case, no relation is derivable. This does not seem to be the usual case in natural language, as can perhaps be seen in the following. As a joke we ask a child, "If Ralph is older than Joe, and Joe is bigger than Steve, who is more handsome, Ralph or Steve?" The humor in this statement derives from the tension between the child's training in combinatorial entailment and the specified absence of relation in this particular instance. If combinatorial entailment did not usually lead to a specific derived relation, there would be no humor in the question.

4.4.3. Transfer of Functions

Relations among stimulus events would be of little importance to psychologists if the other functions (i.e., nonrelational functions) of these events could not themselves be actualized or moderated by these relations. As a psychological matter, we are interested in stimuli not as objects but as events that have psychological functions. Furthermore, the relational functions involved in mutual and combinatorial entailment, when considered on their own terms, are of more direct interest to logicians than to most psychologists. For the concept of relational responding to be relevant to many of the traditional issues in psychology, it must be shown that such responding is relevant to the modification of various nonrelational stimulus functions.

If an event "A" has a psychological function and that event is placed into relation with another event "B," under certain conditions B may acquire a new psychological function. The nature of B's function will depend on its relation to A (i.e., sameness, difference). We will term this acquisition of function of B a *transfer of functions* (although realizing that in many instances the transferred function may not be the *same* function as the function of A). The same is true for event A, as is implied by the concept of mutual entailment.

A given stimulus always has many functions. If *all* functions of one stimulus transferred to another and vice versa, there would no longer be two separate psychological stimuli, by definition. Thus, which functions transfer must be under contextual control. We can represent the transfer of functions this way:

$$C_{\text{func}} \{ C_{\text{rel}} (Af_1 \;|||\; Bf_2r \text{ and } Cf_3r) \}$$

where C_{func} symbolizes the contextual stimuli that select particular psychologically relevant, nonrelational stimulus functions that transfer in a given situation, f refers to stimulus function, the numerical subscripts refer to the specific functions involved, and r refers to the type of relational responding occurring. We can say it this way: Given mutual entailment and combinatorial mutual entailment between A, B, and C, a given function of A entails functions of B and C in terms of the underlying relations. For example, suppose A is specified as smaller than B and B is smaller than C. Suppose that A is given a value function and that this function is relevant to the relation of size between A, B, and C. We might expect that B and C will have ordinally more value than A, to the degree that a response to B or C is an aspect of a relational response to A, B, and C.

As a practical example, consider a child who has learned the value of pennies as measured in how much candy they will buy. Before a child learns the arbitrary relation between pennies and other coins, she or he will prefer a penny over the smaller dime. As the child learns to relate events in terms of the abstract relation of amount, the child will prefer a nickel or a dime over a penny without necessarily having direct experience of the value of nickels or dimes.

The transfer of nonrelational functions observed is always in terms of the underlying relation. Thus, if A and B are opposites and A has positive attributes, B may now have negative attributes. If A and B are in an equivalence class, B may now function in the same way as A.

The kinds of functions that could be involved in the transfer of functions through relational classes are unlimited. Any available function could be involved, as brought to bear by contextual cues. Consider, for example, the perceptual functions of taste, texture, or sight. A person says "picture a lemon." For a verbally able person, the lemon may now be "seen" in the absence of actual lemons. We would interpret this phenomenon as follows: Actual lemons have visual perceptual functions. The word *lemon* and lemons are in a relational class (in this case, an equivalence class). The words *picture a* are a context (C_{func}) in which visual functions are actualized in terms of the underlying relation. In another context (e.g., "imagine tasting a . . ."), other functions (e.g., taste) would be actualized. Transfer of functions, then, refers to the contextual control of all kinds of nonrelational functions in terms of arbitrarily applicable relations.

4.4.4. Relational Frames

We will use the term *relational frame* to designate particular kinds of arbitrarily applicable relational responding. A relational frame is a type of responding that shows the contextually controlled qualities of mutual entailment, combinatorial mutual entailment, and transfer of functions; is due to a history of relational responding relevant to the contextual cues involved; and is not based on direct nonrelational training with regard to the particular stimuli of interest nor to nonarbitrary characteristics of either the stimuli or the relation between them. Given $A\ r_x\ B$, the specific type of relational frame is specified by the nature of r.

An arbitrarily applicable relation can be brought to bear only by virtue of other factors participating in such situations—what was termed C_{rel} before. Some of the contexts may be fairly global and not otherwise linguistic. For example, a teacher may say the name of a novel object using a tone of voice that makes it clear that it is a name that is being said. The tone of voice may function as C_{rel} in this case. The most usual contextual factors, however, are linguistic symbols representing abstracted relations, though more global contexts are also often relevant. These contextual factors actualize relational responding of a certain type: For example, relations of sameness may be readily brought to bear by the symbol *is;* relations of difference by the symbol *is not.*

The types of relational frames must each be under distinctive kinds of stimulus control. There are a number of specific kinds, arranged into several categories (Hayes, S. C., in press a). A few will be mentioned here.

4.4.4a. Coordination. Undoubtedly the most fundamental type of relational responding is that encompassed by the frame we will call *coordination.* The relation is one of identity, sameness, or similarity: This is (or is similar to) that. Much of the earliest language training received by children seems to be of this kind, and thus a relational frame of coordination is probably the first to be abstracted sufficiently that its application becomes arbitrary. It is difficult to imagine a history in a normal language community that would give rise to other kinds of relational frames before that of coordination, although it may be theoretically possible.

The frame of coordination may be thought of as on a continuum from that of identity to that of similarity. In an arbitrarily applicable sense (when the nature of the relation is in no way dependent upon physical properties of the relatae), the distinction between points along this continuum has to do with the nature of the relation and the range of stimulus functions relevant to it. The more *sameness* between two stimuli (in an arbitrary sense), the greater the range of functions that can be derived between participants in this relation. For example, if A is "virtually identical to" B, a wide range of functions of A can be assumed to be actualized for B. If A is "somewhat similar to" B, fewer functions are likely to be actualized.

4.4.4b. Opposition. Another kind of relational frame is that of opposition. In most practical instances, this kind of relational responding is organized around some dimension along which events can be ordered. With regard to some point of reference and an event that differs from that point in one direction along the continuum involved, an opposite differs in the other direction and to about the same degree. The relational frame of opposition typically specifies the dimension of relevance (e.g., "pretty is the opposite of ugly" is relevant only to appearance not to, say, speed), but as an arbitrarily applicable frame, it can be applied even when no physical dimension of relevance has been specified. For example, symbolic logic can specify that A is the opposite of B, without saying which dimension is involved.

4.4.4c. Distinction. Another relational frame is that of distinction. It involves responding to one event in terms of its difference from another, typically also along some specified dimension. Like a frame of opposition, this implies that responses to one event are unlikely to be appropriate in the case of the other, but unlike opposition, the nature of an appropriate response is typically not specified. If I am told only that "this is not warm water," I do not know if the water is ice cold or boiling.

4.4.4d. Comparison. The frame of comparison is involved whenever one event is responded to in terms of a known nonequal and nonopposite quantitative or qualitative relation along a specified dimension with another event. Many specific subtypes of comparison exist (e.g., bigger, faster, better). Some are not obviously an instance of this frame but have the same relational structure (e.g., hierarchical class membership). Although each may require its own history, the family resemblance may allow the more rapid learning of successive members.

4.4.4e. Verbal Control of Frames and Functions. C_{rel} and C_{func} may themselves be verbal events. For example, suppose the word *is* brings to bear a frame of coordination. It could do this directly (i.e., solely through direct experience), but it is more likely that part of the effect is because the word is in a frame of coordination with that frame itself. The capacity of that word to function as C_{rel} may itself then be due to a transfer of functions to the word through an arbitrarily applicable relation. For example, a person may be told that *zook* means *is*. If that person is then told that "this zook a cat," the object and "cat" may enter into a frame of coordination, by virtue of a transfer of contextual control over frames of coordination to "zook" by virtue of yet another frame of coordination (between "zook" and "is").

The same holds true for C_{func}. Often C_{func} is not itself verbal. For example, I may have smelled orange blossoms only once. The wind was blowing at the time. Now I am standing in a windy field and see a sign with the word *orange* on it. It is possible that I might smell orange blossoms (i.e., I "was reminded of the smell"). In this case, the wind may have *selected* among the previously acquired functions of oranges (and thus the word *orange*), by virtue of the previous direct experience. C_{func} can also be a verbal event. Because, in this case, its function may now be entirely indirect, it can be used to *establish* particular functions with regard to particular words. Suppose a person is told "look at Joe." *Look at* is in a frame of coordination with acts of looking. A person could, for example, watch others and say when they are "looking at" each other; "look at" and instances of looking at could be matched readily. The actual function of "look at" in the sentence "look at Joe" is to establish a function with regard to Joe. That is, "look at" is a C_{func} in the presence of which Joe acquires the function of activating looking.

4.4.5. Stimulus Equivalence as a Special Case

In the present analysis, stimulus equivalence is a specific type of relational class built upon a special instance of the frame of coordination. Not all classes built upon a frame of coordination will be equivalence classes. Equivalence is closer to "same" than to "similar." Evidence for this is found in the reflexivity typically seen in equivalence classes.

A stimulus is the same as itself, when it is form that defines the nonarbitrary relation of sameness. All stimuli can show reflexivity in this sense. Such reflexivity is presumably a precondition of arbitrarily applicable relations because mutual and combinatorial entailment require that the same stimulus be seen as the same, regardless of its position or the time of its introduction. For example, if A is defined as the opposite of B, then B is the opposite of A by mutual entailment. The second "A"' must be seen to be the same as the first "A" or no derived relation is possible.

Reflexivity, however, can also be a characteristic of an *arbitrary* relation. If it is specified that $A\ r_x\ B$, we may ask if this entails not just $B\ r_y\ A$ but also $A\ r_x\ A$. A may be the same as A in this *arbitrary* sense. Not all frames of coordination are reflexive, however. If the arbitrary relation by which A and B are coordinated is one of similarity as opposed to identity, $A\ rx\ A$ would mean that A is merely similar to and not the same as A. When a frame of coordination is applied to three or more stimuli and the *arbitrary relation* involves reflexivity as well as mutual entailment and combinatorial entailment, then an equivalence class exists. The problem, however, is that reflexivity as it is measured in matching-to-sample experiments does not distinguish reflexivity based on the nonarbitrary properties of the stimuli in relation and that based on the arbitrary application of relational responding. It is possible to find symmetry and transitivity without reflexivity (e.g., Steele, Hayes, & Lawrence, 1988). This may occur when a frame of coordination changes from one of identity to one of similarity.

4.4.6. How Arbitrary Is Arbitrary?

We have argued that arbitrarily applicable relational responding is probably based on a history of nonarbitrary relational responding. For example, coming into contact with the different physical properties of *hot* and *cold,* fast and "slow," and the like is surely a usual (if not necessary) precondition for deriving the arbitrarily applicable relation of oppositeness. It is an open question whether relational frames can be acquired without such a history. For example, it is possible that a child given only a history of arbitrary matching-to-sample that reinforced symmetry, reflexivity, and transitivity, could derive the frame of coordination and show equivalence classes. In such a case, the child would have had no history of the nonarbitrary relations of sameness based on identical physical forms. Other arbitrary relations might also be trainable in such a manner.

In fact, however, it is very rare that relational frames are *completely* arbitrary. In natural language, words often participate in equivalence classes with events of known physical properties. These properties themselves often define the dimensions of relevance to arbitrary relations. For example, if a person is told that "*xyz* is similar to a hot flame" and "*pqr* is the opposite of *xyz*" then *pqr* is likely to be responded to in terms of the dimension of temperature. The dimension is not completely arbitrary because it is based on the formal characteristics of "hot flames." This nonarbitrary aspect of the relation between *pqr* and *xyz* does not, however, fundamentally alter its arbitrary quality. A person maybe be told that "*pqr* is the opposite of *xyz* on Dimension *x*." Dimension *x* need not be defined for the person to derive relations based on such a statement. Thus we can show completely arbitrary relational responding under some conditions (e.g., abstract mathematics), while acknowledging that such responding usually also involves control by nonarbitrary characteristics of stimuli.

4.4.7. Verbal Stimulation Defined

We are now ready to deal with the issue of verbal stimulation. Recall that our strategy has been to begin with common sense, examine behavioral principles relevant to a commonsense understanding, and then to evaluate the adequacy of the resulting account. The analysis developed so far suggests that there exists a fundamentally different kind of stimulus class based on arbitrarily applicable relational responding. If there is this additional kind of stimulation, it would surely have a profound impact on the organisms sensitive to it (a point to which we will return later). Thus if this kind of stimulation exists, it requires an analysis, whether or not it is termed *verbal.*

The justification for defining verbal stimulation in these terms is (1) only verbal organisms (in a commonsense understanding of that term) show these kinds of relational classes; (2) the processes bear similarities to linguistic situations, such as naming; and (3) the processes involved make sense of the obvious qualities of verbal events: bidirectionality, conventionality, and ineffectuality. Bidirectionality is a defining property of arbitrarily applicable relations. This arbitrariness is a type of conventionality. Ineffectuality also follows from the analysis because the stimulus functions of events in relational frames are derived functions for properly trained organisms; they are not based on the nonarbitrary characteristics of these events otherwise available to impact directly on the world.

In the rest of the chapter and in the next, we will adopt the view that to the degree that a stimulus functions as it does because of its participation in a relational frame, it is functioning verbally. A stimulus can never function only verbally. The perceptual contact one makes with a stimulus, for example, cannot depend completely on the participation of that event in an instance of arbitrarily applicable relational responding because one must contact a stimulus in order to then act relationally with regard to it.

Why distinguish between verbal and nonverbal stimulus events? Because a functional analysis demands categorical constructions on the basis of differences in function, and the difference between verbal and nonverbal stimulation satisfies this criterion. To do otherwise would be imprecise.

4.4.8. Evidence for Relational Frames

We do not have the space available to defend the concept of relational frames fully. A somewhat more detailed empirical defense can be found elsewhere (Hayes, S. C., in press a). A brief litany of the kinds of evidence available is as follows:

1. The analysis provides an explanation for the phenomenon of stimulus equivalence and makes coherent a range of findings relevant to equivalence. This includes the following:

a. *Improvement in testing*. Significant improvements occur during the testing of equivalence relations, even without feedback on performance (e.g., Devany *et al.*, 1986; Lazar, Davis-Lang, & Sanchez, 1984; Sidman *et al.*, 1985). Equivalence is, therefore, not automatic—it requires a context to develop. The relational-frame view would imply that the equivalence test is a contextual source of control over relational responding (C_{rel}).

b. *Control by previous testing*. The relational-frame view would hold that a variety of contextual cues should give rise to relational frames. This is the case. For example, previous testing will give rise to new equivalence classes in a new situation (Devany & Hayes, 1987; Kennedy & Laitinen, 1988).

c. *Conditional equivalence classes*. The development of conditional equivalence classes (e.g., Wulfert & Hayes, 1988) also provides evidence for the contextual control of equivalence.

d. *Transfer of functions*. The analysis holds that a wide variety of functions may transfer through relational classes. So far this has been examined only with equivalence classes but with clear results. Both discriminative control and reinforcement control have been shown to transfer through equivalence classes (Hayes, Devany, Kohlenberg, Brownstein & Shelby, in press; Wulfert & Hayes, 1988).

2. The analysis also applies to other kinds of relations:

a. *Exclusion*. The exclusion effect has been examined in both the behavioral and the cognitive literature (e.g., Hutchinson & McCloskey, 1988; Markman & Wachtel, 1988; McIlvane, Kledaras, Munson, King, de Rose, & Stoddard, 1987). The basic effect is this: A person presented with a novel sample and both a known and novel comparison will tend to relate the two novel stimuli. Suppose a child is shown a cup and previously unknown object (e.g., a metronome). The child knows that the cup is a *cup* but has never heard the word *metronome*. Under such conditions, if the child is asked to "pass the metronome" she will do so and will subsequently relate the object with the new word. The child learned this relation on the basis of "exclusion." In our language, we would explain the effect as follows: The cup and "cup" are in a frame of coordination. Other objects, until and unless they are included in this frame, are potentially in frames of distinction with "cup" and cup. Thus, until the child learns otherwise, the metronome and "metronome" are distinct from the cup. Such a derived relation does not occur because of logic (indeed, it is logically misleading) but because in most contexts it holds true. Thus, when the child is told "pass the metronome," the novel name and the novel object are the only objects that can be in a frame of coordination without violating the assumed frame of distinction. The present view brings together the exclusion and equivalence findings under a coordinating theory.

b. *Additional relations.* The strongest support as yet for a relational theory of stimulus equivalence is the demonstration that subjects with a proper pretraining history will respond in arbitrary matching-to-sample tasks in ways that fit perfectly with the frames of coordination, distinction, and opposition as described earlier (Steele, 1987). This supports the view that stimulus equivalence is but one of the many phenomena that can be derived based on relational frames. None of the available data seems to contradict a relational theory of verbal stimulation, and the studies conducted to test it have been consistently supportive.

5. MEANING AND RULE-GOVERNANCE

Our primary purpose in the present chapter is to apply a relational perspective to the issue of rule-governance. Behavior controlled by verbal stimuli is a different kind of behavior because it involves different psychological processes.

5.1. Speaking with Meaning

Speaking with meaning is not just the act of communicating. Bees communicate with a dance; dogs with a bark; mice with squeaks. Although these events may communicate—and may "mean" something in a nonverbal sense—they do not mean something in a verbal sense. Speaking with meaning exists to the degree that behavior is occurring because the stimulus products of the act participate in relational frames for the speaker-as-listener.

Suppose a person looks at a chair and says *chair*. The word *chair* and the actual chair may participate in a frame of coordination for that speaker (for clarity of example, assume that "chair" is in no other relational classes). To the degree that the act of saying *chair* in this instance is produced and maintained because *chair* is in a relational frame with actual chairs, then to that degree the speaker is speaking with meaning. Verbal meaning, so defined, participates along with other functions of "verbal" events.

This analysis is similar to referential analyses of meaning but not reference in a mentalistic or formalistic sense. According to the dictionary, reference means *in relation to. Relation* itself comes from the Latin word *referre,* or reference. The two are virtually synonymous. Usually, however, relations of reference are conceptualized as references to ideas. The word *chair* may refer to the idea *chair* for example. Others have supposed that "chair" is "associated" with actual chairs, which of course it may be, but this is not what gives it meaning in the linguistic sense. The concept of relational frames puts these constructions in better order. The issue is not association in general but a particular kind of association produced by bringing to bear a history of arbitrarily applicable relational responding. A class of events with particular nonarbitrary qualities (chairs as a natural concept) is in an arbitrary relation with a class of auditory events (the various ways one can say *chair*). The class of words "is associated with" the class of objects in the sense that some of the stimulus functions of each can, in certain contexts, transfer to the other in terms of the underlying relation.

We come at last to the issue of rule-governance. What is a rule, in the present analysis?

5.2. Listening with Understanding

When a person hears a word, some of the functions of that word may depend on the participation of the word in a relational frame with other events. The functions are, in our sense of the term, verbal functions. Verbal understanding is the act of a listener framing events relationally, such that they have these functions.

Understanding in this sense is not a static thing. First, it is a matter of degree. For example, I may "understand" the word *chair* in the sense that the class of words ("chair" said in various ways) participates in a relational frame with a class of actual chairs. Not all of the stimulus functions of the word *chair* in a given instance may be based on relational frames, however. To that degree, or with respect to those functions, my response to chair is not one of understanding. Second, it is multifaceted. Had I been told that chairs can break, I may "understand" the word *chair* in a different way—some of the functions of the word would now depend on the participation of the word *chair* with the word *break* in addition to the relation with actual chairs. Finally, understanding is contextually limited (a point emphasized in the term C_{rel}). As Tichener pointed out in his context theory of meaning, one's understanding of a word dimishes in the context of repeating the word (e.g., "chair") over and over again. In that context, the nonarbitrary functions of the sound of the word come to dominate over the arbitrary relation sustained between the word and actual events.

5.3. Understanding a Rule

From the standpoint of the speaker, a rule is a verbal formula. We have two issues to deal with. First, what does it mean to understand a rule? Second, how can understanding a rule participate in effective action with regard to other events.

In a simple case, understanding a rule is identical to understanding any verbal event. A person says "fire," and all run from the theater. The stimulus functions of the theater (e.g., approach toward the stairs, avoidance areas of the theater far from exits) can be analyzed in terms of the participation of the word fire with actual fires.

A more difficult instance arises when various verbal events are themselves related verbally. A person is told "when the bell rings, get the cake from the oven." Rule understanding in this case is a direct extension of the simpler case.

Let us assume that the word classes *bell, cake, get, go to,* and *oven* each participate in the equivalence classes with the event classes of sounds of bells, actual cakes, actual ovens, and the actual acts of going to things and getting things. The sentence specifies a conditional relation among these verbal classes (*When* bell *then* go to the oven *and* get cake). The words such as *when* and *then* themselves bring additional arbitrary relations to bear on the bell, cake, getting, and oven. For example, the conditional relation specified between the bell and the act of going to the oven is a temporal one—first bell, then go to oven. "Go to" and "get" are verbal C_{func} terms that establish a function for the words *oven* and *cake,* respectively.

Based on the combinatorial entailment and transfer of functions through relational classes, the temporal relation between the bell and the function of going to the oven specified in the rule transfer to the actual bell and actual oven. When the bell now rings, it is no longer the same bell. Some of the stimulus functions of the sound occur because of the participataton of the actual bell in a class with the word *bell.* Some of the stimulus functions of the word *bell* are dependent on its relation to the oven, and the same is now true for the actual bell. When the bell rings, it actualizes the *go-to* function established verbally with regard to the oven. This performance is modeled schematically in Figure 1. In the figure, *r* stands for a relation, *f* for a function.

Understanding a rule is obviously not the same as following it (Parrott, 1987b). Understanding is not, however, a mysterious or "mental" event. It is an action of organizing verbal stimuli into arbitrarily applicable relational networks so that stimulus functions transfer throughout these networks.

When we say that a speaker specifies a contingency, we are implying acts

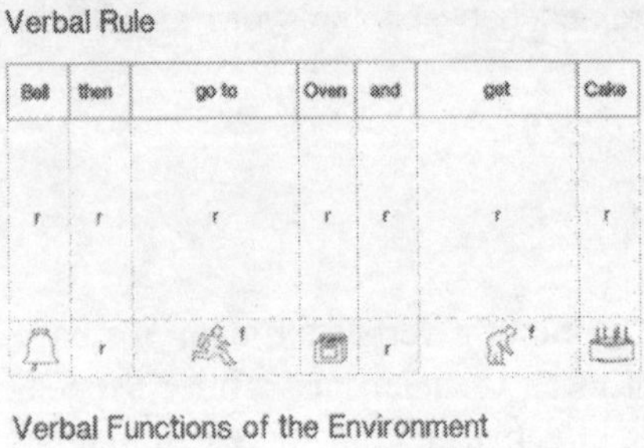

Figure 1. A diagrammatic representation of rule understanding.

on the parts of both speaker and listener—the act of specifying and the act of responding to verbal stimulation, respectively. From the speaker's perspective, the speaker speaks with meaning. Events are "specified" in the sense that events are organized into a relational network. From the listener's point of view, the listener listens with understanding. The listener also organizes events into a relational network.

The kinds of transfer of functions envisioned by this analysis have begun to be examined in the laboratory. It is known that after an equivalence class is formed, if one member becomes discriminative for a response, then other members will also become discriminative for the same response (Hayes, Devany, Kohlenberg, Brownstein, & Shelby, in press; Wulfert & Hayes, 1988). It is also known that reinforcement functions will transfer through these clases (Hayes *et al.*, 1988). Thus, it is possible that instructional control is based on relational classes such as equivalence classes.

5.4. Following a Rule

What remains to be explained is how a person given a rule at Time x comes to respond to stimuli involved in that contingency at Time y (parts of the following are from Parrott, 1987a, b). For example, assume that you are speaking to a newly arrived foreign student who has no experience with rain. At noon you tell the student: "If the sky looks dark when you're ready to leave, take this umbrella." When the student leaves several hours later, having looked outside, she takes an umbrella. At noon, we could say that the student's behavior of listening to the verbal stimulus—the rule—took place. At 6 o'clock, we could say that the student's behavior of taking an umbrella upon looking outside occurred. Yet we know that the student would have no tendency to take an umbrella were it not for exposure to the prior verbal stimulus—so we know that taking the umbrella has something to do with the prior verbal stimulus. How do we explain the fact that verbal stimuli not present in the situation at 6 o'clock are nonetheless exerting control in this situation, although not over the act of listening as they had done at noon but over the act of taking the umbrella? In other words, how do we explain rule-following?

Meaning is a bidirectional affair. Just as some of the functions of the object are present in the interaction with the word, some of the functions of the word are present in the interactions with the object (Hayes, L. J., in press). The present view leads to the conclusion that what we would normally call *nonverbal* events can function verbally, based on their participation in relational classes. This transfer of the functions of words to other events provides the basis for rule-following. Words can alter the functions of events in the world only because these events *are functioning verbally.* It is not a matter of verbal events altering the functions of truly nonverbal events. An event that functions verbally is a verbal event, regardless of its form. When "nonverbal" events have been given new functions by a stated rule, these functions are verbal functions by definition. In other words, the "nonverbal" event has become a verbal event.

Using the example of the foreign student, we may assume that the action taking place upon visual encounter with the dark sky at 6 o'clock is something more than a visual response to the darkness. The dark sky also operates to some extent as would the verbal stimulus *dark sky*. In the original act of understanding, the listener organized events into a network of relations. This organization is brought to bear on the dark sky that comes to "mean" something based on this organization. For example, "dark sky" was prevously organized into a particular relation with verbal stimuli of the forms "leave the house" and "take an umbrella." These words *dark sky* now sustain some of the functions of these other stimuli based on the specified relation. An actual dark sky also sustains some of these functions, based on its relation to "dark sky." The dark sky is functioning verbally, and it is this that enables the rule to be followed (cf. Schlinger & Blakely, 1987).

The effect is that the nonverbal events of leaving the house and taking an umbrella become organized in the same manner as the verbal events. These reponses are occurring in the absence of the stimuli with which they were originally coordinated—the speaker's remark—and instead, are occurring with respect to the specified events themselves.

Actions of this kind do not necessarily require a speaker, however. For example, a person could hear the murmur of the wind and mistakenly take it to be a request for an action of some sort. Thus, a rule from the standpoint of the listener involves the verbal functions of events—not the form of the events themselves. Whenever we speak of rule-governed behavior, therefore, we mean the word *rule* as a function for the listener. This function may or may not be coordinated with a "rule" from the standpoint of the speaker.

We have not as yet accounted for the actualization of appropriate motor functions in rule-governed behavior. We have said only that upon contact with certain events, verbal functions are operative. We will examine this problem in more detail in the next chapter. We assume, however, that the actual taking of the umbrella upon leaving the house would not occur in the absence of the actualization of the verbal functions of the specified events. If the student left the house without the umbrella, we might say that the student "forgot" the instruction (although there are other possibilities). Hence, we are assuming that the actualization of the verbal functions of the referents is necessary for the actualization of the appropriate motor functions. We might say that verbal functions of the specified events provide a context in which the motor functions *may* operate.

6. VERBAL BEHAVIOR

The present analysis suggests a definition of verbal behavior: speaking with meaning and listening with understanding. This definition may be harmonized with the traditional behavior-analytic view, at least to some extent, in the following manner.

Skinner emphasized that verbal behavior requires the mediation of others, and this mediation requires special training. We agree that social mediation is an important aspect of verbal behavior and only when that mediation is based on a particular training history. Skinner, however, did not say what kind of special training was required. As a result, his definition of verbal behavior fails to distinguish it from any learned social behavior (Parrott, 1986).

The present analysis has focused on the nature of the "special training" needed for verbal events to function as they do. In our view, both the speaker and the listener require special training, and of a similar kind. For a mature listener to mediate consequences for a speaker, he or she must respond to speech products in terms of the arbitrarily applicable relations they sustain with other events. For a mature speaker to be understood by listeners, and thus alter their behavior, she or he must learn to produce stimuli that participate in characteristic relational frames for the linguistic community. Each player is behaving verbally. Skinner rejected the notion that "certain basic linguistic processes [are] common to both speaker and listener" (Skinner, 1957, p. 33) but that is precisely the position we are lead to embrace.

The common ground between speaker and listener is not, however, ideas present in the mind; it is the arbitrarily applicable relations sustained by social convention. A verbal community is a social group in which responding to particular stimuli in terms of characteristic relational frames is trained. In France, for example, "pain" and bread are in a relational frame of coordination. In the United States, the same written stimulus is in other relational frames. This conventionality is key to the roles of both speaker and listener. Without a set of conventions shared by speakers-as-speakers and listeners-as-listeners, communication between them could be social but not verbal.

6.1. Why Would Verbal Stimulation Make a Difference?

Human societies differ from those of animals in countless ways, and presumably those differences may be traced to a variety of sources. None seems as significant, though, as the human capacity for language. The development of human language and much of human behavior appears to be interdependent. What is it about verbal behavior, as defined in the present chapter, that could make such a difference? The present analysis of verbal events suggests several reasons why verbal functions differ so profoundly from their nonverbal counterparts.

6.1.1. Indirectness of Stimulus Functions

Verbal stimuli, according to our definition, participate in a network of bidirectional relations from which are derived their many indirect functions. Unless deliberately curtailed, this network of relations, as well as the number of members involved in relational classes within it, is ever increasing. This means, essentially, that verbal stimuli acquire functions from a wide variety of events that make contact with this network of relations, and they do so in a more or less continuous manner (provided one's experience is rich enough to make contact with a wide variety of events). This circumstance accounts for some unusual effects. For example, consider the simple case of an equivalence class containing cats, pictures of cats, the spoken word *cats*, and the letters C-A-T-S. Suppose a child is scratched by a cat and comes to fear them. Now, hearing the words "lets go look at the cats," the child may run away, even though escape in the presence of the word *cats* may have never been reinforced. This kind of effect, although not readily predicted from a traditional behavioral perspective, has already been shown experimentally (Hayes *et al.*, in press).

Further, the more complex the network of relations prevailing for a given individual with respect to some specific verbal stimulus, the more likely it is that that stimulus will acquire functions of events only remotely related to it. This process may explain certain kinds of unusual behaviors frequently observed by clinicians. For example, the word *car* may be in an equivalence class with actual cars. It may also be in a hierarchical class relationship with "transportation vehicles," based on that kind of relational frame. A wide variety of other words may be in the same class, such as boats, planes, and so on. Now suppose a person sees a story about a plane accident on the TV news. The result may be a reluctance to take a long trip in a car. In this case, the network of relations established by the verbal community and operating for this individual, connected an actual plane with an actual car. This analysis does not require "mediation" of events by talking, which is to say, the person may be wholly unaware of the source of the reluctance to travel by car. Such mediation, when it exists and to the extent that it does, is more reflective of the effective process than necessary to it. Relational frames may connect stimuli without mediating responses, although attempting to establish mediating responses may establish relevant relational frames.

6.1.2. Specificity of Functions

Verbal stimulation differs from nonverbal stimulation in another important way: It may be orders of magnitude more specific than nonverbal stimulation, the implication being that the behavior coordinated with it is likewise specific.

A nonverbal stimulus with discriminative function, for example, cannot come to "mean" a specific thing (i.e., control a specific response and only that response) very easily for two reasons. First, all stimuli functioning nonarbitrarily necessarily influence a wide variety of responses. A key light, for example, is not only a stimulus in the presence of which pecking is reinforced, it is also a stimulus that alllows the bird to look at things in an otherwise darkened chamber; it may also elicit an orienting response; it may provide sensory stimulation for glances in its direction; it may make eye movements more likely, and so on. It cannot "mean" just one specific thing. Second, all co-present or proximal events are potentially relevant to stimuli functioning nonarbitrarily, barring phylogenetic restriction. That is, stimulus control over behavior depends on the organism's contact with contingencies, and should those contingencies be probabilistic or involve significant delays, random events may supersede contact with them (Hayes & Myerson, 1986).

Verbal stimuli, from the standpoint of the present analysis, do not have these qualities. Because the formal characteristics of such stimuli are irrelevant to their function, behaviors coordinated with their formal characteristics tend to be extremely weak. As such, verbal stimuli do not "mean" or control the same variety of behaviors as exemplified for nonverbal behaviors previously. On the contrary, verbal stimuli, being arbitrary in form, mean something quite specific. They mean those events that participate in bidirectional relational classes with them and only those events. This circumstance also prevents intrusions in meaning from random event sources, as is often the case with stimuli functioning nonarbitrarily. For example, if a person heard "I'll meet you next Wednesday at noon" and shortly thereafter stepped on a tack, the phrase would be extremely unlikely to become a cue for careful walking.

The conventional or arbitrary character of verbal events provides for specificity of function in another way as well. Because the form of verbal acts is not restricted by the physical properties of stimulating objects, it is free to vary to a much greater extent than is behavior of nonarbitrary form. As a result, an enormous number of forms exist in any given linguistic community, and the number may be expanded in accordance with however fine grained is the perception of the nonlinguistic world to which such forms are bidirectionally related.

6.1.3. *Temporal Relations*

The specificity of verbal functions may overcome the effects of delay in contingent situations, and in doing so prevent control by irrelevant but contiguous events. For example, suppose a person is told, "If you mow my lawn next week while I'm out of town, I'll pay you $20 at the end of the month." When the $20 shows up several weeks later, it is not likely that what was being done immediately before the mail was opened will be made more probable. Rather, it is mowing the lawn when requested that is likely to have been made more probable despite the delay in consequation.

The source of such effects is suggested by the present analysis. Time is a measure of change. An atomic clock, for example, is nothing more than a measure of the orderly change seen at an atomic level. Thus the problem of "delayed" consequences is really a problem in the change of events. Contingencies cannot operate effectively across long time delays because of the effects of these changes.

There are times when such interferences can be greatly reduced. For example, organisms seem prepared to relate food-related cues and food-related consequences. The pheonomenon of taste aversion shows that even extraordinarily long delays can still produce classical conditioning. The phylogenetic contingencies have made nonfood-related cues, and nonfood-related behavior irrelevant to food-related consequences; thus fewer events change across long periods of time that are relevant to the experimentally induced illness. Such an "interference" model of taste aversion (and indeed of delay in general) has received considerable experimental support (Revusky, 1971).

Taste aversion is a phylogenetic example of the reduction of interference. Verbal behavior is an ontogenetic example. It requires a different process but arrives at a similar end point.

Verbal behavior can greatly reduce the number of events relevant to a given consequence, when the consequence is functioning verbally. The $20 that arrived in the mail was not just $20. It was $20 for mowing the lawn. What happened an hour or even a few minutes before the mail arrived is obviously irrelevant to the $20—"obvious" in the sense that the $20 is not in a relational network with these events. In this fashion, verbal events can greatly reduce the problem time (i.e., change) presents to an organism.

6.1.4. *Expansion of Social Influence*

The means by which one organism can influence another is greatly expanded with the advent of verbal behavior. Social influence is possible over a distance, as when one speaks to another over a telephone. Simultaneous influence of many is possible, as when one gives a speech. With written language, the need for temporal and spatial proximity is eliminated. The social impact of the products of verbal behavior can stretch across the centuries and around the world. The result is a flourishing of behaviors that are propagated from person to person and go beyond the lifetimes of the individuals involved—that is, cultural practices become important.

All of this is possible because the products of speaking participate in relational classes for the listener. When means are discovered for making these products permanent or communicable across great distances, nothing new is demanded of the listener. Whether the products of verbal behavior are contiguous with acts of speaking or not is not particularly relevant to the act of listening, and thus the continuing impact of speech is independent of continuing acts of speaking.

6.1.5. Expansion of the Psychological Present

The transfer of functions through relational classes makes possible an expansion of the psychological present peculiar to verbal events. For example, it is only by way of verbal stimulation that listeners can respond with respect to events of the past and future. The past is brought to bear in the present by way of persons' historical contacts with the events spoken of. The functions of those events, having been acquired by verbal stimuli, may operate in the present situation despite the absence of their original event sources. The future, though obviously not functionally available by the same means, depends nonetheless on verbal stimulation to take its place in the present. In this case, the not-yet-existing events of the future are verbally constructed on the model of already-existing events. The participation of these constructions in the present situation, then, enable action with respect to the "future." Likewise, it is only by way of verbal stimulation that distant, remote, intangible, or nonexistent events can operate. In short, the response potential of a verbal organism is not restricted by the objective character of the immediate context, as is the case for nonverbal organisms.

A verbal organism can, by these means, take stock of the past, plan for the future, configure the impact of the not directly confrontable, and otherwise act in what might be considered an intelligent manner. Civilization, in being founded on such acts, eventuates out of social groupings in which verbal behavior has evolved, and it does not do so otherwise.

In sum, verbal stimulation is unlike that of nonverbal events. It is related to behavior in different ways. It exerts a different kind of control over behavior. For this reason, certain terminological distinctions implicating the participation of verbal stimulation would seem useful to make. "Rule-governed behavior'' is one such distinction. According to the present analysis (and in line with Zettle & Hayes, 1982), rule-governed behavior is simply behavior controlled by antecedent verbal stimuli. There may be other kinds of effects of verbal stimulation. For example, behavior maintained by verbal stimuli, operating as consequences for behavior, present another case. Perhaps ''behavior controlled by verbal consequences'' is adequate. We need a general term for the operation of verbal stimulation upon a listener. We suggest *listening*. As such, a nonverbal organism may hear, but only a verbal organism can listen.

7. CONCLUSION

The events of listening, understanding, meaning, and their implications for the actualization of other functions of stimuli—in short, the nature and operations of linguistic events—are not easily dealt with. At least they are not easy to conceptualize from a thoroughly naturalistic perspective. The difficulties involved have been great enough to produce two very different and, from our perspective, equally unsatisfactory solutions. The first of these has been to minimize the difficulty by undermining the complexity of events of this type. Skinner and others of the behavior-analytic tradition have proposed a solution of this sort. Skinner's book *Verbal Behavior* is a remarkable book. It is an attempt to account for verbal behavior by means of well-established principles of nonverbal behavior. It was so well done, that behavior analysts, at least, were quite content with the analysis for decades. Rule-governed behavior and the various theoretical and empirical literatures relevant to it have revealed the shortcomings of the analysis.

The other solution has been to invent structures and processes to account for or otherwise eliminate the difficulties. For example, we can account for the problem of association by inventing structures in which relations among events are stored, and we can explain actions that appear to occur in environments too impoverished to sustain those actions by appeal to these same storehouses. We can invent internal mental or neural processes of understanding—processes of meaning—processes of remembering—anything we want. But the ease with which such processes and storehouses are invented draws them into question. Do explanations of this sort help us to achieve our goals? Or do they just entangle us in even more difficult explanations of the processes and storehouses we invented?

The alternative is to acknowledge the enormous complexity of linguistic events—and thereby avoid oversimplification. The alternative is to construct a thoroughly naturalistic analysis—and in doing so resist the easy fix of a mentalistic account. Whatever its weaknesses, the present analysis has been guided by these two considerations.

8. REFERENCES

Clark, H. H., & Clark, E. V. (1978). *Psychology and language: An introduction to psycholinguistics*. New York: Harcourt Brace Jovanovich.

D'Amato, M. R., Salmon, D. P., Loukas, E., & Tomie, A. (1985). Symmetry and transitivity of conditional relations in monkeys (Cebus apella) and pigeons (Columba livia). *Journal of the Experimental Analysis of Behavior, 44*, 35–47.

Devany, J. M., & Hayes, S. C. (1987, May). *Irrelevant testing can disrupt equivalence: Implications for underlying processes*. Paper presented at the meeting of the Association for Behavior Analysis, Nashville, TN.

Devany, J. M., Hayes, S. C., & Nelson, R. O. (1986). Equivalence class formation in language-able and language-disabled children. *Journal of the Experimental Analysis of Behavior, 46*, 243–257.

Dixon, L. S. (1977). The nature of control by spoken words over visual stimulus selection. *Journal of the Experimental Analysis of Behavior, 27*, 433–442.

Dixon, M. H., & Spradlin, J. E. (1976). Establishing stimulus equivalences among retarded adolescents. *Journal of Experimental Child Psychology, 21*, 144–164.

Gast, D., VanBiervlet, A., & Spradlin, J. E. (1979). Teaching number-word equivalences: A study of transfer. *American Journal of Mental Deficiency, 83*, 524–527.

Hayes, L. J. (in press). Substitution and reference. In L. J. Hayes & P. N. Chase (Eds.), *Dialogues on verbal behavior* (pp.). Hillsdale, NJ: Earlbaum.

Hayes S. C. (in press a). A relational control theory of stimulus equivalence. In L. J. Hayes & P. N. Chase (Eds.), *Dialogues on verbal behavior*. Hillsdale, NJ: Earlbaum.

Hayes, S. C. (in press b). Nonhumans have not yet shown stimulus equivalence. *Journal of the Experimental Analysis of Behavior*.

Hayes, S. C., Devany, J. M., Kohlenberg, B., Brownstein, A. J., & Shelby, J. (in press). Stimulus equivalence and the symbolic control of behavior. *Mexican Journal of Behavior Analysis*.

Hayes L. J., Tilley, K. L., & Hayes S. C. (1988). Extending equivalence class membership to gustatory stimuli. *Psychological Record, 38*, 473–482.

Hayes, S. C., & Myerson, J. (May 1986). *Rules, delays, causes, and specificity*. Invited address presented to the meeting of the Association for Behavior Analysis, Milwaukee.

Hebb, D. O. (1937). The innate organization of visual activity. II. Transfer of response in the discrimination of brightness and size by rats reared in total darkness. *Journal of Comparative Psychology, 24*, 277–299.

Herman, L. M., & Thompson, R. K. (1982). Symbolic, identity and probe-delayed matching of sounds in the bottle-nosed dolphin. *Animal Learning and Behavior, 10*, 22–34.

Hutchinson, J. E., & McCloskey, C. (1988, March). *Teaching retarded children an exclusion strategy for learning new words*. Paper presented at the Gatlinburg Conference on Developmental Disabilities, Gatlinburg, TN.

Kendall, S. B. (1983). Tests for mediated transfer in pigeons. *Psychological Record, 33*, 245–256.

Kennedy, C. H., & Laitinen, R. (1988) Second-order conditional control of symmetric and transitive stimulus relations: The influence of order effects. *Psychological Record, 38*, 437–446.

Lashley, K. S. (1938). Conditonal reactions in the rat. *Journal of Psychology, 6*, 311–324.

Lazar, R., Davis-Lang, D. & Sanchez, L. (1984). The formation of visual stimulus equivalences in children. *Journal of the Experimental Analysis of Behavior, 41*, 251–266.

Lipkens, R., Kop, P. F. M., & Matthijs, W. (1988). A test of symmetry and transitivity in the conditional discrimination performances of pigeons. *Journal of the Experimental Analysis of Behavior, 49*, 395–409.

Mackay, H. A., & Sidman, M. (1984). Teaching new behaviors via equivalence relations. In

P. Brooks, R. Sperber, & C. McCauley (Eds.), *Learning and cognition in the mentally retarded* (pp. 493–513). Hillsdale, NJ: Erlbaum.

Markman, E. M., & Wachtel, G. F. (1988). Children's use of mutual exclusivity to constrain the meanings of words. *Cognitive Psychology, 20,* 121–157.

McIlvane, W. J., Kledaras, J. B., Munson, L. C., King, K. A., de Rose, J. C., & Stoddard. L. T. (1987). Controlling relations in conditional discrimination and matching by exclusion. *Journal of the Experimental Analysis of Behavior, 48,* 187–208.

McIntire, K. D., Cleary, J., & Thompson, T. (1987). Conditional relations by monkeys: Reflexivity, symmetry, and transitivity. *Journal of the Experimental Analysis of Behavior, 47,* 279–285.

Nelson, K. (1974). Concept, word and sentence: Interrelations of acquisition and development. *Psychological Review, 81,* 267–283.

Nissen, H. (1951). Analysis of complex conditional reaction in the chimpanzee. *Journal of Comparative and Physiological Psychology,* 7, 449–516.

Parrott, L. J. (1984). Listening and understanding. *The Behavior Analyst, 7,* 29–39.

Parrott, L. J. (1986). On the differences between verbal and social behavior. In P. N. Chase & L. J. Parrott (Eds.), *Psychological aspects of language: The West Virginia Lectures.* Springfield, IL: Thomas.

Parrott, L. J. (1987a). Reply to Vaughan. In S. Modgil & C. Modgil (Eds.), *B. F. Skinner: Consensus and Controversy* (pp. 277–282). Sussex, England: Falmer Press.

Parrott, L. J. (1987b). Rule-governed behavior: An implicit analysis of reference. In S. Modgil & C. Modgil (Eds.), *B. F. Skinner: Consensus and Controversy* (pp. 265–276). Sussex, England: Falmer Press.

Perkins, F. T. (1931). A further study of configurational learning in the goldfish. *Journal of Experimental Psychology, 14,* 508–538.

Reese, H. W. (1961). Transposition in the intermediate-size problem by preschool children. *Child Development, 32,* 311–314.

Reese, H. W. (1968). *The perception of stimulus relations: Discrimination learning and transposition.* New York: Academic Press.

Revusky, S. (1971). The role of interference in association over a delay. In W. K. Honig & P. H. R. James (Eds.), *Animal memory* (pp. 155–213). New York: Academic Press.

Schlinger, H., & Blakely, E. (1987). Function-altering effects of contingency-specifying stimuli. *The Behavior Analyst, 10,* 41–45.

Sidman, M. (1971). Reading and auditory-visual equivalences. *Journal of Speech and Hearing Research, 14,* 5–13.

Sidman, M., & Tailby, W. (1982). Conditional discrimination versus matching to sample: An expansion of the testing paradigm. *Journal of the Experimental Analysis of Behavior, 37,* 5–22.

Sidman, M., Cresson, O., & Willson-Morris, M. (1974). Acquisition of matching-to-sample via mediated transfer. *Journal of the Experimental Analysis of Behavior, 22,* 261–273.

Sidman, M., Rauzin, R., Lazar, R., Cunningham, S., Tailby, W., & Carrigan, P. (1982). A search for symmetry in the conditional discriminations of rhesus monkeys, baboons and children. *Journal of the Experimental Analysis of Behavior, 37,* 23–44.

Sidman, M., Kirk, B., & Willson-Morris, M. (1985). Six-member stimulus classes generated by conditional-discrimination procedures. *Journal of the Experimental Analysis of Behavior, 43,* 21–42.

Skinner, B. F. (1957). *Verbal behavior.* New York: Appelton-Century-Crofts.

Skinner, B. F. (1966). An operant analysis of problem solving. In B. Kleinmuntz (Eds.), *Problem-solving: Research, method, and theory* (pp. 225–257). New York: Wiley.

Skinner, B. F. (1969). *Contingencies of reinforcement: A theoretical analysis.* New York: Appelton-Century-Crofts.

Skinner, B. F. (unpublished manuscript). Rules and behavior.

Spradlin, J. E. & Dixon, M. (1976). Establishig a conditional discrimination without direct training: Stimulus classes and labels. *American Journal of Mental Deficiency, 80,* 555–561.

Spradlin, J. E., Cotter, V. W., & Baxley, N. (1973). Establishing a conditional discrimination without direct training: A study of transfer with retarded adolescents. *American Journal of Mental Deficiency, 77,* 556–566.

Steele, D. L. (1987). *The relations of same, opposite, and different in arbitrary matching to sample.* Unpublished doctoral dissertation, Department of Psychology, University of North Carolina at Greensboro.

Steele, D. L., Hayes, S. C., & Lawrence, P. S. (1988, May). *Equivalence without reflexivity.* Paper presented at the meeting of the Association for Behavior Analysis, Philadelphia.

Towe, A. L. (1954). A study of figural equivalence in the pigeon. *Journal of Comparative and Physiological Psychology, 47,* 283–287.

VanBiervlet, A. (1977). Establishing words and objects as functionally equivalent through manual sign training. *American Journal of Mental Deficiency, 82,* 178–186.

Vaughn, W. (1988). Formation of equivalence sets in pigeons. *Journal of Experimental Psychology: Animal Behavior Processes, 14,* 36–42.

Wulfert, E., & Hayes, S. C. (1988). Transfer of conditional sequencing through conditional equivalence classes. *Journal of the Experimental Analysis of Behavior, 50,* 125–144.

Zettle, R. D., & Hayes, S. C. (1982). Rule-governed behavior: A potential theoretical framework for cognitive-behavioral therapy. In P. C. Kendall (Ed.), *Advances in cognitive-behavioral research and therapy* (Vol. 1; pp. 73–118). New York: Academic Press.

CHAPTER 6

Rule-Following

STEVEN C. HAYES, ROBERT D. ZETTLE, and
IRWIN ROSENFARB

1. INTRODUCTION

This chapter takes as its starting point the analysis of verbal stimulation and rule-understanding presented in the previous chapter. We consider two topics. First, given that one understands a rule, why might one follow it? Second, how might rule-following interact with other psychological processes in a behavioral episode?

2. THE IMPACT OF RULE-FOLLOWING ON OTHER PSYCHOLOGICAL PROCESSES

It was not too long after the onset of behavior analysis as a distinct area that researchers began to turn their attention from nonhuman to human subjects (e.g., Holland, 1958; Hutchinson & Azrin, 1961). The original intent of much of this work, in a sense, was political. A central strategic assumption of behavior analysis was the continuity assumption: that principles identified with nonhumans would apply, more or less in whole cloth, to the actions of humans (see Hayes, 1987, for a more detailed discussion of the nature and impact of the continuity assumption on behavior analysis). This assumption justified and made coherent the research program of behavior analysis that relied heavily on studies with nonhuman organisms.

STEVEN C. HAYES • Department of Psychology, University of Nevada—Reno, Reno, Nevada 89557. ROBERT D. ZETTLE • Department of Psychology, Wichita State University, Wichita, Kansas 67208. IRWIN ROSENFARB • Department of Psychology, Auburn University, Auburn, Alabama 36849.

It quickly became clear, however, that humans often would *not* show the same kinds of effects of behavioral manipulations (e.g., effects due to simple schedules of reinforcement) even though these effects were nearly ubiquitous in the rest of the animal kingdom. This realization did not challenge the continuity assumption because generalization of behavioral findings from nonhumans to humans was successful often enough, especially with those for whom the environment could be thoroughly controlled. Most behavior-analytic researchers seemed to concluded that relatively simple differences in history or preparation could explain the inconsistencies.

2.1. The Early Period

The original behavior-analytic work on instructions emerged as a natural outgrowth of basic human research. It did so for three reasons. First, it was often more convenient to use instructions with humans to establish performances that then could be studied for other reasons. The fact that these performances were instructionally established often did not seem to be of significant concern, but it meant that instructions were often close by, ready to be examined directly when it occurred to researchers to do so. Second, when instructions *were* examined directly, their effects were often large compared to the impacts of other variables. Third, the relatively atheoretical approach of early behavior analysis allowed instructions to be treated descriptively, and thus research could proceed without waiting for an adequate account of the nature of instructions. Some of the early work simply showed that instructions of a given type had a given effect. What instructions were was not at issue.

Two of the early studies that dealt explicitly with instructions show this latter pattern clearly. In an applied study, Ayllon and Azrin (1964) studied the effects of instructions on 18 psychiatric patients who failed to pick up all their cutlery during mealtime. In the first phase, food or cigarettes were given to subjects if they picked up all their utensils, whereas in the second phase, instructions to pick up utensils were given to all subjects. Results indicated that whereas no change in responding occurred in the reinforcement-only condition, most subjects responded correctly in the instructions-only condition and, after 1 year, one-third of the subjects continued to emit the appropriate response without any explicit reinforcement. (If subjects inquired about the reinforcement contingency during the reinforcement-only condition, they were told that there was no link between their behavior and the reward. Thus it is perhaps not surprising that a change in behavior without the use of instructions failed to take place because in fact instructions were used in both conditions but were at cross purposes.)

Kaufman, Baron, and Kopp (1966) conducted a more basic study looking at the effects of instructions on schedule control. Results indicated that with no instructions, responding was erratic, and control by the schedule was poor. With instructions, however, although the schedule also failed to gain control over behavior, responding appeared to be controlled by the instructions given. For instance, when subjects were told that reinforcement was programmed according to an FI-60 second schedule, the response rate was low and scalloping was occasionally noted. When subjects were told that the schedule was a VR 150, the response rate was high and steady. A second study looked at the effects of instructions on responding during extinction. Subjects were told that reinforcement was available on a variable-ratio schedule. Results indicated that these instructions were able to sustain performance for 3 hours even when no programmed reinforcement was given.

The finding that instructions can exert a powerful and lasting influence over behavior even when the instructions are in opposition to the schedule contingencies intrigued some behavioral researchers, and several studies in the same vein followed over that next few years. These studies, however, were not theoretically driven. They were not geared toward an analysis of the nature of instructions. They simply documented instructional effects. In a sense, *instructions* were treated as an object, not a term that referred to a functional relation between environmental stimulation and the action of the organism. Instructions were things in the world that could be identified by the experimenter by their form; they were given to subjects, and the effects were noted. How they came to operate in this way for human subjects was not at issue.

Several studies in this period have the same quality. Researchers seemed almost surprised at the strong effects instructions could produce, especially when compared to variables that were the stock and trade of behavioral-analytic work with nonhumans. For example, Lippman and Meyer (1967) looked at the effects of different instructions on responding in a FI-20 second schedule. Subjects were either told that reinforcement depended on the passage of time or on the number of responses. Results indicated that all subjects given the time instructions responded as if they were on an FI schedule, whereas subjects given the ratio instructions generally showed a high, steady rate performance. Subjects given minimal instructions responded with either one of the two patterns described but did not show the patterns of FI performance characteristic of nonhumans.

Similarly, Weiner (1970) explicitly looked at the effects of instructions on responding during extinction. One group of subjects was told that they could earn no more than 700 pennies in the experiment, a second group was told they could earn no more than 999 pennies, and a third group was told nothing about the number of pennies they could earn. All subjects were given a 2-hour extinction period after 700 pennies had been earned. Results indicated that responding in extinction was greatest for those subjects given no instructions, was less for those subjects told they could earn 999 pennies, and was the least for those subjects told they could earn only 700 pennies.

2.2. The Period of Stagnation

These early human operant studies showed that instructions can exert a powerful effect on behavior. There seemed, however, to be a sense of embarrassment that instructions could apparently so thoroughly override the effects of direct contingencies. The consistency of contingency effects in the animal laboratory across a wide variety of species was one of their most salient and powerful features. In the late 1960s and early 1970s principles of direct contingency control were forming the basis of early attempts to apply behavioral principles to human affairs. To have them so easily overturned was either an occasion for concern or indifference, depending upon one's view. If these results indicated that very different processes may be involved in human behavior, compared to nonhuman behavior, this would cause concern because it could undermine some philosophical underpinnings of the behavior-analytic perspective. Conversely, if instructional effects and anomalous human operant data more generally were merely due to details of the uncontrolled history of human laboratory subjects or to a powerful form of discriminative control (instructions) that was nevertheless no different in kind from any other type of discriminative control, then these effects were a cause for indifference. Both reactions can be found in the literature of the time. Some early reports termed these effects *remarkable* (Kaufman *et al.*, 1966), whereas in others instructional effects were shrugged off as simple instances of stimulus control (e.g., Ayllon & Azrin, 1964). Most notable by its absence was the failure to consider instruction following as a kind of verbal event. Some behavioral theorists viewed instruction-following as a special kind of responding (Schoenfeld & Cumming, 1963), but even then this special kind of responding was not thought to be verbal in any important sense.

Nonbehavioral authors often saw instructional effects as undermining the validity of behavior-analytic principles as applied to adult humans (e.g., Brewer, 1974). Of course, merely labeling the effects as due to instructions did not explain them. An appeal to simple processes of discriminative control was (and is) attractive to many behavioral theorists, but doing so made the phenomenon relatively uninteresting. Furthermore, the effect of instructions was presumably based on remote sources of control in the history of the individual that were inaccessible to the experimenter. Both of the primary behavior-analytic reactions inhibited successful research in the area: either because it was threatening or unimportant. As a result, the 1970s was a period of stagnancy in which little interesting behavior-analytic work was being done on instructional control. The human operant research that was done largely focused on showing that humans often *did* behave like nonhumans in many situations.

2.3. The Modern Era of Human Operant Research

The shift in perspective that has emerged in human operant research in the late 1970s and the 1980s has involved several aspects. The cognitive trend in basic experimental psychology considerably weakened support for the study of nonhuman behavior as an avenue for the development of findings relevant to human action. Grant money dried up. Student resources were diminished. Some well-known basic behavior analysts began to turn to the study of human behavior (e.g., Rachlin, Catania, Harzem, Sidman). These researchers were not concerned so much with proving the value of the continuity assumption as in an analysis of what they found in the world of human action. Some researchers elaborated on the ways that human and nonhuman data differed. Other began to identify the sources of these differences. Gradually, some researchers began to conclude that the differences between human and nonhuman performance could often be traced in part to the effects of language on human action. The impact of instructions gradually has become a special case of a more general issue: the role of verbal behavior in human performance. It is this exciting "language hypothesis" (Lowe, 1979) that has enlivened the field of human operant psychology and has given the area of rule-governed behavior such a vigorous boost.

2.3.1. Schedule Performance

There are a variety of ways that the role of verbal behavior has been studied, identifed, and explained. One popular preparation, especially early in this modern era, has been the FI schedule because it is a well-established finding that human FI performance (either high, steady rates, or very low rates) differs significantly from responding on an FI by other organisms (e.g., Leander, Lippman, & Meyer, 1968; Lippman & Meyer, 1967; Weiner, 1964, 1965, 1969). There are ways, however, to reduce this effect. In general, human performance is more animallike when steps are taken to reduce counting. A variety of procedures have been used, including the requirement of concurrent verbal tasks such as mental math or reading aloud (e.g., Laties & Weiss, 1963; Lowe, Harzem, & Hughes, 1978) or the use of a response-produced clock (Lowe, Harzem, & Bagshaw, 1978; Lowe, Harzem, & Hughes, 1978). Both have the effect of reducing counting.

It is difficult, if not impossible, to assess whether the failure to count led to the increased temporal control, whether the increased temporal control led to the failure to count, or whether both were caused by some third variable. A variety of other procedures have been used to see if verbal events are responsible for the difference between human and nonhuman FI patterns. It was reasoned that if verbal abilities are involved in the failure to see FI scalloping in most human studies, then preverbal humans should show patterns characteristic of nonhumans. Lowe, Beasty, and Bentall (1983) tested responding on FI-schedules with two human infants, ages 9 and 10 months, respectively. The performances showed clear scalloping and seemed indistinguishable from nonhuman patterns of performance. Lowe *et al.* attributed these scalloping effects to the fact that these children did not develop self-instructions and hence could come under the direct control of the reinforcing contingencies. Developmental studies have shown a gradual transition (especially from about age 2 to age 6 or 7) in performance from the animallike performances of infants to the pattern of adults, both in schedule performance (e.g, Bentall, Lowe, & Beasty, 1985) and in the effects of self-instructions (Bentall & Lowe, 1987).

2.3.2. Contingency Sensitivity

Another preparation has been to expose subjects to changes in contingencies and to assess whether subjects who have had their performances instructed are more sensitive to these changes than those who have not. Catania and his colleagues have shown that more schedule-sensitive performance is obtained by shaping behavior than by instructing it (e.g., Catania, Matthews, & Shimoff, 1982; Shimoff, Catania, & Matthews, 1981). Shimoff *et al.* (1981) compared shaped to instructed performance with low-rate-of-responding schedules. In the first study, low rates were produced through a Random Interval schedule with a superimposed DRL contingency. When the DRL contingency was relaxed, response rate increased for 6 out of 7 shaped subjects who made contact with the schedule contingencies. In contrast, response rate increased for only 4 out of 10 instructed subjects. In a second study, a Random Ratio schedule was used in place of the RI schedule. In this case, an increase in response rate led to an increase in numbers of reinforcers. Rate of responding increase for 4 out of 6 shaped responders after the DRL contingency was relaxed; only 3 of 8 instructed subjects did so. Shimoff *et al.* concluded that insensitivity is a ''defining property'' of instructional control (p. 207).

Similarly, Matthews, Shimoff, Catania, and Sagvolden (1977) taught subjects to respond to a telegraph key by either reinforcing successively closer approximations to a key press or by demonstrating a key press. When responding was established by shaping and a consummatory response was required, ratio schedules maintained higher rates than did interval schedules, a finding similar to that obtained in the animal literature. When responding was established by demonstration, however, ratio and interval schedules produced equivalent rates of responding, and it appeared that subjects were generally insensitive to the schedule requirements.

In these studies, as with many in this line of work, there was considerable overlap between the performances of the subjects exposed to different experimental conditions. In the Matthews *et al.* study, response rate varied considerably from individual to individual (Weiner, 1983). In the Shimoff *et al.* study, one-third of the shaped subjects in Experiment 2 showed no increase in rate of responding when the DRL contingency was relaxed (although some failed to make contact with the change). Furthermore, other procedures (e.g., a long reinforcement history, see Weiner, 1964) also create an "insensitivity" to schedule control. Thus data such as these do not show unequivocally that instructions operate according to different behavioral principles.

2.4. Theoretical Analysis of Verbal Control

Even as behavior analysts have begun to take seriously the possibility that verbal processes are fundamental to an understanding of human behavior, little work has been directed toward an understanding of these processes themselves. Some researchers have attempted to deal with the nature of verbal control, however.

2.4.1. Discriminative Control

One congenial solution to the problem of verbal control is to suppose that it is a matter of discriminative control. Galizio (1979) tested the hypothesis that instructions function as discriminative stimuli. He reasoned that instruction-following if an operant, instruction-following should occur when instructions are accurate and should cease when they are inaccurate. Four experiments were conducted to test these hypotheses. In Experiment 1, the addition of accurate instructions led to quick schedule control over behavior. In Experiment 2, when subjects did not make contact with the schedule contingencies, they remained under instructional control. Inaccurate instruction control broke down, however, when subjects were able to make contact with the schedule contingencies. Instruction-following was brought under stimulus control in Experiment 3. Subjects followed instructions only in the presence of an orange light that signaled that the instructions were accurate and failed to respond to the instructions in the presence of a purple light that signaled that they were inaccurate. In Experiment 4, instructions were not given unless an observing response was emitted. The observing response was readily acquired but only when subjects received accurate instructions. Receiving instructions, therefore, was shown to possess reinforcing consequences.

Galizio concluded that instruction-following is an operant controlled by its consequences. Subjects would follow instructions when they were accurate and would fail to respond to them when they were inaccurate. Subjects would also work to obtain access to accurate instructions. Several difficulties arise with this interpretation, however. First, even within the context of Galizio's studies, instruction-following could not always be interpreted straightforwardly as behavior under stimulus control. For example, in Experiment 1, subjects followed the instructions even though instruction-following did not add to the amount of reinforcement they obtained. Others have shown (e.g., Hayes, Brownstein, Zettle, Rosenfarb, & Korn, 1986, Exp. 2) that inaccurate instructions are followed even when subjects make contact with the inaccuracy.

A bigger problem is this. Even if rule-following can be explained on the basis of discriminative control, this does *not* explain what rules are or how they can be understood in the first place. If rules are nothing more than S^Ds established through direct histories of reinforcement, they should be readily establishable in all kinds of organisms. Few have claimed this is possible. As we argued in the previous chapter, functions can be established in verbal organisms in which the history that lead to these functions does not fit the requirement of discriminative control. Something else seems needed.

2.4.2. Self-Instruction

Another tack has been to explain instructional effects on the basis of self-control. Lowe (1979) suggests that instructions exert a powerful effect on human behavior because they influence self-instructions (cf., Malott, Chapter 8, in the present volume). Evidence for this comes from several sources. Leander *et al.* (1966) and Lippman and Meyer (1967) both gave subjects minimal instructions for responding during FI schedules, and both found that following performance on the schedule, if subjects verbally reported that obtaining the reinforcer was dependent on the number of responses, they responded at a high, steady rate. If subjects, however, reported that the reinforcement was dependent on the passage of time, responding was of a low rate. As has been pointed out elsewhere, however (Weiner, 1983), and as Lowe himself points out, it is difficult to determine if subjects' verbal behavior participates in schedule performance or vice versa. Lowe and colleagues have also shown that training in self-instruction can alter human operant performance (Bentall & Lowe, 1987), but a larger problem still remains. It does little good to explain instructional effects by appealing to self-instructional effects, until self-instruction is itself explained.

3. UNDERSTANDING

What had previously been viewed as a kind of interference, nuisance, or embarrassment—the effects of verbal abilities and instructions on human performance—can instead be viewed as an opportunity to study verbal abilities. This is the shift that defines the modern era of human operant research. Although such a shift is important, other steps are needed before current research being done in the area can contribute to an important advance in our analysis of human action. It is necessary first to understand the behavior of the listener itself. We have developed the case for this in the previous chapter. Second, we must provide a theoretical and empirical account of how and why an understood rule is then actually followed.

We have argued that the behavior of the listener is verbal when events have their effects on the listener because of their participation in equivalence or other relational classes. In our analysis, a verbal rule organizes responding through the participation of events in relational frames. A person "understands" a rule in the sense that the effects of verbal stimuli are based on that organization.

3.1. How Can We Assess Understanding?

Verbal understanding is an act of organization. It is important to assess understanding, primarily because words can occasion actions without it. When that happens, the effects of the words are not verbal effects. For example, I can tell my dog to get my slippers. This is not rule-governed behavior because there are no verbal stimuli involved. Understanding is the behavioral side of what defines stimulation as "verbal." Thus, without an assessment of understanding, we have no rule, whether or not the form of the behavior seen looks like rule-following.

3.1.1. *Verbal Networks*

One way to assess understanding is to examine that organization verbally. The actual act of understanding should not be confused with other behaviors that we may examine to assess that act. Thus verbalization of an organization is not the same as the act of organizing. The method is still useful, however. For example, a person told "when the bell rings, get the cake out of the oven" can show that each of the verbal events involved are being reacted to, in part, based on a network of arbitrary relations that have been established. A person could be asked a series of questions about the rule: "What do you do when the bell rings?" or "When do you get the cake out of the oven?" or "When the bell rings you get what out of the oven?" If a person could not supply the answer to these questions, we would say that the rule was "not understood." More precisely, we may say that the person's understanding of the rule did not correspond to the experimenter's understanding of it.

Because verbal events are members of relational classes, other events in the environment are now also participating in the network of arbitrary relations that has been established. This is important to a fuller explication of what the listener understands to be the case. For example, we could substitute actual objects, or pictures, for the words in the questions above. (This kind of exercise is done often on children's shows such as "Sesame Street," presumably because such an ability is an important building block for following verbal rules.) We could ask, for example, "what do you do when (ring-ring)?", where "ring-ring" is the actual sound of a bell. In this way we can assess whether "nonverbal" events in the environment now are functioning as verbal stimuli. If so, the bell means something in the verbal sense of the word "meaning" developed in the previous chapter.

3.1.2. Transfer of Control

Another way to assess the listener's understanding of verbal events is to examine the transfer of psychological functions through relational networks. For example, suppose Event X has been established as a CS in the presence of which a shock occurs. The person shows a CER to X. We now place X in a frame of coordination with Event Y. If Y is understood verbally—in the sense that Y is related to X, then in relevant contexts, Y should now also function as a CS.

This strategy can be expanded to more complex verbal relational networks. For example, suppose a person suddenly declares, "I am going to stab you in the left arm." Few who understand that statement will fail to show emotional arousal and tension in the left arm. The arousal is not the act of understanding, but it can be shown to depend on such an act if proper controls are used.

3.1.3. The Silent Dog Strategy

Another way to assess understanding is of relevance when that understanding is reflected in the covert verbalizations of the subject. The "silent dog" strategy (Hayes, 1986) is based on the conclusion (Ericsson & Simon, 1984) that if subjects are told to say out loud what they are already thinking verbally (the "talk-aloud" condition), it will have no effect at all on task performance, compared to not stating thoughts aloud. In addition, verbalizing thoughts that are not in the form of words (e.g., information about odors) will usually only slow down task performance and "not change the structure of the process for performing the main task" (Ericsson & Simon, 1984, p. 79).

For example, a subject is asked simply to report aloud what he or she is already saying privately while solving a problem. Under these conditions, concurrent verbalization does not influence task performance. There are at least two possibilities. One is that the verbal report is merely an irrelevant add-on. This could happen either because it is a totally separate response system from that producing task performance or because it is closely controlled by task-relevant variables but does not itself influence these variables in turn. This does not seem likely. If subjects must verbalize thoughts according to a timed schedule, for example, they then *do* interfere with task performance, as does hearing one's own verbalizations, requiring that subjects verbalize motives or reasons for thinking, or requiring verbalization about ongoing perceptual-motor processes (see Ericsson & Simon, 1984, for a review of hundreds of studies that support this conclusion). In addition, the myriad of studies reported in the present volume document the sensitivity of humans to verbal instructions.

A second possibility is that these verbal reports do not alter performance because equivalent events have already influenced task performance; in short, because the behavior is already rule-governed and the verbal report simply describes the rule. Unless other nonverbal processes perfectly mirror rule-governance, we are led to the conclusion that—like Sherlock Holmes's famous case of the silent dog—it is the lack of an effect that shows the effect.

Use of the silent dog strategy requires several interlocking findings. It is a cumbersome method in many ways, but it is the only method we are aware of that claims to be able to identify self-verbalizations with the knowledge that what was reported was actually said. First, it must be demonstrated that the talk-aloud requirement does not influence performance (e.g., by comparing performance under the talk-aloud condition to conditions without the talk-aloud requirement). If talking aloud does influence performance, the evidence (such as it is) for self-rules is eliminated. Second, it must be shown that self-verbalizations are task relevant. Task-irrelevant verbalizations may fail to influence behavior because of that fact alone. For example, working on math problems aloud while driving may not influence driving, but that does not mean that driving is governed by rules having to do with math. It is possible to check for task relevance by showing that the use of the verbal protocols of self-verbalization will influence the specific task in question when used as external rules for other subjects. Third, it must be shown that manipulating a variety of variables that violate the "talk-aloud" conditions (e.g., slowing down reports greatly or requiring verbal inferences about the nature of the task) does reliably produce changes in task performance. This increases the confidence in the task relevance of the verbalizations and shows that self-verbalizations are associated with altered task performance if steps are taken to interrupt the natural flow of self-talk. It is only the entire constellation of results that provides evidence for self-rule-governance. If all three requirements are met, the only plausible explanation for the lack of an effect for requiring subjects to verbalize thought content is that this content is already a participant in the performances seen.

The silent dog method cannot promise to detect all acts of verbal understanding and of self-rule formulation. For example, behavior under verbal control may become automatic with sufficient practice. If so, behavior may be controlled by rules in the remote past and yet produce no current private verbal accompaniments. Similarly, there may be times when requiring verbalization out loud does alter the content of self-verbalization (e.g., when a person is asked to verbalize reactions to a pornographic film in front of others). The method seems well protected against false positives. When it works we can say "yes, this person said that to themselves." Often, however, it may fail to reach any conclusion.

The silent dog method does not assess understanding *per se* but does promise to identify scientifically the content of self-verbalization under some conditions. It can identify the verbal content of some instances of thinking. Knowledge of this content may allow the experimenter to construct plausible accounts of the nature of the subject's understanding of a given rule or task because the relational structure of covert verbalizations can be assumed to correspond somewhat to the relational organization of the act of listening.

4. RULE-FOLLOWING

If a person understands a rule, the events in the environment that participate in the rule by virtue of their arbitrary relation to the words or other symbols in the rule now have verbal functions in terms of the rule. The verbal functions of the previously nonverbal environment help explain why it is possible to move from rule-understanding to rule-following. The behavior of rule-following that occurs in an entirely different context than that in which the rule was delivered is possible because aspects of that new context are functioning as verbal stimuli with effects established by the rule.

This still does not fully explain rule-following, however. When the bell rings, the person may make contact with the altered functions of the oven and cake and still not get the cake out of the oven. The person, for example, could point to the oven if asked "what are you supposed to approach?" and still not approach it. This is essentially a matter of "motivation"—of settings that actualize the nonverbal functions of the verbally involved objects in the environment. To get up and walk toward the oven is a coordination of one's behavior with a different stimulus function of the oven than the function established by virtue of the oven's participation in a relational frame with the word *oven* and through that with the rule. To pick up the cake with one's hands requires the coordination of motor behavior moment by moment with the cake in the context of the oven (reaching down, grasping, lifting, moving out of the hot oven, placing on the top of the oven, letting go). These functions involve the verbal function of the cake but primarily as a matter of coordinating the nonverbal functions of grasping, lifting, and so on.

If these nonverbal functions were not already established, the rule could be understood and nevertheless not lead to effective behavior. A young child might be told that cars are for driving. The acts of driving may have been observed and are understood verbally (for example, one could match the word *driving* to the observed actions and vice versa), but the action of driving has not itself been acquired. If that child is then told "go drive the car to the store,'' effective action may be impossible even if the statement is understood because the nonverbal functions of driving have not yet been established.

If we assume that the rule has been understood and the nonverbal functions needed to follow the rule are available with regard to the events specified in the rule, we still have to deal with the settings that will in fact actualize those nonverbal functions in coordination with the verbal functions. We have to deal with motivation. This is the topic to which we now turn.

4.1. Functional Units of Rule-Following

There are at least three distinct types of rule-governed behaviors organized by the contingencies that motivate action with regard to the rule (see Zettle & Hayes, 1982, for our first analysis of these units and their application to cognitive therapy).

4.1.1. Pliance

The most fundamental unit of rule-governed behavior is pliance, which comes from the word *compliance*. Pliance is rule-governed behavior under the control of apparent socially mediated consequences for a correspondence between the rule and relevant behavior. Thus pliance involves consequences for rule-following *per se* mediated by the verbal community. When a rule functions this way, it is said to function as a ply.

A simple example is as follows: A mother tells her daughter, ''I want you to wear a sweater when you go outside today.'' If the daughter wears the sweater under the control of apparent consequences from her mother (or others in contact with the rule) for following or not following the rule, then this is pliance. Note that we cannot tell from the form of the behavior itself whether or not it is pliance. If the daughter puts on the sweater to show it to a friend, or to cover a torn blouse, or to keep warm, this is not pliance.

If the daughter *refuses* to wear the sweater because of reinforcement obtained for failing to follow parental rules (as in the case of a ''rebellious'' child), this is still pliance—though for convenience we term such effects *counterpliance* to remind ourselves that the form of the rule and the behavior do not match in this case. Clinicians have long claimed that rebellion and conformity were two sides of the same coin. The present analysis concurs because the nature of the contingencies are identical—it is only the valence of the socially mediated consequence that differs.

Counterpliance may not, however, be sensitive to the same experimental manipulations as normal instances of pliance because the ways in which socially mediated consequences are delivered may differ. For example, for a speaker to deliver consequences to me for following a rule, the speaker must know that

I personally followed the rule. In counterpliance, the effects on the speaker caused by my breaking the rule may function as reinforcers for breaking the rule, even if the speaker is unaware that I personally broke the rule. For example, a schoolchild may secretly break a teacher-established rule of silence in the classroom by surreptitiously squeezing a Whoopee cushion. The distress of the teacher may reinforce the rule-breakage (i.e., it may be an instance of counterpliance), but the teacher need not know who made the noise for this effect to occur.

Pliance is probably the most fundamental unit of rule-governed behavior because it is the clearest instance in which the behavior controlled by the rule can be said to be rule-governed. In pliance, there are additional socially mediated contingencies established for a distinct behavioral class: rule-following. All rule-governed behavior makes contact with two types of contingencies: the natural contingencies and those established by the rule and past history with rules. In the case of the natural contingencies, the consequences of an action are determined *completely* by the topography of the action itself in a given situation, not its history or apparent controlling variables. For example, suppose I put my hand through a windowpane. The natural consequences are 100% determined by the form of that action in this situation. The cuts I receive will be produced by the precise manner in which my hand goes through the windowpane. These natural consequences are *exactly* the same if I put my hand through "intentionally" or did it "accidentally," provided only that the form of the response and its relationship to the window remain the same. The window cannot react to why the hand is there, only how it is there.

The distinction between natural contingencies and socially mediated contingencies for rule-following is not the same as the distinction between social and nonsocial contingencies. All verbally established contingencies involve social variables (if only the rule itself), but social consequences can also be natural. For example, the consequences of sexual behavior are socially mediated. Many of them may be natural in that they are determined by the form of the behavior itself. Sexual arousal, for example, is to some degree determined by the topography of sexual stimulation. Other consequences in a sexual situation may be produced by verbally mediated discriminations we make about "why" someone is acting this way (e.g., "I asked him not to do that"). Thus, in pliance the issue is not the type of reinforcement (i.e., social/nonsocial) but the type of contingency. With pliance, the consequences must be socially mediated because only a social/verbal community can discern the presence of a rule and check for behavior that corresponds with it. The fact of social mediation, however, is background; the foreground issue is that the socially mediated consequences are *for rule-following*. The consequences are explicitly designed to organize responding into the class of rule-following (what might be termed obedience, morality, manners, and so on).

Pliance is the most fundamental unit of rule-following for other reasons. It seems to occur first developmentally and probably is the basis for other units of rule-following. Consider the following thought experiment. Imagine a world in which speakers never consequate rule-following. No social reinforcement is provided for responding to speech, even in the simplest ways (e.g., say "Da-Da"). Instead, speakers dispassionately describe natural contingencies only. For example, a speaker may say "%$*%$" meaning "it's cold outside and you'll be warmer if you wear a jacket," or "!@@+" meaning it is 5 hours since you have eaten". Under such conditions it would be difficult if not impossible to acquire language in general and rule-following in particular.

Consider the case when the speaker says "%*@%$," meaning "it's cold outside." The reinforcing effects of wearing a jacket are just as likely when it is cold if the rule is given or when it is not. (You have to remember that the person does not know what "%*@%$" means. For purposes of explanation we have given an English translation but if you think of it in English you will have already understood the rule and you will miss the point). A discriminative stimulus exerts control only because the probability of reinforcement for a given behavior is greater in its presence than in its absence. In the immediate situation (e.g., it is cold outside today), the probability of reinforcement for wearing a jacket is exactly the same in the presence of the rule "$%@$%" as in its absence. It is only in a temporally molar sense that bringing behavior under the control of the rule increases reinforcement. Unfortunately, animals are notoriously inefficient at integrating over long periods—at least until they acquire language. In this case, however, they cannot acquire control by language until they can integrate. In the area of rule-understanding, this paradox is broken by introducing added short-term contingencies for the development of relational frames and thus for the development of relational classes (see Chapter 5 in this volume). The same means seems to be used in the case of rule-following. Children, for example, are told "no," and deviation from the rule is immediately punished ("I told you no!"). Once control by rules is established, the natural consequences of rule-following can also take hold.

Thus, without pliance, we would not be likely to follow rules in the first place even if we could understand them (which without similar social contingencies on relational responding, we would not). In the real world, of course, this discussion is rather academic. Speakers speak because of the effect this has on listeners. In order to give rules that are exclusively maintained by natural reinforcers, the speaker would repeatedly and consistently have to give rules without ever responding to the personal benefits that might come from socially established rule-following. All mands, for example, imply a state of reinforcability in the speaker, by definition. Responses to mands that have the effect of delivering this reinforcer will naturally be reinforced by the speaker, in order to continue this effect. Thus in the natural world there are ample supplies of socially mediated reinforcements, and we would never be able to see if children could acquire language and be controlled by it if there were no social consequences for rule-following.

4.1.2. Tracking

A second unit of rule-following is tracking, to suggest following a path. Tracking is rule-governed behavior under the control of the apparent correspondence between the rule and the way the world is arranged. A rule functioning in this way is termed a *track*. A simple case might be the advice, "The way to get to Reno is to follow I-80." If the listener's behavior is brought under control of the rule because of an apparent correspondence between it and how actually to get to Reno, then this is tracking.

Tracking is sensitive to a host of variables affecting the apparent correspondence between the rule and natural contingencies and the importance of that correspondence. For example, tracking is influenced by the listener's history of making contact with natural consequences by following other rule-givers, the correspondence between the rule and other rules or events in the listener's history, the importance of the consequence implied by the rule, and so on. Note that the speaker does not mediate compliance. Tracking would be as likely to occur if the rule is in a book as if it were given by an actual speaker (assuming similar histories in these two situations).

4.1.3. Augmenting

A third unit of rule-following is augmenting, to suggest a changed or heightened state of affairs. Augmenting is rule-governed behavior under the control of apparent changes in the capacity of events to function as reinforcers or punishers. We originally described this kind of rule-following before behavior analysts had developed a technical vocabulary for such effects. Michael's concept of an "establishing stimulus" (Michael, 1982) has made the definition of an augmental more succinct. An augmental is a verbal stimulus (see previous chapter) that also functions as an establishing stimulus. A rule functioning in that way is termed an *augmental*.

Augmenting is among the most subtle but most important forms of rule-following. Much of media advertising is based on this kind of rule-following. Consider this example: "Aren't you hungry for a Burger King now?" If we assume that the owners of large multimillion dollar corporations are rational businesspersons, we may also assume that this statement, when understood, can be an effective source of control over the purchase of hamburgers. Why would it be?

The statement is unlikely to function as a ply. Others are unlikely to have reinforced burger buying more often in the presence of the commercial than in its absence. If anything, the effect is likely to be the opposite—people might criticize a consumer for being so gullible as to respond to commercial appeals. The statement could function to some degree as a track, essentially specifying the relation between eating a Whopper and removal of hunger. In this analysis, we have to deal with the fact that the commercial is probably heard often. The likelihood of hearing it shortly after a meal is as high as any other time. Thus the commercial cannot specify a contingency reliably. In addition, once the relation between food and hunger reduction is thoroughly learned verbally, a track of that kind is unlikely to influence behavior. No "new information" is presented. For example, a person may be told "that going to school leads to academic degrees." The statement is unlikely to influence behavior as a track if the listener has already been exposed often to that verbal statement of a relation.

It is most likely that the commercial functions as an augmental. The question, "Aren't you hungry," establishes the consequences of eating as more valued for the moment. Unlike the case of pliance and tracking, however, it is not clear how various psychological processes could combine to produce augmenting, even after the rule is understood. In the interests of advancing its empirical examination, we offer one possible process.

Let us examine an instance of appetitive classical conditioning. A previously neutral stimulus reliably precedes a positively valanced UCS. Pavlov's salivation arrangement will do—a bell reliably precedes food. In the natural environment, the organism may also have operant behavior that can produce and is reinforced by the UCS—in this case, ways to produce food. Suppose the CS is presented, but the UCS does not follow. If operant behavior can also give rise to the UCS, the CS will function as an establishing stimulus for that operant behavior. The CS is not a discriminative stimulus because the probability of a given consequence for that operant behavior is the same in the presence of the CS as in its absence. Rats presented with this exact arrangement will, for example, increase their rate of bar pressing to produce food when presented with tones that were previously associated with food in a classical conditioning arrangement, even though the tone has nothing to do with the actual relation between the bar press and food.

To apply this to verbal stimuli is not difficult. Suppose a stimulus is in an equivalence class with the CS. Through the transfer of functions seen in relational classes (see previous chapter), the function of the CS as an establishing stimulus is now transferred to the relational stimulus. The Burger King example seems to fit the description. The commercial presents a visual event (the picture of a Whopper) and a verbal description ("aren't you hungry?"). Both the sight of a hamburger and "feelings of hunger" probably reliably precede consumption of hamburgers. The feelings of hunger cannot be presented directly, but a verbal description of them can be. In radio commercials, even the hamburger itself is described ("a plump, juicy hamburger, hot off the grill," etc.). A good commercial will literally "make your mouth water." Pavlov's dogs did not have a way of earning food in extinction trials, but people do: Drive down to the Burger King.

Augmenting rarely exists in pure form—it is usually mixed with pliance or tracking. Each of these can be affected by augmentals because they each involve implied or specified consequences. An example of how augmentals mix with other units might be the following. An antiabortion appeal is preceded by a song about little children. Later the arguments about abortion keep referring to the death of "unborn children." The initial augmental may create a state of reinforceability that can increase the behavior change potential of these arguments. The common advice to speakers to first "create a need" is reflective of this process.

4.2. Rules as Rules for the Listener

There are probably other units of rule-following, but the three main units previously mentioned seem most distinct and useful. Note that each definition includes the word *apparent*. This is simply to emphasize that rules are antecedent events. The consequences that follow rule-following then affect the future value of certain rules as antecedents for rule-following but not their present value. Their present value is determined by the history of the listener.

It is crucial to realize that the concepts of pliance, tracking, and augmenting are listener-oriented concepts. They are functional units of rule-following, not rule-formulating, stating, or understanding (though they assume each of these). They are not categories of speaker-produced rule-structures. Among other things, this means that speakers cannot reliably produce plys, tracks, and augmentals. It also means that these units cannot be identified from the products of speech (e.g., transcripts). Speakers can produce verbal formulae. These verbalizations may or may not even function as verbal stimuli for a given listener. Regardless of their form, they may or may not function as plys, tracks, or augmentals for the listener.

Thus it is incorrect to attempt to discern the nature of a functional rule, or even its existence, without defining it in terms of the variables controlling the listener's behavior. Rather than claim that a given statement is, say, a track, it is more correct to say that this statement functioned as a track for this listener in this context. Turning types of rules into *stimulus objects,* rather than contextually limited stimulus *functions,* eliminates most of the value of a behavioral perspective on rule-following.

Let us take several examples. A boy named David is playing in his room. He hears a high-pitched, almost frantic voice, seemingly coming from outside the house saying, "David, get out here." It sounds like his mother, and she sounds mad. His history with his mother is that if he does not drop everything and do what his mother said he will be spanked. A spanking is something he would rather avoid, so he leaps to his feet and runs to the frontdoor. As he gets there he realizes that the sound he heard was not his mother but the squeaking of the washing machine. He returns to his room.

This is an example in which the source of verbal stimulation for the listener was not the product of a speaker's verbal behavior. The behavioral episode is an instance of pliance. The squeaking of the washing machine functioned as a ply, in this situation, for this boy, over the behavior of going outside. Obviously, it would be silly to call the squeak a ply based on its form, but that is the point. *Any* stimulus can be the source of verbal stimulation in a given instance. "Rules" as they apply to rule-governed behavior are in the environment–listener interaction, not in the environment as a physicist may examine it.

A second example. A teenage girl is told by her father that she should not go out with a particular boy because he is a juvenile delinquent and will get her in trouble. Let us suppose that the father's statement is under the control solely of his observations of the boy's illegal and dangerous behavior and his observation of the effects of such behavior on others. Now imagine that the teenage girl continues to date the boy in order to "show my father he can't push me around." In this case, the father's statement may be in the form of a description of the natural contingencies, but it has functioned as a ply in this situation, with this girl, over this behavior. The girl is attempting to punish the father's rule-formulation and enforcement through an instance of counterpliance.

In general, of course, rules are produced by speakers. There is nothing wrong with analyzing "rules" from the point of view of the speaker, but this will have little to do with rule-*governed* behavior. From the point of view of a speaker, we might say that a rule has been constructed when a speaker has specified a relation among events. Rules in this sense, however, may or may not govern anything.

4.3. Evidence for the Pliance-Tracking Distinction

Despite their importance, augmentals have hardly been studied within the behavior-analytic community. Pliance and tracking have been examined, however.

There are several controlling variables that may differentiate pliance from tracking (Zettle & Hayes, 1982). Pliance is under the control of socially mediated consequences for a correspondence between a rule and the behavior specified by the rule. Such social mediation is only possible when the mediator (who is usually, although not necessarily, the speaker) has access to the relevant rule and is able to monitor the behavior of the listener. Accordingly, rule-governed behavior that shows sensitivity to these two variables is likely to be an instance of pliance.

One way of assessing this sensitivity is to compare rule-following in a public context, in which both the rule and the relevant behavior are accessible to potential mediators, versus a private context, in which either the rule and/or the relevant behavior are not accessible. For normal instances of pliance, this experimental manipulation should distinguish pliance from other kinds of rule-following.

Three distinct areas of research have investigated the effects of social context on rule-governed behavior. Perhaps the most extensive body of literature in this regard has concerned compliance, obedience, and related social influence processes. Although social psychological research typically has emerged from a nonbehavioral orientation, it has been concerned directly with analyzing the impact of social context and related variables and consequently is relevant to the pliance-tracking distinction.

The remaining two areas of investigation have originated more directly within the behavior-analytic research community. One area has investigated the role of rule-governed behavior in therapeutic process, whereas the other has taken a more basic approach and has employed a human operant paradigm in undertaking a functional analysis of rule-following.

4.3.1. Social Psychological Research

The social psychological literature traditionally has differentiated among three different forms of social influence—conformity, compliance, and obedience (Baron & Byrne, 1984; Deaux & Wrightsman, 1984). Conformity involves adherence to social norms (e.g., Asch, 1956) and is not of direct relevance to this analysis because these norms need not be explicitly verbal. Compliance is regarded as behavior that occurs in response to requests and obedience as behavior that is controlled by commands of others.

Both compliance and obedience essentially are defined as formal rather than functional units of rule-governed behavior. The form of speaker behavior is the defining characteristic that differentiates compliance from obedience. The requests that control compliance typically are in the form of "softened" mands that differ in form from the commands controlling obedience. Within the present analysis, compliance and obedience should not be regarded as instances of pliance unless they show sensitivity to socially mediated consequences for rule-following.

A selective but representative review of the social psychological literature indicates that most instances of compliance and obedience appear to be examples of pliance. Milgram (1969) in his series of laboratory studies on obedience found that subjects were less likely to follow an experimenter's orders to shock another individual when the experimenter was not present or was otherwise unable to monitor the subjects' behavior. A high level of obedience, however, was established when the experimenter returned.

Counterpliance, or what has been called reactance in the social psychological literature (Brehm & Brehm, 1981), often occurs when surveillance is not possible. Pennebaker and Sanders (1976), for example, evaluated the degree to which prohibitions against graffiti writing actually increased this behavior. The greatest increase in graffiti writing occurred in response to strongly worded signs ("Do NOT write on the walls!") attributed to a powerful mediator (the chief of security). In this case, it is the effect due to the powerful mediator that showed the social quality of the rule violation.

Factors other than the lack of surveillance have been shown to be associated with counterpliance. Reactance or counterpliance has been found to occur even when surveillance is present "unless the possible rewards and punishments controlled by the influence agent are important to the target person" (Brehm & Brehm, 1981, p. 156). Stated somewhat differently, counterpliance or reactance occurs when rule-following cannot be monitored or when the contingencies surrounding rule-following are weaker than these controlling rule-breaking (e.g., Bickman & Rosenbaum, 1977; Organ, 1974). Pliance, or what has been termed *reactance suppression* is most likely to result when rule-following can be monitored and the socially mediated contingencies surrounding rule-following are strong (e.g., Dickenberger & Grabitz-Griech, 1972).

Some of compliance and obedience may be regarded as examples of tracking. Research in this area has documented the effects of "information" (following a rule because of a correspondence between the rule and actual contingencies) and expertness (following a rule because the speaker is credible) on compliance and obedience. In the present analysis, these appear to resolve into instances of tracking.

In general, social psychological research appears to support a distinction between tracking and pliance. Several of the variables posited as differentiating pliance from tracking (Zettle & Hayes, 1982) have been identified as important factors in social influence processes. Perhaps further advancement in the ability to predict and control compliance, obedience, reactance, and related phenomena can be attained if social psychologists adopt a more behavioral perspective, or alternatively, if behavior analysts take more seriously the study of social psychological phenomena.

4.3.2. Therapeutic Process Research

Clinical researchers have long been concerned with the role that "nonspecific" social influence effects may play in therapeutic process and outcome. Until recently, however, little attention has been paid to the impact of more "specific" sources of social influence in determining therapeutic process.

Most therapeutic approaches to some degree emphasize the importance of verbal interchange between client and therapist. The fact that most therapies are conducted in a social context permits a social standard for more appropriate client behavior to be established (Rosenfarb & Hayes, 1984). Clients may then show therapeutic change in part because of therapist-mediated contingencies for behavior that matches the established standard. If such a process in fact accounts for therapeutic change, interventions should only be effective when they occur in a public context. Therapeutic change under such conditions would resemble pliance. By contrast, if an intervention is equally effective in a truly private context in which clients believe that their performance cannot be monitored, therapeutic change would be seen as similar to tracking.

The existing research is consistent in indicating that at least three widely used interventions initiate therapeutic change through a process that is associated more closely with pliance than tracking. In an initial study in this area, Zettle and Hayes (1983) compared the efficacy of coping self-statements in a public versus private context. Speech-anxious college students were assigned randomly to a control group, a public coping self-statement group, or a private self-statement group. The two coping self-statement groups received the same coping self-statement and were instructed to repeat it to themselves both before and during speeches. The only difference between the two groups was that the private group was lead to believe that no one, including the experimenter, knew which self-statement he or she had received. This was accomplished by having the subjects select their statements from a container that they were told held different types of statements. In fact, all the statements in the container were identical. Results obtained on both self-report and behavioral measures showed significantly greater improvement for the public coping self-statement group over the control condition. The private group did not differ from the control.

Hayes and Wolf (1984) have found similar effects for coping self-statements in increasing pain tolerance. Only subjects in a public coping self-statement group were able to tolerate a cold-pressor task longer than those within an attention-placebo condition. Rosenfarb and Hayes (1984) have demonstrated that the same process that accounts for the effective use of coping self-statements with adults also extends to their successful application with children. In addition, the results of Rosenfarb and Hayes (1984) suggest that the effect of disinhibitory modeling also may result from specific social influence mechanisms.

Children fearful of the dark were assigned randomly to one of four treatment groups or to one of two control groups. Children in the treatment groups were exposed to either a coping self-statement or a disinhibitory model. Children in the coping self-statement group listened to a tape in which they were instructed in self-statements that previous research had shown to be effective in decreasing fear of the dark (Kanfer, Karoly, & Newman, 1975). Half of the subjects were led to believe that the experimenter did not know which tape they listened to (private context), whereas the other half were told that the experimenter also would listen to the tape (public context). Disinhibitory modeling also was presented in a private versus public context. Subjects watched a videotape of a same-gender coping model entering a dark room while saying aloud thc same self-statements used in the self-statement groups. The effects of coping self-statements and modeling were evaluated against two corresponding control groups. One control group was instructed to use sentences from a children's book as coping self-statements, whereas the other watched a videotape of another child sitting at a desk coloring. Both control conditions were presented in a public context.

Coping self-statements and modeling were found to be equally effective in increasing dark tolerance but only when presented in a public context. Children who received treatment in a public context improved an average of 50 sec in dark tolerance compared to only a 1-sec increase for the two control groups. Treatment conducted in a private context decreased dark tolerance by an average of 2 sec.

The same type of specific social influence process involved in coping self-statements and modeling also appears to account for self-reinforcement effects. The results of a series of studies on self-reinforcement procedures indicated that behavior change only occurred when parts of the procedure occur in a public context (Hayes, Rosenfarb, Wulfert, Munt, Korn, & Zettle, 1985). The most important component of self-reinforcement procedures appeared to be goal-setting. In one study, students enrolled in a program to improve their study skills get goals for a number of modules they would study and for improvement on a test of study skills. Half of the students announced their goals to other members of their group (public context), whereas the other half kept their goals private (private context). Although the two groups did not differ in their goals, the results indicate that the public context group came closer to meeting its goal for number of modules read. The public context group also showed significantly greater improvement than the private context group and a control group, which did not set goals, on a measure of study skills.

Results from a second study suggest that self-consequation does not add to the effect of public goal setting within self-reinforcement procedures. Subjects answering study questions for the Graduate Record Examination were instructed to set goals for the number of correct answers to each reading passage. Half of the subjects set their goals privately and the other half publicly. The context of goal setting was crossed with self-consequation. Half of the subjects were given a supply of edibles that they were instructed to eat in predetermined amounts upon meeting their goals. The rest of the subjects were given an equal supply of edibles that they were told could be eaten whenever they liked.

No effect was revealed for self-consequation or its interactions with the context of goal setting. However, a main effect was obtained for the context of goal setting. Subjects who set their goals in a public context showed a significantly greater increase in the number of correct answers per reading passage than those who set their goals in a private context. Also, only the public context group differed from a control group that did not set goals.

Specific social influence processes appear to account for therapeutic change in all three interventions analyzed thus far. Specifically, therapeutic change appears to occur because of social contingencies surrounding compliance with a social standard. The process has been shown to occur with both children (Rosenfarb & Hayes, 1984) and college students (Hayes *et al.*, 1985; Hayes & Wolf, 1984; Zettle & Hayes, 1983) and occurs whether the social standard is introduced explicitly by an experimenter as in coping self-statements (Hayes & Wolf, 1984; Zettle & Hayes, 1983), implicitly as in modeling (Rosenfarb & Hayes, 1984), or is established by the public expression of the subject's verbal behavior (Hayes *et al.*, 1985). The fact that therapeutic change only occurs in a public context points to a process similar to that in pliance. Such a process should not be viewed as taking anything away from the therapeutic power of coping self-statement, modeling, or self-reinforcement procedures. Rather, the important role that a public context evidently plays in therapeutic process may be maximized to produce even greater therapeutic change in these and other interventions.

4.3.3. Human Operant Research

Human operant behavior differs significantly from the behavior of other species. The effects of instructions, whether introduced by the experimenter or by subjects themselves, appear to be the major factors accounting for such discrepancies in human responding (Baron & Galizio, 1983). The insensitivity to programmed contingencies produced by instructions may be the result of at least two different effects: (1) instructions narrow the range of responding available to make contact with programmed contingencies, and (2) instructions establish additional socially mediated contingencies on responding. The first type of insensitivity may occur with tracking or pliance. The latter is a pliance effect.

A good deal of responding in the human operant situation may constitute pliance (Hayes *et al.*, 1985). Button presses moved a light through a matrix according to a 2-min MULT FR 18/DRL sec. Points worth chances on money prizes were awarded for successfully moving the light through the matrix. The effects of instructions were evaluated by systematically presenting and withdrawing them. An instruction to "Go Fast" was associated with one light and another to "Go Slow" with a different light. The presentation of instruction lights was varied within three conditions. In one condition, only the Go-Fast light was on, in a second only the Go-Slow light was on, and in a third the lights alternated each minute. Because of the multiple schedule that was in effect, the instruction light within each condition was only accurate half of the time. All subjects participated in three successive sessions of 32 minutes each.

Within each condition, half the subjects had all instruction lights turned off after the first session, whereas half stayed on throughout all three sessions.

The most important results involve comparisons between each instruction condition when it was present for either one or three sessions. Large differences obtained in Sessions 2 and 3 after the instruction lights have been withdrawn from half the subjects would suggest that responding had been controlled by socially mediated consequences for rule-following. Such a pattern of responding especially was evident for subjects who were presented with the alternating Go Fast–Go Slow instruction lights for one session. Subjects immediately showed schedule-appropriate behavior when the instruction lights, and thus the possibility of pliance, were removed. By contrast, subjects with the alternating instruction lights for three sessions generally responded in compliance with the lights across all three sessions. The behavior of these subjects showed no sensitivity to the multiple schedule and therefore may be conceptualized as pliance in response to the instruction lights.

Barrett, Deitz, Gaydos, and Quinn (1987) have shown that rule-following is significantly effected by the presence of the experimenter. This can also be interpreted as a pliance effect.

5. DANGERS AHEAD IN THE ANALYSIS OF RULE-GOVERNED BEHAVIOR

Behavior analysis is just beginning to develop a set of preparations and operating assumptions that will serve a basic analysis of human behavior on its own terms. There has been progress, but notable dangers lie ahead as well. A variety of empirical and theoretical cul-de-sacs are ready to ensnare the field.

5.1. Insensitivity

The "insensitivity" literature is misnamed. It is not that people become *insensitive* to direct experience—it is that they are relatively sensitive, under many but probably not all conditions, to control by verbal stimuli. Control by verbal stimuli is itself ultimately based on direct experience, but the experience is now remote, and it is of a special sort, resulting in stimulus control with special properties.

The experimental task is thus *not* to understand the insensitivity effect *per se*. When that is taken as the task, the literature quickly becomes trivialized. For example, papers appear that declare that people are in fact controlled by direct experience, if the direct experiences are salient enough, important enough, or held in place long enough. This may be true, but it misses the point. The value of the so-called insensitivity literature is that it provides a means of studying verbal stimuli and verbal behavior. The insensitivity preparation is a *preparation,* not an end in itself.

The effects of verbal stimuli can be overwhelmed by other variables. This is to be assumed. The field could, however, seek out such findings in order to denigrate the significance of verbal action. This is a mistake. The findings would very likely be found, but they would not thereby explain behavior that *does* involve verbal interaction.

If one is interested in verbal functions, there are times it would be useful to know how verbal relations can be overwhelmed by other events. We could examine when verbal relations become a small or nonexistent part of ongoing human action in order to understand more about these relations themselves. Generally, however, if we are interested in verbal interactions, we should titrate these other variables so that the participation of verbal events can be seen clearly. There is a regrettable tendency for behavior analysts to act as if the domination of strong, direct contingencies over other variables means that these other variables do not exist and do not need to be understood.

5.2. Object-Oriented Accounts

Several studies have shown that instructions can establish performance that appears to be contingency controlled but that is later shown to be verbally governed (e.g., Hayes, Brownstein, Haas, & Greenway, 1986; Shimoff, Matthews, & Catania, 1986; see also Catania, Shimoff, & Matthews, Chapter 4 in the present volume). The definition of verbal stimuli developed in the previous chapter means that even direct contingencies can function as verbal stimuli for humans. This presents a major experimental difficulty is disentangling the nature of verbal control. When direct contingencies dominate over rules, we must still assess the processes through which that domination occurred. It cannot be assumed that "direct contingencies," as an experimental procedure used by the experimenter, function in the same ways or through the same processes for all organisms to which they are applied. If a human, for example, can state the relation between contingent events, these events may function differently than when an organism cannot state the relation between these events.

The experimental and analytic problems this presents to psychology are great, but they cannot be avoided, except by fiat. The silent dog method may be of help. Other methods may appear. Despite its difficulty, the issue cannot be ignored. An experimental manipulation is of interest to psychologists only because of the way in which it impacts on the behaving organism. It is the behavior of the organism that we are studying. To lose that perspective is to confuse objects identified by the scientist with functional relations involving the behavior of the organism studied by the scientist. Thus, for example, it is a mistake to assume that "contingencies" are *things* that impact upon behavior without an analysis of these events from the point of view of the subject. When such an analysis is attempted, the possible participation of verbal events in "contingency control" itself cannot be avoided.

6. FUTURE DIRECTIONS

The literature on rule-governance is at a key stage in its development. Books such as the present volume are beginning to appear. A number of laboratories are actively involved in this research. We would like briefly to suggest several areas of growth for the literature.

First, the rule-governed behavior literature should make better contact with the literature on equivalence, exclusion, and related phenomena. The literature in cognitive psychology has large research areas directed toward an analysis of categories and concepts. The behavioral and cognitive literatures on classes and categories provide the hope of a basic analysis of the nature of rules—an analysis grounded in the nature of verbal stimulation itself. This would also be of use methodologically. Experimental languages could be constructed, for example, in which the direct histories relevant to the classes established are completely known. We would then be in a position to see if rules constructed in these languages operate in particular ways. For example, do rules reduce behavioral variability? Do long-term consequences operate differently when they are part of experimental rules?

Second, we need to develop methods of assessing rule understanding as we have discussed.

Third, we need more experimental attempts to assess and manipulate self-rules. This is a hoary area, but it simply cannot be avoided.

Fourth, we need much better information about the kinds of rules that enhance and restrict sensitivity to other events. Are strategic rules different than prescriptive rules? Are specific rules different than general rules? If so, why? And so on.

Fifth, the applied implications of this work need to be worked out (see Chapters 9 and 10 in the present volume). This is especially important for behavior analysts interested in this area because it is the only thing that ensures an environmentally oriented analysis. Without a close connection to utility, behavior analysis loses its philosophical character (Hayes & Brownstein, 1986; Hayes, Hayes, & Reese, 1988).

7. CONCLUSION

Behavior analysts only fairly recently have attempted to investigate verbal and rule-governed behaviors for their own sake. A human operant paradigm appears to provide an especially attractive preparation against which to evaluate the effects of verbal events. This work is essentially opening up the animal learning tradition to the problems of the human learning area. Both traditions have things to learn from each other.

8. REFERENCES

Asch, S. E. (1956). Studies of independence and conformity: I. A minority of one against a unanimous majority. *Psychological Monographs, 70*(9, Whole No. 416).

Ayllon, T., & Azrin, N. H. (1964). Reinforcement and instructions with mental patients. *Journal of the Experimental Analysis of Behavior, 6,* 327–331.

Baron, R. A., & Byrne, D. (1984). *Social psychology: Understanding human interaction* (4th ed.). Boston: Allyn & Bacon.

Barrett, D. M., Deitz, S. M. Gaydos, G. R., & Quinn, P. C. (1987). The effects of programmed contingencies and social conditions on response stereotypy with human subjects. *Psychological Record, 37,* 489–505.

Bentall, R. P., Lowe, C. F., & Beasty, A. (1985). The role of verbal behavior in human learning. II: Developmental differences. *Journal of the Experimental Analysis of Behavior, 43,* 165–181.

Bentall, R. P., & Lowe, C. F. (1987). The role of verbal behavior in human learning. III: Instructional effects in children. *Journal of the Experimental Analysis of Behavior, 47,* 177–190.

Bickman, L., & Rosenbaum, D. P. (1977). Crime reporting as a function of bystander encouragement, surveillance, and credibility. *Journal of Personality and Social Psychology, 35,* 577–586.

Brehm, S. S., & Brehm, J. W. (1981). *Psychological reactance: A theory of freedom and control.* New York: Academic Press.

Brewer, W. F. (1974). There is no convincing evidence for operant or classical conditioning in adult humans. In W. B. Weimer & D. S. Palermo (Eds.), *Cognition and the symbolic processes.* (pp. 1–42) Hillsdale, NJ: Erlbaum.

Catania, A. C., Matthews, B. A., & Shimoff, E. (1982). Instructed versus shaped human verbal behavior: Interactions with nonverbal responding. *Journal of the Experimental Analysis of Behavior, 38,* 233–248.

Deaux, K., & Wrightsman, L. S. (1984). *Social psychology in the 80s* (4th ed.). Monterey, CA: Brooks/Cole.

Dickenberger, D., & Grabitz-Griech, G. (1972). Restrictive conditions for the occurrence of psychological reactance: Interpersonal attraction, need for social approval, and a delay factor. *European Journal of Social Psychology, 2,* 177–198.

Ericsson, K. A., & Simon, H. A. (1984). *Protocol analysis: Verbal reports as data.* Cambridge, MA: MIT Press.

Galizio, M. (1979). Contingency-shaped and rule-governed behavior: Instructional control of human loss avoidance. *Journal of the Experimental Analysis of Behavior, 31,* 53–70.

Hayes, S. C. (1986). The case of the silent dog: Verbal reports and the analysis of rules. A review of K. Anders Ericsson and Herbert A. Simon, "Protocol analysis: Verbal reports as data." *Journal of the Experimental Analysis of Behavior, 45,* 351–363.

Hayes, S. C. (1987). Upward and downward continuity: It's time to change our strategic assumptions. *Behavior Analysis, 22,* 3–6.

Hayes, S. C., & Brownstein, A. J. (1986). Metalism, behavior-behavior relations and a behavior analytic view of the purposes of science. *The Behavior Analyst, 9,* 175–190.

Hayes, S. C., Brownstein, A. J., Haas, J. R., & Greenway, D. E. (1986). Instructions, multiple schedules, and extinction: Distinguishing rule-governed from schedule controlled behavior. *Journal of the Experimental Analysis of Behavior, 46,* 137–147.

Hayes, S. C., Brownstein, A. J., Zettle, R. D., Rosenfarb, I., & Korn, Z. (1986). Rule-governed behavior and sensitivity to changing consequences of responding. *Journal of the Experimental Analysis of Behavior, 45,* 237–256.

Hayes, S. C., Hayes, L. J., & Reese, H. W. (1988). Finding the philosophical core: A review of Stephen C. Pepper's *World Hypotheses. Journal of the Experimental Analysis of Behavior, 50,* 97–111.

Hayes, S. C., Rosenfarb, I., Wulfert, E., Munt, E., Zettle, R. D., & Korn, Z. (1985). Self-reinforcement effects: An artifact of social standard setting? *Journal of Applied Behavior Analysis, 18,* 201–214.

Hayes, S. C., & Wolf, M. R. (1984). Cues, consequences, and therapeutic talk: Effect of social context and coping statements on pain. *Behavior Research and Therapy, 22,* 385–392.

Holland, J. G. (1958). Counting by humans on a fixed-ratio schedule of reinforcement. *Journal of the Experimental Analysis of Behavior, 1,* 179–181.

Hutchinson, R. R., & Azrin, N. H. (1961). Conditioning of mental-hospital patients to fixed-ratio schedules of reinforcement. *Journal of Consulting and Clinical Psychology.*

Kanfer, F. H., Karoly, P., Newman, H. (1975). Reduction of children's fear of the dark by competence-related and situational threat-related verbal cues. *Journal of Consulting and Clinical Psychology, 43,* 251–258.

Kaufman, A., Baron, A., & Kopp, R. E. (1966). Some effects of instructions on human operant behavior. *Psychonomic Monograph Supplements, 1,* 243–250.

Laties, V. G., & Weiss, B. (1963). Effects of concurrent task on fixed-interval responding in humans, *Journal of the Experimental Analysis of Behavior, 6,* 431–436.

Leander, J. D., Lippman, L. G., & Meyer, M. M. (1968). Fixed interval performance as related to subjects' verbalizations of the reinforcement contingency. *The Psychological Record, 18,* 469–474.

Lippman, L. G., & Meyer, M. M. (1967). Fixed interval performance as related to instructions and to subjects' verbalization of the contingency. *Psychonomic Science, 8,* 135–136.

Lowe, C. F. (1979). Determinants of human operant behavior. In M. D. Zeiler & P. Harzem (Eds.), *Advances in analysis of behavior: Vol. 1. Reinforcement and the organization of behavior* (pp. 159–192). Chichester, England: Wiley.

Lowe, C. F., Harzem, P. & Bagshaw, M. (1978). Species differences in temporal control of behavior. II: Human performance. *Journal of the Experimental Analysis of Behavior, 29,* 351–361.

Lowe, C. F., Harzem, P., & Hughes, S. (1978). Determinants of operant behavior in humans: Some differences from animals.

Lowe, C. F., Beasty, A., & Bentall, R. P. (1983). The role of verbal behavior in human learning: Infant performance on Fixed Interval schedules. *Journal of the Experimental Analysis of Behavior, 39,* 157–164.

Matthews, B. A., Shimoff, E., Catania, A. C., & Sagvolden, T. (1977). Uninstructed human responding: Sensitivity to Ratio and Interval Contingencies. *Journal of the Experimental Analysis of Behavior, 27,* 453–467.

Michael, J. (1982). Distinguishing between discriminative and motivational functions of stimuli. *Journal of the Experimental Analysis of Behavior, 37,* 149–155.

Milgram, S. (1969). *Obedience to authority: An experimental view.* New York: Harper & Row.

Organ, D. (1974). Social exchange and psychological reactance in a simulated superior-subordinate relationship. *Organizational Behavior and Human Performance, 12,* 132–142.

Rosenfarb, I., & Hayes, S. C. (1984). Social standard setting: The Achilles' heel of informational accounts of therapeutic change. *Behavior Therapy, 15,* 515–528.

Schoenfeld, W. N., & Cumming, W. W. (1963). Behavior and perception. In S. Koch (Ed.), *Psychology: A study of a science* (Vol. 5; pp. 213–252). New York: McGraw-Hill.

Shimoff, E., Catania, A. C., & Matthews, B. A. (1981). Uninstructed human responding: Sensitivity of low rate performance to schedule contingencies. *Journal of the Experimental Analysis of Behavior, 36,* 207–220.

Shimoff, E., Matthews, B. A., & Catania, A. C. (1986). Human operant performance: Sensitivity and pseudosensitivity to contingencies. *Journal of the Experimental Analysis of Behavior, 46,* 149–157.

Weiner, H. (1964). Conditioning history and human fixed-interval performance. *Journal of the Experimental Analysis of Behavior, 7,* 383–385.

Weiner, H. (1965). Conditioning history and maladaptive human operant behavior. *Psychological Reports, 17,* 935–942.

Weiner, H. (1969). Human behavioral persistence. *Psychological Record, 20,* 445–456.

Weiner, H. (1970). Instructional control of human operant responding during extinction following fixed ratio conditioning. *Journal of the Experimental Analysis of Behavior, 13,* 391–394.

Weiner, H. (1983). Some thoughts on discrepant human-animal performances under schedules of reinforcement. *Psychological Record, 33,* 521–532.

Zettle, R. D., & Hayes, S. C. (1982). Rule-governed behavior: A potential theoretical framework for cognitive-behavior therapy. In P. C. Kendall (Ed.), *Advances in Cognitive-Behavioral Research and Therapy* (Vol. 1; pp. 73–118). New York: Academic.

Zettle, R. D., & Hayes, S. C. (1983). Effect of social context on the impact of coping self-statements. *Psychological Reports, 52,* 391–401.

CHAPTER 7

Correlated Hypothesizing and the Distinction between Contingency-Shaped and Rule-Governed Behavior

PHILIP N. HINELINE and BARBARA A. WANCHISEN

1. INTRODUCTION

Within our culture, references to consciousness, rational thought, and the use of knowledge are taken as straightforward descriptions of basic human functioning. Within psychology, there has been an enduring controversy over whether such terms qualify as basic explanatory terms, or whether they are misleading intrusions from ordinary language. On one hand, cognitivists have conformed to common usage, encorporating "knowledge," "awareness," and other terms of mentalistic origin into the groundwork of their theories. These concepts are said to *explain* why humans (and sometimes animals as well) behave as they do. On the other hand, behavioral traditions have run counter to these patterns. Many behaviorists have asserted that terms of mentalistic origin are inappropriate to a scientific account.

A different behavioral approach, and the one advocated in this chapter, asserts that a network of basic behavioral principles can be used to understand both the circumstances under which mentalistic terms are used and the phenomena that are identified with them. Thus a behavioral account can address what is involved when people speak of knowing and of being aware (e.g., Hineline, 1983; Skinner, 1963), but only after a network of basic principles has been

PHILIP N. HINELINE • Department of Psychology, Temple University, Philadelphia, Pennsylvania 19122. BARBARA A. WANCHISEN • Department of Psychology, Baldwin-Wallace College, Berea, Ohio 44017.

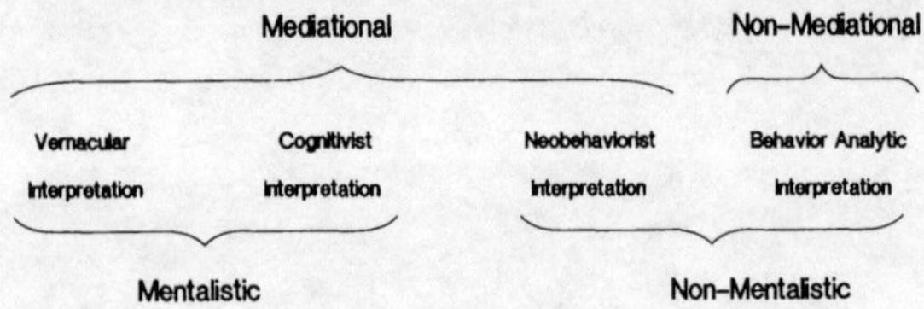

Figure 1. Similarities and differences between four types of interpretation, with respect to two characteristics of theory: mediational versus nonmediational, and mentalistic versus nonmentalistic.

elaborated. We also attempt to show that disagreements between behaviorist and cognitivist traditions can be constructively engaged by identifying similarity between some key features in each type of interpretation. We hope that such comparisons might encourage more cross-talk between the two camps and lead to fruitful experimentation.

2. NONMEDIATIONAL VERSUS MEDIATIONAL, RATHER THAN BEHAVIORIST VERSUS COGNITIVIST

Notions of consciousness and rational thought are encorporated into ordinary language, perhaps because they seem accessible to direct scrutiny. Knowledge is said to consist of information; although it extends beyond immediate awareness, it is considered nonmysterious, a substrate for thought, which may or may not lead to action. Unconscious thought and action are acknowledged, but these tend to be viewed as rather more mysterious. In addition, the dualism of mental causes for physical actions is so engrained in our ways of speaking, that as native speakers we do not intuitively notice it as a problem for explanation. Another characteristic of ordinary-language interpretation also tends to go unnoticed: invoking mediational processes (e.g., thinking, knowing) as essential to explanations of behavior. As schematized in Figure 1, distinctions between mentalistic versus nonmentalistic and of mediational versus nonmediational accounts serve to clarify some general relationships between the interpretive traditions that we shall be discussing. Briefly, this figure shows that cognitivist accounts are both mediational and mentalistic. Behaviorist accounts are always nonmentalistic, but neobehaviorists ascribe to a mediational view as well. The behavior-analytic approach differs more from the cognitivist, in that it is both nonmediational and nonmentalistic. We shall begin with brief characterizations of these positions before moving on to more detailed distinctions.

2.1. Preliminary Sketch of Behaviorist Positions

A traditional behavioristic stance is to begin by rejecting all mentalistic terms as fictions that are not amenable to scientific study. This is a tempting way to begin, for the problem of explaining how mental events can affect physical actions is a classic embarrassment of dualism that points to mentalism as an Achilles' heel of ordinary-language interpretation. And thus, behaviorists are well known for attacking commonsense appeals to consciousness and rationality. Some behaviorists have substantially retained the pattern of ordinary-language interpretation while rejecting its mentalism, by replacing mentalistic constructs with hypothetical but presumably physical constructs whose scientific validity is anchored in operational definitions. This approach has sometimes been called neobehaviorism (e.g., see Kendler & Spence, 1971). In its adherence to those mediational constructs, nonbehavioristic theory has sometimes been blended with cognitive theorizing, as illustrated by Dember's (1974) history of changes in motivational theory.

A characteristic feature of mediational theory, whether cognitivist or neobehaviorist, is that overt behavior is treated mainly as an index of underlying structures and processes posited by the theory. Those underlying entities are given special explanatory status, as accounting for *how* behavior comes to occur. The behavior, then, is of interest as manifestation of brain functions, or as "ambassador of the mind." Questions of what behavior will occur, and when, are left to be derived from the "how account."

Like other behaviorists, B. F. Skinner often has made the rejection of mentalism a prominent part of his position (e.g., Skinner, 1938, 1953, 1974, 1977). However, more than four decades ago, he parted company with the type of behaviorist view sketched before, rejecting the neobehaviorist form of operationism (which he labeled *methodological behaviorism)* in favor of a nonmediational, environment-based account (Skinner, 1945, 1950). This established an experimental and interpretive tradition that has come to be known as behavior analysis. At the same time, Skinner explicitly *included* private events in his behavioristic account. That inclusion became a defining, but not widely understood, feature of "radical behaviorism" as a philosophical position. Private events are those directly available to the organism whose behavior is at issue but not to others who are interpreting the behavior. Among such events are those within the skin. In behavior-analytic interpretation, private events are not presumed to be different in kind from environmental events and overt behavior (Schnaitter, 1978). They are distinguished by their inaccessibility to an observer or interpreter of behavior, not by any special causal role (Skinner, 1945, 1963).

Behavior-analytic theory, then, involves the efficient characterization of environmental events as they interact with behavior and of behavior as it interacts with the environment. Experimental operations and their results directly provide the very warp and weft of a theory that directly describes the interplay between behavior and environment (Hineline, 1984). Psychological process is said to consist directly *in* and of this interplay, extended over time; thus the concepts of behavior analysis comprise a nonmediational theory. This science of behavior (as distinct from the less specific phrase, *behavioral science)* keeps as primary the questions of what an organism will do, and when; questions of *how* are treated as secondary, to be addressed through elaboration of the *what* and *when* relationships of behavior–environment interaction.

Behavior-analytic theory construes events within the organism as activities, rather than as structures or as prebehavioral processes; these are consistent with Skinner's avowed type of theory because they do not refer to "events taking place somewhere else, at some other level of observation, described in different terms, and measured, if at all, in different dimensions" (Skinner, 1950, p. 193). Those activities are proposed to be real events and not mere summarizing, intervening variables (cf. MacCorquodale & Meehl, 1948). For example, the behavior-analytic view accepts that a person might covertly count and that this counting may affect other aspects of the person's behavior. However, whether the counting is covert or overt, whether it involves vocal musculature or only neural activity, the behavior-analytic interpretation gives it no *special* causal status with respect to other behavior. Covert counting affects our other actions just as counting on fingers or computing on a desk calculator might affect our other actions. The organization of covert activity is less affected by environmental constraint: For example, one can imagine treading a set of stairs in random sequence but would be hard put to achieve the corresponding overt behavior. Other properties of covert activity also may differ from overt versions, as when covert computing results in errors that differ from those of overt computing. Nevertheless, the relationships of covert to overt behavior are similar to those of other coordinated activities. They may involve the organization of action, in the same way that placing one foot down affects lifting of the other. This type of interactive relationship is not a causal one.

We shall be discussing rules as they appear in a behavior-analytic account. They are construed as verbal statements whose discriminanda (that is, the events that occasion them) are themselves behavior-consequence relations. Thus in ordinary language, we might speak of rules as describing relationships between actions and consequences. The stating of rules is functionally similar to other discriminative repertoires such as the naming of objects—although, to be sure, rule-stating is more complex than object naming because the discriminanda are relational and therefore more complex. Rule-following involves the rules themselves as discriminanda. A key problem is that of distinguishing the consequences of following a rule from the consequences in the relationship described by the rule (technically, that are discriminative for stating of the rule). In some cases, these consequences are one and the same; In other cases they are not. However, in all cases, rule-governed behavior is distinguished from behavior that is directly shaped and/or maintained by nonverbal contingencies. We shall present these distinctions and the resulting functional categories in greater detail later. For now, the key point is that rules and rule-following come late in the behavioral account and are understood through extensive elaboration of more basic principles.

2.2. Preliminary Sketch of Cognitivist Positions

Although it conforms more closely to ordinary language, the "new mentalism" of cognitivist psychology[1] does not accept all vernacular assumptions. It may finesse the dualistic conundrum of mentally initiated action by positing an identity between mental function and brain function, or by positing a formalism in which structural relationships are identified, with presumed physical bases, but not defined in terms of what they are made of (Putnam, 1973). Cognitivist accounts are inherently mediational, for they assume that explanation of behavior requires description of processes that *underlie* the behavior. Corollary to this, cognitivist accounts typically seem to assume that causation requires contiguously connected events (Lacey & Rachlin, 1978; Morris, Higgins, & Bickel, 1982). We shall describe a specific example of this assumption being the basis for a theorist adopting a cognitivist account in favor of a behavioral one.

In a cognitivist account, the organism is characterized as processing impinging events, evaluating them and deciding upon courses of action. Information-processing models, which have figured prominently in this theorizing, are organized around "working memory" or "short-term memory," which becomes roughly equated with conscious functioning (e.g., see Norman, 1969). This conscious functioning is given a fundamental, decisively controlling role in reactions to stimuli, actions upon knowledge, and in the initiating and monitoring of overt behavior. "Knowledge" is sometimes characterized in terms of internal representations, perhaps subdivided into categories such as procedural versus declarative and episodic versus semantic. Metaknowledge (knowing about knowing) is sometimes invoked as part of conscious functioning, in the selection of alternative strategies. In other cognitivist accounts, knowledge is left more vague, as "information," or even undefined and thus very close to the vernacular notion (e.g., Weisberg, 1980).

Most cognitivist accounts appeal to rules as involved in virtually all levels of functioning. Indeed, rules sometimes are identified as basic units of analysis in cognitivist theory (e.g., Levine, 1966; Siegler, 1983). Sometimes the rules appear to be construed as operative principles in the processes that underlie the organism's most basic functioning—analogous to the machine-language instructions of a computer. More commonly, cognitive theorists treat the rules as entities *used* by the organism in processing input and initiating action. It should

[1]The term *cognitivist* is used here to denote a particular class of interpretations. *Cognitive* will denote a class of phenomena that includes thinking, remembering, problem solving, and the like. The reason for the distinction is that a type of phenomenon need not dictate the specific characteristics of an interpretation of the phenomenon (Salzinger, 1986). Thus there are behaviorist interpretations of cognitive phenomena, just as there are cognitivist interpretations of behavioral phenomena.

be noted that whereas those rules are taken as forming a kind of logic, cognitivist theory does not construe the logic of ordinary human thinking as veridical with formal logic of mathematics or philosophy; rule-use does not imply a strict rationalism.

Recently, vernacular assumptions regarding the degree to which one can be aware of one's own functioning have come into question from several quarters, including social psychology (Nisbett & Wilson, 1977) and the study of problem solving in cognitive psychology (Weisberg, 1980). In addition, some current information-processing models allow for unconscious processing, either via specialized innate cognitive modules (e.g., involved in handling perceptual or grammatical relationships) or via the automaticity of well-learned skills (Kiehlstrom, 1987). However, some have continued to argue for special roles of awareness (e.g., Ericsson & Simon, 1980), and conscious processes are said to be especially involved in the initial acquisition of skills and in the voluntary control of action. Thus cognitivist approaches continue to take rules, knowledge, and consciousness as basic to a person's functioning even if the person is unable to state a rule that accurately characterizes his or her performance. The accurately descriptive rule still may be posited as the operative rule (e.g., see Siegler, 1983). Other aspects of current appeals to consciousness in psychological interpretation are well illustrated in an article by Libet (1985) and its related commentary.

3. SELECTED CONCEPTS FROM BEHAVIOR-ANALYTIC THEORY

In contrast, behavior analysis provides an account of awareness and various forms of knowing, but this approach posits action *without* awareness as more basic—not *based upon* knowledge, but rather, part of the *basis for* the relations that are called *knowing*. The origins of awareness and of logical action are also addressed, in terms of the same principles that apply to more basic functioning. Rules are included in this account, and rule-governed behavior has been a prominent focus of behavior-analytic research. But unlike the rules posited by cognitivist theory, the rules posited by behavior-analytic theory are explicit verbal statements that the person is able to state or are explicitly provided by someone else and that interact with other behavior. They are not construed as principles that are said to underlie verbal statements or other behavior.

We shall proceed by sketching an exposition of behavior-analytic concepts. To clarify fundamental and often misunderstood differences between behavior-analytic and other (including other behavioral) interpretations, we shall include some very basic concepts, as well as elaborations that address domains that are also addressed by cognitivist accounts. As already indicated, we introduce behavior-analytic concepts as predicated upon events distributed over time;

the events of concern are those of behavior and of its surrounding environmental context. Also, we give special emphasis to features that provide informative comparisons with cognitivist theory.

3.1. Open-Loop Relations

Historically, the type of environment–behavior relationship that was clarified first was the reflex relation, whereby discrete responses occur in systematic relation to events that proceed independently of those responses. The fact that the responses do not, in turn, affect the occurrence of the environmental events, identifies this as an *open-loop relation.* In examining such a relationship, an experimenter presents a stimulus from time to time and assesses whether a response reliably occurs only at those times. The stimulus intensity is then varied, and one assesses whether there are corresponding changes in latency and magnitude of the resulting responses (The astute reader may discern closed-loop relations in this experimentation, but they apply to the experimenter's behavior rather than to that of the subject.) Skinner's initial major theoretical contribution was to identify the reflex as a functional environment–behavior relation rather than a structural connection. Skinner also noted that identical stimuli presented successively to the same organism may result in somewhat different responses and that two differing stimuli may each be followed by apparently identical responses. He interpreted these facts as revealing the fundamental nature of the reflex to be a correlation between classes of stimuli and responses, rather than a bundle of stimulus–response connections (Skinner, 1931, 1935). Two far-reaching implications arise from this characterization of the simplest of behavioral relationships. First, the stimulus and response that constitute an observed reflex are not understood through contiguous connection but rather through functional relation. Functional relations allow for causation that spans gaps in time. Second, variability and novelty of behavior are incorporated into the account from its very beginning.

In more complex open-loop relations, environmental events that occur independently of behavior may occur in inexorable sequences rather than as the isolated occurrences that elicit reflex responses. If these sequences systematically affect behavior and especially if that behavior is sensitive to sequential characteristics such as frequency or periodicity, we speak of schedule-induced behavior. It is called adjunctive behavior (Falk, 1966) when the inducing sequence is a by-product of a different environment–behavior relation such as a schedule of reinforcement (a closed-loop relation, which we shall touch upon later). Orderly relations that obtain between characteristics of scheduled sequences of response-independent stimuli and the resulting patterns of behavior are bases for identifying the effective characteristics of the inducing sequence. The resulting behavior-analytic account offers a distinctive interpretation of schedule-induced behavior by focusing upon its functional characteristics without appeal to mediating structures or mechanisms (Hineline, 1986).

Pavlovian conditioning also involves open-loop relationships, for the pairing of, or the contingent relations between stimuli are not affected by occurrence of conditioned or unconditioned responses. Some of the more complex Pavlovian phenomena—blocking, overshadowing, and the like, have been studied mainly in terms of organism-based theory. However, two of the major experimental preparations used for that work—the conditioned suppression procedure (Estes & Skinner, 1941) and the autoshaping procedure (Brown & Jenkins, 1968)—were initially developed within behavior analysis, and the phenomena are readily interpreted within environment-based theory.

Thus reflexive behavior, both conditioned and unconditioned, and schedule-induced or adjunctive behavior constitute the domain of "open-loop" behavior–environment relations where environmental events affect behavior but the behavior does not directly in turn affect the environmental events. These relationships will not be of primary concern in the present account, but they are included here to illustrate how, in even the simplest cases, a conception in terms of functional relations is freed from adherance to connectionistic, contiguous causation, and thus from any necessity of interpreting behavior in terms of mediating, underlying structures—which of course are axiomatic to a cognitivist account. Inclusion of these open-loop behavioral relations also makes the point that behavior analysis, although sometimes characterized as *operant psychology,* is not confined to operant behavior.

3.2. Closed-Loop Relations

The second domain has been more prominent in behavior-analytic accounts. It concerns operant behavior, which is behavior interpreted primarily in relation to its consequences, with antecedent or accompanying events playing supporting, "occasioning," or modulating roles. Its interplay with environmental events involves a distinctive, interactive causal mode characterized as selection by consequences (Skinner, 1981), whereby behavior and its environmental consequences constitute closed-loop relations. The entity that gets selected is quicksilverish: It is never present all at once; although it is patterned, it is *pattern in activity* rather than *structure in stuff.* This core concept of behavior analysis has a subtlety and abstractness that often goes unrecognized. The operant (or more precisely, the operant class) is impalpable through its dispersion. One can look right through a rate of occurrence that is before one's eyes. In contrast, inferred mental events of cognitivist theory can seem to be localized sources of action (thus seeming to preserve contiguous causation), even though they, too, are impalpable, but for a different reason: In principle as well as in fact, they never are directly observed or measured.

The operant can be directly measured, but it concerns bits of history arrayed over time and, to a lesser degree, place. These are not thinglike bits, but rather, verblike occurrences distinguished in streams of activity. Except for this feature, and for its time scale, the concept of the operant class resembles the more familiar concept of *species,* where each individual organism is an historical fact or event of time and place. To constitute a species, the events (organisms) must be real—there is no species of unicorns—and the species is their aggregate. But the whole species, as a piece of the world's history, cannot be collected in one place at one time. Characteristics of the aggregate change over time; indeed, variation within the aggregate is crucial to its evolution, for it evolves through selection of variants. The events that comprise an operant also are real, but they are "pure activity," be they small-scale, as in fine muscular adjustments or firing rates of neurons (Black, 1971; Rosenfeld, Rudell, & Fox, 1969; Shinkman, Bruce, & Pfingst, 1974), or be they intermediate scale, as in opening doors or solving problems; or be they large-scale, as in running marathons or building houses.[2] Variation is an essential characteristic of operants, for like species, operants evolve through selection; *degree* of variability is even a selectable characteristic (Neuringer, 1986). Selection of verblike entities has also been characterized by Dawkins (1981), as occurring with a wide degree of generality, in "survival of the stable."

To identify a particular operant class, one specifies its effects on a set of environmental events—that is, its consequences. As pointed out by Millenson and Leslie (1979), this specification takes either of two forms, the "functionally-defined operant, . . . consisting of all the behaviors that could effect a particular environmental change" or the "topographically-defined operant . . . consisting of movements of the organism that fall within certain physical limits" (p. 77). These two forms can be discerned in descriptions of experimental procedures: For example, in the first case, any response that interrupts light reaching a photocell may produce the specified consequence; in the second case, a particular range of leg movements may produce the consequence. Outside the laboratory, the first case is exemplified by the range of movements that can open a door, and the second is exemplified by the range of movements that a dance teacher accepts as pirouettes. As Millenson and Leslie point out, these two types of specification are not logically independent: A functionally defined operant can, in principle, be translated into topographic terms, because there is a limit to the range of movements that an organism can make that have a specified effect on the environment. Conversely, the measurement of topography can itself constitute a consequent set of environmental events.

Catania (1973) offers a somewhat different distinction that will be crucial

[2]The varying scale of selected events is an issue of discussion in biology, in much the same way that it is an issue within behavior analysis. For relevant discussions, see Dawkins (1982), Smith (1986), and Sober (1984).

to the present discussion: In his terms, both of the previous designations come under the label of *descriptive operants,* as distinguished from *functional operants.*[3] In Catania's terms, a functional operant is a *product of interaction* between a descriptive operant and the environmental events that it affects:

> In . . . a descriptive usage ordinarily found in the methodological sections of experimental reports, the response class is specified in terms of its measured physical properties; for example, a rat's lever-press might qualify as a response in the class only if its force exceeds some minimum value. In the second, a functional usage ordinarily found in the theoretical discussion of experimental findings, the response class is not regarded as an operant class unless its modifiability by response consequences has been demonstrated by experimental data; the lever press typically satisfies this criterion, but would not if the experimenter chose some minimum force that the rat was incapable of exerting. In other words, the first class is the class of responses for which consequences are arranged; the second class is the class of responses generated when consequences are arranged for responses in the first class. The concept of the operant grows out of the relation between these two classes. (pp. 104–105)

Particular operants emerge through selection by consequences, described as reinforcement, if there are increases in the class of behavior producing the consequence. If the consequence results in decreases in the class of behavior, the process is called punishment instead of reinforcement.

Clear illustrations of these relations are provided by operant classes whose descriptive definitions include the time between responses. A classic version is specified in "differential reinforcement of low rate" (DRL), whereby if two occurrences of a specified response are separated by at least *t* seconds, the second occurrence will produce the specified consequence. An example is shown in Figure 2, showing data reported by Richardson and Clark (1976), where in part *A* we see the effects of delivering food only if a pigeon's key-pecks are separated by at least 10 seconds, and in part *B* we see the effects of delivering food only if the same pigeon's key-pecks are separated by at least 20 seconds. Note that although in each condition the modal interresponse time was near the minimum duration that could produce food, interresponse times frequently occurred that were below the range that could produce food. Thus, the temporal distributions of responses varied systematically with the reinforcement contingency (that is, with the variations in *t*), and these distributions included many responses *outside* the categories that could produce the specified consequence. These distributions, in conjunction with the range of topographies that sufficed as key-pecks, constituted functional operants, and in each case the functional operant included behavior that was not part of the descriptive operant.

[3]In this context, Millenson and Leslie, and Catania are using the term *functional* in somewhat different ways, each with ample precedent. Millenson and Leslie's usage derives from biological traditions, whereby one might speak of the function of a behavior pattern, such as chewing, or of an anatomical structure, such as the mandible, addressing its role in the organism's viability. Catania's usage derives from mathematical traditions; functional relations are quantitative relationships between independent and dependent variables.

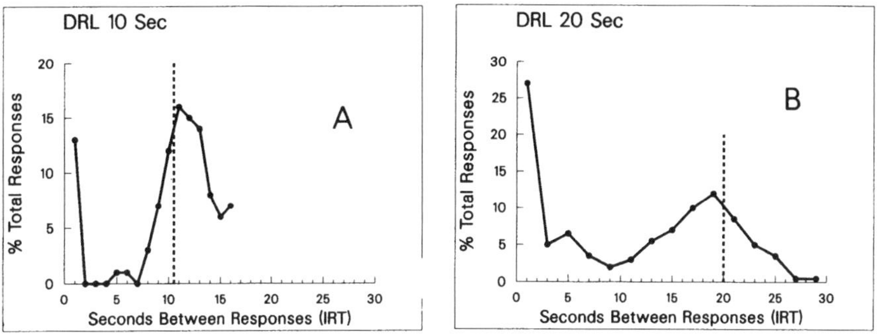

Figure 2. Relative frequencies of interresponse times (pigeons' key pecks) on two schedules that arranged differential reinforcement of low rates (DRL). The left panel shows results when responses separated by at least 10 seconds produced food; the right panel shows results when responses separated by at least 20 seconds produced food. Thus all responses represented to the right of the vertical, dashed lines were reinforced. Each class interval is one-tenth of the schedule value, but the two panels are plotted with identical absolute abscissa scales. (Adapted from Richardson & Clark, 1976; we wish to thank Thomas A. Tatham for preparing these computer-driven plots.)

The relations that constitute an operant also involve a third class of events, called discriminative stimuli, which are said to "occasion" the behavior. Once again, in Catania's (1973) terms, there is a descriptive version and a functional version. Descriptively, the discriminative stimuli for a given operant are events delineating the situation in which the specified behavior produces the specified consequence. When the specified class of behavior has produced the specified class of consequences only within a particular environmental situation, one can assess whether the presence versus absence of that situation affects the occurrence of that behavior. If it does, then one might also experiment further and verify that this is an "occasioning effect," dependent upon the behavior-consequent relation within that situation. This verifies the discriminative property that makes the operant a three-term relation (Skinner, 1938).

But to fully delineate the *functional* operant as a discriminative relation, one must go beyond the mere presentation and removal of the discriminative events; one must also vary them along their various dimensions. Doing this, one is likely to find that stimuli other than the ones previously accompanying the behavior and its consequences also affect the occurrence of the behavior. This result is called generalization. Note that in a behavior-analytic account, behaving similarly in the presence of differing stimuli *is* generalization; generalization is not construed as some underlying connective process.[4] It is also

[4]Similarly, behaving differently with respect to differing stimuli *is* discrimination; discrimination is not construed as separate from the differential behavior. Even if one were to discover differential activity of neurons that reliably preceded or accompanied the overt differential act, that activity, as discrimination, would have no privileged status as compared to the overt act, for both would be comparable behavior–environment relations with similar behavior–environment origins.

customary to assess the degree of behavioral change as a function of degree of stimulus change; the resulting graphical plots are known as generalization gradients. A generalization gradient, then, portrays differences between the descriptive version of a discriminative operant from the corresponding functional version. In practice, completely delineating several orthogonal generalization gradients for a given operant would be an arduous business; however, a rough outline of the range of stimuli included in the discriminative dimension of an operant can be sketched through the presentations and removals of a variety of stimuli, while tracking correlated changes in behavior.

3.3. Paths Not Taken Here

At this point in our exposition, these concepts could be elaborated in any of several directions. (1) A traditional next step would be to systematically address the question, "What if the consequence does not always follow the specified behavior?" and illustrate the development of response patterns over time as behavior interacts with schedules of intermittent reinforcement. To minimize technical detail, we are using only two schedules, DRL (see Figure 2) and Fixed-Interval in our discussions because these two suffice for addressing the issues of concern here. (2) A step in a different direction would illustrate the combining of individual operants into more complex, interrelated networks called repertoires. (3) A third elaboration is to address the traditional domain of "concept formation," which entails the simultaneous development of generalizations within categories and discriminations between categories of discriminative stimuli. This would illustrate another source of novel forms of operant behavior—a point that is relevant here because advocates of the cognitivist approach have asserted that rule-use must be invoked to account for such novelty. (4) A fourth direction concerns processes occurring simultaneously on several scales of analysis—one operant relation may be embedded within a more extended behavioral unit. For example, a malfunctioning carburator may differentially reinforce a new pattern of pedal pushing on the accelerator of one's car, while one continues traveling to a grocery store. More generally, there may be several scales of concurrent behavioral process. In some cases the organization on one scale may constrain the organization at another: In the preceding example (carburetor/grocery store), one might change routes, taking a more lengthy path that entails fewer stop signs. In other cases, the organization at each scale of analysis is quite independent of the others. This raises a fifth general issue, (5) the organization of behavior and the degree to which organization arises through environmental constraint, as opposed to arising primarily in the behavior irrespective of the environment in which it occurs. For example, it is seldom recognized that the linear/ordinal constraint in behavioral chains is a characteristic of the *environmental* side of certain behavior–environment relations, rather than a characterization of the behaving organism.

We lack time and space to systematically address these, so shall thread our way, focusing upon the relationships that will be most germaine to our comparisons of behavior-analytic and cognitivist interpretations. Our ultimate concern here will be characteristically human behavior, but we shall illustrate the basic relations and distinctions through experiments with nonhuman subjects, where rigorous control of experimental histories enables the essential relationships to be cleanly delineated and where it is less tempting to invoke complex functions when simple ones can suffice. The stimuli of concern typically are visual patterns or colors, projected on translucent panels or response keys; the response topographies are selected for convenience—pressing the panel or pecking the key, or pressing a lever or button adjacent to the stimulus. Just as in the case of "box checking" in questionnaires or intelligence tests with humans, the particular form of response is of only incidental interest; we are concerned mainly with the relationships between that response and other events.

3.4. Elaborated Discriminative Relations

In *conditional discrimination,* the contingencies of one discrimination are operative only in relation to a second set of discriminative events. Experimental examples are readily arranged through the matching-to-sample procedure. In the case of pigeons, the subject is first presented a sample stimulus, typically projected on the center response key in an array of 3. A peck on that key produces additional stimuli on the two side keys; one is identical to the sample, and one is different. In a "matching procedure," pecking the key displaying the identical stimulus will be reinforced; in an "oddity procedure," pecking the key with the differing stimulus will be reinforced. Thus, if the sample stimuli are either red or green in successive presentations, reinforcement of pecking the key that displays a green comparison stimulus will be conditional upon presence of a green sample stimulus in the matching procedure and upon the presence of a nongreen sample stimulus in the oddity procedure. Long ago, Cumming and Berryman (1965) found that pigeons perform well on both types of procedures. Nevin and Liebold (1966) added a second order of conditionality to such procedures, also using pigeons as subjects. The sample key could be red or green, and the comparison stimuli were red and green. When a yellow light located above the keys was illuminated, pecking the red or green key whose color was the same as that of the sample would be reinforced; when the yellow light was off, pecking the key with nonmatching color would be reinforced. After some 50 hours of exposure to this procedure, the birds performed at high levels of accuracy in both the matching and the oddity components of that procedure.

The discriminanda for a conditional discrimination need not share physical dimensions with the stimuli that differentiate the alternative operants. For example, Lattal (1975) arranged for the contingency between one response and its consequences to be the basis for a conditional discrimination involving two other responses. A row of three response keys was provided; much of the time, the two side keys were dark, and the center key was illuminated yellow. Two distinct procedures for food delivery with respect to responding on the yellow key were randomly alternated after successive food deliveries. Sometimes, food was delivered according to a DRL 10-sec procedure such as that described with respect to Figure 1. That is, a peck on the yellow key could produce food if at least 10 seconds had elapsed since the preceding peck. Equally often, food was delivered at the end of a 10-sec period in which no pecks had occurred—in this case, food delivery could accompany any behavior other than key pecking, because pecks reset the 10-second timer. Hence, this procedure is called "differential reinforcement of other behavior," or DRO. Conditional discrimination came into play after each food delivery that was arranged according to either the DRL or the DRO procedure: The yellow key became dark, and the two side keys were lighted red and green. If the immediately preceding food delivery had been produced by a yellow-key peck (that is, if the DRL 10-sec contingency had been in effect), a peck on the red key would now produce food. If instead, that preceding food delivery had not been produced by a peck (that is, if the DRO 10-sec contingency had been in effect), a peck on the green key would now produce food. The red- and green-key pecking readily became discriminative operants occasioned by whether or not food deliveries during yellow had been produced by pecks.

An ingenious feature of Lattal's procedure was that similar behavior patterns were reinforced during the two procedures accompanied by yellow—that is, in both cases, a pause of at least 10 seconds was part of the descriptive operant. Furthermore, for one of the birds, the difference between times spent in the DRL and the DRO conditions was less than the difference threshold for temporal stimuli that have been found for pigeons exposed to this range of durations (Stubbs, 1968). Hence, it may have been the contingent relation *per se*—pecks produce food versus food occurs without pecks—that was the effective dimension of the discrimination. Alternatively, it may have been the birds' own immediately prior behavior—pecking versus not pecking—that constituted the functional discriminative event.

A similar procedure has been used, in which the birds' own behavior, rather than a behavior-consequence relation, was explicitly made the discriminadum for a conditional discrimination. Shimp (1983) arranged for intermittent reinforcement of specific classes of interresponse times defined with respect to pecking on a center key. Unlike the standard DRL procedure, each class of interresponse times that could produce the reinforcing consequence had an upper as well as a lower limit. In addition, two distinct ranges were specified in each condition of the experiment, with the longer one always three times the duration of the shorter one (i.e., two descriptive operants were specified; for example, pecks separated by 3–4 sec and pecks separated by 9–12 sec). From time to time (as specified by a variable-interval schedule), a response on the center key whose interresponse time fell within one of the two specified ranges darkened the center key, lighting a red and a green side key. Whether the shorter range or the longer range could produce this effect, was arranged with a random probability of .5. If the immediately preceding center-key peck had been in the shorter range, pecking the green key would produce food; if the immediately preceding center-key peck had been in the longer range, pecking the red key would produce food. Thus, the length of the bird's pause between pecks on the center key was the discriminative stimulus for food-reinforced pecking on the side keys.

Pecks on the side keys were typically well above chance. That is, the patterns of side-key pecking constituted discriminations of the durations of the pauses between the birds' immediately preceding pecks on the center key. One aspect of a bird's behavior was under discriminative control of other aspects of its behavior. Interestingly, the accuracy of this discrimination was not related to the consistency with which the birds spaced their center-key responses within the two specified ranges when the absolute sizes of the pairs of IRT ranges were varied. The contingencies that account for the spaced responding on the center key were distinct from the contingencies that account for the discriminative responding on the side keys, for which the spaced center-key responses were the discriminative events. The experiment can be construed as having arranged a rudimentary self-descriptive language with a two-word vocabulary—and the experiment was presented as showing independence between a pigeon's behavior and self-reports of that behavior. In elaborated human language instead of this rudimentary two-word pigeon vocabulary, the pigeon's side-key pecks were the functional equivalent of "I have just pecked slowly" or "I have just pecked quickly." The "meaning" of the reports is the ancillary relationships whereby its consequences were arranged—that is, in the experimental procedure. Occasionally, humans arrange similar two-word languages for their own reporting—a famous American example being "One if by land, and two if by sea."

3.5. The Origins of Awareness in Behavior-Analytic Terms

The discriminative side-key responding in Shimp's experiment also provides a rudimentary example of a behavior-analytic account of situations where one appropriately speaks of awareness. Skinner (1963) discussed these situations by addressing how it is that we come to "see that we see," sometimes in the sense of "knowing that we see." In its vernacular form, this "language of knowing" is commonly taken as implying a distinct domain of mental activity. However, careful ordinary-language use of those terms *can* be consistent with a behavioral account, provided that each variant of knowing is confined to the specific relations that support it (Hineline, 1983).[5] Thus, if we were to describe Shimp's experiment in terms of the birds' knowing, the spaced pecking on the center key would constitute "knowing which" (which key) and "knowing when" (sensitivity to the spaced-responding contingency). Effective behavior with respect to those contingencies readily occurs without ancillary arrangements for descriptive repertoires (Hawkes & Shimp, 1974; Shimp, 1970). Hence, that behavior need not involve awareness. Only when the separate, "descriptive/discriminative" repertoires are in place does discussion in terms of "knowing that" become appropriate and bring into play a relationship resembling that for which we appropriately speak of being aware. The separate descriptive repertoires require a history of separate, differential consequences such as those which Shimp (1983) arranged for side-key pecking. The specific relationships that were established there would support the statements, "knowing that he pecked quickly" and "knowing that he pecked slowly." Additional contingencies could have been added that would support statements such as "knowing that he knows": This would require an additional set of side keys, whereby pecking one or the other would be reinforced depending upon the accuracy of performance on the initial set of side keys.

The contingencies that produce and maintain these are more elaborated repertoires of description arise through consequences provided by the behavior of other organisms. This, following Skinner's original formulation (Skinner, 1957), is taken as the defining feature of verbal behavior. Thus, outside the laboratory, a verbal community provides consequences contingent upon a child's behavior that is occasioned by queries such as "Where did you go?" or "What have you been doing? Asking those questions is the prompting of conditional discriminations, analogous to the experimenter's lighting up sets of side keys; the consequences of the resulting verbal reports are distinct from the consequences of the "going" or "doing" that are the discriminanda occasioning the reports. In a behavioral account, the discriminative repertoires that constitute such reports are viewed as the origins of awareness—awareness of self and of other events and relations. Later, even at the university level, we see the effects of differential consequences coming to bear on the repertoires of "knowing that you know"—as in knowing whether one has studied sufficiently, or whether

[5]The language of knowing, then, becomes objectionable when it trivializes the more complex meanings of what it is to know, by gratuitously implying complex forms of knowing when simpler forms would suffice for the facts at issue.

one's answer on an examination effectively addressed its questions. Thus one's awareness continues to be refined and elaborated.

3.6. Rules and Rule-Governed Behavior

We have already described the operant as a three-term, discriminative relation and have pointed out that its discriminative dimension can be based upon discrete objects or upon lights, tones, and the like. Outside the laboratory, these discriminative repertoires may arise through direct differential contingencies of the physical/biological world—as in the case of learning to eat strawberries only after their visual characteristics have changed. Reinforcement of this and of other nonsocial operants need not involve any organisms other than the one whose differential behavior is under consideration. However, discriminations among discrete objects and their characteristics also are shaped and maintained through consequences supplied by a verbal community. Thus a child learns color naming as discriminative responding in relation to particular environmental dimensions that constitute a stable relation within the verbal community. To the extent that such naming is independent of particular reinforcers, it satisfies Skinner's definition of *tact* (Skinner, 1957). Other naming may occur in relation to particular reinforcers, thus establishing the functional responses known as *mands*.

Tacts and mands can also be under discriminative control of *relations*. For example, Lamarre and Holland (1985) showed that young children could learn the phrases "on the right" and "on the left" as mands or as tacts.[6] And finally, when the discriminative stimuli for tacts and mands are the relationships that we call contingencies of reinforcement, we enter the behavioral account of rules and rule-governed behavior. Thus Skinner (1969) defines *rule* as a contingency-specifying stimulus. Skinner has argued at great length that behavior under discriminative control of rules is distinct from behavior controlled directly by the contingencies that the rules specify—as, for example, one's speaking German by following the rules in a grammar book will differ from one's speaking German that is shaped and maintained directly by consequences supplied by the German-speaking community.

It should be noted that the stating of a rule can occur either as tact or as mand; these are distinguishable in terms of the consequences *to the speaker* of a listener's behavior with respect to the stated rule. If the listener's rule-following reinforces the speaker's rule-stating, the rule-stating is a functionally a mand. If the listener's rule-following is of no particular consequence to the speaker,

[6]They also showed that these tact and mand relationships were learned independently of each other even though the forms of the responses were identical, showing, once again, that the meanings of the utterances were in their relationships with other events, rather than in their structures.

the rule-stating is functionally a tact. Typically in these cases, the consequence of a listener's behaving in accordance with rule-as-mand is supplied by the speaker. And typically, the consequence of a listener's behaving in accordance with rule-as-tact arises from environmental contingencies that are independent of the speaker. Skinner has not supplied labels for the functional categories of listeners' behavior, Zettle and Hayes (1982) have filled this gap, by denoting as *pliance,* the listener's behaving with respect to rule-as-mand, and as *tracking,* the listener's behavior with respect to rule-as-tact.

3.7. Rules as Defined by Dual, Converging Sets of Contingencies

Zettle and Hayes (1982) have also proposed a slightly different basis for defining rule-governed behavior, suggesting that "rule-governed behavior is behavior in contact with two sets of contingencies, one of which includes a verbal antecedent" (p. 78). They use the example of someone being reminded that he or she should fast on a particular day. Although fasting would probably have intrinsically aversive consequences (a nonverbal contingency), following the rule and fasting would be reinforced through social (possibly religious) contingencies. They suggest that rule-governed behavior requires self-awareness and is only possible in verbal organisms. As noted in our earlier discussion, we also would attribute awareness to dual sets of contingencies, one of them as discriminandum for the other, which would necessarily be verbal. However, it would not be "self" as discriminandum, but rather, separate contingencies involving behavior whose reinforcers need not be of verbal origin.

Zettle and Hayes also distinguish between rules supplied to a listener by a speaker and self-generated rules, although the latter repertoires are first established through interactions with others. One can be aware of—that is, have tacting repertoires with respect to—events other than contingencies of reinforcement and of events quite unrelated to oneself *per se,* so rule-governed behavior is not synonymous with or coextensive with awareness. When describing rules, one is aware of them (by definition); when following rules, one may not be aware of them. Zettle and Hayes also note that it is more difficult to tell whether a self-rule "governs" overt behavior (same variables affecting both) or whether it is "merely a collateral response," which is to say, a part of the functional operant that is not part of the descriptive operant.

4. CHARACTERISTICS OF COGNITIVIST INTERPRETATION

As behavior analysts, it is not for us to attempt a systematic exposition of cognitivist theory. Instead, we shall identify what seem to be its essential assumptions and features, with special emphasis on ones that enable specific comparisons with behavior-analytic theory. Some of these are explicitly stated in cognitivist discourse, but others must be discerned as underlying, perhaps axiomatic assumptions.

4.1. Basic Assumptions of Cognitivist Theory

Kiehlstrom (1987) characterized his view of the field as follows: "Cognitive psychology comes in various forms, but all share an abiding interest in describing the mental structures and processes that link environmental stimuli to organismic responses and underlie human experience, thought and action" (p. 1445). The concern with mental structures and processes is explicitly stated, and it is also made explicit that cognitivist theory is mediational theory. However, Kihlstrom's statement seems not to acknowledge that it is *assuming* a distinct domain of structures and processes. Even more subtly, the statement assumes that environment–behavior relationships require connective linkages. These assumptions, particularly the former, often go unnoticed because they also are implicit in ordinary language. If the additional assumptions were being acknowledged, the statement would read something like: ". . . abiding interest in describing mental structures and processes that are hypothesized as providing needed links between . . ."

The presumed locus of agency, or causation, is quite explicit in most cognitivist accounts. For example, Fodor (1981) writes in terms of mental representations and says that his theory about thinking "construes the concept of causal role in such a way that a mental state can be defined by its causal relations to other mental states" (p. 118). Shepard and Metzler (1971), presenting a series of classic studies, write of "mental rotation" as an example of how mental representations can be moved, manipulated, and transformed within the individual's mind. Clearly, the organism is characterized as actor upon his or her own mental knowledge. Similarly, Weisberg (1980) discusses the person as acting upon acquired knowledge.

4.2. Some Major Distinctions within Cognitivist Theory

These characterizations also apply to information-processing models of the sort described by Norman (1969) that have continued to be prominent in cognitivist theory. The computer metaphor is adopted to describe thinking, with the inputting of information into memory storage and subsequent retrieval and manipulation of that information by the organism. Filters and search processes are proposed for encoding and retrieval. The conceptions of memory—iconic, short-term, and long-term—construe information or content as distinct from activity whereby that content is acted upon or processed. The content is often taken as representation of the external world; however, such appeal to representation need not imply exact copies, for as Siegler (1983) states:

> People often assume that accurate encoding of information—i.e., accurate mental representation of objects and events in a particular situation—is automatic, and that the way in which we perceive an object or event is the way that it objectively is. Ample evidence exists, however, that much of the way we encode information is not innate and that great changes in methods of encoding can occur within an individual's lifetime and over historical periods. (p. 636)

Thus, whereas veridical representation of the world is not assumed and it is acknowledged that prior learning can shape how new information is obtained, the account still construes human functioning as the construction and manipulation of representations, through encoding of input, storage, retrieval, and reorganization of information.

Siegler asserts that strategies people use to learn new information are based upon knowledge acquired so far, which suggests another prominent cognitive concept, that of metacognition, introduced by Flavell (1971). Elaborating this notion, Kluwe (1982) characterizes two kinds:

> (a) the thinking subject has some knowledge about his own thinking and that of other persons;
> (b) the thinking subject may monitor and regulate the course of his own thinking, i.e., may act as the causal agent of his own thinking. (p. 202)

Both characterizations, but the second in particular, suggest a role of awareness as a special order of thinking that has causal status in relation to other thinking. Cognition is to be distinguished from metacognition in that cognition includes stored memories or knowledge about a topic, the basic processes whereby those are acquired, and the operations upon the knowledge or memories. Metacognition is cognition about cognition—about one's skills used in thinking and the monitoring of one's own thinking skills and strategies.

A related distinction is one between "declarative" and "procedural" knowledge. Although there are a number of characterizations of this distinction, Kluwe (1982) seems to suggest that declarative knowledge, the information stored in memory, is part of the cognitive domain, whereas procedural-knowledge includes processes that act upon this knowledge and thus is metacognitive. He concludes:

> It is important that human beings understand themselves as agents of their own thinking. Our thinking is not just happening, like a reflex; it is caused by the thinking person, it can be monitored and regulated deliberately, i.e., it is under the control of the thinking person. (p. 222)

These distinctions hint at a new kind of dualism—a dualism that splits mental activity into two separate domains: automatic/unconscious and conscious/intentional. The major point, however, is that metacognitive activities are seen as intrinsically involving awareness and as having a special, causal role in the thinking process, and that causation is construed as within the person.

4.3. Unconscious Functioning, According to Cognitivist Theory

Recently unconscious processes have been given greater consideration in cognitivist models, as indicated by Kihlstrom's (1987) essay addressing unconscious versus conscious processes in contemporary cognitivist theory. Kihlstrom notes that, in traditional information-processing models, consciousness is identified with attention and rehearsal—which is to say, with short-term or working memory, where those processes are said to occur or be directed. In addition, he reports that recent models of information processing distinguish declarative knowledge (episodic or semantic in nature) from procedural knowledge, which consists of the skills, strategies, and rules that act upon declarative knowledge. Consciousness is still identified with working memory, with the dual assumptions that one's declarative knowledge is stored there and that one can be aware of it. However, unlike Kluwe's conception of procedural knowledge as similar to metacognition, which we noted, Kihlstrom's description portrays procedural knowledge as inaccessible to introspection and thus to awareness. This provides for a greater degree of unconscious processing than was accommodated by more traditional models.

Kihlstrom also describes a recent generation of structurally different models that also entail greater provision for unconscious processing. These models are based on parallel distributed processing, whereby various systems are presumed to operate quite independently, with only some of them accessible to awareness and subject to voluntary control:

> Both the number of simultaneously active processing units and the speed at which they pass information along themselves may exceed the span of conscious awareness. . . . By virtue of massive parallelism, processing systems tend to reach a steady state very rapidly, within about half a second. At this point of relaxation the information represented by the steady state becomes accessible to phenomenal awareness. Information may also reach consciousness if the relaxation process is slowed by virtue of ambiguity in the stimulus pattern; in this case, however, the contents of consciousness will shift back and forth between alternative representations. (p. 1446)

Reviewing these as well as more conventional processing models, and reviewing relevant research on perception and memory, Kihlstrom concludes:

> One thing is now clear: consciousness is not to be identified with any particular perceptual-cognitive functions such as discriminative response to stimulation, perception, memory, or the higher mental processes involved in judgment or problem-solving. All of these functions can take place outside of phenomenal awareness. Rather, consciousness is an experiential quality that may accompany any of these functions. The fact of conscious awareness may have particular consequences for

> psychological function—it seems necessary for voluntary control, for example, as well as for communicating one's mental states to others. But it is not necessary for complex psychological functioning. (p. 1450)

Thus, although at least some contemporary cognitivist accounts allow for extensive unaware functioning—in parallel distributed processing, in the automaticity of well-practiced skills, and in some versions of procedural knowledge, a primary controlling role is retained for conscious, "executive functioning." The decisions involved in reacting to nonroutine events or in learning new relationships are still construed very much as within more traditional models. And it can be expected that some cognitive theorists will continue adhering to traditional conceptions that give a privileged role to conscious operations of working memory.

4.4. Rules in Cognitivist Theory

Another prominent theme in cognitivist theory and research is the study of rules, which are taken as fundamental to much of human functioning and even have been proposed as the primary units for analysis. In conceptions that are patterned after computer models of information processing, rules are treated as analogous to the computer's machine-language instructions—that is, as elemental descriptions of how cognition is accomplished. In other cognitivist accounts, rules are closer to propositional forms, which suggest declarative knowledge, but are still part of procedural knowledge—as in rules for acting upon visual representations or for generating sentences in the past tense. Procedural knowledge, then, is construed as involving the application of rules, and metacognition suggests the knowing of, awareness of, and choice among rules to apply. However, it is not uncommon for a theorist to assert that a rule is operative even though the person in question describes a quite different basis for his or her action. All that seems to be required for a cognitivist to invoke a rule is that the putatively operative rule be consistent with the action to be accounted for (e.g., Siegler, 1983).

The usual arguments for taking rule-use as fundamental, appeal to performance with respect to novel stimuli (in the sense that the individual has not encountered them before) or to the production of novel responses (doing what one has not done before). Thus Siegler (1983) uses the example of children learning to speak who make predictable errors of past tense, saying "goed" instead of went and "runned" instead of ran—words that they would not have learned by listening to others speak. In addition to predicting patterns of error, rule-use is invoked to account for the fact that a linguistically competent human can (at least in principle) generate any of an infinite number of novel sentences, all of which are grammatical. The issue, then, concerns novelty in orderly behavior, and the argument reveals an ironic "tight determinism" as implicit within cognitivist accounts. The infinite novelty is impressive only if one assumes that the utterances have tightly related, contiguous proximal causes—leading one to be concerned with where the novelty comes from. The irony, then, is that these assumptions of tight, rather mechanistic determinism are part of an account that places causation of action within the person, suggesting personal agency that conforms to the cultural assumptions of free will and personal responsibility. As we have described before, the behavior-analytic approach encorporates variability and novelty into the definition of its most basic concepts; for the behavior analyst, novel actions are not a serious interpretive problem. In addition, as we have described earlier, in a behavior-analytic account, generalizations described by a rule (as in speaking with the suffix *-ed* in all of one's utterances concerning past events) do not necessarily imply the behavior of using that rule.

Finally and most fundamentally, as we noted earlier, cognitive interpretations begin with the questions of *how* the organism does what it does; the question is answered in terms of processes that are said to underlie or mediate the behavior. The emphasis on mediation follows, in part, from a pervasive assumption, that the causes of behavior must be contiguous with that behavior. (Lacey & Rachlin, 1978; Morris *et al.*, 1982).

4.5. Cognitivist Assumptions in Criticisms of Behaviorist Accounts

Cognitivist assumptions also are revealed in criticisms or rejections of alternative positions. The assumptions often are introduced in rather casual fashion, as illustrated by Fodor's (1981) comparison of cognitivist and behaviorist positions: "In the cognitive sciences, at least, the natural domain for psychological theorizing seems to be all systems that process information" (p. 118); and three pages later: "An important tendency in the cognitive sciences is to treat the mind chiefly as a device that manipulates symbols" (p. 121). These informal phrasings, "natural" . . ."seems to be" . . . "tendency," belie the importance of the notions they introduce, for these seem to become Fodor's implicit bases for rejecting a behaviorist view. To be sure, Fodor also states an explicit basis, by describing radical behaviorism as unable to handle even the simplest of (first-order) conditional discriminations. However, that part of his argument is wholely untenable, for at its time of writing, it ignores at least 15 years of systematic behavioral research addressing conditional discriminations. And as we approach 30 years of such research, the implications of complex fifth- and sixth-order conditionality are a topic of contemporary interest in behavior analysis (e.g., see Sidman, 1986).

Another example of unacknowledged assumptions underlying a cognitivist rejection of the behaviorist view can be discerned in Chomsky's (1959) famous critique of Skinner's *Verbal Behavior*. MacCorquodale (1970) identifies a variety of ways in which that critique was irrelevant to Skinner's book: "Chomsky's actual target is only about one-half of Skinner, with the rest a mixture of odds and ends of other behaviorisms and some other fancies of vague origin" (p. 83). One of these was especially perplexing to behaviorists, that being drive-reduction theory, to which Chomsky devoted a six-page refutation, even though Skinner has always implacably opposed that theory. Chomsky failed to understand or acknowledge the status of the reinforcement concept as a theoretical primitive in Skinner's theory—a status comparable to that of "transformation" in Chomsky's theory. For Chomsky, as for other cognitivists, it is *axiomatic* that explanations of behavior must be founded upon processes internal to the behaving organism. Hence, to him, it apparently seemed essential, if reinforcement were to be seriously considered, that it would have to be evaluated in terms of some underlying process—and thus drive-reduction was selected as the best-known candidate to criticize, even though it derived from *neobehaviorism,* which as we have noted earlier, is a form of behaviorism that is quite distinct from behavior analysis, in that it is predicated upon mediational processes.

A commonly asserted basis offered by cognitivists for favoring their viewpoint over a behavioral one is the occurrence of actions that do not have evident causes in their immediate environments. The assertion, then, is that such behavior must be accounted for in terms of proximal mediating process within the organism. In this maneuver, the behaviorist position is portrayed as requiring close, one-to-one connections between stimuli and responses and between responses and consequences. But it is the *cognitivist* interpretation, along with the neobehaviorist one, that requires contiguous connections. To the extent that it is well understood, behavior-analytic theory is untouched by such arguments. However, it is not widely recognized how this is the case, so we shall present a detailed example here, as documentation of cognitivist assumptions and as illustrating how behavior analysis handles a type of data that cognitivists take as supporting their assumptions:

In his presentation, *A Cognitive Theory of Learning,* Levine (1975) describes a sequence of experiments and data as leading him from a behavioral to a cognitivist theory of learning, through two fundamental shifts: The first was a shift from "response hypotheses"—a characterization of learning as selection among response biases such as choices of particular stimuli or particular response locations (each to the exclusion of all else)[7]—to "prediction hy-

[7]Levine's initial position focused upon "response sets," a label that suggests a behaviorist position. However, the notions that Levine so designates must not be confused with the response classes that define an operant, for "response sets were conceived of as automatic and rigid, the response pattern appearing regardless of feedback" (p. 146). These notions were derived from the work of Harlow (1959) and of Krechevsky (1932), with a declared affinity to mathematical models such as that of Bower and Trobasso (1964), all of which were far removed from the tradition of behavior analysis. A behavior analyst would characterize these patterns of position- or stimulus-preference as biases, not as operants (e.g., see Baum, 1974), and surely not as hypotheses, for this last term would be taken as implying the behavior of verbally stated rules.

potheses''; these were construed as the subjects' expectancies regarding contingencies of the experiment. The second shift was from hypothesis as response pattern to hypothesis as ''*determinant* of a response pattern, as a mediating process that results in the particular response pattern'' (p. 150).

Levine's experiments used college students as subjects, confronted them with choices between pairs of symbols, and provided consequences of the experimenter saying ''right'' or ''wrong.'' In some cases, there were sequences of as many as four ''blank trials'' without those consequences, but these sequences were presented only after ''the subject was told that during the next few cards the experimenter would not say anything, that because this was a test he [the subject] was to try to get 100% correct'' (e.g., pp. 155, 163). The fact that extended response patterns such as alternation between stimulus choices were readily learned and the fact that such patterns remained stable over the sequences of ''blank trials'' were taken as invalidating traditional conditioning theory. Levine proposes that ''the hypothesis, rather than the specific choice on a particular trial, is regarded as the dependent variable, i.e., as the unit of behavior affected by the reinforcements.'' He asserts that the experimenter's saying ''right'' on a given trial ''is virtually universally regarded as a reinforcement of that response'' (p. 168), with the result that the learning of alternating patterns of responding should be viewed as paradoxical to an account predicated on reinforcement of behavior.

From these procedures, results, and considerations, Levine finds it compelling to shift the definition of hypothesis ''from a behavior pattern to a mediating process of which the behavior pattern is a manifestation,'' making much of the fact that ''a distinction is explicitly made between Predictions (manifested during Outcome problems, in behavior contingent upon outcomes) and Response-sets (manifested in behavior which is always independent of outcomes)'' (p. 169). Furthermore, he assumes that for reinforcement of behavior to be the appropriate interpretation, there must have been disruptions of response pattern resulting from the sequences of four trials without reinforcement. Because such disruptions did not occur, Levine concludes that on the ''blank trials,'' of which the subjects were forewarned by verbal instruction, no outcome must function as reinforcement.

Clearly, if Levine had entertained a less simplistic version of behavioral theory, it need not have been abandoned for the reasons he indicated. First, he had directly, verbally instructed his subjects to tolerate intervals of nonreinforcement (so this was an issue of rule-governed, rather than contingency-maintained behavior); second, even considering the behavior in terms of its direct consequences, Levine clearly did not take into account the massive literature on intermittent reinforcement—including intermittent reinforcement of performance in conditional discriminations such as maching-to-sample (e.g., Boren, 1973; Davidson & Osborne, 1974; Ferster, 1960). Third and most directly, Levine did not recognize that a behavior-analytic account readily handles extended behavior patterns such as alternation between responses, by considering larger functional units of behavior: Configural patterns can function as discriminative stimuli; concept formation is readily studied within the context of behavioral theory, as discrimination between categories and generalization within categories (e.g., Herrnstein, 1979; Vaughan & Herrnstein, 1987). And as we have noted earlier, extended patterns of behavior can be selected as operants. As stated by Morris *et al.* (1982), "if one fails to find an immediate stimulus that controls a response, perhaps the response is only an element of a larger functional unit which is controlled by currently operative variables not immediately attendant to that element" (p. 120). Such considerations of scales of analysis are not peculiar to behavior analysis, for they also are of fundamental concern in the analysis of selective processes in biology (Smith, 1986).

This example, which is provided by Levine's choice between theories, illustrates the fact that cognitivist accounts seem not to entertain the possibility that causation over temporal distance can be left as such—that there can be an "extended psychological present" in which time-past and time-present can be brought together in one's interpretation without the artifice of present-constructed (or reconstructed) representations of past events. Stated differently, it appears to be an axiomatic (and from a behavior-analytic perspective, rather hidebound) assumption of mediational, cognitivist theory that the causes of behavior must be temporally and spatially contiguous with that behavior. To a cognitivist, the intangibility of localizable mental causes is less discomfitting than the diffuse remoteness of historical causes in the environment.

5. CONFLICTING INTERPRETATIONS OF CONDITIONING EXPERIMENTS

Many of the direct, substantive arguments that have occurred between theorists of the behaviorist and cognitivist traditions have concerned the interpretation of human performance on operant conditioning procedures. In a well-known example, Greenspoon (1955) asked subjects to generate words aloud for 50 minutes. Whenever a plural noun was emitted, the experimenter said "um-hum." Greenspoon reported a systematic increase in the occurrence of plural nouns and concluded that this result demonstrated the conditioning of verbal behavior without the subjects' awareness.

5.1. A Cognitivist Proposal: Awareness through Correlated Hypothesizing

In response to Greenspoon's experiment, several cognitivists (Adams, 1957; Dulany, 1961; Spielberger & DeNike, 1966) proposed, in direct opposition to

Greenspoon's interpretation, that in experiments such as Greenspoon's, human subjects are aware of experimental contingencies and that this is essential to the conditioning effects even though the awareness may not be accurately related to the contingencies. They suggested that a subject may employ a "correlated hypothesis" when participating in an experiment. For example, Spielberger and DeNike (1966) propose that if a subject were exposed to the Greenspoon procedure in which saying plural nouns is reinforced, the subject might list varieties of fruits such as "apples, pears, peaches" and thus receive the maximum number of reinforcers. In reporting a replication of Greenspoon's experiment, Dulany (1961) states that the subject will sometimes report that certain categories produce reinforcers and will continue to respond with words from these categories. Accordingly, when the "umhum" consequence ceases that is a cue for the subject to move to another category. It is clear that, following this strategy, the subject will continue to maximize payoff without running out of plural nouns. The subjects are said to be formulating hypotheses, following them as provisional rules, and changing them when they are contradicted by outcomes.

As Spielberger and DeNike (1966) point out, behavioral accounts of verbal conditioning assume that reinforcement can produce an increase in the saying of plural nouns before awareness of the contingency occurs. They say, "On the other hand, it is argued in cognitive explanations of verbal conditioning that awareness precedes performance increments" (p. 314), and they assert the importance of assessing when, within the session, more accurate description of the contingencies (awareness) occurs. They cite an experiment by DeNike (1964) in which subjects were exposed to Greenspoon's basic procedures but were also required, upon presentation of a flash of light, to write down "thoughts about the experiment." This signal occurred after every 25 words were emitted, irrespective of the particular words. "Unaware" and control subjects did not increase emission of plural nouns, whereas increases were seen in "aware" subjects as a function of the accuracy of their verbal reports. Spielberger and DeNike conclude that, although there might be some instances of learning without awareness (they use the examples of shifting gears and nailbiting), probably most verbal conditioning occurs with awareness.

In answer to these criticisms, behaviorists responded by proposing that in asking subjects about the experiment, the cognitive psychologists were probably prompting the subjects' reactions of awareness at that point (e.g., Greenspoon, 1963). For example, in exit interviews, the subjects, upon being asked about what was going on in the experiment, may have realized at that point what the experimenter had been doing during the session, even though they were not engaging in such descriptive formulations during the session. A similar case could be made regarding the DeNike (1964) study, in that taking written protocols during the session could invoke awareness, thus changing the properties of the Greenspoon procedure.

5.2. Behavioral Experiments Minimizing the Role of Awareness

In addition, other experiments reported by behaviorists during this period were accomplished with unobtrusive experimental procedures. For example, Centers (1963) conducted an experiment in the "waiting room" to his laboratory to minimize, if not eliminate, subject awareness of the contingencies. When each of the 49 subjects arrived (individually) at the laboratory, a confederate (an undergraduate with special training) was already there, who said:

> Hi. I'm Johnny Martin and am going to be in the experiment with you. You must have just missed Dr. Centers. I came early and Centers told me the machine had broken down and that he had to go downstairs to get someone to fix it. He said he ought to be right back, but if he isn't we are to wait for a half-hour before we can leave. We'll get full credit for the experiment even if he doesn't come. (p. 237)

The 30-minute "waiting period" was divided into three 10-minute phases. A baseline rate was assessed on three targeted categories of utterance: opinion statements, the offering of information, and the asking of questions. The confederate responded to all three with general attention but, when called upon, would speak noncommittally. In the second phase, the confederate reacted to each of the three types of utterance by nodding, agreeing, and/or restating what the subject had said. Importantly, instead of a stereotyped "uh huh," which had been specified as the reinforcer in Greenspoon's experiment, the putative reinforcers were varied, presumably making them less obtrusive and more like the social reinforcers that are assumed to occur in nonexperimental situations. The last 10 minutes of the procedure was the extinction phase during which the confederate either disagreed, disapproved, or did not respond to the targeted operants. Results were clear and systematic with respect to the conditioning of opinion and information statements, but no significant result was obtained with respect to the behavior of questioning.

This study avoids some of the problems inherent in conducting research in sterile laboratory settings with stereotyped reinforcers, although the procedures are less precisely implemented and specified. The confederate must make "snap judgments" and attempt to perform consistently while directly involved with the subject. Centers reported a residual problem related to awareness, in that some subjects were "suspicious"; however, he also reported that they later accepted the confederate's explanation that they had been in the "control condition" of the experiment and, furthermore, that they did not show any signs of knowing that their behavior was being conditioned.

One way to alleviate the "suspicion" dimension (and hypothesizing that might accompany it) would be to remove the study from the laboratory entirely. Salzinger and Pisoni (1960) achieved this, in interviewing 26 hospital patients who were suffering from a variety of illnesses such as pneumonia, arthritis, and appendicitis. Interviewers told each patient that the hospital was interested in determining the types of questions that should be included in their medical admissions questionnaire. The targeted verbal operant was comprised of self-descriptive "affect statements" not including statements about intellectual or physiological states. Salzinger and Pisoni limited the response class to statements beginning with "I" or "we," for example: "I am upset," "I am satisfied," "We enjoyed it."

The interview lasted 30 minutes and baseline, reinforcement, and extinction phases each lasted 10 minutes. In the baseline phase, the interviewer asked questions without reacting to the answers. In the conditioning phase, each "affect statement" was reinforced with any of several agreement phrases (e.g., "uh huh," "I see," "yeah"). During the extinction phase, answers produced no such reactions on the part of the interviewer. Affect statements occurred least frequently in the first phase, most frequently in the conditioning phase, and intermediately during extinction. Although this study is, in some ways, less complicated than that of Centers (1963), basically the same result was seen. Thus it appears that in "normal conversation," a participant's categories of utterances are quickly shaped by the reactions of the other speaker. The selection of these complex and subtle categories of behavior goes on without accurate awareness of what the other person is reinforcing.

Experiments that do not explicitly involve verbal behavior may provide even more convincing evidence of reinforcement of human operant behavior without its being dependent upon the subjects' awareness of closely correlated features of the procedure or of their behavior. For example, Hefferline, Keenan, and Harford (1959) recorded electromyographic responses corresponding to a thumb twitch that was too small to produce overt movement and then established a narrow range of such responses as an operant class: Thumb twitches could eliminate or prevent noise that was superimposed on recorded music. The subjects were found to be unable to report the ongoing relationships or even the kind of behavior that was involved. That experiment has been replicated recently by Laurenti-Lions, Gallego, Chambille, Vardon, and Jacquemin (1985), who used a similar but improved experimental design and modern computer-based technology. They obtained similar results, with even more convincing evidence of the subjects' inability to describe the experiment as having anything to do with their hands.

Furthermore, a related experiment by Hefferline and Pererra (1963) suggests that a varient of their conditioning procedure could actually generate new sensory perceptions, raising the provocative possibility that operant conditioning can shape a process that for cognitivists is a presumed basis for, and thus prior to, the processes that constitute awareness. Hefferline and Pererra established electromyographically recorded thumb twitches in the subject's left hand as discriminative stimuli for reinforced overt key pressing with the right hand, again with the subjects remaining unable report that a thumb twitch was involved. That is, the experimenter presented a tone whenever the left thumb muscle had twitched, and overt key presses with the right hand could produce money only if they occurred within 2 seconds of the tone. Then the intensity of the tone was gradually reduced to zero; the subjects continued to press the key only when the thumb twitches had occurred (no other presses were reinforced) and reported that the tones were becoming difficult to hear. When the experimenters reintroduced the tone, its onsets were slightly after the thumb twitches (due to the experimenter's reaction time in detecting the twitch via oscilloscope and turning on the tone), and the subjects reported hearing two tones in rapid succession. In the behavior-analytic account, hearing is behaving, and the "conditioned hearing" suggested by this study awaits further investigation.

5.3. The Continuing Dispute about Awareness

In experiments such as these, the subjects' reports do not describe contingencies resembling or clearly related to those specified by the experimenters. We have found no cognitivist discussions addressing these particular experiments. However, Brewer (1975) presents a methodologically oriented review of both Pavlovian and operant conditioning of human behavior, adhering to the awareness-based position that we outlined before. One part of his argument is an attempt to place behaviorists in the position of having to prove an unconditional negative—that there is no possibility of any kind of awareness operative in the effects of a conditioning experiment. Of course the experimenters have not prevented the subjects from being aware of *some* aspects of the experimental situations, and one might propose that the subjects are, in at least an informal sense, hypothesizing about what will produce rewarding consequences. The second part of Brewer's argument is to present experiments indicating a decisive role of verbally mediated effects in conditioning. The conditioning account that he challenges is construed as molecular, mechanistic theory—making no distinction between a neobehaviorist conception and a behavior-analytic one such as the one we have outlined. In particular, Brewer fails to acknowledge the behavior-analytic account of verbal behavior as derived from conditioning principles. Thus he takes any demonstrations of instructional control as evidence exclusively favoring cognitivist theory.

From a behaviorist viewpoint, the first part of Brewer's argument merely reflects gratuitous assumptions. Brewer accepts the vaguest of relationships between verbal reports (often prompted after the experiment) and experimental conditions as enabling those relationships to account for the detailed effects of those conditions. Hence the inferences are tantamount to *assuming,* rather than demonstrating, that aware, logical functioning must be primary in human action. In addition, a great deal remains unspecified in Brewer's version of cognitivist theory—such as what consciousness *is* that gives it a special causal role.

There is no indication of how expectations are generated, and especially, how they translate into actions. Virtually always, those terms seem to be mere labels, borrowed from the vernacular, for sensitivity to environmental events. The second part of Brewer's argument was out of touch with the behavior-analytic theory of its time and has been made thoroughly obsolete by subsequent behavior-analytic developments regarding the interactions between verbal and nonverbal behavior—developments that we shall describe later.

Perhaps the disagreements we have been addressing cannot be resolved because they arise from directly conflicting axiomatic assumptions. More optimistically, one might hope that the arguments concerning awareness could be put aside because, as we noted earlier, recent cognitivist accounts have allowed for a greater role of unconscious functioning: Kihlstrom's (1987) review of research from the *cognitivist* tradition thoroughly undermines half of Brewer's (1975) argument against behaviorist interpretation. However, contemporary cognitivist accounts appear to retain a decisive, "executive" role for conscious functioning, so the behaviorist/cognitivist disagreement on these issues remains active. Still, there is basis for further comparison of and discussion between the two viewpoints: The behavior-analytic conception includes principles and distinctions addressing behavior such as that invoked in cognitivist arguments that we have just reviewed. That is, the "correlated" aspect of correlated hypothesizing as proposed by the cognivist has a fairly precise counterpart in a behaviorist distinction that we outlined earlier, between descriptively specified and functionally specified operants. In addition, a contemporary behavior-analytic account of rule-governed and other verbal behavior includes repertoires of rule-generating as well as of rule-following, which address both the "hypothesizing" part of correlated hypothesizing and the actions that the cognitivist assumes as following from the hypothesizing. These aspects of the behaviorist account, to which we now turn, might be appreciated from a cognitivist viewpoint and lead to more clearly articulated differences between, if not partial reconciliation of, the two positions.

6. CORRELATED HYPOTHESES AS FUNCTIONAL OPERANTS?

As we described earlier, a descriptive operant includes only the parts of the repertoire that can actually produce the consequent events that are maintaining the operant. A functional operant includes behavior maintained by those consequences—behavior that produces them and perhaps additional behavior that cannot produce the consequences under the specified contingencies that identify the corresponding descriptive operant. The cognitivist interprets the subject's behavior as resulting from his/her hypothesizing about the situation. In designating a putative hypothesis as "correlated," it is asserted that there is *some* overlap between the behavior designated by the hypothesis and behavior that can actually produce the consequences. But "correlated" also indicates that some features of the behavior designated by the hypothesis are irrelevant to the consequence. Clearly, there is a resemblance between the aggregate of "procedure and resulting correlated hypothesis" and the aggregate of "descriptive operant and functional operant." To examine that resemblance more closely, we consider the two conceptions as applied to an actual experiment.

Bruner and Revusky (1961) studied the behavior of four male high-school students who were presented with a keyboard with four keys, each of which buzzed when pressed. Importantly, presses on only one particular key would produce reinforcers: a bell, red light, and increment of a counter accompanied each earning of 5 cents, and the subjects were told that the counter would keep track of total earnings. First, an operant level of key pressing was obtained for each subject, then low rates of responding were established by reinforcing the first three responses that were spaced by at least 8.2 seconds (DRL schedule). Eighty subsequent reinforcers were delivered contingently upon interresponse times between 8.2 and 10.25 seconds. Finally, there was a 2-hour extinction period. The experimenters found that each subject engaged in a consistent repetitive pattern of pressing on the three inconsequential keys and that doing so maintained temporal spacing that efficiently met the DRL requirement on the key that produced reinforcers. Subjects were interviewed upon conclusion of the experiment, and none said anything about the passage of time. Instead, each subject identified a particular pattern of presses as being required, specifying patterns that included the buttons defined as nonfunctional by the procedure.

No doubt, a cognitivist account of these results would attribute the subjects' performances to correlated hypothesizing, identified by the subject's descriptions—the formulating of provisional, verbally stated rules that are continually adjusted on the basis of outcomes. The experimenter cannot prevent the subject from being aware nor prevent that aware functioning from affecting other behavior. The fact that the subject's stated hypothesis or "rule" includes statements about the additional response keys, which had no role in the experimenter-arranged contingencies, would not be seen as preventing the rule to be given a causal role in the subject's behavior.

Analogously, the behavior analyst's distinction between a functional operant and its corresponding descriptive operant depends partly upon the fact that some of the behavior maintained by the consequences cannot produce the consequences. Thus the extra-key responding in those experiments would be part of the functional operants but not part of the descriptive operants—just as in Figure 2, which we presented earlier, responses with short interresponse times were part of the functional operant maintained by a DRL schedule even though they could not produce the reinforcers arranged by that schedule.

Could it be, then, that from the behavior analyst's viewpoint, the subject's hypothesizing and interrelated behavior, as proposed by the cognitive theorist, are included in a single functional operant? That when generating and then following a rule includes some behavior that can and some that cannot produce the consequence, it is all part of a single operant class because it varies as a whole aggregate, selected by the consequence? If so, one might be tempted to conclude that the behavioral and cognitive accounts are equivalent descriptions that differ only in that one attributes control to internal processes and the other attributes control to the environment. However, there are bases within the behavioral interpretation for not treating the functional operant as undifferentiated aggregate when there is substantial disparity between the descriptive and the functional operant and especially when both verbal and nonverbal behavior are involved.

6.1. Multiple Scales of Analysis

Some distinctions can be made within the functional operant that do not appeal to verbal behavior but rather to distinct properties (and perhaps adaptive roles) of the parts of that operant that are not essential to producing the consequence. Also, if verbalizing is only incidentally involved, it can be viewed as part of the functional operant. On the other hand, if verbal behavior is functionally involved, the behavior-analytic account distinguishes between the behavior of stating rules, the behavior of following rules, and the behavior described by rules, which are distinct operant classes. As we described earlier, each of these is identified as having separate properties that originate in distinct environmental contingencies in the individual's history, even though the three types of behavior may have overlapping consequences in the situation where they are being interpreted. We shall address first the nonverbal components of functional operants, then incidental verbalizing, and then functionally distinct subclasses of verbal behavior.

Bruner and Revusky's (1961) behavioral interpretation of their experiment identified a functional role for the responding on the procedurally nonfunctional buttons but did not invoke a separate category for verbal hypothesizing. That is, they designated the patterns of pressing the ineffective buttons as "collateral chains" of behavior that aided the functional spacing of responses that *could* produce the reinforcers. They did not include the subjects' verbal descriptions (which were recorded after the experimental procedure was over) as part of the collateral behavior. The collateral behavior was said to be maintained through chaining and conditioned reinforcement: "Thus, these unsolicited, 'impromptu' responses became a functional chain of conditioned reinforcers which successfully maintains DRL performance" (p. 350). The role of the collateral behavior was thus characterized as a mediating one, but with mediation not being an appeal to underlying process nor to particularly human characteristics. Ferster and Skinner (1957) had provided the precedent: "Behavior occurring between two instances of the response being studied . . . which is used by the organism as a controlling stimulus in subsequent behavior'' (p. 729).

Bruner and Revusky supported their interpretation by relating it to the literature on nonhuman behavior, pointing out the similarity between their results and those reported by Wilson and Keller (1953) from an experiment that exposed laboratory rats to DRL contingencies. There, nose pokes, grooming, and climbing occurred in stereotyped sequences that were interpreted as collateral chains whose components constituted conditioned reinforcers that helped to maintain the performance. A functional, mediating role of such collateral behavior was demonstrated by Laties, Weiss, Clark, and Reynolds (1965), who took advantage of the fortuitous pattern of a rat's behavior on a DRL schedule, whereby between lever presses the rat stereotypically (and gently) nibbled along the length of its tail. Through various manipulations, Laties *et al.* demonstrated the role of this pattern in the DRL performance—for example, when they suppressed the tail nibbling by painting the tail with cycloheximide (''a substance that dissuades rats from chewing wires coated with it''), the rat's temporal distribution of responding was temporarily disrupted, with a resulting decrease in the frequency of reinforcement.

Considered as a whole, collateral behavior can still be seen as part of a functional operant: Whether to change the scale of analysis, subdividing the behavior into chained components, is an issue of identifying whether the behavior is in fact organized as chaining principles predict and of discovering whether a smaller scale of analysis gives improved predictions. In advocating smaller-scale analyses, some theorists place priority on bridging gaps in time: We have tried to show that this is not essential to a behavior-analytic account and that organization at a molar level is valid in itself. Others have looked to smaller-scale analysis as being potentially more complete because it specifies molecular patterns as well as molar relationships. Contemporary molar/molecular arguments within behavior theory entail much more quantitative sophistication than we have indicated here, but these basic strategic issues remain unchanged and have much in common with biologists' arguments regarding the sizes of units in genetic selection (Smith, 1986).

An alternative nonverbal account also attends to detailed, molecular patterns of behavior that cannot affect the arranged consequences—such as the pressing on nonfunctional buttons in Bruner and Revusky's experiment. If the subject's verbalizing is merely incidental to performance, this account includes the verbal behavior as well. That is: Behavior that is not included in the descriptive operant is said to be superstitious—adventitiously reinforced by the environmental consequence of the whole sequence. The slightly pejorative connotation of the term *superstition* lends emphasis to the fact that the extra button pressing had no direct effect on the procedural events. To the extent that the focus is on *particular* patterns as well as their being patterns whose occurrence is not necessary for producing the reinforcer, behavior analysts have tended to relegate them to a nonfunctional, rather than mediating role. Thus, especially during the 1960s and mid-1970s, in experiments on nonverbal behavior such as the work of Bruner and Revusky, the subjects' accompanying verbal behavior was seen as superfluous to their nonverbal performances. It was relegated either to a superstitious role or to that of collateral behavior whose particular origins or characteristics were given little importance. This, of course, was supported by research, some of which we have already described, indicating that reinforcement effects are not dependent upon verbal processes.

6.2. Multiple Converging Relationships: Verbal Behavior, Including Rules

Although contemporary behavior analysts still see verbal behavior as substantially based on reinforcement, rather than vice versa, recent behavior-analytic research on human behavior has given much greater emphasis to verbal behavior as interacting with nonverbal behavior. The shift of emphasis was prompted by the fact that when adult humans are exposed to schedules of reinforcement contingent upon responses such as button or panel pressing, the resulting patterns of repetitive responding are quite different from those consistently observed in a wide variety of nonhuman species (for a review, see Lowe, 1979). Fixed-interval schedules provide typical examples: Instead of responding with gradually increasing frequency as each interval progresses, adult humans either pause extensively, typically emitting only one response per reinforcer, or they respond indiscriminately at high rates with no evident sensitivity to the size of the scheduled interval. Fergus Lowe and his colleagues (Bental, Lowe, & Beasty, 1985; Lowe, Beasty, & Bentall, 1983) examined this difference as a function of age of human subjects, finding that for young infants (e.g., 2 years of age), the FI response patterns are indistinguishable from those observed with nonhuman subjects. With children ranging from 5 to 9 years of age, the responses patterns are like those of adults. In between, children aged 2½ to 4 years gave intermediate and less consistent patterns. These researchers have interpreted those results, along with results of verbal "self-instructional training" (Bentall & Lowe, 1987) as indicating a primary role of verbal functioning in adult human performance.

Catania, Matthews, and Shimoff (1982) introduced a technique for more directly analyzing the role of verbal behavior with respect to nonverbal behavior under schedules of reinforcement. They intermittently asked their subjects to emit guesses regarding the experiment at various points during experimental sessions and examined the effects of shaping the subjects' guesses via separate contingencies of reinforcement, as compared with providing prescriptive statements as instructions. It appears that shaping of the subject's guesses has more consistent effects on related schedule performance than does the provision of comparable descriptions as instructions. Additional work with this technique has compared different types of shaped guesses, such as contingency descriptions versus performance descriptions (e.g., Matthews, Catania, & Shimoff, 1985).

Thus behavior analysts construe the subject's verbal descriptions—including descriptions of rules—as behavior distinguishable from behaving with respect to the rules or to the relationships described by the rules. They are not alone in this, for there is ample precedent in social psychology to study the relationships between what people say and what they actually do in relation to what they say. It is widely acknowledged that there are numerous cases of noncorrespondence between saying and doing. Most obviously, a person might lie, saying one thing as a result of one set of contingencies and then not perform what was said, as a result of a different set of contingencies. More subtly, a subject's statements may be affected by the presence or other involvement of an experimenter, as in the "demand characteristics" studied by Orne (1962). Studies of these effects focus on overt verbal behavior and overt "doings" and determine the lack of correlation between the two; a cognitivist might argue that the subject's covert/private hypothesizing is not subject to such distortions. However, as Nisbett and Wilson (1977) showed in some detail, adult experimental subjects often are not aware of the discrepancies between what they say and what they do. Lloyd (1980) also reviews a variety of experiments illustrating the dissociability of doing and saying about doing.

In addition, studies from a behaviorist perspective have shown that "saying in accurate relation to doing" is a skill that children can readily be taught through use of reinforcement procedures. (e.g., Bem, 1967; Rogers-Warren & Baer, 1976) and that accurate performances of this kind do not automatically occur in the absence of supporting contingencies of reinforcement. Relatedly, such functional, "self-instructional" repertoires have been a continuing focus of applied behavior analysis (e.g., Guevrmont, Osnes, & Stokes, 1988). We have already described the supporting interpretive concepts, in terms of distinct but converging sets of contingencies leading to rule-governed behavior.

Behavior analysts assume that these effects, although demonstrated in the laboratory, commonly occur in the world at large. It follows that prior to an adult human subject's participation in an experiment, that person's repertoires of rule-generating and rule-following have been well established. The making up of rules and following them, the changing of rules, and the reinforcing of each others' following of arbitrary rules—all of these are readily observed in children's play. Even the intersection between conflicting rules can be the basis for play, as in the children's game, "Captain, May I?" The subject also has a history of encountering new situations in which instructions are given, with varying degrees of consistency in the consequences of heeding those instructions. Formal schooling as well as interactions with parents and peers frequently include training in formulating provisional rules for solving problems. Thus it is no surprise—and it is readily accounted for in behavioral terms—that when exposed to the procedure of an experiment, the person might generate a provisional description based on the initial few events of the experiment and proceed by acting in relation to that description. As we noted earlier, Zettle and Hayes (1982) provide a detailed behavioral account of such sequences, keeping distinct at least two functional categories of generating rules (manding and tacting) and of following rules (pliance and tracking). Behaviorist accounts of such behavior have often identified rule-governed behavior as relatively insensitive to its direct consequences (e.g., Shimoff, Catania, & Matthews, 1981).

7. DETAILED COMPARISON OF THESE COGNITIVIST AND BEHAVIORIST ACCOUNTS

Of course the behavior characterized just now is strongly suggestive of the "correlated hypothesizing" that we described earlier as part of the cognitivist interpretation for cases in which subjects do not accurately describe contingencies that appear to be affecting their performance. So once again we ask whether the behaviorist and cognitivist accounts are converging on virtually equivalent interpretations.

One major point of similarity that we have not emphasized occurs in instructed learning. For example, consider someone learning to drive a car with standard transmission: In behavior-analytic terms, there would be a transition from rule-governed to contingency-shaped behavior. The new driver initially acts with respect to instructions that are discriminative stimuli provided by someone else. He or she then rehearses the rules while practicing, thus producing discriminative stimuli for appropriate sequences of actions. However, the direct consequences of those actions gradually take over and shape the behavior of skilled driving; the driver no longer rehearses the rules while driving. In fact, thinking about (generating verbal descriptions of) the details of what one is doing at that point would probably disrupt the smoothness of the ride. A cognitivist version has been provided by Anderson (1980, p. 225) encorporating the distinction between declarative and procedural knowledge. Again, it is said that the person would think about the rules involved: how to properly engage the clutch, manipulate the stick shift, and the like. Initially, progress would be slow, shakey, and full of errors. In time, as the driving skill is honed, the driver no longer rehearses each step and just allows the arms and legs to coordinate with each other. This stage would then be called procedural knowledge, once the use of declarative knowledge subsides.

7.1. Summary of the Cognitivist Account

Other points of comparison can be clarified by briefly reviewing the two positions. To summarize some characteristics of the cognitivist view: There must be some overlap, but not necessarily identity, between circumstances as described by the person's hypotheses and the actual circumstances of the situation in which the person is functioning. If rewards (or "confirmations") are not forthcoming, hypotheses are said to change before the corresponding overt performance does. Although a cognitivist might agree that behavior maintained even though it cannot produce the arranged consequences might be aptly called collateral behavior, that theorist would distinguish the collateral behavior from the correlated hypothesizing that presumably mediates it. The cognitivist accounts that have appealed to correlated hypothesizing tend to assume that a person's performance follows more or less directly from the person's verbal descriptions (declarative knowledge; hypotheses) regarding situational requirements. Thus cognitivist theory is often rather vague regarding disparities between those descriptions and the performance rules or procedural knowledge that result in actual behavior. When the subject's descriptions correspond neither to the procedure nor to the observed performance on the procedure, this difference is acknowledged, but the subject may be said to be *really* following other rules that the experimenter has identified as consistent with the observed performance. Rules, then, remain central to cognitivist interpretation, whether or not the subject can describe them. The ultimate criterion for judging a rule as operative is its consistency with observed performance, irrespective of what the person says about it. Although this is consistent with rules being viewed as mediating behavior rather than being part of the behavior itself, it reduces the interpretive status of conscious-correlated hypothesizing, and the exact conceptual nature of what is meant by "rule" and what is involved in rule-using or rule-following becomes difficult to pin down. Descriptions of the nature and role of consciousness also have become increasingly variable across cognitivist accounts, with greater roles given to unconscious processing, as we described earlier. However, problem solving, decision making, and new learning seem to be reserved for conscious, "executive functioning."

7.2. Summary of the Behaviorist Account

Reviewing some corresponding aspects of the behaviorist account: Catania's (1973) distinction between descriptive and functional operants coincides nicely with the "correlated" part of correlated hypothesizing. Furthermore, if the subject's verbalizing is construed as incidental and thus not functioning discriminatively in the form of rules, the verbalizing and related nonverbal behavior may be considered part of a unitary functional operant. The verbalizing, then, would be construed as collateral, or perhaps even as less functional, superstitious behavior. Historically, for situations with contingencies contingent only upon nonverbal behavior, verbal functioning was often relegated to the superstitious role, emphasizing the fact that in the behaviorist account, verbal behavior is said to be based upon conditioning rather than vice versa.

When verbal behavior is given distinct functional roles in the behaviorist account, the stating of rules could be aptly characterized as hypothesizing. However, although the cognitivist construes hypothesizing as mediating process that underlies behavior, the behavior analyst construes it as behavior. We described the operant as a three-term, discriminative relation and pointed out that its discriminative dimension can be based upon discrete objects, lights, tones, and the like, but its discriminanda can also involve relationships between events, such as contingencies of reinforcement or aspects of one's own behavior. Repertoires involving these last two may or may not interact with other behavior, and whether they do is said to be based upon distinct sets of contingencies in the individual's conditioning history concerning relationships between the behavior of stating rules, the behavior of following rules, and contingency-shaped nonverbal behavior.[8] Thus, when a person's verbalizing is discriminative for related, nonverbal behavior, one is no longer dealing with a unitary functional operant. The correlated hypothesizing, as behavior, would be one operant class (manding, tacting), and the related performance would be a distinct operant class, that of rule-following (more specifically, tracking, or pliance).

7.3. Intersection of the Two Accounts

Comparison of these two summaries yields the following:

1. Neither account requires the person's stated rules to correspond exactly to the procedure or situation in which the person is functioning. Correlated hypothesizing, directly verified as ongoing activity, is an acceptable notion from both viewpoints.
2. To the extent that details of the verified hypothesizing correspond exactly to details of the related performance with respect to procedure, the two accounts could be very similar. The cognitivist would subdivide the person's functioning into overt performance and mental activity. The behaviorist would subdivide it into the distinct but related repertoires of rule-stating and rule-following. It would be difficult but

[8]It should be noted that some contemporary behavior-analytic accounts of verbal functioning, although retaining a prominent role for reinforcement principles and their traditional elaborations that we have described above, have also begun to include additional principles related to equivalence classes, which appear to be unique to humans (e.g., see Sidman, Rauzin, Lazar, Cunningham, Tailby, & Carrigan, 1982), may be the basis for symbolic relations (Sidman, 1986) and appear to be correlated with the development of linguistic functioning (Devany, Hayes, & Nelson, 1986). Although these could be used for further elaboration of the workings of rule-governed behavior, especially to account for rule-following in novel situations, they have not been included here because at their present degree of development, they do not change our basic arguments.

interpretively important to distinguish the hypothesizing from performance, verifying that they were not a single functional operant. (Techniques for achieving this have been described by Shimoff, Matthews, and Catania, 1986, and by Hayes, Brownstein, Haas, and Greenway, 1986, which we shall describe later.)

3. To the extent that one can verify that correlated hypothesizing is actually occurring but that it is not veridically related to the *performance* that it is proposed to account for, the cognitivist interpretation in terms of correlated hypothesizing is seriously undermined, and is untenable as an alternative account of operant behavior. That type of result, which cognitivists do acknowledge as occurring (e.g., see Siegler, 1983), requires them to allow for substantial unconscious functioning.

Any of several behavior-analytic accounts could be valid here: If it were found that the verbalizing was irrelevant to performance, the verbalizing and other performance could be independent operants, or the verbalizing could be superstitious, incidental part of a unitary functional operant. If, on the one hand, the performance were affected by the verbalizing but was not veridically related to the description, the verbalizing could be collateral (e.g., effective as a result of the time it occupies) or functionally a rule but accompanied by an inadequate repertoire of rule-following.

8. ADDITIONAL EXPERIMENTAL TECHNIQUES ADDRESSING HYPOTHESES AND RULES

There are a few types of evidence that might facilitate detailed evaluations such as those outlined here, but in specific cases rather than in abstract, general ones. The first is to consider the relationship between "saying and doing," another is to evaluate possible cases in which verbal reports can and do disrupt performance, and, finally, there could be other techniques for distinguishing specific instances of rule-governed and contingency-shaped behavior.

We have identified some of the studies of disparity between what people do and what they say about what they do (e.g., Lloyd, 1980; Nisbett & Wilson, 1977). Although behavior analysts find this work useful for assessing some of the roles of verbal behavior in other behavior, we have noted that cognitivist accounts typically give interpretive primacy to specification of rules that are inferred (by the interpreter) from the behavior in question, even if these are inconsistent with what the experimental subjects say about what they do. Hence, data of these kinds are unlikely to resolve disagreements between the two viewpoints.

A second approach has been pointed out recently by Hayes (1986). One can first establish and evaluate performance within a situation and then explicitly prompt the subject's verbal stating of hypotheses. If the person has been verbally hypothesizing all along, the overt stating of the hypotheses should result in no appreciable change in the related performance. One might thus conclude that the hypothesizing was involved even when not prompted and made overt. On the other hand, if performance changes, then one might argue that hypothesizing, as a separate activity, was not previously involved in the performance.

Conversely, one might try disrupting performance by providing a concurrent verbal task that would compete with hypothesizing in relation to the experiment. If the behavior were not under verbal control, it could perhaps continue without disruption. Of course, there are limits to the independence of verbal and nonverbal repertories, as when a verbal argument might interfere with one's driving a car. Furthermore, the exact nature of the disruption may be difficult to identify. For example, Laties and Weiss (1963) exposed subjects to a signal-detection task in which signals were presented according to a FI schedule; they were concerned to evaluate the roles of behavior that the subjects emitted during the intervals. They found that when the subjects were required to do successive substractions from 1,000 during the interval, the spacing of responses changed. Clearly, the subjects' behavior of subtracting interfered with behavior involved in the spacing of button presses. Part of the behavior interfered with could be the correlated hypothesizing itself. Or if we assume, as the authors did, that patterns such as singing and counting played a collateral role in the spacing of button pressing and further that it was disruption of those patterns that resulted in changes produced by adding the concurrent substraction task, there still remain two alternative interpretations. According to one, those patterns in themselves constituted the difference between the descriptive and the functional operant, and no correlated hypothesizing need be involved. According to the other interpretation, correlated hypothesizing could specify singing and counting as part of the contingency. Yet another interpretation that includes correlated hypothesizing would have the hypothesis specifying time, and the singing and counting would be an explicit technique for timing and thus spacing one's responses.

Other techniques for distinguishing rule-governed and contingency-shaped behavior have been emerging within basic behavioral research on human behavior. Two examples are provided by Shimoff, Catania, and Matthews (1986) and by Hayes, Brownstein, Haas, and Greenway (1986). In the former, the subjects were explicitly taught provisional descriptions of contingencies, and then their guessing was shaped during occasional interruptions of a multiple schedule of reinforced button pressing, in a manner that resulted in behavior that mimicked conventional schedule performances, producing apparent sensitivity to the differences between schedules. Then, carefully chosen manipulations of the schedules were introduced, in ways that would result in one change if the behavior were rule-governed and a different change if it were contingency shaped. The former proved to be the operative principle. The study by Hayes *et al.* employed instructions of varying degrees of accuracy with respect to complex schedules of reinforced button pressing. These were carefully chosen in such a way that responding during subsequent extinction procedures revealed whether the behavior had been rule-governed or contingency shaped.

The logic of these techniques bears some similarity to that of work described by Siegler (1983), which is presented in the cognitivist tradition, as assessing children's knowledge and the teaching of new knowledge in problem solving. He presented children with carefully devised sets of "balance-beam" problems that enabled him to discern, through the patterns of the children's errors, which of several possible rules (that had been provisionally identified by the experimenter) might be operative in the children's performances. Although Siegler's stated rationale and interpretations seem inimical to behavior analysis, the actual research is strongly reminiscent of behaviorally based teaching. That is, Siegler demonstrates the importance of making changes that permitted success through relatively small changes between the child's currently inferred hypothesis and the hypothesis that could cope with a new problem. Whether one treats the hypotheses as operants (verbally stated rules), or whether one focuses on the child's direct interactions with the environment, this is the venerable behaviorist principle of "shaping through differential reinforcement of sucessive approximations." There is even a more refined point of similarity between this and traditional behavioral work: That is, special procedures were used to teach the child to attend to particular dimensions of the problem—such as the weights of the stimuli or their distances along the balance beam. Although Siegler uses the cognitivist characterization of "encoding" of a dimension, the effects were identical with what a behavior analyst would call discriminative control by, or sensitivity to, a stimulus dimension. In addition, it should be pointed out that a major focus of behavioral work in this domain has been to develop a person's new repertoires *without* the necessity of producing errors, even for the evaluation of those repertoires. Touchette (1971) demonstrated an ingenious way of achieving this when shifting the child's sensitivity from one stimulus dimension to another. Behavioral work on programmed instruction, beginning more than three decades ago, has focused on achieving the same with respect to complex concepts (Skinner, 1961, 1968).

9. CONVERGING BUT DISTINCT INTERPRETATIONS

It is not surprising that when a given experiment is interpreted by both behaviorists and cognitivists, they often draw rather different conclusions. Early arguments between proponents of the two positions revolved around the notion of awareness or consciousness in human behavior during conditioning experiments. The cognitivist account took awareness as a fundamental feature of primary memory and as a theoretical primitive in interpretations of human learning. More recently, cognitivists have conceded that at least some unconscious learning occurs, and it is widely acknowledged that a person may not be able to describe the rules (which at least sometimes are formally equivalent to hypotheses) that a cognitivist would say the person is following.

The behavior-analytic account also has evolved during the past two decades. Although B. F. Skinner's systematic interpretation of verbal behavior had been published in 1957, the researchers who were interpreting human behavior on schedules of reinforcement during the 1960s gave accounts that treated verbal functioning as irrelevant or superfluous. More recently, behavior analysts have focused on the interplay between verbal and nonverbal behavior during experimental procedures, and some aspects of this verbal functioning have been occasions for behavior analysts to appropriately speak of awareness.

Hence, the two types of interpretation have converged somewhat, each allowing that a person learns through being aware or unaware, depending on the circumstances. We may all agree that in laboratory experiments, adult subjects are typically aware of the experimenter and may try to "second guess" the rules of the experiment. The dividing question is, what *is* that process? Is it close to primary process in human behavior, to the point of being prior to language? Or is it based on the contingencies of verbal behavior? The two positions still differ regarding the origins of awareness and the degree to which it is fundamental and in the way to characterize the roles of language. As the behaviorist account is elaborated to deal with the verbal domain in greater detail, or if cognitivist research comes to address nonverbal behavior–environment relations as arrayed over time, additional similarities may emerge between the cognitivist and behaviorist accounts: The data should require this to be true. However, given their differing starting points and given the differences between what each accepts as explanation, the two types of interpretation are likely to remain distinct.

10. REFERENCES

Adams, J. (1957). Laboratory studies of behavior without awareness. *Psychological Bulletin, 54,* 383–405.

Anderson, J. R. (1980). *Cognitive psychology and its implications.* San Francisco: W. H. Freeman

Baum, W. M. (1974). On two types of deviation from the matching law: Bias and undermatching. *Journal of the Experimental Analysis of Behavior, 22,* 231–242.

Bem, S. L. (1967). Verbal self-control: The establishment of effective self-instruction. *Journal of Experimental Psychology, 14,* 485–491.

Bentall, R. P., & Lowe, C. F. (1987). The role of verbal behavior in human learning: III. Instructional effects in children. *Journal of the Experimental Analysis of Behavior, 47,* 177–190.

Bentall, R. P., Lowe, C. F., & Beasty, A. (1985). The role of verbal behavior in human learning: II. Developmental differences. *Journal of the Experimental Analysis of Behavior, 43,* 165–181.

Black, A. H. (1971). The direct control of neural processes by reward and punishment. *The American Scientist, 59*, 236–245.

Boren, M. C. P. (1973). Fixed-ratio and variable-ratio schedules of brief stimuli in second-order schedules of matching to sample. *Journal of the Experimental Analysis of Behavior, 20*, 219–234.

Bower, G., & Trobasso, T. (1964). Concept identification. In R. C. Atkinson (Ed.), *Studies in mathematical psychology* (pp. 32–96). Stanford: Stanford University Press.

Brewer, W. F. (1975). There is no convincing evidence for operant or classical conditioning in adult humans. In W. B. Weimer & D. S. Palermo (Eds.), *Cognitive and symbolic processes* (pp. 1–56). Hillsdale, NJ.: Erlbaum.

Brown, P. L., & Jenkins, H. M. (1968). Auto-shaping of the pigeon's key-peck. *Journal of the Experimental Analysis of Behavior, 11*, 1–8.

Bruner, A., & Revusky, S. H. (1961). Collateral behavior in humans. *Journal of the Experimental Analysis of Behavior, 4*, 349–350.

Catania, A. C. (1973). The concept of the operant in the analysis of behavior. *Behaviorism, 1*, 103–116.

Catania, A. C., Matthews, B. A., & Shimoff, E. (1982). Instructed versus shaped human verbal behavior: Interactions with nonverbal responding. *Journal of the Experimental Analysis of Behavior, 38*, 233–248.

Centers, R. (1963). A laboratory adaptation of the conversational procedure for the conditioning of verbal operants. *Journal of Abnormal and Social Psychology, 67*, 334-339.

Cumming, W. W., & Berryman, R. (1965). The complex discriminated operant: Studies of matching-to-sample and related problems. In D. Mostofsky (Ed.), *Stimulus generalization* (pp. 284–330). Stanford: Stanford University Press.

Chomsky, N. (1959). *Verbal Behavior*, by B. F. Skinner. *Language, 35*, 26–58. Reprinted as item A-34 in the Bobbs-Merrill Reprint Series in the Social Sciences, and in J. A. Fodor and J. J. Katz, (1964) *The Structures of language: readings in the philosophy of Language*. Englewood Cliffs, NJ: Prentice-Hall.

Davidson, N. A., & Osborne, J. G. (1974). Fixed-ratio and fixed-interval schedule control of matching-to-sample errors by children. *Journal of the Experimental Analysis of Behavior, 21*, 27–36.

Dawkins, R. (1981). Selfish genes and selfish memes. In D. R. Hofstadter & D. C. Dennett (Eds.), *The mind's I: Fantasies and reflections on self and soul* (pp. 124–144). New York: Basic Books.

Dawkins, R. (1982). *The extended phenotype*. Oxford: Oxford University Press.

DeNike, L. D. (1964). The temporal relationship between awareness and performance in verbal conditioning. *Journal of Experimental Psychology, 68*, 521–529.

Dember, W. N. (1974). Motivation and the cognitive revolution. *American Psychologist, 29*, 161–168.

Devany, J. M., Hayes, S. C., & Nelson, R. O. (1986). Equivalence class formation in language-able and language-disabled children. *Journal of the Experimental Analysis of Behavior, 46*, 243–257.

Dulany, D. E. (1961). Hypotheses and habits in verbal "operant conditioning." *Journal of Abnormal & Social Psychology, 63* (2), 251–263.

Ericsson, K. A., & Simon, H. A. (1980). Verbal reports as data. *Psychological Review, 87*, 215–251.

Estes, W. K., & Skinner, B. F. (1941). Some quantitative properties of anxiety. *Journal of Experimental Psychology, 29*, 390–400.

Falk, J. L. (1966). Schedule-induced polydipsia as a function of fixed-interval length. *Journal of the Experimental Analysis of Behavior, 9*, 37–39.

Ferster, C. B. (1960). Intermittent reinforcement of matching to sample in the pigeon. *Journal of the Experimental Analysis of Behavior, 3,* 259–272.

Ferster, C. B., & Skinner, B. F. (1957). *Schedules of reinforcement.* New York: Appleton-Century-Crofts.

Flavell, J. H. (1971). First discussant's comments: What is memory development the development of? *Human Development, 14,* 272–278.

Fodor, J. A. (1981). The mind-body problem. *Scientific American, 244,* 114–123.

Greenspoon, J. (1955). The reinforcing effect of two spoken sounds on the frequency of two responses. *American Journal of Psychology, 68,* 409–416.

Greenspoon, J. (1963). Reply to Spielberger and DeNike: "Operant conditioning of plural nouns: A failure to replicate the Greenspoon effect." *Psychological Reports, 12,* 29–30.

Guevremont, D. C., Osnes, P. G., & Stokes, T. F. (1988). The functional role of preschoolers' verbalizations in the generalization of self-instructional training. *Journal of Applied Behavior Analysis, 21,* 45–55.

Harlow, H. F. (1959). Learning set and error factor theory. In S. Koch (Ed.), *Psychology: A study of a science. Vol. 2. General systematic formulations; learning and special processes* (pp. 492–537). New York: McGraw-Hill.

Hawkes, L., & Shimp, C. P. (1974). Choice between response rates. *Journal of the Experimental Analysis of Behavior, 21,* 109–115.

Hayes, S. C. (1986). The case of the silent dog—verbal reports and the analysis of rules: A review of Ericsson and Simon's *Protocol analysis: Verbal reports as data. Journal of the Experimental Analysis of Behavior, 45,* 351–363.

Hayes, S. C., Brownstein, A. J., Haas, J. R., & Greenway, D. E. (1986). Instructions, multiple schedules, and extinction: Distinguishing rule-governed from schedule-controlled behavior. *Journal of the Experimental Analysis of Behavior, 46,* 137–147.

Hefferline, R. F., Keenan, B., & Harford, R. A. (1959). Escape and avoidance conditioning in human subjects without their observation of the response. *Science, 130,* 1338–1339.

Hefferline, R. F., & Pererra, T. B. (1963). Proprioceptive discrimination of a covert operant without its observation by the subject. *Science, 139,* 834–835.

Herrnstein, R. J. (1979). Acquisition, generalization, and discrimination reversal of a natural concept. *Journal of Experimental Psychology: Animal Behavior Processes, 5,* 116–129.

Hineline, P. N. (1983). When we speak of knowing. *The Behavior Analyst, 6,* 183–186.

Hineline, P. N. (1984). What, then, is Skinner's operationism? *Behavioral and Brain Sciences, 7,* 560.

Hineline, P. N. (1986). Re-tuning the operant-respondent distinction. In Travis Thompson & M. D. Zeiler (Eds.), *Analysis and integration of behavioral units* (pp. 55–79). Hillsdale, NJ: Earlbaum.

Kendler, H. H., & Spence, J. T. (Eds.). (1971). *Essays in neobehaviorism: A memorial volume to Kenneth W. Spence.* New York: Appleton-Century-Crofts.

Kihlstrom, J. F. (1987). The cognitive unconscious. *Science, 237,* 1445–1452.

Kluwe, R. H. (1982). Cognitive knowledge and executive control: Metacognition. In D. F. Griffin (Ed.), *Animal mind-human mind* (pp. 201–224). New York: Springer-Verlag.

Krechevsky, I. (1932). "Hypotheses" in rats. *Psychological Review, 39,* 516–532.

Lacey, H. M., & Rachlin, H. (1978). Behavior, cognition and theories of choice. *Behaviorism, 6,* 177–202.

Lamarre, J., & Holland, J. G. (1985). The functional independence of mands and tacts. *Journal of the Experimental Analysis of Behavior, 43,* 5–19.

Laties, V. G., & Weiss, B. (1963). Effects of a concurrent task on fixed-interval responding in humans. *Journal of the Experimental Analysis of Behavior, 6,* 431–436.

Laties, V. G., Weiss, B., Clark, R. L., & Reynolds, M. D. (1965). Overt "mediating" behavior during temporally spaced responding. *Journal of the Experimental Analysis of Behavior, 8,* 107–116.

Lattal, K. A. (1975). Reinforcement contingency as discriminative stimulus. *Journal of the Experimental Analysis of Behavior, 23,* 241–246.

Laurenti-Lions, L., Gallego, J., Chambille, B., Vardon, G., & Jacquemin, C. (1985). Control of myoelectrical responses through reinforcement. *Journal of the Experimental Analysis of Behavior, 44,* 185–193.

Levine, M. (1966). Hypothesis behavior by humans during discrimination learning. *Journal of Experimental Psychology, 71,* 331–338.

Levine, M. (1975). *A cognitive theory of learning.* Hillsdale, NJ: Erlbaum.

Libet, B. (1985). Unconscious cerebral initiative and the role of conscious will in voluntary action (and related commentary). *Behavioral and Brain Sciences, 8,* 529–566.

Lloyd, K. E. (1980). Do as I say; not as I do. *New Zealand Psychologist, 9,* 1–8.

Lowe, C. F. (1979). Determinants of human operant behavior. In M. D. Zeiler and P. Harzem (Eds.), *Advances in analysis of behaviour (Vol. 1): Reinforcement and the organization of behaviour* (pp. 159–192). Chichester and New York: Wiley.

Lowe, C. F., Beasty, A., & Bentall, R. P. (1983). The role of verbal behavior in human learning: Infant performance on fixed-interval schedules. *Journal of the Experimental Analysis of Behavior, 39,* 157–164.

MacCorquodale, K. (1970). On Chomsky's review of Skinner's *Verbal Behavior. Journal of the Experimental Analysis of Behavior, 13,* 83–99.

MacCorquodale, K., & Meehl, P. E. (1948). On a distinction between hypothetical constructs and intervening variables. *Psychological Review, 55,* 95–107.

Matthews, B. A., Catania, A. C., & Shimoff, E. (1985). Effects of uninstructed verbal behavior on nonverbal responding: Contingency descriptions versus performance descriptions. *Journal of the Experimental Analysis of Behavior, 43,* 155–164.

Millenson, J. R., & Leslie, J. (1979). *Principles of behavioral analysis* (2nd ed.). New York: Macmillan.

Morris, E. K., Higgins, S. T., & Bickel, W. K. (1982). Comments on cognitive science in the experimental analysis of behavior. *The Behavior Analyst, 5,* 109–125.

Neuringer, A. (1986). Can people behave "randomly?": The role of feedback. *Journal of Experimental Psychology: General, 115,* 62–75.

Nevin, J. A., & Liebold, K. (1966). Stimulus control of matching and oddity in a pigeon. *Psychonomic Science, 5,* 351–352.

Nisbett, R. E., & Wilson, T. C. (1977). Telling more than we know: Verbal reports on mental processes. *Psychological Review, 84,* 231–259.

Norman, D. A. (1969). *Memory and attention: An introduction to human information processing.* New York: John Wiley & Sons.

Orne, M. T. (1962). On the social psychology of the psychological experiment: With particular reference to demand characteristics and their implications. *American Psychologist, 17,* 776–783.

Putnam, H. (1973). Reductionism and the nature of psychology. *Cognition, 2,* 131–146.

Richardson, W. K., & Clark, D. B. (1976). A comparison of the key-peck and treadle-press operants in the pigeon: Differential-reinforcement-of-low-rate schedule of reinforcement. *Journal of the Experimental Analysis of Behavior, 26,* 237–256.

Rogers-Warren, A., & Baer, D. M. (1976). Correspondence between saying and doing: Teaching children to share and praise. *Journal of Applied Behavior Analysis, 9,* 335–354.

Rosenfeld, J. P., Rudell, A. P., & Fox, S. S. (1969). Operant control of neural events in humans. *Science, 165,* 821–823.

Salzinger, K. (1986). *Cognitive problems, behavioral solutions.* Paper presented at the Behaviorists' European Summer Academy, Bad Kreuznach, Germany, June 1986.

Salzinger, K., & Pisoni, S. (1960). Reinforcement of verbal affect responses of normal subjects during the interview. *Journal of Abnormal and Social Psychology, 60,* 127–130.

Schnaitter, R. (1978). Private causes. *Behaviorism, 6,* 1–12.

Shepard, R. N., & Metzler, B. (1971). Mental rotation of three-dimensional objects. *Science, 171,* 701–703.

Shimoff, E., Matthews, B. A., & Catania, A. C. (1986). Human operant performance: Sensitivity and pseudosensitivity to contingencies. *Journal of the Experimental Analysis of Behavior, 46,* 149–157.

Shimoff, E., Catania, A. C., & Matthews, B. A. (1981). Uninstructed human responding: Sensitivity of low-rate performance to schedule contingencies. *Journal of the Experimental Analysis of Behavior, 36,* 207–218.

Shimp, C. P. (1970). The concurrent reinforcement of two interresponae times: Absolute rate of reinforcment. *Journal of the Experimental Analysis of Behavior, 13,* 1–8.

Shimp, C. P. (1983). The local organization of behavior: Dissociations between a pigeon's behavior and self-reports of that behavior. *Journal of the Experimental Analysis of Behavior, 39,* 61–68

Shinkman, P. G., Bruce, C. J., & Pfingst, B. E. (1974). Operant conditioning of single-unit response patterns in visual cortex. *Science, 184,* 1194–1196.

Sidman, M. (1986). Functional analysis of emergent verbal classes. In T. Thompson & M. D. Zeiler (Eds.), *Analysis and integration of behavioral units* (pp. 213–245). Hillsdale, NJ: Erlbaum.

Sidman, M., Rauzin, R., Lazar, R., Cunningham, S., Tailby, W., & Carrigan, P. (1982). A search for symmetry in the conditional discriminations of rhesus monkeys, baboons, and children. *Journal of the Experimental Analysis of Behavior, 37,* 23–44.

Siegler, R. S. (1983). How knowledge influences learning. *American Scientist, 71,* 631–638.

Skinner, B. F. (1931). The concept of the reflex in the description of behavior. *Journal of General Psychology, 5,* 427–458.

Skinner, B. F. (1935). The generic nature of the concepts of stimulus and response. *Journal of General Psychology, 12,* 40–65.

Skinner, B. F. (1938). *The behavior of organisms.* New York: Appleton-Century-Crofts.

Skinner, B. F. (1945). The operational analysis of psychological terms. *Psychological Review, 52,* 270–277, 291–294.

Skinner, B. F. (1950). Are theories of learning necessary? *Psychological Review, 57,* 193–216.

Skinner, B. F. (1953). *Science and human behavior.* New York: Macmillan.

Skinner, B. F. (1957). *Verbal behavior.* New York: Appleton-Century Crofts.

Skinner, B. F. (1961). Why we need teaching machines. *Harvard Educational Review, 31,* 377–398.

Skinner, B. F. (1963). Behaviorism at fifty. *Science, 140,* 951–958.

Skinner, B. F. (1968). *The technology of teaching.* New York: Appleton-Century-Crofts.

Skinner, B. F. (1969). *Contingencies of reinforcement: A theoretical analysis.* New York: Appleton-Century-Crofts.

Skinner, B. F. (1974). *About behaviorism.* New York: Knopf.

Skinner, B. F. (1977). Why I am not a cognitive psychologist. *Behaviorism, 5,* 1–10.

Skinner, B. F. (1981). Selection by consequences. *Science, 213,* 501–504.

Smith, T. L. (1986). Biology as allegory: A review of Elliott Sober's *The nature of selection. Journal of the Experimental Analysis of Behavior, 46,* 105–112.

Sober, E. (1984). *The nature of selection: Evolutionary theory in philosophical focus.* Cambridge, MA: MIT Press.

Spielberger, C. D., & DeNike, L. D. (1966). Descriptive behaviorism versus cognitive theory in verbal operant conditioning. *Psychological Review, 73,* 306–326.

Stubbs, A. (1968). The discrimination of stimulus duration by pigeons. *Journal of the Experimental Analysis of Behavior, 11,* 223–238.

Touchette, P. E. (1971). Transfer of stimulus control: Measuring the moment of transfer. *Journal of the Experimental Analysis of Behavior, 15*, 347–354.

Vaughan, W., & Herrnstein, R. J. (1987). Choosing among natural stimuli. *Journal of the Experimental Analysis of Behavior, 47*, 5–16.

Weisberg, R. W. (1980). *Memory, thought, and behavior*. New York: Oxford University Press.

Wilson, M. P., & Keller, F. S. (1953). On the selective reinforcement of spaced responses. *Journal of Comparative and Physiological Psychology, 46*, 190–193.

Zettle, R. D., & Hayes, S. C. (1982). Rule-governed behavior: A potential theoretical framework for cognitive-behavioral therapy. In P. C. Kendall (Ed.), *Advances in cognitive-behavioral research and therapy, volume I* (pp. 73–118). New York: Academic Press.

CHAPTER 8

The Achievement of Evasive Goals

Control by Rules Describing Contingencies That Are Not Direct Acting

RICHARD W. MALOTT

1. INTRODUCTION

Why do we have so much trouble with procrastination? Why do we have so much trouble leading healthy lives of proper diet and exercise, to floss our teeth, to wear seat belts, to stop smoking? Why do we have so much trouble doing what we know we should? Perhaps an even more difficult question: Why do at least a few others have so much less trouble with procrastination, proper diet and exercise, flossing, wearing seat belts, and not smoking?

The answer to these questions may help us understand both the major and minor behavior problems we encounter in our normal, everyday lives in a variety of settings, such as the home, the school, and the workplace. Though outside the scope of the present chapter, the answer might also help us understand much of the pathological behavior with which psychologists are traditionally concerned—the behavioral or psychological problems of people labeled neurotic, retarded, and even psychotic.

More generally, this chapter addresses the following problem: The complex behaviors I mentioned involve striated muscles and thus are probably operant behaviors. So we should be able to demonstrate their operant nature by showing that their likelihood is increased or decreased as a result of their outcomes. However, I will argue that, to be effective, those outcomes must be immediate, probable, and sizable. Furthermore, I will argue that we often end up with maladaptive behavior, when important outcomes are not immediate, probable, and sizable. In addition, I will consider ways in which outcomes

---

RICHARD W. MALOTT • Department of Psychology, Western Michigan University, Kalamazoo, Michigan 49008.

might indirectly control rule-governed behavior, even though they are not immediate, probable, and sizable. First, let us consider the need for immediate, probable, and sizable outcomes. (For more details of this analysis, see Malott, 1984, 1986.)

2. CONTINGENCIES THAT ARE NOT DIRECT ACTING

First, let us divide behavioral contingencies into two general classes, according to the relationship between the outcome and the response that produces that outcome (the causal response). One class consists of contingencies that are direct acting, and the other class consists of contingencies that are not. A *direct-acting contingency* involves outcomes that function as behavioral consequences for the causal response class. (A stimulus or event functions as a *behavioral consequence* if it will reinforce or punish a response.) For example, touching a hot stove produces the outcome of a burn that will effectively punish the touching response. In the following sections, I will argue such outcomes are effective because they are immediate, probable, and sizable. (I use *outcome* as a generic term to refer to the results of responding that may either be behavioral consequences or may be neutral, that is, that may neither reinforce nor punish the preceding response class.)

A *contingency that is not direct acting* involves outcomes that do not function as effective behavioral consequences for the causal response. I will argue that such outcomes are ineffective either because they are too delayed, too improbable, or too small (though perhaps of cumulative significance). For example, consider the dental-flossing contingency: Daily flossing produces the outcome that your teeth and gums will be much healthier than otherwise. I suggest that this contingency is not direct acting because the improved health is too delayed and a single flossing produces too small an effect on dental health, though the healthy outcome accumulated from a lifetime of flossing is considerable. We will now consider, individually the effects of delayed, improbable, and small but cumulating outcomes.

3. DELAYED OUTCOMES

In this section, we will consider evidence for and against the argument that outcomes of our actions must be immediate, if they are to reinforce or punish those actions. In doing so, we will look at human behavior in our contemporary environment, behavior in the laboratory, and behavior in more natural or primitive environments, including behavior involved in the bait-shy phenomenon. We will also consider interpretations in terms of response specificity and in terms of the correlation-based law of effect. Because this is a more controversial issue, we will address the evidence for and against the deleterious effect of delays in greater detail than for the deleterious effects of low probability and small, but cumulatively significant, outcomes.

3.1. Human Behavior

3.1.1. *The Ineffectiveness of Delayed Reinforcement and Punishment of Human Behavior*

Many everyday observations suggest that the delayed outcomes of our actions are ineffective as behavioral consequences for those causal actions; only immediate outcomes appear to function as effective behavioral consequences. This may be true even when the delayed outcomes are quite harmful. For example, consider nicotine, alcohol, caffeine, and other such drugs. The often small, but immediate, outcomes of using those drugs act as powerful rewards, maintaining their use in spite of their often devastating but delayed outcomes. Furthermore, delayed outcomes seem no more effective as behavioral consequences when they are quite favorable. For example, consider doing physical exercise or dental flossing. Their low frequency of occurrence suggests that their extremely worthwhile, but delayed, outcomes do not reinforce the causal actions; instead exercise and flossing are often suppressed by their small, but immediate, aversive outcomes, by their interference with the attainment of competing rewards, and by the effort involved. (I define *reward* as a stimulus condition organisms tend to maximize contact with, a slightly more general definition than positive reinforcer, which is procedurally defined only in terms of the reinforcement procedure. Similarly, I define *aversive stimulus* as a stimulus condition organisms tend to minimize contact with. [For more discussion of these definitions, see Malott, Tillema, & Glenn, 1978, Chapter 1].)

3.1.2. *The Importance of Knowledge of the Contingency*

However, there are many everyday occasions when human behavior appears to be controlled by delayed reinforcement and punishment. Therefore, many behavior analysts and cognitive behavior modifiers seem to take the commonsense view that knowledge of delayed behavioral outcomes will somehow allow those delayed outcomes to reinforce and punish the causal behavior. I address this view in a review of a textbook on behavior analysis (1988, pp. 141–142):

> Delayed outcomes do not reinforce or punish behavior. Most behavior analysts know this and so do their grandmothers. However, they forget this restriction, when applying behavior analysis to everyday life, a cornucopia of delayed outcomes. And at first glance, the Baldwins (Baldwin & Baldwin, 1986) seem to follow suit—for

> example: "Receiving an award for breaking a track record provides positive reinforcement for regular exercise and training" (p. 14). However, the outcome comes too late to reinforce the exercise and training.
>
> Later the Baldwin's even acknowledge that, "Generally, operant conditioning is most likely to occur when reinforcers and punishers follow immediately after an operant" (p. 32). Didn't they see their inconsistency? Yes; on the next page they say, "Delayed consequences can cause operant conditioning if a contingent, causal relationship between a behavior and its consequences is detected." Thus the Baldwins surge way ahead of the rest of the pack, but they have not yet reached the finish line. They have not done a behavior analysis of how knowledge of the causal relationship allows the delayed consequence to control future occurrences of the causal response class. (p. 141)

3.1.2a. A Theory of the Relation between Knowledge and Delayed Reinforcement and Punishment. Hayes and Myerson (1986, May) do offer an analysis of the effects of knowledge of the causal relation. I will deal in some detail with their analysis because it is a careful explanation of how knowledge might facilitate delayed reinforcement and punishment. In other words, they provide an explanation of what many others take for granted. However, before considering their analysis of the role of knowledge of the contingencies, it may help to examine their analysis of the deleterious effects of delays.

3.1.2b. Competing Behaviors and the Effects of Delayed Outcomes. Hayes and Myerson (1986, May) also argue against the notion that the delayed delivery of outcomes can normally reinforce the causal response class. They point out that it does not make evolutionary sense for every outcome to affect all responses that precede it; too many irrelevant and even inappropriate responses would be affected. Furthermore, they suggest that no combination of known principles of behavior could account for the differential effects of such delayed outcomes, if those effects were to occur. However, they also suggest that the reduced effectiveness of delayed reinforcement and punishment may result from the learning of incompatible responses; the delay may have no direct effect on the reinforcing or punishing value of the delayed outcome. In other words, they propose that there is no fundamental gradient of delay, just more opportunity for competing responses to be reinforced.

3.1.2c. A Critique of the Theory of Competing Behaviors. From the intuitive, subjective point of view of introspective behaviorism, it does not seem reasonable to suggest that a reward delivered a year from now will strengthen all of the intervening classes of behaviors occurring during that 1 year interval and prior to it as well. The only thing that would prevent the organism from running off in a thousand different directions at once would be the physical impossibility of it all.

More importantly, the notion of increasing the likelihood of competing behaviors seems useful only in the context of a gradient of the effects of behaviorally effective delayed consequences. If we have a gradient, then we would expect, for instance, that the irrelevant response classes temporally closest to the delivery of the reward would be more affected by that reinforcer than would be the more distant causal response class. In addition, the resulting increased frequency of occurrence of the irrelevant response would prevent the causal response class from increasing in frequency as much as it would otherwise. So the analysis in terms of competing responses does not seem to replace the analysis in terms of gradients of delay, if an assumption of gradients of delay is needed for the competing-response analysis to work.

Furthermore, if there were no gradient of delay, all responses would increase in likelihood equally, regardless of their temporal proximity to the delivery of the reward. No response would increase differentially. Under such conditions, it would seem that operant conditioning could never be demonstrated, and the rat would starve to death in the test chamber. The only defense between the rat and starvation is the possibility that no other response would be associated with reinforcement as frequently as the causal bar-press response (W. Fuqua, personal communication, May 27, 1986). However, that defense seems a weak one when the instrumental response has a low operant level, as is often the case for the animal in the operant test chamber, for example. In summary, the notion of interference does not seem to me to be a good substitute for the notion of a gradient of delay.

3.1.2d. An Introduction to the Behavioral Concept of Rules. The Hayes and Myerson theory of response selectivity, as well as much of the remaining analysis in this chapter, makes use of the behavioral concept of rule; so a few comments about this concept also seem in order before directly addressing their theory: By *rule,* I mean a verbal description of a behavioral contingency. For example, "If you touch that stove when it's hot, you'll burn yourself." Or, "Tell that joke to Jim, he'll like it." A behavioral contingency consists of a response, an outcome, and a discriminative stimulus in the presence of which the response will produce that outcome. For example, in the presence of a hot stove, touching that stove will produce an aversive burn. Or in the presence of a receptive audience, telling a joke will produce a rewarding laugh.

This definition is only a slight extension of Skinner's 1969 formulation. Although Skinner (1969) discusses rules merely as "contingency-specifying stimuli" (e.g., p. 157), his examples all involve verbal stimuli. Therefore, they seem in keeping with the present spirit of not considering simple, nonverbal stimuli as rules. For example, we would not consider an example of a rule to be the green key light associated with the opportunity for reinforcement of the key peck response in the operant test chamber (Malott, 1982a, May).

The concept of control by rules or rule-governed behavior may help behavior analysts address many of the questions previously of concern only to cognitive psychologists (e.g., Skinner, 1969). In other words, rules provide a behavioral mechanism for understanding how thoughts or self-talk might control goal-oriented behavior. However, we should not confuse the present use of *rules* with the cognitivist's use. The present use of *rule* is as a verbal description of a contingency; and the verbal statement is typically thought of as a discriminative stimulus, though it might be more appropriately thought of as a motivating operation. Cognitive psychologists use the concept of rules and hypotheses to account for the orderly behavior of nonverbal animals, as well as verbal human beings, in problem-solving and learning experiments. In some instances, their use of *rule* or *hypothesis* may be no more than a description of an orderly pattern of behavior, for example, "switch to the left operandum, if responding to the right operandum was not reinforced on the previous trial." However, in other instances, cognitivists seem to use *rule* and *hypothesis* as an intervening variable to actually explain that orderly pattern of behavior. In either case, that is not the same as the present use of *rule* because it is not a verbal description of a contingency, at least not from the point of view of a nonverbal animal.

3.1.2e. The Theory of Response Selectivity and Rule-Governed Behavior. Hayes and Myerson (1986, May) attempt to account for the control-delayed outcomes sometimes seem to exert over causal response classes in human behavior. They say what is needed is a way to prevent irrelevant, potentially interfering responses from being reinforced or punished by the outcome in question, even when the outcome is closer to the irrelevant responses than to the relevant response. They suggest that rules might perform this selective role in the following manner: When a rule is stated to or by the person, that rule-statement prevents the specified outcome from reinforcing or punishing response classes not specified in the rule, thereby leaving the specified response class as the only one to be affected.

Hayes and Myerson propose that this mechanism of selectivity may result from the person's sensitivity to stimulus-equivalence training. (In stimulus-equivalence training, neutral Stimulus A is made equivalent to discriminative Stimulus B and then functions in much the same discriminative way as B.) They suggest that the statement of a rule is a form of verbal stimulus-equivalence training. However, according to their theory, the rule-statement seems more analogous to stimulus-nonequivalence training. In other words, the rule-statement does not establish the delayed outcome as equivalent to an immediate outcome for the causal response. Instead, the rule establishes the delayed outcome as not being equivalent to an immediate outcome for all other responses, for the irrelevant, noncausal responses. The statement of the rule "A causes B" converts B into the equivalent of a behaviorally ineffective outcome for all responses except the causal response class, A.

In any case, their analysis may go considerably beyond the laboratory demonstrations of stimulus equivalence training, where stimuli are established as equivalent in terms of their function as discriminative stimuli (e.g., Sidman, Rouzin, Lazer, Cunningham, Tailby, & Carrigan, 1983). In other words, Hayes and Myerson are going beyond the establishment of stimuli as equivalent in terms of their function as discriminative stimuli, when they suggest equivalence in terms of their function as conditioned rewards and conditioned aversive stimuli.

Clearly, with the right rules and the right conditions, a delayed outcome does appear to control behavior almost as if it were a direct-acting, behaviorally effective consequence reinforcing or punishing that behavior. However, that does not mean the delayed outcome controls the response by actually reinforcing or punishing that response class; instead, another mechanism might be involved.

In summary, the theory of response selectivity seems to rest on two assumptions: (1) All responses are equally affected by rewards and aversive stimuli, regardless of the time delay between those responses and stimuli; and (2) as a form of stimulus-equivalence training, rules restrict the reinforcing and punishing effects of those stimuli to the response classes specified in the rules. I am skeptical of both assumptions for two reasons: First, they are assumptions and not laboratory-derived principles. Second, they do not account for the control of behavior when a rule has been stated prior to the first opportunity to emit the behavior.

3.1.3. The Correlation-Based Law of Effect

Alternatively, we could call on the correlation-based law of effect to account for the control that delayed outcomes might exert over human behavior. The correlation-based law of effect states that the molar relation between response and reinforcement is responsible for instrumental behavior and that simple response-reinforcement contiguity is neither sufficient nor necessary (Baum, 1973). In other words, responding will be maintained, if rewards are delivered at a higher rate during periods of time when that responding occurs at a higher rate, though those rewards may never immediately follow the responses. For example, if your floss your teeth at a high rate (once a day) and if you get approval from your dental hygienist at a high rate (once every 6 months), then this correlation between the high rate of flossing and high rate of dental-hygienist approval will be sufficient to reinforce the act of flossing.

Even if we were to assume a correlation-based law of effect (and many molecular-oriented behavior analysts do not), the natural outcomes of many of our everyday behaviors are so greatly delayed (days, weeks, months, and years) that they are way outside the range of temporal relations studied in the laboratory from a correlation-based view. Thus it might require excessive faith in the power of extrapolation to suggest that any evidence for the correlation-based law of effect from the laboratory would be relevant to such everyday human behaviors.

Furthermore, even if we were to make that considerable extrapolation, we would still have to account for why those delayed outcomes would not affect all behavior, why their effects would be largely restricted to the causal response class. Such an accounting would be especially difficult if there are high probability behaviors in the organism's repertoire that might be as frequently associated with the delayed outcome as is the causal response class. (As mentioned before, Hayes & Myerson, 1986, address this problem; however, the earlier objections to their interpretation still apply.)

3.2. Basic Research

There is at least one major problem with the previously cited everyday observations of the ineffectiveness of the delayed delivery of behavioral consequences: The outcomes are often not only delayed, but they are also the cumulative product of many individually insignificant outcomes. For example, the outcome of smoking cigarettes is cumulative in the sense that no single puff of a cigarette will have much effect; only after smoking many packs, over many years, will the harmful effects appear; and even then, some of those effects may not only be delayed but may also be improbable, for example, lung cancer. So it may be that in these everyday examples, the lack of control of the outcome may be more a result of its small and cumulative nature or its low probability than it is a result of its delay. Laboratory research may more effectively eliminate this confounding of delay with the effects of small and low probability.

As Malott and Garcia (in press) state:

> From Watson to the present, the issue of delayed reinforcement (and punishment) has been under debate. Several behaviorists have argued that a stimulus does not have to immediately follow the response to reinforce or punish that response (Rachlin, 1974; Rachlin & Green, 1972; Solnick, Kannenberg, Eckerman, & Waller, 1980). Others have argued that close temporal contiguity between response and the forthcoming stimulus is essential for that stimulus to control the response (Banks & Vogel-Sprott, 1965; Camp, Raymond, & Church, 1967; Cohen, 1968; Renner, 1966; Spence, 1947; Trenholme & Baron, 1975).

3.2.1. Early Research

> Spence (1947) suggested [that learning does not occur] . . . under conditions of delay of primary reinforcement but instead through contiguous presentations of conditioned reinforcers. Indeed most classical experiments on delayed reinforcement have struggled with the difficulty of controlling the influence of the conditioned reinforcers when studying the effects of delayed reinforcement (Williams, 1973, pp. 38–40). Williams (1973, pp. 40–41) reported Keesey's (1964) experiment as the study that most effectively controlled the influence of secondary reinforcers. And

> perhaps as a result, Keesey found little reinforcement after 5 second's delay. Considerable subsequent research has demonstrated an inverse relation between delay of reinforcement and rate of responding and a positive relation between delay of punishment and rate of responding (Camp *et al.*, 1967; Cohen, 1968; Renner, 1966; Trenholme & Baron, 1975). (Malott & Garcia, in press)

Ferster's (1953) research suggests that where appreciable effects of delayed outcomes have been demonstrated with infrahumans, the causal response may have produced an immediate stimulus change that was terminated with an effective behavioral outcome.

Williams (1973, pp. 41–42) further points out:

> During delays before reinforcement, animals usually engage in some form of stereotyped, superstitious behavior—"superstitious" because it is in no way responsible for the presentation of the reward. . . . These chains of superstitious behavior help the animal to pass time while reinforcement is delayed. With humans, however, such time intervals are mediated by more complicated forms of behavior. People will continue to engage in goal-directed behavior, sometimes for years, because they have been told or know that they will eventually receive reward.

In summary of the earlier work, events that immediately followed the causal response had most likely become learned rewards and probably maintained that response. Furthermore, the response classes were generally well established with immediate rewards, before the delay was introduced.

3.2.1a. Chaining and Everyday Human Behavior. We should pause a moment to consider, the previous quote from Williams (1973, pp. 41–42). It may be misleading, to the extent that it implies that human beings engage in elaborate chains of behavior, superstitious or otherwise, chains that mediate the delay between the response and the outcome. Delays of hours, let alone years, may normally be too long to be explained by such a mechanism. (It is important to consider this issue because many behavior analysts have informally presented similar mediation interpretations of the effects of outcomes of such extreme delays.) One problem with such an analysis is that the superstitious chain of behavior must be either homogeneous (the pigeon keeps pecking the key); or, if it is heterogeneous, it must be stereotyped (a repetitive ritual) in order to bridge the gap. Otherwise the terminal reward would not be able to establish the intermediate learned rewards presumably needed to reinforce such a stimulus response chain.

If the chain consists of a sequence of identical responses, then the pairing of the terminal instance of those responses with the ultimate behavioral consequence would eventually establish each of those identical responses as a learned behavioral consequence and would allow its occurrence to reinforce or punish the causal response it immediately followed. If the chain consists of a sequence of heterogeneous responses, then many more pairings of the chain would be needed, as the links further from the ultimate behavioral consequation gradually acquired their value as learned behavioral-consequences and (through pairing) passed that value on to successively more distant links in the chain. Unfortunately, that would take a much larger number of pairings than is likely to occur in our everyday world. However, an even greater problem is that we never engage in either homogeneous response chains or stereotyped heterogeneous response chains of any duration; our hours and days and years are filled with too much variety. In addition, we often engage in extended, goal-directed activity that is novel, that cannot be accounted for in terms of past reinforcement of the total chain of the sequence of behaviors leading to that outcome, that goal.

3.2.2. *Current Research*

Malott and Garcia (in press) also state:

> In much contemporary research on the effects of delayed outcomes, the interest has shifted from the effects of a particular combination of time delay and outcome size to the concurrent effects of competing contingencies involving different combinations of time delays and outcome sizes. This is studied with concurrently-presented chained schedules. Wasserman and Moore (1986, May) reviewed such research suggesting that it is the immediate outcome, not the delayed outcome that controls the behavior of animals in experimental settings. . . . Wasserman and Neunaber (1986) have also shown that humans will respond, if the response will produce a more immediate presentation of a conditioned reward (the turning on of a light associated with the presentation of points). . . . Hineline (1970, Experiment 1) [demonstrated] the reinforcing effect of shock delay,

thereby indirectly suggesting a decrease in the effectiveness of delayed aversive outcomes.

The laboratory data may still be viewed by some as equivocal; however, in my view, these data provide little support for the idea that delayed outcomes of more than a few seconds are effective behavioral consequences; and what support they do provide comes from situations irrelevant to the common, everyday events we normally encounter, especially those involving outcomes with extremely long delays.

In any case, there are two reasons why the experimental results with infrahumans may not be too relevant to many of the normal, delayed outcomes humans experience: First, the outcomes of our actions may be delayed by hours, days, weeks, or even years; however, the infrahuman research normally deals with delays of only a few seconds, and even then the effects are weak or equivocal. Second, as mentioned earlier, the intervals between the causal action and the outcomes would contain a wide variety of other actions that would vary greatly from time to time, thus making it unlikely that a superstitious response chain would develop to support the causal response class.

3.3. The Natural Environment

From a commonsense point of view, it seems unlikely that organisms have evolved so that delayed outcomes would have much direct effect, if any, on the response classes that produce them; otherwise those delayed outcomes would surely affect all behaviors that preceded them by comparable delays; and most of those behaviors would have no causal relationship with the delayed outcomes. However, the value of the direct-reinforcing and direct-punishing effects of immediate behavioral consequences is that the response that just precedes an event is most likely the one that caused that event. So it is functional for outcomes to have direct reinforcing and punishing effects on the immediately preceding class of responses. In the same way, most responses that occur some time before an event probably did not produce that event; so it is also most often functional that such delayed events have no direct reinforcing or punishing effects on such response classes; otherwise accidental reinforcement and punishment would lead to a disfunctional chaos.

While discussing the natural or evolutionary environment, we will now consider two phenomena behavior analysts often offer as proof of the general efficacy of delayed reinforcement and punishment in the natural environment. I will argue otherwise. Then we will speculate about the need for the behavior of early human beings to be under the control of delayed outcomes.

3.3.1. Instinctive Control

Behavior does sometimes produce important delayed outcomes, for instance, infrahuman behaviors such as seasonal nest building, food storage, and procreation, behaviors often called "instinctive." It is then disfunctional for the delayed outcomes not to affect those classes of responses that produce them. What mechanism might allow such response classes to be controlled by their outcomes?

If we view those behaviors as operant behavior, then I believe we must find immediate, highly probable, and sizable outcomes to function as behavioral consequences for those response classes. "Instinctive" operant behaviors might be similarly controlled by immediate behavioral consequences that have evolved phylogenetically because of their effects on the survival of the species. For instance, the responses of copulating, nursing, and brooding may be maintained by certain immediate tactile, olfactory, and thermal outcomes that function as instinctive behavioral consequences. In other words, the behavioral consequences become effective only as a result of precurrent hormonal actions, often correlated with seasonal changes, hormonal actions that function as motivating operations (Michael's establishing operation, 1982) to increase the reward value of those particular tactile, olfactory, and thermal stimuli. Though more complex, we might eventually be able to analyze goal-oriented response sequences such as next building in a similar manner.

In summary, perhaps in their natural or evolutionary environments, infrahumans achieve the long-range outcomes of survival and procreation through the effects of immediate behavioral consequences, often of an instinctive, or hormonally induced, periodic nature (Malott & Whaley, 1976, Chapter 6). There seem to be little if any data directly addressing the issue of immediacy of reinforcement and the operant nature of so-called instinctive behaviors; yet this view might provide a fruitful framework for a reexamination of many of the traditional areas of animal behavior.

3.3.2. The Bait-Shy Phenomenon

> Hayes and Myerson (1986, May) point out that, at times, the outcomes of the organism's actions are delayed and it would benefit that organism or the species if those outcomes did appropriately affect the causal response class. They offer the bait-shy phenomenon as an example of this. . . . (The bait-shy phenomenon [also called taste aversion learning] consists of the avoidance of nonpalatable or toxic foods with which the animal has had previous contact [Fantino & Logan, 1979, 344–347]. (Malott & Garcia, in press)

In the case of taste aversion learning, nauseous stimulation will suppress the consumption of food primarily of the same flavor and secondarily of the same smell as food eaten before the nauseous stimulation, even if the time lapse is several hours. This makes evolutionary sense. In the natural environment, the poisonous food often takes a few hours to produce a nauseous effect, and yet it would be to the advantage of the organism if the nauseous stimulation would suppress further eating of that food.

3.3.2a. Incentive Modification versus Behavior Modification. Taste aversion learning is of concern to the present analysis because psychologists have often offered learned taste aversion as proof that delayed behavioral consequences can effectively reinforce or, in this case, punish the causal response, the ingestion of the food. (See Adams, 1980, pp. 142–143, for an example of the assumption that taste aversion demonstrates delayed punishment.) From this assumption, some have informally argued that delayed reinforcement and delayed punishment can, in fact, explain the sorts of problems the current analysis addresses.

However, Garcia, Lasiter, Bermudez-Rattoni, and Deems (1985) suggest that learned taste aversion is an example of "incentive modification," not behavior modification. In other words, the pairing of the taste and the illness establishes the taste as a learned aversive stimulus that will, in the future, punish the response that produces it. The pairing does not establish the taste as a warning stimulus or cue that will decrease the frequency of the ingestion response, such a decrease being a result of previous delayed punishment in the presence of that cue. They say the pairing of neutral stimuli with damage to external tissue of the organism will establish such a cue; however, the pairing of taste and odor with visceral distress will establish a learned aversive stimulus that will later punish the consummatory response.

This is an interpretation of the bait-shy phenomenon as taste aversion based on learned aversive stimuli. Note that this interpretation does not make the phenomenon any less interesting; it just takes the problem out of the camp of delayed punishment and puts it into the camp of the delayed establishment of learned behavioral consequences—a small step for behavior analysis but at least a mild relief for my particular theoretical emphasis on the need for immediacy for effective punishment and reinforcement.

In keeping with this analysis, Bolles (1985) notes that the smell and taste that have been paired with visceral distress affects not only consumption but also approach and withdrawal. This suggests that the incentive value of the smell has been modified to now be aversive; it now punishes the approach response, as well as the consummatory response; and its reduction now reinforces the withdrawal response; however, other interpretations are possible.

(This notion that there is nothing unique about the consummatory response is in keeping with the usually successful practice of behavior analysts to assume that operant behaviors are arbitrary, that any one is readily substitutable for another, as in the case of the operant response of following an imprinted stimulus; in that case a key peck response, for instance, can substitute for the response of following the imprinted stimulus [Bateson & Reese, 1969]. Thus we would expect that the contingent presentation of the aversive smell or taste would punish an ongoing bar-press response maintained by some independent reinforcement schedule.)

In any case, the incentive-modification interpretation of taste aversion learning also suggests we should not consider such learning as an example of delayed punishment but rather as an example of delayed incentive modification. Therefore, we should not consider taste aversion learning as evidence that delayed reinforcement and delayed punishment can explain the sorts of problems with which this current chapter is concerned.

3.3.2b. Two Kinds of Learning. Furthermore, Garcia *et al.* (1985) argue for two kinds of learning, one involving internal-homeostatic systems, as in the case of taste aversion learning, and the other involving external coping mechanisms, as in the case of dental flossing. They say the principles describing one kind of learning are not the same as those describing the other kind of learning. In addition,

> Michael (1986, May) has suggested that the effects of taste aversion are a result of unique phylogenic programming and not a contradiction of the general need for close contiguity between response and behaviorally-effective consequence. Whether the

> bait-shy phenomenon involves unique phylogenic programming [either in terms of the delayed establishment of learned aversive stimuli or in terms of delayed punishment] or can ultimately be understood in terms of more typical behavioral principles, this phenomenon does not necessarily support the notion that the delayed delivery of behaviorally-effective consequences can normally affect the causal response class. (Malott & Garcia, in press)

3.3.3. *Early Human Beings*

What about the behavior of primal, preverbal human beings, human beings in their natural, evolutionary environment, in the environment where our species evolved? Instinctive behavioral consequences seem to be less relevant to our species; in other words, the immediate rewarding and aversive stimuli for human beings seem to be more or less continuously functional rather than seasonal. Probably the human species was well enough adapted to its natural environment that immediate behavioral consequences, both unlearned and learned, insured that members of the species ate, copulated, nursed, and sought shelter in a manner that allowed them to survive.

In that natural environment, the evolving human species did not have much of a problem with the deleterious drugs and food that plague their lives today, nor with high-speed automobiles and seat belts, with the sedentary life, with the need to write a book or an article, or to finish a dissertation. The problem the human species currently faces is how to survive in an environment they themselves have changed so drastically, an environment where their original, relatively simple, preverbal systems of behavioral consequences are no longer appropriate.

Perhaps even early, verbal hunters and gatherers had little need for dealing with outcomes of any significant delay because their environments seem to have been exceptionally provident, with food almost immediately ready for the taking (Harris, 1977, p. 10). However, probably human beings needed to have their actions controlled by delayed outcomes when the carrying capacity of the environment decreased to the point of forcing them to shift from hunting and gathering to intentional farming (Harris, 1979, p. 87). The delay between intentional planting and harvesting almost insures a need for the behavior of planting to be under the control of delayed outcomes (Malott, 1980–1981b). (By *intentional* I am attempting to exclude that precursor to farming that may have involved the accidental spreading of seed by the consumer of the food.)

3.4. Rule-Control

I have suggested that delayed outcomes do not function as behavioral consequences for the acts that produce them; and yet sometimes human beings do act in a manner that optimizes those delayed outcomes, maximizing the favorable ones and minimizing the unfavorable ones. How do they do this? A main tenant of the present analysis is that human beings optimize outcomes by following instructions or rules that specify the outcomes of their actions; in other words, it is not the delayed outcomes but rather the rules stating those delayed outcomes that more directly control the actions. For instance, even though the outcome is delayed, most human beings would probably follow this rule: "You just won the grand prize. If you fill out this simple form, you will get $100,000 in cash, as a tax-free gift. However, due to administrative red tape, it will take 9 or 10 months before we will be able to deliver the money." Or consider these less dramatic, but more realistic examples: "Put this 10-pound turkey in the oven now, and it will be ready to eat in 3 hours." Or, "Be sure to close the windows because it's supposed to rain tonight." And, "Take this medicine, and you will feel better in a few hours." (See Michael, 1986, for another theoretical analysis of the repertoire-altering effects of remote contingencies.)

All of these examples involve rules that are easy to follow, even though the rules specify outcomes that are too delayed to act as direct behavioral consequences; in other words, the outcomes are too delayed to reinforce or punish the causal responses. It seems plausible that human behavior can be controlled by rules, instructions, or guidelines specifying the outcomes of various actions. Thus the delayed outcomes may not control the behaviors that produce those outcomes. Instead the rules specifying those outcomes (or a combination of the rules and their outcomes) may do the controlling. (In later sections, we will consider the processes underlying this rule control.)

However, other rules often exert poor control over our actions, even when they specify immediate outcomes; these rules specify outcomes that are either improbable but large or probable but so small that only their cumulative effects are significant. We will next consider improbable outcomes.

4. IMPROBABLE OUTCOMES

4.1. Basic Research

Behavioral consequences that are delivered intermittently are often less effective than ones delivered consistently or continuously. This contradicts the popular misconception suggesting otherwise. This misconception may result from the use of explanatory fictions or intervening variables like *response strength.* Traditionally, behavior analysts seem to have thought that intermittent reinforcement increases response strength. (However, see Nevin, 1979, for a thoughtful use of the concept of response strength as related to resistance to change.) In fact, the intermittent presentation of behavioral consequences only increases two dependent variables. It increases the time and number of responses before the history of such a presentation loses its control, once the presentation is stopped. This phenomenon is often called *resistance to extinction*—another potentially dangerous construct. Even resistance to extinction decreases as reinforcement becomes increasingly intermittent, at least for variable interval schedules of reinforcement (Nevin, 1979, pp. 123–124), though perhaps not for ratio schedules of reinforcement (p. 132).

Furthermore, the high rate of response during intermittent reinforcement may be an artifact. It may be largely due to our failure to take into account the disruptive effects of the consummatory response. The consummatory response interrupts the high rate of responding during consistent or continuous reinforcement. In fact, response rate decreases, as reinforcement becomes more intermittent (decreases in probability) for variable interval schedules of reinforcement (Nevin, 1979, pp. 121–122); this supports the notion that the lower rate of responding during the reinforcement of each response is an idiosyncratic artifact of the consummatory response. However, the rate of response does increase as probability of reinforcement decreases on ratio schedules of reinforcement (Nevin, 1979, p. 132), within the range of probability values studied (e.g., 1.0 to .025), but undoubtedly the rate of response would eventually start to decrease as the probability of reinforcement approached zero (extinction). Furthermore, the low probability events of concern in this chapter will often be much lower (much closer to zero) than those studied in the laboratory, for example, the probability of an automobile accident.

Furthermore, high-probability behavioral consequences should always have the more powerful effect when competing against low-probability behavioral consequences in a concurrent schedule of reinforcement or punishment. This agrees with the large amounts of data supporting variations of Hernstein's matching law applied to schedules of reinforcement (de Villiers, 1977). This also agrees with Azrin and Holz's (1966) review of the literature supporting the decreasing effect of punishment when it occurs less frequently.

4.2. The Natural Environment

In the natural settings where organisms evolved, improbable outcomes usually should not effectively reinforce or punish acts that immediately preceded the delivery of those outcomes. Otherwise the organism would be too susceptible to control by events that only accidentally followed that response and were not really caused by the response class. In other words, most improbable events that follow an action may not, in fact, be caused by that action but instead may be only a coincidence; so such events should not affect the organism as if they were causally related to the organism's actions. (This is not to say that an improbable outcome does not have some reinforcing or punishing effects on the causal response but rather that those effects are normally so small as to be insignificant, when the probability of the outcome is low.)

4.3. Human Behavior

In the everyday, human environment, we see many instances we can interpret as examples of the ineffectiveness of the improbable or intermittent delivery of outcomes. For example, people with broken toes persist in acting in a carefree manner that only occasionally result in painful outcomes. We see other examples of the ineffectiveness of intermittent punishment in the persistence of lying, cheating, stealing, speeding, driving without seat belts, and frequent violations of safety regulations in work settings.

As a further example, consider two incompatible, concurrent responses—writing an article and daydreaming. Often it is with only the greatest difficulty that we manage to interrupt our reverie with a bit of work. We can account for this difficulty in terms of the discrepancy in the consistency of reinforcement for the two concurrent responses: Daydreaming may produce frequent rewards, with each new thought effortlessly producing another reward, such as amusement, excitement, or novelty, whereas the thoughts involved in writing may produce rewards only intermittently, as the author struggles to develop or present a new concept.

Brigham (1982, pp. 42–43) also points to the problems caused by improbable outcomes:

> The immediate contingencies involve small consequences, either positive or negative, while the delayed consequences are all major but potential. Cases are well documented of individuals who smoked two packs of cigarettes a day throughout their adult life and who died of old age at 95 without any health problems related to smoking. Similarly, regular visits to the dentist will not guarantee the avoidance of serious dental problems.

(In this quote, Brigham uses *potential* to mean "with a probability less than 1.0.") However, the probability of the delayed consequences is often sufficiently high that the problem may be more related to something else. (I believe that something else is the smallness of the outcomes immediately contingent on the relevant response, as we will discuss shortly.)

4.4. Rule-Control

Not only do improbable outcomes often fail to reinforce or punish the causal response class, but many important outcomes are so intermittent, so improbable that a person may never have had direct contact with them; and yet the person would benefit, if the possibility of contacting those outcomes controlled his or her actions. However, potential outcomes cannot affect our actions, but rules specifying these low-probability, potential outcomes can exert control. For instance: "You can avoid being hit by oncoming traffic, if you stop at the intersection and look both ways." "You can avoid losing a finger, if you use a stick to guide the wood through the bench saw."

Now we will consider one final class of outcome that frequently fails to exert direct control over our actions, though we would often benefit if they did.

5. CUMULATING OUTCOMES

5.1. Human Behavior

In the area of self-management, self-control, and rule-governed behavior, behavior analysts mainly address the problem with delayed outcomes and whether or not they control behavior: "The majority, if not all, of the situations where the individual is said to have a self-control problem involve some difference between the immediate consequences of a response and its delayed consequences" (Brigham, 1982, pp. 40–41). Similarly, Rachlin and Green (1972, p. 22) are committed to an analysis in terms of "a choice between an immediate small reward and a delayed large reward."

However, in most everyday instances, people do not have problems with delayed outcomes but rather with small and cumulating outcomes. For example, consider dental flossing: The problem is not that the person flosses once and 6 months later gets a clean bill of health from the dental hygienist; and the problem is not whether or not that clean bill of health will or will not reinforce that single instance of flossing. The delayed clean bill of health does not result from a single day's flossing. Instead, the problem is that each response of moving the dental floss (or even each episode of daily flossing) produces an outcome that is too small to reinforce the act of maintenance flossing, regardless of whether or not that outcome is immediate or delayed. A similar analysis applies to the consumption of some prescribed medications and some nutritious foods, as well as the performance of physical exercise.

All of the preceding examples involved immediate outcomes that are too small to reinforce the behavior that produces them. However, the same sort of analysis applies to events that are cumulatively harmful, though the harmful effects from each instance are too small to punish the behavior that produces them. Examples might involve the consumption of substances that are cumulatively quite harmful, though the negative effects from each instance are too small to suppress the act of consumption when concurrent rewards maintain that consumption. For example, consider the harmful outcomes of smoking: The harmful outcomes from a single puff, or even from a whole cigarette, are normally too small to punish the habitual smoker's smoking. Furthermore, these harmful outcomes are too small, regardless of whether or not those outcomes are immediate or delayed. Yet the accumulation of those small and insignificant outcomes become harmfully significant, after a person has smoked many cartons of cigarettes. However, that cumulative, significantly harmful outcome often fails to control the behavior that generates it. A similar analysis applies to the consumption of other harmful substances such as caffeine, alcohol, sugar, cholesterol, excessive salt, and excessive fat.

As a further example, consider this little acknowledged but more obvious example—the person who continues to eat, even though he or she is already uncomfortably full. According to the present analysis, that glutton is behaving so irrationally because each bite of food has such a small impact on his or her discomfort and, at the same time, produces such a rewarding taste. Again significant discomfort results, only as the small outcomes of each bite cumulate.

In summary, often outcomes are immediate and certain; and yet each outcome is too small to function as an effective behavioral consequence (reward or aversive stimulus); each individual outcome is without behavioral effect, even though the cumulative results of the repetition of many such outcomes has a large effect on the person's well-being.

5.2. Basic Research

Little basic research seems to deal with small, cumulating outcomes. However, we might consider a hypothetical animal experiment, using an operant chamber. Each bar press would produce a pellet of food and a subthreshold increment in the intensity of a continuously ongoing electric shock. Eventually the cumulative level of shock would probably become so severe it would disrupt all ongoing behavior, including bar pressing, but not as a punisher. Yet it seems likely that the proper control procedures would demonstrate that the small, response-contingent increments in shock intensity would not be sufficient to punish the causal bar-press response. This would then be an experimental instance of the behavioral ineffectiveness of small outcomes that have considerable cumulative significance.

The total accumulation of shock would, no doubt, act as effective behavioral consequences, if those total amounts had been contingent upon each individual bar-press response, even though each individual, small, cumulative outcome would not be large enough to function as a behavioral consequence, that is, not large enough to punish the causal response class.

Some experimental evidence, however, does indirectly support this analysis. Four-year-old children did not procrastinate on tasks when they were told they needed to do the task immediately, though they were also told they would not get their reward for the task until a later day. However, they often did procrastinate to the point of failing to do the tasks when they were told they could do the tasks whenever they wanted to. Under the first condition, the deadline condition, off-task behavior of a minute or so might have resulted in a significant outcome—a loss of the opportunity to get the future reward. However, under the no-deadline condition, off-task behavior of a minute or so would usually only have a small, insignificant outcome—a slight increase in the delay to the reward. Sufficient procrastination, to the point where the task was never completed, would and did cumulate to produce the sizable outcome of loss of the opportunity to get the future reward. These data suggest that the small but cumulatively significant outcome did not effectively control the children's behavior (Braam & Malott, 1986).

5.3. The Natural Environment

If the assumption is correct that small, cumulative outcomes are ineffective as behavioral consequences, then we might ask, how have organisms managed to survive? Perhaps there is less need for such behavioral consequences in the natural environment where the species evolved. Many outcomes that are only cumulatively harmful are much rarer in the natural environment, for example nicotine, caffeine, and alcohol; and others that are present, like mercury, may normally be unlikely to be accumulated to toxic levels.

Furthermore, outcomes that are only cumulatively beneficial may also be much rarer; for instance, prescribed medications are not available in the natural environment. In addition, other outcomes that are only cumulatively beneficial may occur for other reasons; for instance, the taste of nutritious foods may be a sufficient reward to maintain their consumption when they are not competing with more tasty but less nutritious, human-manufactured foods.

As another example, the physiological reaction called the activation syndrome has been hypothesized to be sufficiently rewarding to maintain physical exercise (Malott & Whaley, 1976, pp. 513–515; Malott *et al.*, 1978, pp. 54, 81), even though the health benefits of an individual instance of exercise may be too small to reinforce that behavior. For instance, those built-in biological reactions have been hypothesized to reinforce the caged hamster's running in an activity wheel. (Incidentally, it might be interesting to see if the animal could be satiated on the activation syndrome with some other means such as drugs, with the result that its rate of physical exercise would decrease.) In addition to the activation syndrome, extrinsic rewards, such as the procurement of food and the avoidance of harm, may maintain considerable physical exercise in the natural environment.

In summary, perhaps our behavioral insensitivity to cumulatively important outcomes is of major concern only in the contemporary, human-made environment.

5.4. Rule-Control

Though small, cumulating outcomes may not function as behavioral consequences, some human beings do effectively cope with them, on a daily basis. Such small cumulating outcomes involve the food, drugs, and poisons they should avoid, no single instance being that crucial, the medications and nutritious foods they should consume, again no single instance being that crucial, and the exercise they should do, the teeth flossing they should perform, and the various tasks they should not procrastinate on, though no single instance is that crucial. So how do human beings cope with such outcomes? Once again, rule-control may be the answer: "Don't ever eat, drink, or smoke these things, or you'll harm your health." "Do eat and drink those things, every day, and you'll maintain your health." "Exercise 30 minutes 5 days a week, and you'll achieve good cardiovascular fitness." "If you got 'em, floss 'em." "Don't put off until tomorrow what you can do today." (Note that last two rules only imply the antecedents and outcomes.)

Of course many of the contingencies with which we must cope have the features of all three problem areas; they are combinations of delayed, low-probability, small but cumulative outcomes. For example, consider the relation between what we eat and our having a heart attack: It is far from certain that the heart attack will occur; if it does occur, it will probably be sometime in the future; and no single meal matters that much. In fact, many of the examples we considered earlier actually involve two or more of these problem features.

6. RULES SPECIFYING CONTINGENCIES THAT ARE NOT DIRECT ACTING

6.1. How Do Rules Control Behavior?

The analysis of the preceding sections has suggested that rule control is essential, if human beings are to deal effectively with their human-made environment. Therefore, in the remaining sections, we will consider, in more detail, rule-control and its role in helping human beings deal with delayed, improbable, and small, cumulating outcomes.

I hope this analysis of the control of rules describing contingencies that are not direct acting will help us better understand processes that do not involve any obvious, direct-acting contingencies. To date, such contingencies have been frequently misanalyzed by behavior analysts. Behavior analysts often treat them as if they were simple direct-acting contingencies. Many behavior analysts attempt to understand such contingencies in terms of straightforward generalizations of the processes involved in infrahuman behavior. Of course the basic procedures and processes of behavior analysis ultimately account for the control of such rules and contingencies. However, I think the analysis is far from straightforward. (Michael, 1986, has also discussed the problem of such misanalyses of contingencies that are not direct acting.)

6.1.1. The Rule as a Cue

At least two analyses suggest why rules control our actions. According to the most common analysis, people have a behavioral history that has established rules as a generalized stimulus class. In the presence of this stimulus class, the response class of following such rules has been supported by an effective behavioral consequence, namely the specified outcome. This is essentially Skinner's position (1969, p. 148). For instance, we might be told this rule: "If you aren't careful, you're going to get shocked." Then, if we continue in our careless manner and get shocked, the rule will be more likely to function as an effective warning stimulus in the future. The natural outcomes of complying with such rules or failing to comply with them suffices to establish these rules as effective cues (discriminative stimuli).

(The shock rule is an example of the kind of rule Zettle & Hayes, 1982, call a track; in the terms of the present analysis, a *track* is a rule that specifies a natural, nonsocially mediated outcome that might function as an effective behavioral consequence. However, their use of the concept of a track seems as applicable to rules describing contingencies that are not direct acting as it is to direct-acting contingencies, at least from the point of view of this analysis.)

However, there may be a problem with the interpretation of a rule as a cue. A *cue* (discriminative stimulus) is a stimulus in the presence of which a particular behavioral contingency is more likely to be operative. (Many behavior analysts also require that the stimulus actually exert stimulus control over the relevant behavior.) However, concerning the shock rule, it we act carelessly, in the presence of live wires, we are likely to get shocked, regardless of whether or not the rule has been stated. So, from that point of view, the rule does not seem to function as a cue; it is not a stimulus in the presence of which a particular behavioral contingency is more likely to be operative.

We might be able to justify a somewhat different interpretation of the rule as a cue. We might argue that rule-compliance is maintained because compliance with the rule does increase the likelihood of socially mediated reinforcement or decrease the likelihood of socially mediated punishment. An example would be where parents reinforce or punish compliance with requests. Suppose a parent told a child to get ready for bed. That parent would then more likely praise the child for getting ready for bed than if the child randomly got ready for bed throughout the day. The parent would also more likely nag at the child for failing to get ready than at times when the parent had not made the request (an implicit rule statement).

This sort of social contingency probably plays a major role in the acquisition of control by rules, and it also probably plays a role in the maintenance of such control. (This is an example of the kind of rule control Zettle and Hayes, 1982, call *pliance*. In the terms of the present analysis, a *ply* is a rule that controls behavior because compliance with that rule will generate social approval and failure to comply will generate social disapproval.) Note that the socially mediated behavioral consequence is not the same as the outcome specified in the more typical track-type rule such as the one about electric shock.

Furthermore, rule-compliance might even maintain in some settings without the need for an increased likelihood of socially mediated reinforcement or punishment, just as generalized imitation is maintained in settings that will clearly produce no added or extrinsic reward. Baer and Deguchi (1985) argue that this generalized imitation is maintained by a learned reward, the class of stimuli resulting from a match of the imitator's behavior to the model's behavior. Malott (1987, May) has pointed out that this is similar to the pigeon's key peck being maintained by the learned reward of the sound of the food magazine and light flash. This occurs, even though the setting is discriminably different from the one in which that learned reward is paired with food (Zimmerman & Hanford, 1966). In the same way, we might argue that a symbolic match of the behavior with the rule would generate a learned reward and the lack of a match would generate a learned aversive condition.

Alternatively, we might be able to justify an interpretation of the rule as a cue as follows: Across settings, rules that warn about the dangers of shock have been stimuli in the presence of which shock is more likely to occur. So in that sense, the shock contingency is more likely to be operative in the presence of the rule, and thus the rule functions as a cue. The rule would be a cue, even though in any individual situation, the shock contingency would be no more likely to operate, even if the rule had been stated. In other words, the shock rule will function as a cue, even though the live wire will shock you, whether or not the rule has been stated.

6.1.2. *The Rule as a Motivating Operation*

Alternatively, we might consider the rule as a motivating operation (establishing operation) rather than as a cue. In other words, the statement of the rule might establish certain stimuli as more effective behavioral consequences; that is, the statement of the rule might make those stimuli more rewarding or more aversive. The statement of the rule might increase the reward value of stimuli immediately resulting from compliance with the rule, and the statement might increase the aversive value of stimuli immediately resulting from noncompliance with the rule. In turn, the rule-statement's function as a motivating operation would result from a behavioral history involving reinforcement for compliance and punishment for noncompliance. (For more details, see Malott, 1986, pp. 210–212.)

As an instance of the statement of a rule as a motivating operation, consider the previous example. Perhaps the statement of the rule about the electric shock increases the aversiveness of the stimuli resulting from careless behavior. Those stimuli might be proprioceptive and visual stimuli associated with carelessness. Then in that context, any careless act, would produce aversive stimuli; and those aversive stimuli would tend to punish carelessness, even if the person did not act careless enough to get shocked. In a sense, the person would be avoiding the learned aversiveness of careless behavior rather than the unlearned aversiveness of the electric shock. (Hayes, 1987, also considers the motivating function of rules he calls augmentals.)

As another example, consider this rule: "If you don't start working, you're not going to finish writing your article on time." Again, that contingency is operative, regardless of whether or not the rule is stated. However, its statement may act as a motivating operation, increasing the aversiveness of the stimuli associated with not working on the article. Then starting to work will reduce that aversiveness which will in turn reinforce working.

Note that the example of writing the article involves a contingency that is not direct acting because the article's timely completion is a delayed outcome. Also any given instance of working will probably have only a minimal effect on that outcome. However, the electric-shock example might involve a direct-acting contingency because the electric shock would certainly be immediately contingent on a sufficiently careless act, and it might also be a sizable and even probable outcome. So the motivating-operation interpretation might account for the effectiveness of rules describing direct-acting contingencies, as well as those describing rules that are not direct acting.

6.1.3. Automatic Behavioral Consequences

The analysis of both the example of carelessness with live wires and procrastination of writing assumes that the statement of the relevant rule functions to establish effective built-in or automatic contingencies (Vaughan & Michael, 1982), possibly involving nonverbal aversive states often labeled *fear* or *guilt,* states resulting from our failure to comply with a rule. In addition, the statement of the rule might establish the reinforcing condition of "good feelings" when we do comply. Presumably behavioral consequences associated with these automatic contingencies would have acquired their value as aversive stimuli or as rewards through a behavioral history involving paring with other aversive stimuli or rewards, such as parental disapproval or approval.

6.1.4. Self-Given Behavioral Consequences

We, ourselves, might be a source of another set of behavioral contingencies that could play a role in maintaining control by rules. These contingencies are somewhat different from the automatic contingencies just discussed, though they might also involve behavioral consequences whose effectiveness was established by the statement of the rule that would function as a motivating or establishing operation. This class of self-given contingencies is in the form of covert statements of four general types:

1. Rewarding thoughts (self-statements) about our following a rule: for example, "Spend as much of your time as you can writing, so you can get a better understanding of your topic and perhaps complete a publishable manuscript." The self-given reward for following the rule might be: "I'm really doing a good job staying on task this morning; I've done more writing today than I did all last week." Such rewarding thoughts might deal only with compliance and involve no reference to the natural outcome of following the rule, in this instance the completion of a publishable manuscript and an increased understanding.

Masters and Santrock (1976) provide some evidence that such self-statements reinforce the behavior on which they are contingent. They found that 4-year-old children persisted longer on an effortful, repetitive handle-turning task, when they made a pleasant or positive statement to themselves (e.g., "This is fun, really fun!") as opposed to an unpleasant, negative statement (e.g., "Ugh! This is no fun") or a neutral statement (e.g., "Two-one, two-one, two-one"). Incidentally, the positive statements were at least as effective in producing persistence (presumably reinforcing the behavior) when they were irrelevant to the task (e.g., statements about ice cream or pancakes with syrup).

As the authors point out:

> It is important to note, however, that the contingency itself was not systematically varied. . . . [Furthermore,] recent studies of affect induction (Moore *et al.*, 1973; Underwood *et al.*, 1973) have shown the powerful effects of children's positively or negatively toned thoughts which do not occur with any contingent relationship to the behaviors they control. (p. 347)

In other words, the Masters and Santrock experiment did not demonstrate that the positive statement actually had to be contingent on the effortful response for that response to persist, that is, that self-reinforcement actually occurred.

However, to return to our struggling writer, we might ask the following question: If self-congratulation is reinforcing, why does not the person simply sit around thinking those self-congratulatory thoughts all day, without actually doing any writing? The answer may be that self-approval is a conditional learned reward, conditional on having done something worth approving of or at least something close enough to meritorious that the person can justify the giving of that self-approval (Malott *et al.*, 1978, pp. 15–16).

2. Aversive thoughts about our failure to follow the rule: for example, "I'm really doing a poor job this morning; I've spent more time daydreaming than thinking about my writing." Again, no reference is made to the natural outcome of following the rule.

3. Rewarding thoughts about how our current actions are leading toward

the accomplishment of the outcome stated in the rule: for example, "I've really made a lot of progress today; I've learned a lot, and I've gotten the paper much nearer completion." Reinforcing thoughts might also stress the aversive outcomes we are avoiding; that is, "If I keep working at this rate, I probably won't lose my job."

4. Aversive thoughts about how our current actions are not leading toward the accomplishment of the favorable outcome: for example, "If I don't get to work, I probably will lose my job." Or "If I don't get on task, I'll never get this written."

The previous statements of self-praise might function as conditional learned rewards that could reinforce compliance with the rules, whereas the previous statements of self-criticism might function as conditional learned aversive stimuli that would punish noncompliance. In addition, those statements of self-criticism might establish an aversive condition that could be escaped by rule-compliance and that would therefore reinforce such compliance. This aversive condition might be similar to or identical to the aversive conditioned involved in the automatic contingencies previously discussed.

Of course, rule-compliance could be supported by all three classes of contingencies, that is social contingencies, automatic contingencies, and self-delivered behavioral consequences in the form of thoughts.

The notion of self-reinforcement (and, by implication, self-punishment and automatic reinforcement and punishment) has evoked considerable debate (Bandura & Mahoney, 1974; Catania, 1975; Goldiamond, 1976; Hayes & Zettle, 1980–1981; Malott, 1980–1981a, 1982a, b).

6.1.4a. Inadequate Causal Analyses Involving Private Events. As Hayes (1987) has pointed out, people often provide inadequate causal analyses of behavior by citing reasons involving private events, like their feelings and thoughts, for example, "I argued with him because I was angry." However, their citation of private events makes the analysis no less adequate than, "I argued with him because it was hot and humid," even though we are now dealing with nothing but public events. Both analyses are unsatisfactory to a radical behaviorist, who, as Hayes says, will only accept a causal analysis in terms of behavioral contingencies. However, from my perspective, that does not rule out the causal importance of contingencies involving rule-governed behavior and private events, for example, automatic and self-given behavioral consequences such as feelings and thoughts.

Hayes also points out that the misanalysis of private events causes many clinicians to attempt to eliminate aversive private thoughts and feelings by asking their clients to follow rules, where in fact direct manipulation of contingencies might be more effective. In other words, when mind over matter fails, we should try contingencies. However, again from my perspective, that still does not rule out the causal importance of contingencies involving rule-governed behavior and private, automatic and self-given behavioral consequences such as feelings and thoughts.

6.1.4b. The Ineffectiveness of Self-Reinforcement: Self-Reinforcement and Public Commitment. Hayes, Rosenfarb, Wulfert, Munt, Korn, and Zettle (1985) demonstrated that the college student's public commitment to achieve self-selected academic goals greatly enhances the achievement of those goals, for example, answering multiple-choice questions over material just read and answering vocabulary and content questions over material read throughout a 36-day period. However, private commitment has no effect. They theorized that, in the student's past, public commitment has been a discriminative stimulus for social reinforcement of achievement and social punishment of nonachievement of those publicly committed goals; therefore the student's current achievement is a result of the discriminative control exerted by the current public commitment.

In this context, the experimenters further demonstrated the lack of effect of instructions to eat self-delivered M&Ms, raisins, or peanuts each time the student met his or her personal goal of the number of correct answers to six multiple-choice questions following each passage of reading. (The student preselected the choice and amount of the edible.) These instructions had no effect on the percentage of correct answers, regardless of whether the student had stated the goal publicly or privately.

However, in an ancillary experiment, they demonstrated the effectiveness of an experimenter's delivery of those edibles contingent on each correct answer to the multiple-choice questions. These students answered more questions correctly than did a yoked control. From this, the experimenters seem to conclude that the edible was a reinforcer or reward of sufficient magnitude in the previous experiment but that the self-delivery of that reward prevented it from reinforcing the behavior that would result in an increase in the number of correct answers, though the experimenters do not specify what that behavior is.

As in most research, however, alternate interpretations are possible, especially for those of a theoretical orientation somewhat different from the experimenters. First, in the ancillary experiment, perhaps the experimenter's implicit acknowledgment of the student's correct answers reinforced that correct answers. Perhaps the edible was irrelevant. In that case the failure of self-reinforcement in the main experiment might still be attributable to the lack of an effective reward. (This possibility of social reinforcement is especially cogent in the context of the experimenters' earlier theorizing about the power of the mere hint of social approval or social disapproval.)

Second, even if the edible was the crucial reward in the ancillary experiment, it was made contingent on a different response class than in the main experiment—each correct answer, in the ancillary experiment versus the achievement of the goal of a specified percentage correct for each set of six questions, in the main experiment.

Third, in the main experiment, it is not clear that the students had not satiated or partially satiated themselves with the edible during the baseline phase when they were instructed to consume the food ad lib. In which case, we would not expect food reinforcement to work, regardless of the mechanism of delivery. (I once had an overly fed grade-school student say he would keep working on the problems, if I would stop giving him those damned raisins each time he got one right.)

Fourth, in the experimental phase of that experiment, it is not clear that the students actually followed their instructions; it is not clear that they actually ate the food contingent on attaining their goals and that they refrained from eating the food in the absence of that goal attainment. Such a failure to follow those instructions would vitiate a test of the efficacy of self-reinforcement.

Although these experiments seemed to address the theoretical question of whether the self-delivery of a reward eliminates its effectiveness in a reinforcement procedure, and although the experimenters seemed to conclude that it did, they then go on to argue that it does not—that self-reinforcement can probably occur. On the one hand, "Overall, the two experiments make more plausible the view that self-reinforcement procedures work by setting a socially available standard against which performance can be evaluated" (Harper *et al.*, 1985, p. 201). On the other hand:

> In external reinforcement, however, a consequence not earned is a consequence lost. In self-reinforcement, usually at best a consequence not earned is a consequence delayed, because the subject owns the consequence to begin with. For example, in Experiment 1, the students knew they could leave with the leftover food they did not use as a consequence. It is not clear that external consequation would be effective under similar circumstances. (p. 211)

That seems more like a flaw in the experimental design than an intrinsic flaw in the process of self-reinforcement; on the other hand, the experimenters could have imposed a limited hold on the edibles. They then say:

> Our results do not suggest, however, that self-consequation cannot add to goal setting under certain circumstances. . . . [if] public availability ensures consistent use of the stated consequences . . . [but] these conditions are uncommon or may even be nonexistent . . . [and] you are probably going to cheat on the contingency anyway. (p. 211)

In other words, there is nothing theoretically wrong with the concept of self-reinforcement, but it may be difficult to use as a behavior modification procedure because of the dangers of dishonestly consuming unearned rewards.

I agree with their analysis. I agree that self-reinforcement works; and I agree that behavior modification procedures based on the self-delivery of M&Ms may sometimes require more policing than they are worth, though perhaps not always; Sohn and Lamal (1982) review several studies showing that self-reinforcement procedures can greatly reduce the amount of external monitoring needed. However, I suspect more subtle forms of self-reinforcement may pervade our lives, especially reinforcement by the removal of aversive consequences, such as aversive thoughts about the results of failing to comply with rules specifying contingencies that are not direct acting.

Incidentally, Sohn and Lamal (1982) say:

> The expressions of skepticism [about self-reinforcement] . . . can be . . . based on a logical analysis of the concept of SR [self-reinforcement] . . . the appropriateness of the designation of *self-reinforcement* after a study of the closeness of fit between SR as it is generally defined and the critic's judgment of what is the behavior-modifying mechanism in a 'true' SR situation (e.g., Catania, 1975; Goldiamond, 1976; Rachlin, 1974). The hallmark of this . . . type of skepticism is its a priori nature. (pp. 179–180)

The previously sighted logical analysis by Hayes *et al.* (1985) seems to place them reluctantly in the category of *a priori* believers in the possibility of self-reinforcement, in spite of the tone of their empirical work. I willingly place myself in that same category.

6.1.4c. The Ineffectiveness of Self-Reinforcement: A Critical Review of the Literature on Self-Reinforcement. Sohn and Lamal (1982) go on to provide a foundation for their own "expressions of skepticism . . . based on an examination of the empirical research on SR" (p. 179). Their main reason for rejecting the empirical evidence for self-reinforcement is that the experimental procedures in the research they carefully review do not meet the requirements specified by the

> apt delineation of . . . [the] characteristics of the SR situation . . . in the following statement by Morgan and Bass (1973: "It is therefore crucial that the subject understand and believe that he truly does have complete control over all contingencies and could, if he wishes, cheat or reward himself at any time without bringing about any other contingent external consequences of either a reinforcing or punishing nature." (pp. 120, 181)

Largely on the basis of Morgan and Bass's apt delineation (19 out of 44 studies), Sohn and Lamal conclude:

> Our search for evidence relevant to the proposition that the SR situation possesses a reinforcing capability has uncovered . . . very little that supports the credibility of this proposition. . . . SR studies are found to have used procedures or situations which are at variance with the most widely accepted definition of the SR situation (p. 195). . . . In view of the present findings, we believe there is no justification for speaking of SR in a way that suggests that it possesses the functional properties of reinforcement, that is that it is the analogue of external reinforcement. (p. 196)

I question their conclusions on two grounds: First, I do not accept their "widely accepted definition of the SR situation." (Furthermore, neither does

Skinner, as I will argue later.) I agree that "It is . . . crucial that the subject understand and believe that he truly does have complete control over all contingencies and could, if he wishes, cheat or reward himself at any time. . . ." (However, I would rephrase this to exclude the subject's understanding and beliefs. I would do so because their inclusion does, for example, *a priori* rule out animal research on the topic. At least they rule out animal work, unless we talk in terms of the animal's understanding and beliefs; and I would rather not.)

My main concern is with the restriction that this cheating be allowed "without bringing about any other contingent external consequences of either a reinforcing or punishing nature." True, self-reinforcement of only deserving responses is more intriguing when it occurs in the absence of external contingencies, but I suspect that a self-delivered M&M will reinforce the previous response regardless of the deserving nature of that response.

Second, I think Sohn and Lamal misapply their agreement "with the conventional wisdom that you cannot prove the null hypothesis" (p. 195). In the present case, this means "that you cannot prove self-reinforcement has no effect." The conventional wisdom applies to research where no statistically significant differences were found between various conditions (only 8 out of 44 studies in their review). However, Sohn and Lamal assert the null hypothesis (that self-reinforcement is not effective) in studies where statistically significant differences were found (36 out of 44 studies). In other words, according to their criteria, the crucial experiments have yet to be done. They ask the question, "Is there any evidence that SR is able to affect behavior through a reinforcing capability that it possesses?" (p. 179). They answer, *no*. However, I ask the question, "Is there any evidence that SR is not able to affect behavior through a reinforcing capability that it possesses?" On the basis of their literature review, I believe both they and I would also have to answer *no*. In other words, which question we ask may well reflect the *a priori* theoretical orientation, mentioned earlier. Some of us have to be convinced that self-reinforcement does work, others of us that it does not work. From my point of view, their review provided convincing, though somewhat confounded, evidence that self-reinforcement does work.

6.1.4d. The Quest for the Ultimate Cause and the Missing Link. Arguments against self-reinforcement (and presumably self-punishment) are also made in the context of arguments against including the person's own initial behavior as part of the cause of later behavior. Such an argument concludes that you cannot include the person's initial self-delivery of behavioral consequences as part of the cause of later rule-governed behavior.

Hayes and Brownstein (1986) suggest that we should not explain a person's good performance in playing squash by noting that the performance resulted from the person's previously having learned how to play racquetball. Presumably, they would have preferred us to say that the good squash performance resulted from the events that led to the learning of racquetball. They would prefer this because such events are closer to the ultimate cause.

However, I would argue in support of the intervening link in the chain as a useful proximal cause. But First, let us slightly vary their example. Few people would object to saying that one of the reasons the person plays squash well is because he or she is in good physical condition. True, the fact that the person is in good physical condition is because that person had previously been involved in a rigorous running program. Nonetheless, the good physical condition is a crucial link in the causal chain; if the running program had somehow occurred without producing the good physical conditioning, the person would not now play squash as well. Furthermore, the good physical condition could have resulted from other aerobics programs such as swimming or biking.

If we accept the good physical condition as a proximal cause in the causal chain, without reference to the specific source of that condition (earlier exercise), we should also accept having learned to play squash as a proximal cause. We should not be confused by the fact that having learned squash is a behavioral condition, whereas aerobic fitness is a physical condition.

Thus we might argue that some of the characteristics of the organism result from previous conditions. Furthermore, we might then think of those characteristics as links in a causal chain, linking the previous conditions to the current performance of the organism. So we might refer to these characteristics in accounting for current performance, either with or without reference to the antecedent condition that produced the more proximal condition of the organism? Similarly we might argue that having self-delivered behavioral consequences contingent on performance is part of a causal chain that now affects current performance.

Furthermore, it is true that we may be concerned with the early links that dispose the organism to act in a way that will ultimately result in some particular terminal behavior. However, I also think we should fill in that causal chain. Such filling in is part of our job as scientists, even though in the short run, it might sometimes be more technologically expedient to concern ourselves only with the early links and perhaps be ignorant of intervening conditions. In other words, we can stick the key in the ignition of our automobile and start it running and drive to the market without having the slightest idea of the processes going on inside the engine. Nonetheless, as scientists, we should be curious about the intervening links. We should be especially curious when those events lie more or less in the same domain, that is, when they are at our current level of analysis, for example, when we have behavioral events involved in the causal chain between external environmental events and external behavioral events.

6.1.4e. The Role of Private Events in a Natural Science. Note that the intervening links can be either public or private. Hayes and Brownstein (1986) object to them in either case. Many methodological behaviorists are especially concerned when those intervening links are private. However, I do not stand alone among behaviorists willing to consider private events:

> Behaviorists have, from time to time, examined the problem of privacy, and some of them have excluded so-called sensations, images, thought processes, and so on, from their deliberations. When they have done so not because such things do not exist but because they are out of reach of their methods, the charge is justified that they have neglected the facts of consciousness. The strategy is however, quite unwise. It is particularly important that a science of behavior face the problem of privacy. It may do so without abandoning the basic position of behaviorism. Science often talks about things it cannot see or measure. (Skinner, 1969, pp. 227–228)

However, we should not misinterpret Skinner by assuming that he argues that private events are important causes of behavior:

> Although Skinner's analysis of private events is considered by many to be one of his most valuable contributions, it would be a mistake to assume that for him, private stimuli are of great importance in human life. For Skinner, the main reason for dealing with private stimuli is to put them in proper perspective, which represents a considerable reduction in their significance from the essential causal role they are thought to play in traditional and common sense accounts. (Michael, 1985, p. 117)

More specifically, we should not misinterpret Skinner by assuming that he argues that self-given behavioral consequences will reinforce or punish behavior, regardless of whether they are public or private events, as Brigham (1982) correctly points out. Concerning the self-delivery of a reward, following a meritorious act, Skinner says:

> Something of this sort unquestionably happens, but is it operant reinforcement? It is certainly roughly parallel to the procedure in conditioning the behavior of another person. But it must be remembered that the individual may at any moment drop the work in hand and obtain the reinforcement. We have to account for his not doing so. It may be that such indulgent behavior has been punished—say, with disapproval—except when a piece of work has just been completed. The indulgent behavior will therefore generate strong aversive stimulation except at such a time. The individual finishes the work in order to indulge himself free of guilt (Chapter XII). The ulitmate question is whether the consequences has any strengthening effect upon the behavior which precedes it. Is the individual more likely to do a similar piece of work in the future? It would not be surprising if he were not, although we must agree that he has arranged a sequence of events in which certain behavior has been followed by a reinforcing event. (1953, p. 238)

I agree with all of Skinner's analysis, except I would be surprised if the individual were not more likely to do a similar piece of work in the future. I would be surprised if the delivery of a reinforcer did not reinforce the behavior, even though the inappropriate, immoral, or illegal taking of unearned reinforcers is suppressed by the threat of punishment. In fact, I am surprised that Skinner would not be surprised. Is that not how society works? In other words, the delivery of money reinforces behavior, even though stealing that money is suppressed by the threat of punishment. Of course, we could readily answer this question about the deleterious effects of aversive control. All we would need would be three rats, a Skinner box, two levers, a food dispenser, and a shock grid. In fact, I think others have already answered the question: Sohn and Lamal (1982) report 19 studies where the self-delivery of a reward produced an increased performance relative to control groups, even though there may have been some sort of external, explicit, or implicit coercion toward honesty.

Notice, by the way, that the position of Skinner and that of Sohn and Lamal may be just the opposite: On the one hand, Skinner seems to me to ague that a history of external coercion toward honesty might eliminate the effectiveness of self-reinforcement, even if it were now in the form of internal coercion; but he implies that if such coercion did not eliminate the effectiveness, then the procedure would meet his standards for self-reinforcement. On the other hand, Sohn and Lamal argue the external coercion is why so called self-reinforcement works, but the presence of that coercion causes the procedure not to meet their standards for self-reinforcement. They do not address the issue of internal or self-delivered coercion.

Although Skinner advocates a complete analysis of private events, as indicated in the first paragraph of this section, Hayes and Brownstein (1986) also advocate a complete analysis in the other direction, saying, "behavioral analyses that implicate 'covert behavior,' rather than 'mental events,' are equally incomplete if they fail to extend the analysis to environmental variables" (p. 187). I agree, though such analyses are not necessarily useless or invalid, just incomplete. Their warning is more than justified because, historically, that sort of incomplete analysis has satisfied much of psychology, perhaps even the majority of the field of psychology. Nonetheless, it seems equally incomplete to leave out the intervening covert (or overt) behavior; and in terms of a scholarly search for knowledge, it would be equally unfortunate. We should note, however, that in spite of their concern with public, environmental events, Hayes and Brownstein were advocating "a behavioral analysis of private events" and not advocating that we should ignore private events. I am simply extending their position to include an analysis of the self-delivery of behavioral consequences as an important private (or public) event in an important causal chain.

6.1.5. *Summary of How Rules Control Behavior*

For much contemporary human behavior, often the natural contingencies involve outcomes that are delayed, improbable, or small and of only cumulative significance. Therefore, they cannot effectively reinforce or punish that behavior. So I infer that the behavior must be under the control of rules. Usually those rules describe this contingency that is not able to reinforce or punish the causal response. However, even these rules will not control behavior without some sort of effective behavioral consequences. So I also infer that control by such rules is supported by self-given or automatic reinforcement or punishment. This reinforcement often involves the termination of an aversive condition initiated by the statement of the rule.

I am suggesting that rules control behavior, often not because they function as cues associated with the outcome specified in the rule, as might at first glance appear to be the case. Instead, rules probably control behavior because they function as motivating operations increasing the effectiveness of behavioral consequences immediately contingent on compliance and noncompliance with those rules. (The increased importance of the rule-statement as a motivating operation and not as a cue seems especially clear with regard to rules specifying contingencies that are not direct acting.) However, all of this rule-control seems to require a highly developed repertoire on the part of the person whose behavior is being controlled; so we will consider this prerequisite repertoire in the next section.

6.2. Prerequisites for Control by Rules Specifying Contingencies That Are Not Direct Acting

From the perspective of the current analysis, there seem to be five behavioral prerequisites for effective control by rules specifying indirect-acting contingencies. They are:

1. Specific rules must be able to control behavior.
2. Novel rules must be able to control behavior.
3. Performance must evoke accurate self-evaluation.
4. Self-evaluation must evoke the self-delivery of behavioral consequences.
5. Effective behavioral consequences must be available.

The first two prerequisites deal with rules either as cues or as motivating operations, depending on your point of view. (For a related analysis, see Kanfer & Gaelick, 1986.) We will now look at these five prerequisites in more detail.

6.2.1. Specific Rules

First, specific rules need to control behavior by functioning either as verbal cues or as verbal motivating operations; that is, the person needs to have the necessary verbal skills, for instance, to be able to comply with specific instructions and requests as a result of training with those specific rules. This can be established by reinforcing acts of compliance and punishing acts of noncompliance, in the presence of those rules, for example, "Open your workbook, Johnny. . . . Good for you for opening your workbook."

6.2.2. Generalized Rule Control

Second, generalized rule control needs to be effective; that is, the person needs to be able to comply with novel instances of general classes of rules, even though he or she has not been trained with that particular novel instance. For example, we would have generalized rule control if the following occurred: We said, "The way you put your new car in reverse is to push down on the gear shift, and then move it to the left and back"; then after a little practice, the person got his or her Volkswagon in reverse.

Is the requirement of generalized rule-control redundant? In other words, if it is rule-control, then it must be verbal, as suggested earlier in the definition of a rule. What does it mean for stimulus control or motivational control to be verbal and not merely simple cue control or respondent control, as when the pigeon pecks the key in the presence of a green light? According to at least some scholars, verbal control must be productive; in other words, a rearrangement of the components of such stimuli (e.g., words) must appropriately control behavior in novel settings (Hayes, 1987, March; Hockett, 1960; Whaley & Malott, 1971, pp. 257–261). Furthermore, the notion of novelty in productive verbal control is similar to novelty in generalized rule-control. In other words, novel verbal stimuli or novel rules must accurately control behavior. However, it seems feasible that at least a rudimentary productive language control might be established, without the generalization of rule-control based on that language. For example, for some individuals some novel descriptive statements (tacts) might control their actions, even though novel rules (mands) might not. Therefore, the requirement of generalized rule-control does not seem redundant with the verbal nature of rules.

The first prerequisite, control by specific rules, is needed if a person is to acquire generalized rule-control, because generalized control should result from the establishment of control by a large number of specific rules. This should take place in much the same way other conceptual behavior is often acquired: Appropriate behavior is reinforced in the presence of a wide variety of instances of a concept, and inappropriate behavior is extinguished or possibly punished. As a result, eventually that appropriate behavior will occur in the presence of novel instances of the same concept, and inappropriate behavior will not (Whaley & Malott, 1971, Chapter 9). (Note that we can also establish conceptual control by giving rules or definitions of concepts, but that seems like getting the cart before the horse in the establishment of initial rule-governed behavior.)

As an example of the development of conceptual control, the concept of "picture of people" can develop stimulus control over the behavior of a pigeon, if we reinforce proper identification of a wide variety of pictures of people. Eventually novel instances of the stimulus class *pictures of people* come to exert stimulus control over the pigeon's behavior, that is, the pigeon comes to be able to identify novel instances of pictures of people (Herrnstein & Loveland, 1964; Siddall & Malott, 1971).

In much the same way, rules might gradually come to control our actions, until eventually, even novel rules exert effective control. This should be the case whether the rules function as cues or as motivating operations. However, I should point out that, at present, it is only an assumption that generalized motivating operations can be established in the same manner as generalized stimulus control (i.e., conceptual control); I know of no direct empirical evidence. (Incidentally, I am using *rule* in the most general sense to include not only rules that describe the nature of things but also instructions and requests. I am doing this because rules, instructions, and requests all seem to control behavior in much the same way.)

This analysis also assumes that rules acquire their effectiveness either as cues or as motivating operations through the direct involvement of behavioral consequences. The behavioral consequences would be those consequences specified in the rule, in the case of direct-acting contingencies. They would be added consequences (often delivered by the parent), in the case of both rules specifying contingencies that are direct acting and rules specifying contingencies that are not direct acting.

These two prerequisites of control by specific rules and control by general classes of rules are essential if our behavior is to be most effectively controlled by rules describing direct-acting contingencies as well as indirect-acting contingencies. However, the remaining prerequisites are more important for control by rules describing indirect-acting contingencies and especially when there is no one else to deliver the supportive behavioral consequences. In other words, these remaining prerequisites may constitute the repertoire needed for effective self-management.

6.2.3. *Self-Evaluation*

I assume that control by rules not specifying direct-acting contingencies involves self-reinforcement or self-punishment. Therefore, the third prerequisite is that we need to be able to self-evaluate our performance, that is, determine whether or not our behavior matches the rule. We probably need to self-evaluate, if we are to deliver behavioral consequences contingent on our compliance or noncompliance with the rule. This would seem to be the case especially when we self-deliver praise or aversive thoughts or when we stop thinking aversive thoughts (e.g., when we finally comply with a rule).

Perhaps we also need to self-evaluate, even when the delivery of behavioral consequences happens automatically (e.g., with the termination of possibly unconscious aversive feelings such as anxiety or guilt), though this is much less clear. For example, a writer might need to evaluate whether he or she has written enough for the day to stop writing without evoking those aversive feelings. Suppose the rule were, "Write 300 words every day, if you want to be a productive scholar." In this case the writer would need to count the words before the stopping of the writing would not automatically produce an aversive condition.

Presumably self-evaluation is itself operant behavior and, as such, also needs behavioral consequences for its maintenance. So the question again arises, what are the consequences, and who or what delivers them? Let us return to the writer. The writer makes a self-evaluation response, an observing response, because that observing response is occasionally reinforced with an all-is-clear signal, a cue in the presence of which the writer can terminate writing without the punishment of aversive feelings.

A hypothetical, experimental analog might be the pigeon in an operant chamber that would peck an observing key. That observing response would turn on either a red light or a green light. The red light would turn on, when a punishment contingency was in effect for pecking a food-producing key (the dangerous periods). The green light would turn on, when the punishment contingency was not in effect (the safe periods). The occasional presentations of the green light might be sufficient to maintain the pigeon's observing response. Similarly, the occasional presentation of a word count of at least 300 words might be sufficient to maintain the writer's observing or self-evaluation response.

A real experiment somewhat analogous to our problem of self-observation or self-evaluation showed that human beings would make an observing response that sometimes produced a stimulus in the presence of which an "avoidance" response would prevent an aversive condition (the loss of rewards) (Baron & Galizio, 1976). This supports the notion that human beings might also make a self-evaluation response if it sometimes produced a stimulus in the presence of which a termination response would not produce an aversive condition (aversive feelings).

Of course the writer may stop writing and not contact that aversive condition; in other words, it may not be aversive to stop writing in the absence of clear evidence of completion of the task (the 300 written words). This brings us to what I assume to be our next prerequisite for the effective control of rules specifying indirect-acting contingencies.

6.2.4. Delivery of the Behavioral Consequences

The fourth prerequisite is that differential behavioral consequences be delivered, immediately contingent on our compliance or noncompliance with the rule. It is not crucial whether those behavioral consequences be self-delivered thoughts or automatic, nonverbal ones like general aversive states such as anxiety. In other words, it is not enough that we be able to self-evaluate our compliance because without the delivery of an appropriate behavioral consequence, we would stop complying with rules describing indirect-acting contingencies—extinction would occur.

6.2.5. *Effective Behavioral Consequences*

Finally, for effective behavioral consequences to be delivered, they must exist, whether those consequences are of the automatic, nonverbal sort, or whether they are self-statements or thoughts. We need the appropriate behavioral history to establish such outcomes as effective behavioral consequences; for example, thinking, "I sure did let people down, when I failed to prepare my lecture," will not be aversive, without the proper behavioral history, without such thoughts having been paired with aversive events in the past. Similarly, the writer needs to have had aversive events paired with past failures such as failing to meet the day's quota of words, if that failure is to be aversive in the present.

Incidentally, informal introspective behavior analysis has suggested the following: Many of us procrastinate on such tasks as writing chapters, grading papers, and preparing lectures until we get dangerously near the deadline for the completion of those tasks. Then, as we have so often done in the past, we state a rule specifying an aversive consequence that will befall us if we fail to complete the task on time. However, on this occasion that rule-statement acts as a motivating operation that establishes not working on the task as a very aversive condition. Then, and only then (more or less), will working on the task allow us to escape a sufficiently aversive condition that we will in fact start to work. Prior to the proximity of the deadline, the aversiveness of the condition established by the rule-statement was not sufficient to reinforce escape through productivity.

Further introspection suggests, at least to me, that the self-delivery of rewards may play a much less important role in the compliance with rules specifying contingencies that are not direct acting—the main source of reinforcement is the removal of the aversive condition associated with noncompliance (a condition the aversiveness of which was established by the statement of the relevant rule). For the present analysis, it is not crucial whether that aversive condition is an automatic result of noncompliance or a result of a self-statement (a thought). So I am suggesting that the sort of automatic reinforcement or self-reinforcement (negative reinforcement) that probably maintains control by rules has little to do with people giving themselves M&Ms every time they comply with those rules; and it seems to be automatic reinforcement or self-given reinforcement involving the delivery of rewards (positive reinforcement) that so many behaviorists find methodologically or philosophically offensive. We all seem to be more comfortable with aversive control.

6.2.6. *Summary of the Prerequisites for Control by Rules Specifying Contingencies That Are Not Direct Acting*

In summary, we may need the following prerequisites, if our behavior is to be adequately controlled by rules describing indirect-acting contingencies, that is, contingencies with delayed outcomes, low probability outcomes, or small and only cumulatively significant outcomes; we need (1) specific rule control, (2) generalized rule control, (3) self-evaluation, (4) delivery of behavioral consequences, and (5) effective behavioral consequences. Furthermore, compliance with such rules is probably maintained by the reinforcement resulting from the termination of aversive, private conditions associated with noncompliance.

Now this may all seem precarious and fragile. It may seem too easy to disrupt the proper balance of the complex prerequisites for effective control by rules describing contingencies that are not direct acting (those contingencies that do not reinforce or punish the causal response class). I think the balance probably is at least as precarious as it seems. The difficulty many authors have in writing (for example, chapters for scholarly books) might attest to this fragility.

6.3. How Do Contingencies That Are Not Direct Acting Control Behavior?

Thus far, we have analyzed how *rules* describing contingencies that are not direct acting might control behavior. Now we ask the following questions: How do *outcomes* that are not direct acting affect the control such rules exert over our actions. Outcomes that are not direct acting (with regard to the causal response) are too delayed, or too improbable, or too small to reinforce or punish that causal response class. Nonetheless, they sometimes do seem to influence behavior. How? (Note that this analysis distinguishes between how rules control our behavior and how the outcomes in the contingencies described by the rules affect the control exerted by those rules.)

6.3.1. *Outcomes That Confirm Rules*

What happens when the outcome predicted by the rule is confirmed? What happens when you do not have cavities after 6 months of flossing? Of course it would probably depend on your previous rate of cavities, but a dramatic improvement might be effective in maintaining rule-compliance. In the same way, an auto accident with or without seat belts fastened might affect the probability of our stating and following the seat-belt rule. So a striking outcome for compliance or noncompliance with a rule may be important.

The occurrence of the predicted outcome of a rule describing contingencies that are not direct acting might affect rule-control in at least two ways: It might affect the likelihood that we would state the rule when the appropriate occasion arose in the future, and it might affect the likelihood that we would follow the rule once it had been stated. First let us consider the effects on our likelihood of stating the rule at a later time.

6.3.2. *The Likelihood of Stating the Rule*

6.3.2a. Stating the Rule Immediately after Confirmation. We might repeat the statement of the rule right after a confirming outcome, and this repetition might make it more likely we would state it again the next time a similar occasion arose. However, why would we repeat the rule immediately after an outcome? Such a repetition of the rule probably does not automatically result from the outcome; we probably do not always say to ourselves, "I must remember to floss," right after our dentist discovers another cavity; and we probably do not always say to ourselves, "I must remember to buckle up," right after an accident. However, a special behavioral history might make us more likely to state the rule following a confirming outcome. Essentially we may be following a problem-solving strategy, one where significant outcomes act as cues for statements about how to prevent or achieve those outcomes in the future. Our following that strategy would probably be a product of modeling and of social consequences related to conspicuously following the same strategy in the past. (See Baer & Deguchi, 1985, for a review of generalized imitation that seems relevant to the problems of delayed and private imitation raised by the present analysis.)

Informal observation suggests that the behavioral history that generates this sort of ad-hoc, problem-solving analysis, especially of our failures, is, indeed, so special that many people rarely engage in such analyses. A much more common approach is to find someone else to blame, to rationalize out of the responsibility for our own failure. This might result from a behavioral history that punishes acknowledgment of responsibility, rather than one that supports that acknowledgment along with an analysis of what rules to follow to prevent such failure in the future, for example the rules of flossing and buckling up.

6.3.2b. Rule Control Resulting from Stating the Rule Immediately after Confirmation. Suppose the statement of the rule does occur after an episode involving the relevant contingency. Then we must ask how that statement makes it more likely that we will state the rule the next time it is appropriate, for example, that we will state the seat-belt rule the next time we get into a car. In some way, that earlier statement of the rule might cause the stimuli associated with getting in the car to act as an effective cue for stating the rule again.

(Another interpretation might be that we do not state the rule on the next appropriate occasion, that instead the initial statement of the rule causes compliance on the next occasion without any restatements of that rule. However, such stimulus control or action at a distance seems unlikely, at least to me.)

The stimuli associated with getting in the car might come to function as cues in at least three ways:

1. The actual car was part of the stimulus present when we had stated the rule earlier and in the presence of which that statement might have evoked some self-given or automatic reinforcement. Then simple physical stimulus generalization might account for the next statement of the rule on entering the car. (Note that we may still need to invoke some sort of self-given or automatic reinforcement here because often we will be alone when it is appropriate to state the rule. The sources of social consequences that were essential for acquisition of this rule-stating repertoire will often not be present at a later date.)
2. We had an image of the car when we stated the rule earlier, so stimulus generalization from the image to the actual car could account for the next statement of the rule.
3. Entering the car evokes a verbal statement involving the car that in turn could function as a cue for the rule that contains words about entering the car; for example, the first time we might have said, "When I get into the car, I must always buckle up." So now, as we get into the car, we might say to ourselves, in essence, "I'm getting into the car." That statement, in turn, might cue our stating the remainder of the rule, "I must buckle up."

6.3.3. *The Likelihood of Following the Rule*

How could the occurrence of the predicted outcome affect the likelihood that we would later follow the rule when stated? It seems plausible that the occurrence of the outcome could affect the value of the self-given or automatic behavioral consequences immediately contingent on compliance or noncompliance with that rule. This could happen under four different conditions:

1. The presentation of a reward contingent on following the rule.
2. The avoidance of an aversive event contingent on following the rule.
3. The presentation of an aversive event contingent on failure to follow the rule.
4. The loss of a reward contingent on failure to follow the rule.

We will now consider those four conditions in detail.

6.3.3a. The Presentation of a Reward Contingent on Following the Rule. Suppose the predicted outcome were a reward that in fact was attained, though its attainment was too delayed or too infrequent to appreciably reinforce the response that actually produced it. To understand the impact of such an outcome, we might first consider the factors controlling the following of a rule describing an indirect-acting contingency of that sort. For example, "Work hard and you'll get a raise." What happens when we tell ourselves that rule at the appropriate time? Remember, I am assuming that only outcomes in addition to the ones described by rules of this sort will reinforce rule-following. Furthermore, we are now considering only the case where there is no outside intervention from another person, so we need to provide our own effective behavioral consequences.

Those behavioral consequences we provide can be either aversive, rewarding, or both. We can say, "I'd be a fool not to work hard now, so I can get my raise," thereby setting up an aversive condition that working hard would terminate. Or we might have a history of self-congratulation when we correctly follow rules, so that the statement of a rule is a generalized cue associated with self-given rewards for compliance.

How might the attainment of the outcome affect the value of a self-given aversive consequence. Success might cause us to think something of this sort, "Now that I got paid off for it the last time, I know the rule is really true; and I really can do it; so I'd be an even greater fool, if I didn't work hard," thereby possibly setting up a slightly more aversive condition to be escaped by hard work.

How might success affect the value of a self-congratulatory reward? It seems likely that a successful outcome would have little effect on the value of the self-given reward if the congratulations were of this sort: "Congratulations for following the rule because it's usually a wise strategy to follow rules; and being able to follow rules of this sort is no easy trick." Though success might increase the reward value of implicitly labeling our selves as wise.

It is also possible that we might imagine the rewarding features of the raise, contingent upon working hard; and those images might have increased reward value as a result of having received a previous raise. However, the problem is that having such images might not be contingent upon working hard; rather it might be just as likely to occur prior to working, or after we have failed to work hard. So in that case, any increased rewarding value of the image would have little impact on the following of the rule, because the image would be noncontingent.

6.3.3b. The Avoidance of an Aversive Event Contingent on Following the Rule. Keller and Schoenfeld (1950, p. 314) point out that animal research shows that successful avoidance prevents the pairing of the "warning" stimulus with the unlearned aversive stimulus being avoided. They then cite research suggesting that this lack of pairing in turn causes the warning stimulus to lose its learned aversiveness. As a result, the animal is less likely to make the response that escapes the warning stimulus and simultaneously avoids the unlearned aversive stimulus. This then results in increased pairing of the two stimuli, increased aversiveness of the warning stimulus, and increased avoidance responding. Such a cyclic process continues indefinitely. (This analysis assumes that the repeated occurrence of a learned aversive stimulus will reduce its aversiveness, if that stimulus is not occasionally paired with another aversive stimulus, often an unlearned aversive stimulus.)

If Keller and Schoenfeld's analysis is correct, successfully avoiding the aversive event might produce a decrease in the conditioned aversiveness of the relevant thoughts at the time the rule should be followed, thereby making the rule less likely to control our behavior. So following rules that specify aversive outcomes might tend to be somewhat cyclic as contacts with the aversive event temporarily increase rule-following. However, generalized rule-control, based on support from following other rules, might tend to attenuate the amplitude of that cycle.

On the other hand, in the classic research of Solomon and Wynne (1953), a dog's successfully avoiding an aversive shock did not produce a decrease in the conditioned aversiveness of the associated warning light and did not, thereby, make the light less likely to control the dog's avoidance behavior, even though the dog experienced over 500 trials without pairing with the electric shock. Solomon and Wynne theorized that the short latencies of the avoidance response did not leave the warning light on long enough for it to loose its aversive value from lack or pairing with the shock. So promptly following rules that specify aversive outcomes also might tend to persist, in spite of lack of contact with the aversive outcome specified by the rule. In other words, if you comply immediately, you terminate noncompliance before it loses its learned aversiveness.

6.3.3c. The Presentation of an Aversive Event Contingent on Failure to Follow the Rule. Suppose the predicted outcome were an aversive event contingent on failure to follow the rule and suppose that aversive event had occurred, for example, we had gotten a painful cavity. Thinking about the painful cavity at the time we should floss our teeth might set up an aversive condition most readily escaped by actually flossing our teeth, that is, by complying with the flossing rule. We might state to ourselves something like the following, though no doubt in a more abbreviated form: "Before I get dressed, I'd better floss my teeth; otherwise I might forget; and the result of too much forgetting might be another cavity." The mention of another cavity might evoke an aversive condition that we can attenuate by getting out the floss.

(Note that I am not trying to bridge a delay between the failure to floss and the aversive cavity, nor am I trying to bridge a delay between the act of flossing and a subsequent relatively pleasant visit to the dentist. Instead, I am trying to account for how our last visit to the dentist might affect our current flossing. The action at a distance I am trying to account for is not the time between the flossing and the dentist but rather the time between the dentist and the flossing.)

6.3.3d. The Loss of a Reward Contingent on Failure to Follow the Rule. Finally, suppose the predicted outcome were a rewarding event we had failed to get because we failed to follow the rule. What effect would that have? What happens when we do not work hard enough to get the proffered raise? Loss of a reward or failure to get a reward seems to act as an aversive event. So such an outcome might increase the aversiveness of our thoughts about failing to work diligently, and thus we would be more likely to terminate such aversive thoughts by working more industriously when those thoughts occurred.

The question is, how would an actual aversive event, like the loss of a reward, increase the aversiveness of our thoughts about that event, like thinking about failing to work hard enough to prevent that loss? Presumably a neutral or even mildly aversive event will increase its aversiveness as a result of pairings with other more aversive events. So, our thinking about such losses might in some way have been paired with the actual loss. Or perhaps thinking about future losses would evoke some of the aversiveness of that past event.

6.3.3e. Summary of the Effects of Outcomes That Confirm Rules. In summary, it seems plausible that outcomes that are not direct acting can affect rule-following. Such outcomes might affect the likelihood that we will state the rule at the appropriate time. Those outcomes might also affect the likelihood that we will follow the rule once we have stated it. We may be more likely to state the rule at the proper time, if we have previously stated it right after the operation of an indirect-acting contingency. This increased likelihood is because the stimuli present when we first stated the rule are similar to stimuli when it is next appropriate to state that rule; those stimuli could be part of the external environment, imaginal, or verbal.

These outcomes might also affect the likelihood that we will follow the rule we have stated. Experiencing the previous indirect-acting contingency might affect the value of the self-given behavioral consequence that was immediately contingent on complying with the rule; this could often occur as an increase in the aversiveness of thoughts that could be terminated by following the rule. The increased aversiveness could result, regardless of whether that rule dealt with increasing rewarding outcomes or decreasing aversive outcomes. These outcomes might also increase the reward value of statements given after the following the rule.

6.3.4. Outcomes That Disconfirm Rules

Suppose a rule is disconfirmed; what happens? An analysis similar to the one applied to confirmatory outcomes suggests that we would be less likely to state the rule, and if we did state the rule, we would be less likely to follow it because the reinforcing behavioral consequences would be less effective.

However, if the outcome were stated as a probability, the rule might be more likely to continue to control our actions, when that outcome fails to occur—for example, "floss and you probably won't have cavities." Then even if you do have cavities, that should not be too devastating to the rule. In fact, many rules that maintain considerable amounts of behavior are difficult to disprove. For example, "Pray and you'll go to heaven."

6.3.4a. Human Operant Research. Though not directly dealing with this issue, Galizio (1979) studied the effects of disconfirmation of rules describing direct-acting contingencies. In his experiments, rules he gave the subjects lost control over the subjects' behavior when compliance with those rules produced a conspicuously greater loss of rewards that did noncompliance. (Such noncompliance might have been compliance with alternative, subject-generated rules.) However, the rules generally maintained control when their disconfirmation was less conspicuous.

In another series of human operant experiments, rules describing direct-acting contingencies did not lose their control, even when they had been disconfirmed. For example, the subjects were instructed to press a response button slowly in order to earn conspicuous but intermittently presented rewards. However, they continued to press the button slowly, even after the program had been changed, without their being informed; the program was changed so that now more rapid responding would produce those rewards (Shimoff, Catania, & Matthews, 1981).

It is not clear from the article how great the variability of the subjects' response rates were; in other words, it is not clear how often the subjects responded rapidly enough that they would have violated the old rule, produced a reward for more rapid responding, and thus actually disconfirmed that old rule. Therefore, it is not clear to what extent the rule was actually disconfirmed, even though the variability in the speed of responding for an uninstructed control group was great enough that the contingencies of reinforcement produced a marked increase in their speed of responding. In other words, it is not clear whether the rules produced a decrease in the variability of the speed of responding or a decrease in sensitivity to the direct-acting contingencies that were actually contacted.

However, even if the rules did produce a decrease in sensitivity to changes in direct acting contingencies of reinforcement, in this and other human operant experiments using variations on the classical schedules of reinforcement, it might be premature to conclude that "insensitivity is a defining property of instructional control." In other words, research of this sort should not cause us to predict that people would go broke putting quarters in nonfunctional vending machines, even though the instructions on the machine clearly say, "Insert quarter here." Instead we might expect that such a conspicuous disconfirmation would greatly attenuate that instructional control. Perhaps rule-generated insensitivity is a common occurrence in the human-operant laboratory where rewards are typically presented with a low probability; but that does not mean a similar insensitivity occurs in our everyday world where rewards are typically presented with a high probability; for example, moving a fork full of mashed potatoes toward our mouth will almost always be reinforced by the taste of the potatoes; and perhaps that is why we usually do not try to transport our peas with a knife, though such a task would be more characteristic of life in the human operant laboratory (Malott, General, & Snapper, 1973, Chapter 3). For another noninstance of insensitivity of instructional control, ask any halfway perceptive grade-school teacher what happens to instruction-generated discipline the moment he or she steps out of the room.

Furthermore, even if this insensitivity of rule-governed behavior is more general than the preceding paragraph suggests, it might still be premature to conclude with too much finality that "insensitivity is a defining property of instructional control," especially with the implication that such a conclusion has anything to do with the fundamental nature of human beings. It might instead be that the behavioral history of most college sophomores has been such that compliance with instructions produces more rewarding stimuli and fewer aversive stimuli than noncompliance, even when the contingencies of reinforcement and punishment of the moment might suggest otherwise. It might be that compliance with rules is itself rule-governed. It might be that insensitivity of instructional control is a cultural artifact and not a fundamental issue in behavior analysis. It might be that, with little difficulty, the researchers in the human operant laboratory could provide their subjects with a history that would produce a generation of college sophomores for whom instructions would produce hypersensitivity to the direct-acting contingencies of reinforcement and punishment rather than insensitivity.

In fact, other human-operant research suggests the possibility that sensitivity to the direct-acting contingencies could, in deed, result from a behavioral history (Hayes, Brownstein, Haas, & Greenway, 1986). Subjects who showed apparent sensitivity to changes in contingencies within the first phase of an experiment also usually showed apparent sensitivity to the subsequent changes in contingencies between the two phases of the experiment; however, those who failed to demonstrate sensitivity in the first phase usually failed to demonstrate sensitivity in the second phase. Perhaps some subjects acquired their sensitivity during the first phase that then allowed them to respond differentially during the second phase. Or the sensitivity in the two phases of the experiment might also have resulted from factors prior to the experiment.

The second phase of the experiment was extinction. That is such a conspicuous change in contingencies that it is hard to imagine the subjects could not tact it. In fact, in their procedure section, the authors mention that some of the subjects attempted to communicate with them or to leave the experimental space during this extinction phase. It would be interesting to know if the majority of those subjects were the sensitive subjects.

Social context (awareness of being observed by the experimenter) has a considerable effect on the experimental performance of human subjects (Rosenfarb & Hayes, 1984; Zettle & Hayes, 1983). So some of these human-operant results might also be due to their social context; the insensitivity to conspicuous contingencies might be due to rules the subjects give themselves, for example, "I should keep responding, even though I'm no longer getting anything, because this must be what the professor (experimenter) wants." If so, it would seem insensitive of us to suggest that the subjects are insensitive to the experimentally manipulated contingencies.

In summary, this analysis of some of the human operant literature suggests the following: Although the possibility has been raised that disconfirmation of rules has little or no impact on rule control, as behavior analysts, our common sense should prevail because such disconfirmation is crucial in many important aspects of our everyday life.

7. OTHER APPROACHES TO SELF-MANAGEMENT AND RULE-GOVERNED BEHAVIOR

Many scholars have dealt with issues similar to those in this chapter; however, it seemed necessary to present the current theoretical framework, before comparing and contrasting some of those approaches with the current approach.

7.1. Environmental Restructuring

Brigham (1982) builds on Skinner's (1953, Chapter 15) approach to self-control. Skinner talks about changes the individual makes in the environment that will in turn produce changes in the behavior of the individual—for example, the individual could change the environment by leaving a reminder note to take out the garbage on the way to the car; the reminder note could in turn change the behavior of the individual by increasing the likelihood of the individual's taking out the garbage.

According to Brigham, "The major behavior for analysis in self-management is self-observation . . . to analyze the behavior/environment interdependencies . . . the recognition of mutual influences of the individual's responses on the environment and the effect of the environment on his or her responses" (p. 50). Rather than self-reinforcement, Brigham recommends the reinforcement of others so they will in turn act in such a way as to reinforce the behavior the individual wishes to increase—for example, the college student might arrange reinforcing study dates rather than try to self-reinforce studying.

Although this approach to environmental restructuring is an important contribution to our field, I do not think it gets to the most difficult problem of self-management, the problem of concern in this chapter—for example, two people individually stand in front of their bathroom mirrors; they have just brushed their teeth; the dental floss is conspicuously at hand; both people know the importance of daily flossing; one flosses daily, and the other flosses annually, at best. Why?

7.2. Human Operant Research

Human operant research on rule-governed behavior seems mainly concerned with rules describing direct-acting contingencies, the discovery of such rules by the subject, and the ignoring of old rules or the discovery of new rules when those direct-acting contingencies have changed (e.g., Bentall, Lowe, & Beasty, 1985; Catania, Matthews, & Shimoff, 1982; Galizio, 1979; Kaufman, Baron, & Kopp, 1966; Lowe, Beasty, & Bentall, 1983; Matthews, Catania, & Shimoff, 1985; Shimoff *et al.*, 1981; Vaughan, 1985). It is sometimes unclear whether this work is primarily concerned with an analysis of the way rules control significant human behavior in the normal human habitat or with a demonstration of the phylogenic continuity of the effects of schedules of reinforcement. In any event, interesting and important as this work clearly is, it does not directly apply to the problems of dental flossing.

The dental flosser is in a position human beings often find themselves in. Often human beings receive rules from a higher authority—the elders, the church, or science. Often the humble individual cannot discover the correct rules (for example, it takes well-trained scientists and millions of dollars to discover the correct rules describing the relation between smoking and health). In such a position, the individual knows the rule, believes the rule, but may still not be able to follow the rule.

7.3. Animal Operant Research

Malott and Garcia (in press) discuss some relevant animal operant research as follows:

> Rachlin and Green (1972) designed and studied a fascinating, though complex, animal analog of self-management involving delayed outcomes. The analog has a great deal of convincing face validity. It is based on the every day observation, that we can chose the path of righteousness instead of the path of least resistance when we are temporally removed from the temptations that might lead us astray. For example,

we will be more likely to start our rainy-day, payroll-deduction savings account when we are in the personnel office, not when we are in the pub on Friday evening with our pay check in hand, even if the personnel officer is standing next to us in the pub offering a payroll-deduction form and ball-point pen.

Rachlin and Green studied the variables controlling a pigeon's pecking one key that would put itself into a condition where further key pecking would produce a 20-sec delay but a large reward (analogous to payroll-deduction savings) and its pecking another key would put it into a condition where further key pecking would produce a more immediate but smaller reward (analogous to many beers). Malott and Garcia (in press) then analyzed the experiment as an example of a psychophysical procedure:

> Even if we can account for Rachlin and Green's results by a common-sense Fechner's law analysis, the question remains, is their procedure a reasonable analog to the sort of self-management or self-control procedures human beings use? We think not. Rachlin and Green offer as an example the worker who signs up for automatic deposit from payroll into a savings account. We think the outcome of the larger, though delayed reward (savings plus interest) is too delayed to reinforce the act of signing up; the delay will normally range from a few weeks, before the worker receives a bank statement showing the accumulated interest, to a few years, before the worker actually spends the accumulated interest. In view of the other animal work on delayed reinforcement, it seems unreasonable to assume that Rachlin and Green's pigeons would continue to peck either key if the delay were extended from 20 sec to 1 week.
>
> But this whole analysis is almost academic and boarders on teleology, when we consider that we may be talking about a new worker who has never established a savings account, let alone a payroll-deduction program. We now have to account for his or her emission of this complex sequence of responses before the opportunity for it to have been reinforced, regardless of the delay.
>
> We propose that, whether we are talking about an experienced saver or a novice, we can more readily understand the act of establishing a savings program as an act controlled by its immediate consequences, perhaps the termination of an aversive condition (feelings or thoughts accompanying noncompliance with a good rule or fear of an impoverished future), or by the presentation of a rewarding condition (thoughts of self-righteousness).

7.4. Public Goal Setting

I agree with Hayes *et al.* (1985) that in many situations, public goal setting is a powerful tool for the behavior modifier—in many situations, but not in the privacy of the bathroom, not in the land of the normal, middle-aged dental flosser whose parents have long since stopped monitoring their offspring's efforts at dental hygiene. (Or, if public commitment is relevant there, its effectiveness will require some fairly subtle behavior analysis.) A small amount of daily flossing does occur. I suspect it receives most of its support from the immediate termination of private micronightmares. I suspect flosser are active in public goal setting.

In summary of the other approaches, they all represent impressive theoretical and experimental analyses, and they all deal with important behavioral issues; however, none seem to effectively address the major problem of control by rules describing contingencies that are not direct acting—the lonely flosser.

8. CONCLUDING REMARKS

Human beings have created an environment in which biologically important outcomes of their actions often fail to function as behavioral consequence for those actions. This failure occurs either because the outcomes are too delayed, too improbable, or too small and of only cumulative significance. However, rule-statements sometimes cause verbal human beings to act in ways that will produce more beneficial outcomes and fewer harmful outcomes, even though those outcomes still may not function as behavioral consequences for the causal acts. Thus the chances of success and survival will increase both for human beings as individuals and for human beings as a species, to the extent that appropriate rules govern their actions. Rule-control may be the major factor that allows humanity to survive the world human beings have created. However, a special behavioral history is required for a person to acquire the repertoire needed for their behavior to be under the control of such rules; therefore such control is often far from perfect. (See Hayes, 1987, for an analysis of the negative side of rule-governed behavior, the control over maladaptive behavior exerted by inappropriate rules.)

Several theorists have attempted to account for those occasions where delayed outcomes seem to control our behavior; and some have also attempted to account for those occasions where delayed outcomes seem to have failed to control our behavior. However, to my knowledge, none have also attempted to account for those occasions where improbable outcomes and small but cumulatively significant outcomes control our behavior or fail to do so. In other words, theorists seem to have misanalyzed the problem of evasive goals, thinking that it is a problem of delayed outcomes; but according to the present analysis, it is the improbable and small outcomes, not the delayed outcomes, that cause humanity so many problems. Therefore, this analysis is a preliminary attempt to provide a more comprehensive and also more detailed analysis of the control exerted by rules describing contingencies that are not direct acting.

ACKNOWLEDGMENTS

I gratefully acknowledge Jack Michael's valuable feedback throughout the development of this chapter. I also appreciate the helpful comments by Joseph Parsons and Maria Emma Garcia on the penultimate draft of the chapter.

9. REFERENCES

Adams, J. A. (1980). *Learning and memory: An introduction*. Homewood, IL: Dorsey.

Azrin, N. H., & Holz, W. C. (1966). Punishment. In W. K. Honig (Ed.), *Operant behavior: Areas of research and application* (pp. 380–447). New York: Appleton-Century-Crofts.

Baer, D. M., & Deguchi, H. (1985). Generalized imitation from a radical-behavioral viewpoint. In S. Reiss & R. Botzin (Eds.), *Theoretical issues in behavior analysis* (pp. 179–217). New York: Academic Press.

Baldwin, J. D., & Baldwin, J. I. (1986). *Behavior principles in everyday life*. Englewood Cliffs, NJ: Prentice-Hall.

Bandura, A., & Mahoney, M. J. (1974). Maintenance and transfer of self-reinforcement functions. *Behavior Research and Therapy, 12*, 89–97.

Banks, R. K., & Vogel-Sprott, M. (1965). Effect of delayed punishment on an immediately rewarded response in humans. *Journal of Experimental Psychology, 70*, 357–359.

Bateson, T. G., & Reese, E. P. (1969). The reinforcing properties of conspicuous stimuli in the imprinting situation. *Animal Behavior, 17*, 692–699.

Baum, W. M. (1973). The correlation-based law of effect. *Journal of the Experimental Analysis of Behavior, 20*, 137–153.

Bentall, R. P., Lowe, C. F., & Beasty, A. (1985). The role of verbal behavior in human learning: II. Developmental differences. *Journal of the Experimental Analysis of Behavior, 43*, 165–181.

Bolles, R. C. (1985). Introduction: Associative processes in the formation of conditioned food aversion—An emerging functionalism? *Annals of the New York Academy of Sciences, 443*, 1–7.

Braam, M., & Malott, R. W. (1986, May). *Rule-governed behavior in preschool-aged children*. Poster presented at the meeting of the Association for Behavior Analysis, Columbus, OH.

Brigham, T. (1982). Self-management: A radical behavioral perspective. In P. Karoly & F. H. Kanfer (Eds.), *Self-management and behavior change: From theory to practice* (pp. 32–59). New York: Pergamon Press.

Camp, D. S., Raymond G. A., & Church, R. M. (1967). Temporal relationship between response and punishment. *Journal of Experimental Psychology, 74*, 114–123.

Catania, A. C. (1975). The myth of self-reinforcement. *Behaviorism, 3*, 192–199.

Catania, A. C., Matthews, B. A., & Shimoff, E. (1982). Instructed versus shaped human verbal behavior: Interactions with nonverbal responding. *Journal of Experimental Analysis of Behavior, 38*, 233–248.

Cohen, P. S. (1968). Punishment: The interactive effects of delay and intensity of shock. *Journal of Experimental Analysis of Behavior, 11*, 789–799.

de Villiers, P. (1977). Choice in concurrent schedules and a quantitative formulation of the law of effect. In W. K. Honig & J. E. R. Staddon (Eds.), *Handbook of operant behavior* (pp. 233–287). Englewood Cliffs, NJ: Prentice-Hall.

Fantino, E., & Logan, C. A. (1979). *The experimental analysis of behavior*. San Francisco: W. H. Freeman.

Ferster, C. B. (1953). Sustained behavior under delayed reinforcement. *Journal of Experimental Psychology, 45*, 218–224.

Garcia, J., Lasiter, P. A., Bermudez-Rattoni, F., & Deems, D. A. (1985). A general theory of aversion learning. *Annals of the New York Academy of Sciences, 443*, 8–21.

Galizio, M. (1979). Contingency-shaped and rule-governed behavior: Instructional control of human loss avoidance. *Journal of the Experimental Analysis of Behavior, 31*, 53–70.

Goldiamond, I. (1976). Self-reinforcement. *Journal of Applied behavior Analysis, 9*, 509–514.

Harris, M. (1977). *Cannibals and kings: The origins of culture*. New York: Random House.

Harris, M. (1979). *Cultural materialism: The struggle for the science of culture*. New York: Random House.

Hayes, S. C. (1987, March). Rules are not just discriminative stimuli. In M. L. Sundberg (Chair), *Rule-governed behavior*. Symposium conducted at the meeting of the Northern California Association for Behavior Analysis, San Mateo.

Hayes, S. C., & Brownstein, J. A. (1986). Mentalism, behavior-behavior relationships, and a behavior-analytic view of the purpose of science. *The Behavior Analyst, 9*, 175–190.

Hayes, S. C., Brownstein, A. J., Haas, J. R., & Greenway D. E. (1986). Instructions, multiple schedules, and extinction: Distinguishing rule-governed behavior from schedule control. *Journal of the Experimental Analysis of Behavior, 46*, 137–147.

Hayes, S. C., & Myerson, J. (1986, May). *Time, specificity, rules, delays, and causes*. Paper presented at the meeting of the Association for Behavior Analysis, Milwaukee, WI.

Hayes, S. C., Rosenfarb, I., Wulfert, E., Munt, E. D., Korn, D., and Zettle, R. D. (1985). Self-reinforcement effects: An artifact of social standard setting? *Journal of Applied Behavior Analysis, 18*, 201–214.

Hayes, S. C., & Zettle, R. D. (1980–1981). Behavioral causes and self-reinforcement revisited: A re-reply to Malott. *Notes from a Radical Behaviorist, 2*(26). (Available from Department of Psychology, Western Michigan University, Kalamazoo, MI 49008.)

Hineline (1970). Negative reinforcement without shock reduction. *Journal of the Experimental Analysis of Behavior, 14*, 259–268.

Hockett, C. F. (1960). Logical considerations in the study of animal communications. *Animal Sounds and Communications, 7*, 392–429.

Kanfer, F. H., & Gaelick, L. (1986). Self-management methods. In F. H. Kanfer & A. P. Goldstein (Eds.), *Helping people change: A textbook of methods* (pp. 283–345). New York: Pergamon Press.

Kaufman, A., Baron, A., & Kopp, R. E. (1966). Some effects of instructions on human operant behavior. *Psychonomic Monograph Supplements, 1*, 243–250.

Keesey, R. (1964). Intracranial reward delay and the acquisition rate of a brightness discrimination. *Science, 143*, 702.

Keller, F. S., & Schoenfeld, W. N. (1950). *Principles of Psychology*. New York: Appleton-Century-Crofts.

Lowe, C. F., Beasty, A., & Bentall, R. P. (1983). The role of verbal behavior in human learning: Infant performance on fixed-interval schedules. *Journal of the Experimental Analysis of Behavior, 39*, 157–164.

Malott, R. W. (1980–1981a). Self-reinforcement, ultimate causes, and Skinner's analysis. *Notes from a Radical Behaviorist, 2* (26). (Available from Department of Psychology, Western Michigan University, Kalamazoo, MI 49008.)

Malott, R. W. (1980–1981b). The natural evolution of rule-governed behavior: A speculative account. *Notes from a Radical Behaviorist, 2*(15) (Available from Department of Psychology, Western Michigan University, Kalamazoo, MI 49009.)

Malott, R. W. (1982a, May). Skinner on issues relevant to rule-governed behavior. In M. E. Vaughan (Chair), *On rule-governed behavior*. Symposium conducted at the meeting of the Association for Behavior Analysis, Milwaukee, WI.

Malott, R. W. (1982b, May). Some theoretical considerations about rule governed behavior. In L. Parrott (Chair), *Rule-governed behavior*. Symposium conducted at the meeting of the Association for Behavior Analysis, Milwaukee, WI.

Malott, R. W. (1984). Rule-governed behavior, self-management, and the developmentally disabled: A theoretical analysis. *Analysis and Intervention in Developmental Disabilities, 6*, 53–58.

Malott, R. W. (1986). Self-management, rule-governed behavior, and everyday life. In H. W.

Reese & L. J. Parrott (Eds.), *Behavioral science: Philosophical, methodological, and empirical advances* (207–228). Hillsdale, NJ: Lawrence Erlbaum.

Malott, R. W. (1987, May). *Conditioned behavioral consequences: Hedonic or instrumental.* Paper presented at the meeting of the Association for Behavior Analysis, Nashville, TE.

Malott, R. W. (1988). Can we really apply behavior analysis to everyday life? *Contemporary Psychology, 33,* 141–142.

Malott, R. W., & Garcia, M. E. (in press). *Private events and rule-governed behavior.* In L. J. Hayes & P. Chase (Eds.), *Dialogues on verbal behavior.* Hillsdale, NJ: Erlbaum.

Malott, R. W., & Whaley, D. L. (1976). *Psychology.* Holmes Beach, FL: Learning Publications.

Malott, R. W., General, D., & Snapper, V. (1973). *Issues in the analysis of behavior.* Kalamazoo, MI: Behaviordelia.

Malott, R. W., Tillema, M., & Glenn, S. (1978). *Behavior analysis and behavior modification: An introduction.* Bridgewater, NJ: F. Fournies.

Masters, J. C., & Santrock, J. W. (1976). Studies in the self-regulation of behavior: Effects of contingent cognitive and affective events. *Developmental Psychology, 12,* 334–348.

Matthews, B. A., Catania, A. C., & Shimoff, E. (1985). Effects of uninstructed verbal behavior on nonverbal responding: Contingency descriptions versus performance descriptions. *Journal of the Experimental Analysis of Behavior, 43,* 155–164.

Michael, J. (1982). Distinguishing between discriminative and motivational functions of stimuli. *Journal of the Experimental Analysis of Behavior, 37,* 149–155.

Michael, J. M. (1985). Behavioral analysis: A radical perspective. In D. L. Hammonds (Ed.), *Psychology and learning: Master lecture series, Volume 4* (pp. 95–121). Washington, DC: American Psychological Association.

Michael, J. (1986, May). Principles of Behavior Analysis. In *Newcomer's Series.* Symposium conducted at the meeting of the Association for Behavior Analysis, Milwaukee, WI.

Michael, J. (1986). Repertoire-altering effects of remote contingencies. *Analysis of Verbal Behavior, 4,* 10–18.

Moore, B. S., Underwood, B., & Rosenhan, D. L. (1973). Affect and altruism. *Developmental Psychology, 8,* 99–104.

Morgan, W. G., & Bass, B. A. (1973). Self-control through self-mediated rewards. In R. D. Rubin, J. P. Brady, & J. D. Henderson (Eds.), *Advances in behavior therpay, Volume 4* (pp. 117–126). New York: Academic Press.

Nevin, J. A. (1979). Reinforcement schedules and response strength. In M. D. Zeiler & P. Harzem (Eds.), *Reinforcement and the organization of behavior* (pp. 117–158). New York: John Wiley & Sons.

Rachlin, H. (1974). Self-control. *Behaviorism, 2,* 94–107.

Rachlin, H., & Green, L. (1972). Commitment, choice and self-control. *Journal of Experiential Analysis of Behavior, 17,* 15–22.

Renner, K. E. (1966). Temporal integration: Relative value of rewards and punishments as a function of their temporal distance from the response. *Journal of Experimental Psychology, 71,* 902–907.

Rosenfarb, I., & Hayes, S. C. (1984). Social standard setting: The Achilles heel of informational accounts of therapeutic change. *Behavior therapy, 15,* 515–528.

Shimoff, W., Catania, A. C., & Matthews, B. A. (1981). Uninstructed human responding: Sensitivity of low-rate performance to schedule contingencies. *Journal of the Experimental Analysis of Behavior, 36,* 207–220.

Siddall, J. W., & Malott, R. W. (1971). Acquisition of the people concept in pigeons. *Psychological Record, 31,* 3–13.

Sidman, M., Rouzin, R., Lazer, R., Cunningham, S., Tailby, W., & Carrigan, P. (1983). A search for symmetry in the conditional discrimination of rhesus monkeys, baboons, and children. *Journal of the Experimental Analysis of Behavior, 37,* 5–22.

Skinner, B. F. (1953). *Science and human behavior*. New York: Macmillan.

Skinner, B. F. (1969). *Contingencies of reinforcement*. Englewood Cliffs, NJ: Prentice-Hall.

Sohn, D., & Lamal, P. A. (1982). Self-reinforcement: Its reinforcing capability and its clinical utility. *The Psychological Record, 32*, 179–203.

Solnick, J. V., Kannenberg, C. H., Eckerman D. A., & Waller, M. B. (1980). An experimental analysis of impulsivity and impulse control in humans. *Learning and Motivation, 11*, 61–67.

Solomon, R. L., & Wynne, L. C. (1953). Traumatic avoidance learning: Acquisition in normal dogs. *Psychological Monographs, 67*(No. 354).

Spence, K. W. (1947). The role of secondary reinforcement in delayed reward learning. *The Psychological Review, 54*, 1–8.

Trenholme, I. A., & Baron, A. (1975). Immediate and delayed punishment of human behavior by loss of reinforcement. *Learning and Motivation, 6*, 62–79.

Underwood, B., Moore, B. S, & Rosenham, D. L. (1973). Affect and self-gratification. *Developmental Psychology, 8*, 208–214.

Vaughan, M. (1985). Repeated acquisition in the analysis of rule-governed behavior. *Journal of the Experimental Analysis of Behavior, 44*, 175–184.

Vaughan, M. E., & Michael, J. L. (1982). Automatic reinforcement; An important but ignored concept. *Behaviorism, 10*, 217–227.

Wasserman, E. A., & Moore, J. (1986, May). *Some comments on the temporal law of effect*. Paper presented at the meeting of the Association for Behavior Analysis, Milwaukee, WI.

Wasserman, E. A., & Neunaber, D. J. (1986). College students responding to and rating of contingency relations: The role of temporal contiguity. *Journal of Experimental Analysis of Behavior, 46*, 15–35.

Whaley, D. L., & Malott, R. W. (1971). *Elementary principles of behavior*. Englewood Cliffs, NJ: Prentice-Hall.

Williams, J. L. (1973). *Operant learning: Procedures for changing behavior*. Monteray, CA: Brooks/Cole.

Zettle, R. D., & Hayes, S. C. (1982). Rule-governed behavior: A potential theoretical framework for cognitive-behavioral therapy. In P. C. Kendall (Ed.), *Advances in cognitive-behavioral research and therapy, Volume 1* (pp. 73–117). New York: Academic Press.

Zettle, R. D., & Hayes, S. C. (1983). Effect of social context on the impact of coping self-statements. *Psychological Reports, 52*, 391–401.

Zimmerman, J., & Hanford, P. V. (1966). Sustaining behavior with conditioned reinforcement as the only response-produced consequence. *Psychological Reports, 19*, 391–401.

PART III

APPLIED IMPLICATIONS OF RULE-GOVERNANCE

CHAPTER 9

Some Clinical Implications of Rule-Governed Behavior

ROGER L. POPPEN

1. INTRODUCTION

It is not difficult to be a behaviorist in accounting for "normal" behavior. Men and women normally perform daily tasks that earn a livelihood, maintain health, and sustain social relationships. The controlling influences of salary, nutrition, and attention are apparent and require little psychological interpretation. "Abnormal" behavior that is not closely related to prevailing contingencies presents a puzzle. Why do some intelligent, capable people engage in behavior that results in loss of livelihood, health, and relationships? Clinicians for years have struggled to explain and treat this "neurotic paradox" (Mowrer, 1948). Two general strategies have developed, one focusing on environmental events in a person's history, and the other on various internal states that are a product of those experiences. Behavior therapy has accommodated both points of view in a sometimes uneasy alliance.

Recently, behavior therapy has been regarded as having undergone a "cognitive revolution," in which earlier models of classical and operant conditioning have given way to theories of cognitive operations (e.g., Rosenbaum, Franks, & Jaffe, 1983). Although operant procedures and concepts have revolutionized the education and treatment of individuals over whom a great deal of environmental control exists, they have had little impact on the treatment of "neurotic" outpatients. The clinician has little control over, and indeed, little access to, the environments of his/her clients. Instead, verbal procedures have been developed that serve to mediate the observation and treatment of the client.

ROGER L. POPPEN • Behavior Analysis and Therapy Program, Rehabilitation Institute, Southern Illinois University, Carbondale, Illinois 62901.

Figure 1. The cognitivist view of behaviorism.

Such radical behaviorist conceptualizations as verbal behavior, private events, and rule-governed behavior could be very useful in verbally based treatment strategies, but therapists, of "behavior" as well as "psycho-" persuasion, have developed their own separate concepts of emotions and cognitions. The purpose of this chapter is to show that both cognitivists and behaviorists have much in common and that an alternative exists to devisive debate.

Cognitive psychologists frequently misrepresent radical behaviorism, portraying it as a "black box" psychology or as espousing peripheral S–R connectionism (Figure 1). For example, in his introduction to the collection of papers from the First World Congress on Behavior Therapy, Cyril Franks states,

> Metaphysical or radical behaviorism, with its denial of the very existence of mental states, and its non-mediational, antimentalistic bias, is incompatible with the everyday practice of clinical behavior therapy in the eighties, involving, as it does, cognition, awareness of self, and the like. (Rosenbaum *et al.*, 1983, p. 6)

Albert Bandura (1977, p. 192) interprets discriminative stimuli as "stimuli [which] are automatically connected to responses by their having occurred together." He accuses radical behaviorism of "unidirectional environmental determinism," that is, neglecting the fact that peoples' behavior affects their environment and, in general, regarding humans as passive, reactive machines (Bandura, 1978).

On the other side of the battle line (e.g, Skinner, 1977), cognitive psychology is regarded as no different from ancient concepts of mentalism (Figure 2). Having written extensively on "private events," Skinner rejects them as "causes" of, or in more technical terms, independent variables that affect overt behavior (e.g., Skinner, 1969, p. 258; 1977). They are criticized on the following grounds: (1) It is a logical fallacy *(Post hoc ergo propter hoc)* to assume that just because an event occurs prior to a second event, it is the cause of the second event (Skinner, 1974, p. 9). Precedence is but one of the criteria for causality, necessary but insufficient. (2) People are likely to have difficulty discriminating and hence be unreliable in reporting their private experiences. Skinner (1969, p. 227 ff.) has described the "problem of privacy" as a problem for the verbal community, which does not have direct, independent access to the internal experiences of an individual and thus must rely on unreliable collateral public accompaniments to teach him/her to discriminate what is going on inside. (3) As a result of the problems in verification, internal events can be invented, by oneself or by others, to have just the properties needed to account for public behavior (Skinner, 1977). Spurious causes are free for the asking. (4) Appealing to inaccurate or invented internal events diverts inquiry from the factors responsible for the behavior, namely past and current contingencies (Skinner, 1977).

2. THE PROBLEM OF HISTORY

The clinician has problems of access and verification not only with events happening within an individual's skin but also with events in an individual's past. The behaviorist's appeal to history, rather than internal states, as the locus of critical controlling variables, does not solve these problems. Skinner's criticisms of precedence not proving causality, unreliable reporting, spurious invention, and diversion may be leveled as easily at history as at private events. In seeking information on either private events or past events, the clinician often must rely on the client's verbal report of those events.

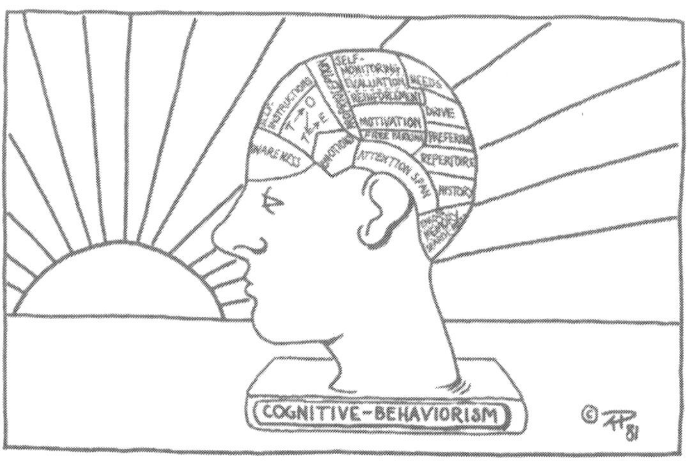

Figure 2. The behaviorist view of the cognitive revolution: The new phrenology.

The *tact* is a useful conceptualization of verbal reports of events with which an individual has exclusive or special contact (Skinner, 1957). A person's verbal community provides differential reinforcement for correspondence between events and the reporting of them. The establishment of tacting for past events may be easier than for private events because in some instances the verbal community has been in direct contact with prior events. Sharing recollections is one way in which tacting the past is developed. A mother may prompt a child to "tell daddy where we went this morning" and provide corrective feedback. Other means of verification include seeking products of past events. A parent may verify a child's report of school performance by looking at homework and report cards. Collaborative reports of others who shared a particular event are sought out. The process of reinforcing accurate tacts of past events continues throughout a person's life. Agencies such as credit departments, graduate schools, journal editors, and the Internal Revenue Service are interested in accurate tacts of educational and financial history. Outside of these special agencies, the verbal community relies on intermittant corroborations by chance witnesses and consistencies in the telling and retelling of an event. "Telling the truth" is a social virtue, by which members of the verbal community are exhorted by story and example to engage in a generalized response class of accurately tacting past events, but like most virtues, it is one that is frequently violated.

There are two major sources of inaccuracy in tacting historical as well as private events. The first is the limited repertoire. Whereas private events may be vaguely and inconsistently learned, past events may not have "made an impression," to use the metaphor of the clay tablet. For example, "eyewitness" accounts of exciting events are notoriously idiosyncratic and inaccurate (Loftus, 1979).

The other major factor is contingencies for inaccuracy. Just as internal events may be invented or misconstrued when there are immediate reinforcers for doing so, historical events may likewise be forgotten, constructed, or confabulated depending on the contingencies. Skinner (1957) has described the "audience control" of verbal behavior. What a person says, in this case about a past event, is only partially determined by that event; other important variables include the contingencies wielded by his/her current audience and by similar audiences in the past. For example, when a person remembers something previously forgotten under the careful guidance of a therapist, he/she is not dredging up memories from some remote corner of the brain but is responding to the cues and consequences of the questioner. The reconstruction of past experience under the influence of hypnosis is especially subject to questioner influences (Hilgard & Loftus, 1979). The warm, accepting, noncritical demeanor of a therapist is an audience designed to facilitate accurate tacts of past and private events. But the tendancy to tell what the therapist wants to hear (or what he/she does not want to hear in cases of "resistance") is an ever-present problem.

The concept of "history" as an accessible event evaporates under this schema. In analyzing a tact of a historical event, the therapist is left with the inaccessible event, inaccessible prior audiences, and the current audience contingencies. In practice, we ask the person to report the event, past audiences, and perhaps even judgments of his/her certainty about the reports; we weigh the congruities of these reports in light of the current audience contingencies and our own experience with such events, audiences, and judgments; and we accept or reject the report and administer consequences accordingly. As with tacts of private events, this is an approximate affair.

Another avenue lies in the experimental analysis of learning histories. Behavior analysis has made only a few steps down this road. Early experimental work avoided the problems of history by employing naive, nonhuman organisms and research designs that eliminated the effects of earlier experience on later behavior by focusing on "steady-state" performance. Harold Weiner's pioneering research with human subjects opened the door to the study of "history" as an important variable in itself (e.g. Weiner, 1969). He demonstrated lawful relationships between performance on current schedules of reinforcement as a function of experience on prior schedules of reinforcement. It has been proposed that such history effects are mediated by a person's verbal statements of the contingencies (Lowe, 1979; Poppen, 1972, 1982a,b). This proposition will be developed further in a later section of this chapter. For now, this research affirms our belief in the importance of learning history in accounting for behavior, but it also implies the importance of verbal behavior in conjunction with history. And, to date, research has only begun to scratch the surface of the "problem of history."

In summary, the invocation of history as an observable, and therefore preferable, alternative to private events is of little advantage when faced with an individual with whom we have had no prior contact. A therapist, of course, attempts to ascertain relevant history, subject to the limitations described here. But we should also recognize that the results of that history may be currently represented by certain "states" of the individual that can be assessed through physiological recording or through self-report. Today's hunger results from yesterday's deprivation, today's toothache from yesterday's neglect, today's guilt from yesterday's punishment, today's belief from yesterday's indoctrination. Such states do indeed "fill the gap" between past causes and current behavior and are important for that reason. When distal events are remote, complex, and inaccessible, proximal events are all the more useful. As Skinner (1974, p. 31) noted:

> A behavioristic analysis does not question the practical usefulness of reports of the inner world that is felt and introspectively observed. They are clues (1) to past

Table 1
A Taxonomy of Behavior, Consisting of Four Major Modalities, Each of Which Contains Members That Are Publicly Observable (Overt) and Privately Observable (Covert)

Behavior	Function	Overt	Covert
Motoric	Moves body	Walking	Relaxing muscles
Verbal	Mediates social reinforcement	Speaking	Silent reading
Visceral	Maintains homeostasis	Sneezing	Mouth watering
Observational	Seeks stimuli	Touching	Imaging

behavior and the conditions affecting it, (2) to current behavior and the conditions affecting it, and (3) to conditions related to future behavior.

Having come full circle, perhaps it is time to examine again the role of private events and the nature of "causality." Rather than avoiding cognitive approaches, they may be seen as providing useful information on the role of private events in human behavior. At the risk of rejection by both camps, an attempt at compromise is in order. To that end, a broadly sketched framework, which may serve to encompass both cognitive and behaviorist concepts, is presented.

3. A BEHAVIORAL TAXONOMY

A commonly employed distinction made by behavior therapists is that of *behavior, cognitions,* and *feelings,* reminiscent of the ancient triumvirate of body, mind, and spirit. In this context, behavior refers to publicly observable performances and pronouncements, cognitions refers to covert thoughts and images, and feelings refers to emotions or physiological arousal. Table 1 offers a taxonomy of behavior, derived from the radical behaviorism of B. F. Skinner (1953, 1957, 1969, 1974), which cuts across these traditional distinctions and provides a more fine-grain analysis. For example, behavior commonly termed *emotional* has a large visceral component but consists of much more than a particular pattern of gut reactions: motoric behavior, such as tensing up, running away or lashing out; verbal behavior, such as statements of fear or rage; and observational behavior, such as focusing on feelings of pain or the object of affection. Similarly, cognitive behavior is a complex class that involves both verbal and observational behaviors. For example, as I write this, I covertly rehearse various statements, or covertly construct a drawing, imagining the reactions of an audience, before setting pen to paper. (Popular references to "left-brain" and "right-brain" activity seem to be an attempt to physiologize the verbal and observational aspects of "cognitive" behavior).

3.1. Four Modalities of Behavior

3.1.1. Motoric Behavior

Overt motoric behavior topographically involves the skeletal muscular system; it functions to move one's body, or parts of it, through space, and also serves to manipulate one's physical environment. Most of the experimental literature on operant conditioning concerns this behavior modality. Covert motoric behavior also involves the muscular system but below the level of publicly observable movement. Examples of covert motoric behavior include an orchestra conductor covertly beating time, or an athlete, such as a weightlifter, covertly rehearsing a sequence of movements prior to public performance. Individuals may be trained to engage in covert motoric behavior, as for example in progressive muscle relaxation training, and to verbally report (be aware of) such behavior. Edmund Jacobson (1938) invented electromyography to provide an objective measure of covert motoric behavior, though, as Skinner (1969, p. 226) noted, "the scales read by the scientist are not the same as the private events themselves."

3.1.2. Verbal Behavior

Verbal behavior has been defined functionally as behavior dependent upon socially mediated consequences (Skinner, 1957). It is the primary means of manipulating, and being manipulated by, one's social environment. Topographically it involves both production, through spoken, written, or gestural means, and reception, through auditory, visual, or in rare instances, tactile means. The structural analysis of verbal behavior, that is, grammar, is the subject matter of psycholinguistics. (The relationship between functional and structural approaches to language are exemplified in the work of Brown, 1973, and Segal, 1975).

Covert receptive verbal behavior involves silently reading, watching signs or gestures, or listening to another's speaking, but covert production involves both "speaker" and "listener" within the same skin. "Thinking," following John B. Watson's attempts to measure subvocal speech, is often described as covert verbal behavior. One can, of course, "think out loud," but the audience is oneself rather than others. In either case, the function of such behavior is to consider several alternatives before overtly committing oneself to a particular course of action or overt statement.

3.1.3. Visceral Behavior

Visceral behavior topographically involves the activity of glands and smooth muscles and functions primarily to maintain physiological homeostasis. Visceral systems in chronic disequilibrium are termed *stress,* and the newly emerging field of behavioral medicine seeks to relate stress to environmental events and other behaviors. For example, cardiovascular and other disorders of "Type-A" individuals is related to demanding, competitive environments and high-rate, rigorously scheduled behavior. Visceral behavior is usually thought of as covert but may be overt, for example, when one cries, blushes, or has an erection. As with covert muscle activity, covert visceral responses may be made overt by means of special equipment. Biofeedback represents a therapeutic application of operant procedures to electronic amplifications of visceral behavior (Miller, 1978).

3.1.4. Observational Behavior

Observational behavior functions to seek out or select among discriminative stimuli. Overt observational behavior topographically consists of orienting one's receptors, such as turning one's ears toward the source of sound, focusing one's eyes, running one's hand over a surface, or sniffing the air. Covert observational behavior includes "attending," as when one selectively listens to the woodwinds in a symphony orchestra or tastes the amount of oregano in the spaghetti sauce. Such behavior puts one in contact with discriminative stimuli, making further behavior possible. Thus it serves an important mediating function in sequences of responding.

A person may also "see in the absence of the thing seen" (Skinner, 1974, p. 82), though modalities other than visual are also involved. Such behavior influences further behavior in a manner similar to observing external stimuli. Thus one can "re-view" the route from one's home to the office or "re-call" the sound of a loved one's voice. Covert observational behavior seems especially susceptible to influence by verbal behavior of others. "Imagery" as employed in therapy involves colorful description of either relaxing or arousing scenes.

3.2. Causality

A complete account of behavior requires the specification of environmental antecedents and consequences. For example, verbal behavior implies a social environment that includes the occasion in which one speaks or writes and the audience reactions to one's efforts. "Emotional" behavior implies arousing events and consequences for behaving emotionally. To the behaviorist, the cause, or the independent variables that control behavior, resides in the environment.

But there are different levels at which causality may be assessed. For example, a pigeon may peck a key, or a motorist may proceed across an intersection, when a green light is illuminated. At one level, the causes for these behaviors are the differential reinforcement contingencies concerning green lights in each organism's learning history. At a another level, the green light itself is said to control or influence behavior. Next, consider the case in which the motorist consults a written list of directions as he finds his way along an unfamiliar route. His verbal behavior of reading the directions affects his driving behavior. There are historical variables responsible for his directions reading, just as there are for the controlling influence of green lights, but at the level of immediate performance, his driving may be said to be a function of his reading. Finally, consider the case in which there are no written directions but the driver covertly recites directions he has been given earlier. Here again, at the level of immediate performance, one behavior, driving, is influenced by, in a sense "caused" by, the behavior of reciting.

Behavior in any of the eight categories described may be linked to any other in chains of various lengths, periodically punctuated by contacting discriminative and reinforcing events in the environment. For example, the verbal behavior of assuming various facial expressions of emotion may result in specific visceral responses (Ekman, Levensen, & Friesen, 1983). Verbally induced observational behavior (imagery) also results in patterns of visceral behavior (Lang, Kozak, Miller, & Levin, 1980). Imagery can also serve as the basis of verbal behavior or other types of artistic productions. Verbal and observational behaviors occurring in response to the muscle tension, visceral arousal, and the other elements involved in "pain" greatly influence further pain behaviors, such as escape, relief seeking, or complaining (Turk, Meichenbaum, & Genest, 1983). A patient suffering with back pain may withdraw to bed, observing his symptoms and reviewing limitations, resulting in still greater distress. The contingencies of social attention may be important in this case, but effective treatment would also have to address the patient's motoric, verbal, visceral, and observational responses to discomfort.

The goal of therapy is to teach behavior that in turn influences further behavior outside the office. For example, a driving phobic may be taught the motoric and visceral skills of relaxation that then affect her visceral, verbal, and motoric behavior while in the car. A pain patient may be taught observational skills of distracting imagery, again influencing his visceral, verbal, and motoric behavior at home. As will be detailed in the following sections, verbal behavior is especially important as a mediating link between behavior modalities and between behavior and the environment.

3.3. Summary

A rapprochement between cognitivist and behaviorist positions may be possible through a finer-grain analysis of behavior and a multilevel view of "causality." As outlined in Table 1, behavior takes many forms and serves

Figure 3. The impact of behaviorism on modern society.

many functions. Vague terms such as *cognitions* or *emotions* would be better replaced by defining the topographic and functional aspects of the behavior modalities involved. However, behavior analysis has paid relatively little attention to verbal and observational behaviors, which constitute the primary area of interest to cognitive therapists (Figure 3). Radical behaviorism offers many formulations that both experimental and applied behavior analysts could employ in addressing the problems that cognitive therapists have been facing for years.

In this respect, arguments over the "ultimate" locus of causal variables are of little help. Short of chemical or electrical stimulation of the nervous system, the therapist has no direct means of controlling behavior and must rely on environmental manipulation. Neither can the therapist undo a client's learning history; we can only add and never subtract. For practical purposes, the locus of control is the part of the client's social environment mediated by the therapist. At another level, effective therapy requires "self" control, whereby the client implements the relaxation, imagery, or verbal appraisal so as to influence his/her own behavior.

4. RULE-GOVERNED BEHAVIOR

As originally formulated by Skinner (1969, Chapter 6), a rule functions as a discriminative stimulus (SD), an antecedent correlated with the availability of reinforcement. It differs from a simple SD in that it is a verbal statement of a contingency relationship between behavior and the environment. That is, rather than an arbitrary signal that would require specific training to discriminate, a rule employs the existing verbal repertoire to establish behavior directly. For example, a red light may be placed at an intersection as an SD to control pedestrian behavior, or a sign displaying the rule "Don't Walk" may be employed. In its most complete form, a rule may state the time, place, and other antecedent conditions appropriate for the behavior; the topography, rate, duration, and other features of the response class; and the type, quantity, quality, and schedule of the consequences. Such precision is rare, and most rules are only a partial statement of contingencies, leaving the person to gather the remainder from other aspects of the environment and his/her past history. A complete specification of the "Don't-Walk" rule would state "don't walk across this intersection when this sign is lighted, or else you may be struck by a vehicle or arrested for jay walking." Indeed, a rule is usually a boiled-down, short-hand statement of a contingency and may specify only one aspect of one term of the three-term contingency: for example, the antecedent ("Hospital Zone"), the behavior ("Don't Walk"), or the consequence ("Win $1 Million!").

Another similarity of a rule to a discriminative stimulus is that its effectiveness in controlling behavior depends on the consequences for responding or not responding to the rule (Skinner, 1969). Consequences for rule-following are mediated by two sources, and rules may be distinguished by taking into account the agent delivering the rule and the agent delivering reinforcement. Table 2 outlines the possible combinations.

In the first instance, the consequences are mediated only by the physical or social environment, whereas the rule-giver is indifferent as to whether the person follows the rule or not. In the "Don't Walk" example, one source of reinforcement for rule-following is mediated by the vehicles whizzing through the intersection. The signal post itself is completely indifferent to pedestrian behavior. Skinner terms this kind of rule *advice*. Zettle and Hayes (1984) term it a *track* that highlights the tactlike function of the rule-giver. Like a tact, a track is under stimulus control of the environment, but the aspect of the envi-

Table 2
Categories of Rules as Defined by the Sources of Reinforcement for Rule-Following

	Consequence mediator		
	Environment	Rule-giver	Rule-governed behavior
Rule 1: Track[a] (advice)	+[b]	0[c]	Tracking
Rule 2: Ply[b] (command)	0[c]	+[b]	Pliance
Rule 3: Congruent	+[b]	+[b]	Congruence
Rule 4: Contrant	+[b]	−[d]	Contrance

[a]In contrast to Zettle and Hayes (1984), these terms are used to designate a class of rules rather than rule-governed behavior.
[b]Rule-following is consequated by positive or negative reinforcement or by punishment.
[c]No consequences for rule-following; the source is indifferent.
[d]Consequences which affect rule-following in a direction opposite that of (+) (e.g., punishment rather than reinforcement).

ronment being tacted is a behavioral contingency. *Tracking* is rule-governed behavior that is reinforced by the consequences of responding to tacts of contingencies provided by the verbal community.

For a second type of rule, the consequences are mediated only by the social agent delivering the rule. In the "Don't Walk" example, another source of reinforcement is mediated by a police officer, a social agent whose job is to enforce compliance. Even though the intersection may be devoid of traffic, the noncompliant pedestrian may receive a ticket. Skinner terms such a rule a *command;* Zettle and Hayes call it a *ply* and relate it to the mandlike verbal behavior of the agent. Like a mand, a ply specifies what would be reinforcing for the speaker (the rule-giver), but in this case, what is reinforcing is the compliance of the listener (the rule-follower). In addition, a ply expresses or implies speaker-mediated reinforcement for listener compliance. *Pliance* is rule-governed behavior that is reinforced by the rule-giver (or an agent of the verbal community issuing the ply) for conformity to behavior specified by the rule.

In many cases, consequences are mediated by both the rule-giver and the environment, a sort of combined track and ply. A rule for which the consequences from both sources are complementary is termed a *congruent* in Table 2. In this case, both the rule-giver and the environment administer reinforcement for rule-following. Doing well in school may satisfy both parental admonitions and gain social approval and scholarship money. Rule-following of this sort can be called *congruence.*

Finally, the consequences administered by the two sources may be in conflict; this is termed a *contrant* in Table 2. In this instance, one agency administers reinforcement, and the other administers punishment for engaging in the rule-specified behavior. One who does well in school may earn the approval and avoid the criticism of parents but be shunned by classmates as a "teacher's pet" or a "nerd." Rule-following that results in conflicting consequences can be termed *contrance*.

Laboratory studies of rule-governed behavior have shown rules to be a potent source of control (Lowe, 1979; Poppen, 1982a). Experimenter instructions may be regarded as a track, specifying some aspect of the response-reinforcer relationship. When there is a conflict between such tracks and the actual schedule of reinforcement, the instructions often prevail (Kaufman, Baron, & Kopp, 1966; Lippman & Meyer, 1967). The lack of sensitivity of human performance to reinforcement-schedule parameters has been attributed to experimenter instructions (Matthews, Shimhoff, Catania, & Sagvolden, 1977). Instructions intended as a general track ("Press the key to earn points") may instead generate pliance, as the subject presses at high rates in order to please the experimenter.

4.1. Some Examples of Rules

Instances of tracks abound. All written instructions are tracks, from books promising self-awareness, fulfillment, and weight loss, to road maps, cookbooks, and owner's manuals for electronic appliances. Weather reports, telephone directory assistance, help with homework, and directions in a strange locale can all be tracks. Such rules specify or imply reinforcement for tracking but are indifferent to whether or not we follow them and our success or failure in doing so. Some rules may have the formal aspect of tracks but on closer analysis turn out to be plys (Zettle & Hayes, 1984, speak of "Trojan tacts"). A man may seemingly tact the caloric content of a dessert to his girlfriend or comment on the attractiveness of a slender movie actress, subtly issuing the ply "don't get fat or I will withdraw my affection."

Threats are plys that specify or imply aversive consequences for noncompliance. Thus ply-governed behavior is often avoidance of threatened aversive events, or, where possible, avoidance of the agent mediating the consequences. A highway speed limit is a societal ply that may be followed to avoid the response cost of a ticket, or a driver may take an unpatrolled route to avoid the agent who administers the consequence for noncompliance. Ubiquitous observation is necessary to insure total pliance to threats, for example, "Big Brother" in Orwell's *1984*. Intermittent consequation is a less costly way to maintain compliance and also has the advantage of increasing resistance to extinction and perhaps reducing avoidance of the consequating agent. A lead foot might avoid a road that is always policed but would be more inclined to observe the limit on one that was patrolled on a variable interval. Avoidance behavior that is maintained by the "nonoccurrence" of an event is notoriously persistent. The rule "Don't talk back" maintains meekness at considerable strength by virtue of not generating criticism or disagreement.

Plys that control behavior through positive consequences can be termed *bribes*. An exasperated parent may yell, "Shut up or I'll spank you!", whereas a more enlightened one might offer, "Be quiet for the next half hour and I'll give you an ice cream." Business and political relationships are often based on this rule of mutual back scratching. Plys in personal relationships replace material with social reinforcers. We have expressions of thanks, appreciation, and love for those who do our bidding. "Be a darling and let mommy rest" is a ply that offers affection rather than ice cream.

Many rules of the ply form are designed to be *congruant* with the delayed or intermittent environmental consequences of an act. That is, the immediate speaker-mediated consequences are intended to supplement the "faulty" environmental ones. Parental admonitions often follow this line. Rules about playing in the street, associating with disreputable chums, wearing warm clothing, eating vegetables, and similar burdens of childhood are plys under the control of immediate parental consequences but also are tracks of the long-term natural consequences of health and well-being. Many rules and laws are "for our own good" to prevent exposure to the harmful natural consequences of unbridled behavior, for example, motorcycle-helmet and drunk-driving laws. In other instances, plys may be disguised as congruants to promote compliance. Parents may enforce strict curfew and social behavior rules, ostensibly to protect their child from harmful influences but in reality to maintain their authority and control. Congruants may have once specified environmental contingencies that are no longer effective. For example, religious dietary laws may have once promoted health practices that are no longer relevent under modern conditions. The rule "Don't talk to strangers" is functional for a 6-year-old but less so for a college freshman. "Growing up" is a process of determining which congruants actually specify environmental contingencies and which are only parental plys. Persons who question authority, who "have to find out the hard way," are seeking out the natural contingencies beyond those mediated by the rule giver.

Contrants are rules for which the rule-giver and the environment provide opposing consequences. For example, a parent may issue the contrant, "Don't play with yourself," opposing the joys of genital self-stimulation with the threat of punishment. Contrants not only function to forbid people to forgo immediate pleasures but can force them into aversive situations. Military orders are of this nature; a soldier following orders may place his life in jeopardy, yet this extreme environmental consequence is overridden by those mediated by the rule-giver. A rule may be a congruant with respect to the long-term consequences of behavior, as described, but thereby oppose and serve as a contrant with respect to the immediate consequences. Playing in the street, taking candy from strangers, or watching TV instead of doing homework are immediately reinforcing; parental injunctions specify additional immediate punishing consequences to counteract these reinforcers, as well as specifying the long-range benefits to the child. Because the primary function of a contrant is to overcome the environmental contingencies of behavior, contrants are important in an analysis of "abnormal" behavior.

4.2. Self-Rule-Governed Behavior

Rules arise initially from one's verbal community. Parents, peers, schoolteachers, TV, radio, books—sources of rules pervade a person's environment. Rules are portable. Once provided by the external verbal community, one can then repeat them to oneself. Rules once under external control are then said to be "internalized," with the "speaker" and "listener" within the same skin (Skinner, 1957). Much training is provided to encourage such self-instruction. Parents ask children to rehearse a rule ("What are you supposed to do if a stranger wants you to get into his car?") to increase its effect when the parent is not present. Meichenbaum observed chronic schizophrenic patients spontaneously repeating rules given them in training sessions and developed a "self-control" program based on echoing teacher instructions (Meichenbaum & Cameron, 1973).

Rules are also derived from one's own observations of and interactions with environmental contingencies. The verbal community provides us with a kind of metarule: "Extract rules." That is, we are taught to tact contingent relationships that affect our own and others' behavior. One may derive rules about people ("It's no use talking to her") and situations ("I can't resist chocolate") based on one's idiosyncratic experiences. These rules then serve to guide one's own behavior in similar situations.

Poppen (1982a) has suggested that the "history effects" observed in laboratory studies of human operant behavior (Duvinsky & Poppen, 1982; Poppen, 1972, 1982; Weiner, 1964, 1969, 1970) are instances of self-rule-governed behavior. The subject derives a self-track based on observation of his/her responding and its relation to the contingencies. Tracking persists, even when contingencies change so that the rules are less accurate than when they were initially developed, as long as there is some minimal payoff for responding in the same old way (Schwartz, 1982; Weiner, 1970). Behavior is changed, and presumably a person's rules, only when the old patterns result in extinction or response cost. To date, subjects' statements of contingencies have been studied only in retrospect (Duvinsky & Poppen, 1982; Harzem, Lowe, & Bagshaw, 1978). Even though there is close correspondence between statements of perceived response-reinforcer relationships and actual motor performance, this does not prove that a controlling relationship exists between verbal and motor behavior. Research is needed that examines the concurrent development of contingency statements and motor performance and their persistence when contingencies change.

4.2.1. Reinforcement for Self-Rules

Inevitably, conflicts arise between rules from various sources as well as between rules and contingencies. Further rules are developed to deal with these conflicts, to provide clarity and simplicity in confusing and complex situations (''What would mother think?'' ''When in Rome, do as the Romans do.'' ''If in doubt, don't.'' ''Go with the flow.'') A major reinforcing consequence of rule-governed behavior, apart from that specific to the rule, is the reduction of conflict that a rule provides. Ambiguity and indecision are aversive, and a rule that allows action in such a situation, even though it may not be the ''best'' action in terms of possible outcomes, may control behavior nonetheless.

Self-tracking is reinforced by the environment just as following tracks from any other source. Before a trip, one may review an infrequently traveled route by systematically recalling the landmarks and turns, just as one could consult a map or ask a friend for directions. In all cases, the reinforcing consequence is the timely arrival at one's destination. But whereas the map or the friend are indifferent as to whether or not one made the trip, a person who follows his own advice is interested in the outcome. When the speaker and listener are in the same skin, the ''speaker'' as well as the ''listener'' is affected by the consequence. Thus, in addition to the consequences mediated by the environment for self-tracking, the person may add self-evaluative comments (''Boy, I really blew that; what a dope!'' or ''Way to go; I've got this beat!''). Such statements may be congruent with the environmental consequences, or they may stand in contrast (''I don't care what they say; I still think I was right!''). Reinforcing oneself for adhering to a plan of action shades tracking into self-pliance.

A ply has been defined as a rule in which the rule-giver (or agent) mediates the consequences for conforming to the requested action. A self-ply suggests that the individual consequates his/her own behavior for conformity to self-administered command. A self-ply may occur when immediate environmental consequences are absent, remote, or obscure, specifying oneself as the reinforcing agent under these circumstances. Or a self-ply may be congruent with environmental consequences, as when an athlete tells himself, ''Just play the way Coach tells you.'' More often, probably, self-plys occur in opposition to immediate environmental consequences. A person may endure social criticism by covertly stating, ''I won't compromise my religious beliefs.'' An author may be ''his own worst critic,'' ignoring the positive statements of others and downgrading his efforts. Self-plys are likely in situations in which the immediate environmental contingencies suggest one course of action but the self-ply recommends another (''I will not have a cigarette!'' ''I will be calm and cool when I meet him'').

Skinner developed the concept of rule-governed behavior in the context of his analysis of ''problem solving'' (1969). A ''problem'' exists when environmental contingencies demand a course of action that an individual is ill-equipped

Table 3
A Comparison of A-B-C Analyses of Ellis and Skinner

Ellis	Skinner
A—Activating event (losing one's job)	Antecedent event (losing one's job)
B—Belief ("This is unbearable")	Behavior (sadness, avoidance)
C—Consequence (sadness, avoidance)	Consequence (attention, support)

to perform or when high-probability behavior results in aversive consequences, extinction, or response cost. In such circumstances, a person is especially likely to "stop and think," to "re-view" the available contingencies and his/her behavioral options, and to formulate a plan of action, a rule. However, such rules may be inaccurate or short-sighted, literally out of touch with long-term consequences of behavior, leading to further problems rather than solutions. Skinner observed that "when contingencies change and the rules do not, rules may be troublesome rather than helpful" (1969, p. 141). The troublesome beliefs and expectancies described by cognitive behavior therapists may be formulated as self-rules that are in conflict with a person's contingencies. The systems developed by these therapists and theorists can be included in the behaviorist framework as analyses of and programs for changing the rules that govern behavior.

5. RATIONAL-EMOTIVE THERAPY

Historical precedence in cognitive approaches to behavior change belongs to Albert Ellis (Ellis & Harper, 1961; Ellis & Grieger, 1977). Ellis's citation of the Greek philosopher Epictetus serves as a summary statement for all cognitive therapies: "It is not the events which occur that upset us, but our *view* of these events." This assertion of internal rather than external control may be upsetting to behaviorists but that upset may be relieved by some cognitive restructuring (i.e. verbal translation).

Table 3 contrasts Ellis's A-B-C Framework with Skinner's three-term contingency. Point A in Ellis's system refers to an "activating event or experience," analogous to Skinner's antecedent events. To use an example from Ellis, being fired from a good job would be an activating event. Both approaches assume that an individual's history—prior learning experiences as well as genetic factors—contributes to the current situation. Ellis focuses on how historical factors result in an individual's irrational belief system, whereas Skinner emphasizes how they build discriminative stimuli and a behavioral repertoire. And both approaches indicate that the current situation cues a complex sequence of behavior. Ellis states that external events "significantly contribute to but do not actually cause'' one's reactions, whereas Skinner has noted that discriminative stimuli control in the sense of influence, rather than elicit, behavior.

Point B refers to one's ''belief'' about that event, for example: ''I *desperately needed* that job! It is *absolutely awful* that I lost it! I'm *totally incompetent* for losing it! I'll *never* find one as good!'' These beliefs, then, generate the emotional and behavioral ''consequences'' at Point C, such as feelings of depression, complaining, and inertia in seeking another job. Point C in the Skinnerian system, the environmental consequences of behavior, are not considered at all by Ellis. This emphasizes the degree to which behavior is divorced from the environment in a cognitivist system. Although it often appears that consequences exert little effect on ''neurotic'' behavior, it is more likely that their effect is subtle and idiosyncratic (Goldiamond, 1974). And, as will be shown, even cognitive therapies make use of environmental consequences.

All of the events at Ellis's Points B and C can be considered ''behavior,'' as described previously in Table 1. Ellis proposes a chain, in which a ''belief'' (covert verbal behavior) generates both ''feelings'' (covert visceral and observational reactions) and overt action, apparently in tandem. Skinner has often asserted that covert thoughts and feelings do not ''cause'' overt action but that private and public responses occur ''collaterally,'' both under the control of environmental contingencies. As stated earlier, a solution to this dispute may be that none of the particular combinations is the general case but that a variety of controlling relations within and among various behavior modalities may be established.

Self-rules, as described in the previous section, comprise one type of controlling relation that is consistent with both approaches. One's ''belief'' about a situation may be translated into one's statement of contingent relations between behavior and environment in that situation. To take the example in Table 3, losing one's job generates covert and overt verbal responses that serve as discriminative stimuli for further action (or inaction). Some rules surrounding job loss might include: ''No work means extreme hardship for myself and my family. No work means no respect from my family and friends. I do not have the skills to find or keep a job. A life of hardship and no respect is not worth living.'' These rules are discriminative for complaints and withdrawal and fairly accurately describe the consequences of depressed behavior. Another person might react to job loss with different rules: ''No work means I can collect unemployment, go on vacation, sleep 'til noon, and watch soap operas.'' This person's emotional demeanor would clearly be different from that of the first, though he/she would be equally avoidant in seeking new employment. The reason for these different rules, of course, lies in each person's history, which, as described earlier, is not directly accessible. RET is notably ahistorical and does not focus on how an individual came to his/her current beliefs or the contingencies maintaining them. Indeed, according to Ellis, humankind is afflicted with irrational thinking, and it is a wonder how anyone copes without a course in RET.

5.1. Irrational Beliefs as Rules

Irrational beliefs can be considered to be inaccurate statements about contingencies. Of the hundreds of beliefs Ellis states that he has observed in his clients, he groups them into four, colorfully named, major categories: (1) "musturbation," (2) "awfulizing," (3) "can't-stand-it-itus," (4) "damnation."

The first category seems to describe rules that simplify or regularize complex and conflicting contingencies. The examples given by Ellis and Grieger (1977, pp. 12–13) reflect rigid statements of antecedents, behaviors, and consequences that *should* prevail: "I must do well and win approval for my performances, or else I rate as a rotten person"; "Others must treat me considerately and kindly, in precisely the way I want them to treat me; if they don't, society and the universe should severely blame, damn, and punish them . . ."; "Conditions under which I live must get arranged so that I get practically everything I want comfortably, quickly, and easily; . . . and life proves awful, terrible, and horrible when I do not get what I prefer." Musturbation appears to involve plys, to oneself or to others, for consistent, if not continuous, schedules of reinforcement. Because real-world contingencies are not consistent with those demanded by the person, the rules are often stated in the negative: "I never perform well enough"; "Nobody ever appreciates me"; "I'm always treated unfairly." Thus the rules take the form of contrants, in which the environment is described as mediating extinction and punishment, with the rule-giver demanding reinforcement and exerting countercontrolling punishment. The same contrants may be issued towards oneself: "I am incompetent"; "I deserve to suffer"; or in Ellis's terms, "I'm a turd."

The other categories seem to be attempts to strengthen the consequences in favor of the rule-giver. "Awfulizing" is a way in which a person seeks confirmation that events *should* be different. This may take the form of complaining to others, a ply in which approval by the sufferer is contingent on agreement that things are indeed awful, and in turn the sufferer is reinforced by the agreement of others. "Misery loves company" is a maxim describing this relationship. The person may also selectively review events in his/her past history or seek out vicarious environments through books, TV, and movies that confirm that the discrepancy between what is and what ought to be is untenable. "Can't-stand-it-itus" ups the ante by including the person's emotional responses. The rule seems to be that emotional intensity further confirms the rightness of one's belief. A tantrum may at some point have been effective in changing external contingencies, and others may agree or be sympathetic with a person who is very upset. "Damning" is the administration of additional, countercontrolling, punishing verbal consequences to force the contrary contingencies into line with the musturbatory rule.

Faced with a conflict between contingencies and statements about those contingencies, why does a person not change his rules rather than "irrationally" stick to them? First, the rules are not in total disagreement with external contingencies. One at times is unrecognized for accomplishments, is treated unfairly, makes mistakes, or acts foolishly, which is consistent with rules about the negative aspects of oneself and the environment. On the other hand, "musterbation" rules demanding hard work and perfection occasionally pay off. People who "must succeed" are often successful in some areas, such as business, but carry this rule over to personal relationships where it is less effective. The verbal community models and reinforces rules such as "You can be whatever you want if you want it badly enough."

Secondly, consistency (pliance) itself may be reinforcing. Doing poorly is reinforcing, in a perverse way, if it is consistent with a rule. This could be called the "I-told-you-so" phenomenon. "Expect the worst," "Whatever can go wrong will go wrong," and other worst-case strategies allow the person to prepare for yet another rotten day. Pleasant surprises can be taken in stride better than unpleasant ones. Such pessimism and negative expectations can become self-fulfilling prophecies, as people seek out situations in which the outcomes will be consistent with their rules.

Third, one may get attention, support, reassurance, or sympathy for being upset or victimized. Proclamations of unfairness or of one's own limitations may also allow one to avoid onerous situations or to receive special considerations. Finally, the rules are likely to be incompletely spelled out, and thus fine-grain inconsistencies with prevailing contingencies are not obvious.

5.2. Changing Rules

The therapy portion of RET is consistent with the analysis of "beliefs" as oversimplified contingency statements. Ellis proposes two major procedures to change beliefs and, thereby, feelings and behavior. The first is verbal, the second is experiential. The goal of both is to force the person to more closely examine the discrepancies that exist between actual contingencies and his/her descriptions of them.

First, Ellis verbally attempts to restructure the person's belief system. To his A-B-C framework, he adds a fourth component: *D* for detecting, disputing, debating, discriminating, and defining (Figure 4). *Detecting* refers to the therapist convincing the person that he/she is, in fact, engaging in irrational thinking. The therapist is a powerful member of the verbal community and uses that authority to persuade a client that his/her beliefs are responsible for discomfort. Ellis notes that people are often "unaware" of these beliefs; that is, they do

Figure 4. Albert Ellis disputes and debates.

not immediately verbalize such rules. Reading material describing RET tenets is frequently assigned. The therapist reinforces client pliance to the rule: "Emotional upset is a result of what you tell yourself about an event." The therapist reviews the client's verbal descriptions of upsetting situations and points out examples of "musturbating," "awfulizing," and so forth.

Disputing and debating are verbal reinforcement procedures by which the therapist challenges the rules that have been discovered. The client is asked to defend "logically" why he/she believes events *must* happen in a particular way and why it is *awful* when they do not. Such challenges are punishing, and the therapist models and reinforces statements of new rules. The client is taught to discriminate and define individual instances of events occurring, some good and some bad, rather than simplistic *always* and *never* formulations of contingency statements. In a similar fashion, the client is taught the difference between *preferences* and *shoulds*. Thus the client is provided with new rules to make finer-grain analyses of contingencies rather than the broad overgeneralizations of his/her old rules.

5.3. Changing Behavior

Concurrently with the verbal analyses of past situations, the therapist assigns "homework," encouraging the client to practice "thinking, emoting, and behaving" in a different way in troublesome situations. If a client has a history of avoiding such situations, these assignments serve to encourage him/her to engage in new behavior, such as asking for a date or a raise, staying alone in the dark, or looking for a new job. These experiences then serve as the subject for analysis in the therapy session. The client thus imitates the verbal behavior of the therapist and is differentially reinforced for doing so. The process serves as a type of contingency analysis, though the environmental reinforcing consequences of overt behavior are not explicitly addressed. As a means of teaching new, more accurate contingency statements, then, an important element is omitted, or at best only indirectly included.

It would be extreme to say that RET focuses only on teaching a person to think and feel differently about troublesome situations, in effect teaching acceptance of the status quo. By teaching more accurate rules, the assumption is that the client will behave more effectively. But like Tolman's rat, "lost in thought at the choice point," it is not clear how covert rules translate into overt behavior. Discriminative stimuli control behavior only when they have been established by the contingencies of reinforcement. What are the contingencies operating in RET?

First, there are heavy therapist-mediated consequences for the client to verbalize and act in accordance with "rational" rules. At an early stage, the new rules are contrants, with the therapist opposing the environmental contingencies selected by the client. Secondly, by reducing the punishment mediated by the client, in the form of "damning" him/herself and others, it is more likely that suppressed behavior will appear and be reinforced. Thirdly, by questioning *shoulds* and *always,* the client learns that simple continuous schedules of reinforcement, punishment, or extinction are not the case, thereby coming in contact with the more complex schedules that operate in his/her environment. Finally, by exposure to previously avoided situations, the client comes under the control of naturally reinforcing consequences, such as obtaining a job, getting a date, or having parents treat him/her as an adult. All these factors serve to maintain new, more adaptive behavior as well as more accurate statements of contingency relationships.

This analysis reveals two deficits in RET. First, as shown in Table 3, it ignores the environmental consequences of behavior. Some environments may be extremely punishing or extinguishing. It is always wise to select environments that will be the most reinforcing in order to establish new skills. It almost seems that Ellis tries to teach folks that it does not matter what happens to them as long as they think rationally about it (Figure 4).

A second problem is that RET depends entirely on the client's existing repertoire. Clients may have problems asking for a date, applying for a job, talking about their feelings, or picking up a snake because they do not have the requisite skills. Rather than making assumptions, it would be important to assess the client's repertoire and environment before attacking his/her statement of contingencies or assigning "homework." More overt behavior therapy, such

Table 4
Sequence of Behavioral and Environmental Events in Bandura's "Self-System"

Antecedent	Behavior (Covert)	Behavior (Overt)	Consequence	Behavior (Covert)
Stimulus	Contingency statement Self-efficacy Outcome expectancy	Action	Outcome	Self-regulation Self-observation Self-evaluation Self-consequation

as training in assertiveness, communication, parenting, relaxation, or sexual responsivity, is often needed. Such an approach is not incompatible with RET but emphasizes the need to go beyond a strictly verbal approach.

On the other hand, it is important to asses clients' beliefs and expectations, their rules, when implementing any behavior change program. Weight loss will not make one universally attractive, time management will not make one effortlessly efficient, parent training will not make one's kids into angels, pain management will not make one immune to discomfort. Clients who seek treatment for these reasons and therapists who provide treatment unaware of these beliefs are both likely to be unsuccessful. Behavioral programs based strictly on contingency management cannot assume that clients' statements of those contingencies will be accurate. RET is a reminder of the importance of consistency between rules and contingencies.

6. SELF-EFFICACY THEORY

Albert Bandura (1976, 1977, 1978, 1981, 1982) has developed a "self-system" theory and research program that provides a framework for other behavior and cognitive therapy systems. Like other cognitivists, he interpolates covert behavior between the occurrence of an environmental antecedent event and overt action, which serves to mediate that action. Compared to Ellis's "irrational beliefs," this intermediate behavior consists of a longer chain of components. In addition, after overt behavior and the environmental consequences for that behavior have occurred, Bandura proposes covert postactivity evaluation behavior. The sequence is outlined in Table 4.

6.1. A Behavior Chain

6.1.1. Statement of Contingencies

The initial reaction to "stimuli that either signify events to come or indicate probable response consequences" is a "cognitive representation of the contingencies'' (Bandura, 1977). By substituting the word *verbal* for *cognitive,* this is the general definition of a rule. In other words, the initial reaction to a discriminative stimulus may be a covert verbal statement of the contingencies. Two categories of rules are distinguished at this stage, one focusing on behavior and the other on consequences.

The first category of rules is termed *self-efficacy,* defined as the degree to which a person believes he/she can ''successfully execute the behavior required to produce the outcomes.'' This appears to be an instance of a self-ply that specifies that one's behavior conform to a particular plan of action. For example, ''I know that I can do well on the test'' specifies that one needs to perform at a certain level of competence. Persons low in self-efficacy indicate that their behavior is not in compliance with standards necessary to satisfy prevailing contingencies.

A second category of rules is termed ''cognitive representations of future outcomes,'' or *outcome expectations,* defined as ''a person's estimate that a given behavior will lead to certain outcomes.'' In other words, an individual may track the nature of the consequences, such as type, schedule, immediacy, or probability, pursuant to a given course of action. As noted earlier, in a world of delayed, concurrent, and conflicting consequences, rules about outcomes serve an important clarifying function.

Both classes of rules are needed to effect the initiation and maintenance of behavior. When the two are congruent, action is likely to proceed smoothly. A young man whose statements about his behavior are positive (e.g., ''I'm an attractive guy''), as are his statements about consequences (''MaryAnn will probably go out with me''), is likely to have little difficulty in following through and, in this example, asking for a date. Likewise, a person may have low self-efficacy (e.g., ''I cannot carry a tune'') but also negatively evaluate the consequences (''Singing in the choir is boring.'') and experience no problem or discomfort. Problems arise when contrants occur. A person's self-efficacy rules may be very strong (e.g., ''I am a very good carpenter''), but his/her outcome tracking is very weak (''There are no jobs in the building industry''), leading to ineffective and, perhaps, negative emotional behavior (''There's just no use looking for work''). Or, a man may have very strong outcome expectations (e.g., ''Going to the prom is a lot of fun'') but have low regard for his own behavior (''I can't dance or talk to girls''), also leading to ineffective action and negative feelings.

Bandura is careful to point out that self-efficacy and outcome-expectation rules are not in themselves sufficient determinants of behavior. He states:

> Expectations alone will not produce desired performance if the component capabilities are lacking. Moreover, there are many things that people can do with certainty of success that they do not perform because they have no incentives to do so. Given appropriate skills and adequate incentives, however, efficacy expectations are a major determinant of people's choice of activities, how much effort they will expend, and of how long they will sustain effort in dealing with stressful situations. (1977, p. 194)

The "appropriate skills," of course are a product of one's learning history, and "adequate incentives" refer to current environmental contingencies. To this mixture Bandura adds self-efficacy rules as a catalyst that results in overt verbal and motor behavior.

6.1.2. Overt Behavior

The overt behavior Bandura is concerned with generally involves complex sequences requiring sustained effort. Tasks faced by his research subjects include interacting with feared animals and performing arithmetic computations. Other researchers have observed assertive social interactions, smoking cessation, and physical exercise (Bandura, 1982). Tasks are often divided into hierarchies according to level of difficulty. Dependent measures include number of tasks or level attained, rate, and duration of effort. Overt performance is an important determinant of self-efficacy rules.

6.1.3. Outcomes

The environmental consequences of overt behavior are difficult to discern in much of Bandura's research. Subjects are described as "successfully" completing tasks, implying social approval by the experimenter. As with Ellis, this reflects the cognitivist's lack of concern with environmental events. The lack of attention to environmental consequences arises from Bandura's focus on internal mechanisms of self-reinforcement, described later. Environmental and social consequences are recognized as important determinants of "outcome-expectation" and "self-evaluation" rules.

6.1.4. Self-Regulation

Bandura (1978) emphasizes the ongoing interaction between behavior and environment by expanding on behavior occurring in response to reinforcing consequences. In the interaction of behavior and environment, the occurrence of a reinforcer may be regarded as an "antecedent" that controls another sequence of action. In addition, complex behavior may involve continuous evaluation and adjustment. The self-regulation sequence listed in Table 4 may occur after overt action but prior to environmental consequences, maintaining behavior until a particular outcome is achieved. Or it may occur after an environmental consequence.

The first component of the self-regulation response sequence is *self-observation*. This may be regarded as covert observational behavior, the discriminative stimuli for which are the person's own motoric, visceral, or verbal behaviors. Bandura notes that behavior varies on a number of dimensions. "Depending on value orientations [arising from one's history] and the functional significance [environmental consequences] of given activities, people attend selectively to certain aspects of their behavior and ignore variations on nonrelevant dimensions'' (Bandura, 1978).

Observing one's own behavior leads to the next step in the sequence, *self-evaluation.* This takes the form of a self-ply to compare one's current performance with certain standards of behavior. Whether or not performance results in environmental consequences often is not the only, or even the most important, standard for judging the adequacy of an activity, according to Bandura. For example, a student may receive an A on a test but not evaluate himself positively because he had to ''work harder than everybody else'' or ''I just expect A's.''

Contingent upon meeting (or failing to meet) particular performance standards, the person then engages in *self-reinforcement,* or more generally, self-consequation. This may take the form of either verbal statements, such as self-praise or self-damnation (as Ellis described) or administering some environmental consequence, such as taking a coffee break or staying home from a movie. Depending on one's self-evaluation and consequation, a person may persist in the face of immediately punishing consequences, or he/she may give up easily and fail to obtain an available reinforcer that requires more persistence.

A great deal of debate has centered on ''self-reinforcement'' (Bandura, 1976, 1978, 1981; Catania, 1975, 1976; Goldiamond, 1976a,b; Jones, Nelson, & Kazdin, 1977; Mahoney, 1976; Nelson, Hayes, Spong, Jarrett, & McKnight, 1983; Thoreson & Wilbur, 1976). The behaviorists have concluded that environmental variables are critically important, whereas the cognitivists have concluded that internal variables are critically important. On close examination, there does seem to be agreement on the following points: (1) People often engage in self-administration of verbal and material consequences contingent on meeting performance standards; (2) this activity influences the rate or persistence of the consequated behavior; (3) the self-consequation repertoire arises from a learning history involving modeling and differential reinforcement for meeting social standards; (4) the self-consequation rules require occasional contact with externally mediated contingencies. Dispute centers around the nature of the influence and the extent of external contact, but the previously mentioned features have been empirically demonstrated and provide clinically useful procedures.

6.2. Behavior Change

Bandura does not provide a new therapy program to effect change in efficacy rules. Rather, he provides a framework to show how a variety of existing behavior therapy techniques affect self-efficacy and thereby change behavior. He proposes that behavior therapy procedures change behavior in one of four modalities. The change in behavior in a particular modality then serves as a "source of information," a basis for changing the self-efficacy rules (Bandura, 1977).

The four "sources of information" consist of the following:

1. "Performance accomplishments," in which procedures such as participant modeling or *in vivo* desensitization encourage a person to overtly perform a previously avoided activity
2. "Vicarious experience," in which procedures such as live or filmed models demonstrate behavior that a person avoids
3. "Verbal persuasion," in which procedures such as RET induce a person to talk more rationally about his or her behavior and environment
4. "Emotional arousal," in which procedures such as systematic desensitization or biofeedback teach a person to remain calm in problematic situations

A striking feature of Bandura's system is that the four sources of information for formulating efficacy rules closely correspond to the four categories of behavior proposed in Table 1. "Performance accomplishments" may be seen as "motoric behavior," "vicarious experience" as "observational behavior," "verbal persuasion" as "verbal behavior," and "emotional arousal" as "visceral behavior." Bandura seems to be proposing that efficacy rules are based on people's plys for their own behavior in these four areas. Therapy consists of inducing people to behave appropriately in one or more of these areas *and to see that they are doing so*. The therapist thus serves as the member of the verbal community who not only teaches people more adaptive behavior but teaches them to extract rules about their own behavior.

6.2.1. Motoric Behavior

Bandura (1977) reviews a number of behavior therapy studies in support of the view that the most powerful means of changing people's rules about their own abilities, and hence their subsequent performance, comes from their actually engaging in the requisite behavior and achieving successful outcomes. At first glance, this merely seems to be inserting a gratuitous cognitive step into the behavioral truism that the best predicter of future behavior is past behavior. Teach people effective behavior and they will continue to behave effectively. However, he cites evidence that suggests that certain behavior is rule-governed rather than just past-contingency-governed.

Bandura (1982; Bandura, Reese, & Adams, 1982) describes a series of experiments in which subjects systematically progressed through an 18-step hierarchical task, observing and handling snakes and spiders. After each trial they reported which steps they thought they could accomplish, and they rated their confidence in performing them. It was found that people's statements of self-efficacy did not simply parallel training experience and that such statements were more closely related to test performance (handling a novel animal) than were the number of tasks completed in training. According to the sequence outlined in Table 4, it is hypothesized that people observed their own behavior, evaluated it, and translated it into a new efficacy rule. In an initial step toward studying this process, two subjects were asked to speak aloud their thoughts as they went through the training steps. Efficacy statements improved, were held in abeyance, or declined, as a function of activity of the snake and their observations of their ability to cope with a situation, even though all task outcomes were rated "successful." Much more research of this nature is required to determine the role of such rules in the control of behavior, as opposed to inferring the action of cognitive constructs.

6.2.2. *Observational Behavior*

People observe others engaging in certain behaviors, as well as the antecedents and consequences of those behaviors, and thereby change their own behavior. The advertising industry attests to the power of this mode of behavior change. Bandura (1982; Bandura *et al*,. 1982) proposes that changes in overt activity due to observing others are mediated by efficacy rules. Even though a person does not immediately engage in an activity that is observed, providing no opportunity for reinforcement, the verbal community can determine the likelihood of future behavior by asking the person to state his/her efficacy rule. In one of the experiments described before, subjects observed a model handle a spider until they stated that they could perform low or medium levels of interaction with the spider (high levels were not sought because of the need for lengthy modeling or actual practice). Subjects' test performance corresponded to their statements of efficacy. No data are presented on the extent of modeling necessary to obtain the stated levels of efficacy, though it is apparent that more modeling was needed to obtain medium than low levels. The implication, however, is that efficacy statements derived from observational behavior were a better predictor of actual performance than was total amount of observation.

6.2.3. *Visceral Behavior*

As stated earlier, *emotion* is a complex behavior class involving responses in all modalities. Bandura uses the term to refer to autonomic arousal (visceral behavior) and to self-reports of fear (verbal behavior). Bandura proposes a two-way relationship between efficacy rules and visceral arousal. First, like other cognitivists, Bandura suggests that efficacy plys mediate visceral arousal—"by conjuring up fear-provoking thoughts about their ineptitude, individuals can rouse themselves to elevated levels of anxiety that far exceed the fear experienced during the actual threatening situation" (1977, p. 199). In the research described, subjects' fear ratings, both while anticipating and actually performing a task, were closely related to their efficacy statements. In a further study, measures of heart rate and blood pressure were also highly related to subjects' efficacy statements (Bandura, 1982; Bandura *et al.*, 1982).

On the other hand, visceral arousal, as a "source of information," influences efficacy rules. People who feel calm in a situation are more likely to state confidence in their ability than when they feel upset. However, because people cannot clearly discriminate visceral cues, the relationship between arousal and self-efficacy rules or behavior is often unreliable. Bandura and Adams (1977) performed systematic desensitization until subjects reported no upset while imagining a snake. After treatment, however, subjects varied widely in their self-efficacy rules, and their performance was more consistent with their efficacy statements, rather than their lack of upset, in behavioral tests.

6.2.4. *Verbal Behavior*

Pep talks, encouragement, reassurance, and "positive-thinking" promotions are widely employed in athletics, business, counseling, and friendly advice. Ellis's RET makes extensive use of this modality. In effect, the instructor is providing a verbal model of a rule to be adopted by the listener. The "you-can-do-it!" instruction generates an "I-can-do-it!" echoic by the recipient. The assumption is made that the person has an adequate repertoire but just needs a kick in the self-efficacy to get behavior underway. More elaborate instructions may be given in an attempt to establish a skill. Skinner's analysis of rules and contingencies is largely concerned with the issues involved in establishing a repertoire through verbal means. A great deal of social influence occurs through instructional control. The "nonspecific effects" of various therapies can be attributed to explicit and implicit self-efficacy rules provided by the therapist. On the other hand, by the time clients seek professional help they may be largely refractory to such rule-induction procedures.

Bandura (1977) notes that rules generated in this fashion are not likely to be as effective as those arising from actual experience. He reviews a number of behavior therapy studies employing placebos and expectancy manipulations, concluding that they exert little or no effect. As with any procedure, instruction will be effective to the extent that it can induce a client to engage in the requisite behavior, receive reinforcing outcomes, and thereby change his/her rules.

6.3. Discussion

Bandura, like Ellis and other cognitive theorists, proposes that a person's initial response to a problematic situation is a verbal reaction that mediates subsequent behavior. (According to the analysis presented earlier, the initial responses to a situation are not necessarily verbal; they may as well be motoric, visceral, observational, or some combination.) These statements fall into two broad classes, concerning either one's behavioral adequacies or the nature and schedule of environmental consequences. Bandura focuses on self-evaluative rules, whereas Ellis emphasizes, in addition, the importance of rules about consequences. All systems agree that when a person has strong views that his/her behavior is inadequate, or the environment is unjust or impoverished, negative emotions and ineffective behavior will occur. Ellis describes how these rules may be inaccurate, reflecting extreme demands for perfection and reinforcement. Treatment involves verbal analyses of clients' rules to bring them more in line with existing capabilities and reinforcers. In contrast, Bandura is more concerned with actually training behavioral skills, either through practice or observation, and implies that people will modify their self-efficacy rules and outcome expectancies, in the "self-regulation" stage (Table 4), without any additional therapist intervention.

The emphases of Ellis and Bandura are complementary. A major deficit in Ellis's system, mentioned earlier, is that it assumes that the client has an adequate behavioral repertoire. Such may not be the case. A client may be a social klutz, experience frequent panic attacks, or have no skill in speaking assertively. Behavior therapy techniques to train more effective behavior, as advocated by Bandura, provide the client with the opportunity to see that he/she is *sometimes* successful and not *always* a failure. On the other hand, people may need a therapist's verbal guidance in order to recognize that their behavior is acceptable and their environment adequate. People's operative rules at the "self-regulation" stage may be as faulty as those at earlier stages of a problem-solving episode. Maintenance of behavior change requires not only that people behave effectively but that their rules reflect that fact.

To the behavior analyst, it is apparent that cognitive approaches neglect environmental consequences of behavior. This is apparent in Ellis's system (Table 3), and although "outcome" is mentioned in Bandura's system (Table 4), it is not accorded nearly as much significance as "self-reinforcement." One reason for this neglect is that the therapist has minimal access to or control over the client's environment. Yet reinforcement is an integral part of treatment. The therapist provides social reinforcement in behavior rehearsal procedures, such as assertiveness training. And, though assessed through verbal report rather than direct observation, more benign environments are selected for the client to test nascent skills in "homework" assignments. Finally, the procedures of "self-control" are often useful, in which the client is taught to rearrange the contingencies in his/her own environment.

7. CONCLUSIONS

The goal of this chapter has been to provide a common framework, allowing researchers, clinicians and theorists from various points on the behavioral map to speak to one another. Recognition and analysis of the four modalities of behavior, and their interrelations, are steps in that direction. It would seem that effective therapy requires attention to all four modalities of human behavior, as well as to environmental contingencies, recognizing the limitations of verbal reports of history and private events. Research on the development and function of rules is in its infancy; this chapter has made many assertions in the absence of empirical evidence. Cognitive approaches emphasize the central importance of rules as mediators among various modalities of behavior, whereas behavioral approaches have focused on teaching specific skills and constructing more congenial contingencies. At present, the best therapy seems to be to teach people adaptive skills where needed, in any or all behavioral modalities, to teach them to program a more reinforcing environment where possible, and to teach them to make accurate, positive verbal appraisals of the relationship between the two.

8. REFERENCES

Bandura, A. (1976). Self-reinforcement: Theoretical and methodological considerations. *Behaviorism, 4,* 135–155.

Bandura, A. (1977). Self-efficacy: Toward a unifying theory of behavior change. *Psychological Bulletin, 84,* 191–215.

Bandura, A. (1978). The self-system in reciprocal determinism. *American Psychologist, 33,* 344–358.

Bandura, A. (1981). In search of pure unidirectional determinants. *Behavior Therapy, 12,* 30–40.

Bandura, A. (1982). Self-efficacy mechanism in human agency. *American Psychologist, 37,* 122–147.

Bandura, A., & Adams, N. E. (1977). Analysis of self-efficacy theory of behavior change. *Cognitive Therapy and Research, 1,* 287–308.

Bandura, A., Reese, L., & Adams, N. E. (1982). Microanalysis of action and fear arousal as a function of differential levels of perceived self-efficacy. *Journal of Personality and Social Psychology, 43,* 5–21.

Brown, R. (1973). *A first language: The early stages.* Cambridge: Harvard University Press.

Catania, A. C. (1975). The myth of self-reinforcement. *Behaviorism, 3,* 192–199.

Catania, A. C. (1976). Self-reinforcement revisited. *Behaviorism, 4,* 157–162.

Duvinsky, J., & Poppen, R. (1982). Human performance on conjunctive fixed-interval fixed-ratio schedules. *Journal of the Experimental Analysis of Behavior, 37,* 243–250.

Ekman, P., Levenson, R. W., & Friesen, W. V. (1983). Autonomic nervous system activity distinguishes among emotions. *Science, 221,* 1208–1210.

Ellis, A., & Grieger, R. (1977). *Handbook of rational-emotive therapy.* New York: Springer.

Ellis, A., & Harper, R. A. (1961). *A guide to rational living.* Englewood Cliffs, NJ: Prentice-Hall.

Goldiamond, I. (1974). Toward a constructional approach to social problems. *Behaviorism, 2,* 1–84.

Goldiamond, I. (1976a). Self-reinforcement. *Journal of Applied Behavior Analysis, 9,* 509–514.

Goldiamond, I. (1976b). Fables, armadyllics, and self-reinforcement. *Journal of Applied Behavior Analysis, 9,* 521–525.

Harzem, P., Lowe, C. F., & Bagshaw, M. (1978). Verbal control in operant behavior. *Psychological Record, 28,* 405–423.

Hilgard, E. R., & Loftus, E. G. (1979). Effective interrogation of the eyewitness. *International Journal of Experimental & Clinical Hypnosis, 27,* 342–357.

Jacobson, E. (1938). *Progressive relaxation.* Chicago: University of Chicago Press.

Jones, R. T., Nelson, R. E., & Kazdin, A. E. (1977). The role of external variables in reinforcement. *Behavior Modification, 1,* 147–178.

Kaufman, A., Baron, A., & Kopp, E. R. (1966). Some effects of instructions on human operant behavior. *Psychonomic Monograph Supplements, 1* (No. 11).

Lang, P. J., Kozak, M. J., Miller, G. A., & Levin, D. N. (1980). Emotional imagery: Conceptual structure and pattern of somato-visceral response. *Psychophysiology, 17,* 179–192.

Lippman, L. G., & Meyer, M. E. (1967). Fixed-interval performance as related to subjects' verbalization of the contingency. *Psychonomic Science, 8,* 135–136.

Loftus, E. F. (1979). *Eyewitness testimony.* Cambridge: Harvard University Press.

Lowe, C. F. (1979). Determinants of human operant behavior. In M. D. Zeiler & P. Harzem (Eds.), *Reinforcement and the Structure of Behavior.* New York: Wiley & Sons.

Mahoney, M. (1976). Terminal terminology: A self-regulated response to Goldiamond. *Journal of Applied Behavior Analysis, 9,* 515–517.

Matthews, B. A., Shimoff, E., Catania, A. C., & Sagvolden, T. (1977). Uninstructed human responding: Sensitivity to ratio and interval contingencies. *Journal of the Experimental Analysis of Behavior, 27,* 453–467.

Meichenbaum, D., & Cameron, R. (1973). Training schizophrenics to talk to themselves. *Behavior Therapy, 4,* 515–534.

Miller, N. E. (1978). Biofeedback and visceral learning. *Annual Review of Psychology, 29,* 373–404.

Mowrer, O. H. (1948). Learning theory and the neurotic paradox. *American Journal of Orthopsychiatry, 18,* 571–610.

Nelson, R. O., Hayes, S. C., Spong, R. T., Jarrett, R. B., & McKnight, D. L. (1983). Self-reinforcement: Appealing misnomer or effective mechanism? *Behaviour Research & Therapy, 21,* 557–566.

Poppen, R. (1972). Effects of concurrent schedules on human fixed-interval performance. *Journal of the Experimental Analysis of Behavior, 18,* 119–127.

Poppen, R. (1982a). Human fixed-interval performance on concurrent schedules: A parametric analysis. *Journal of the Experimental Analysis of Behavior, 37,* 251–266.

Poppen, R. (1982b). The fixed-interval scallop in human affairs. *The Behavior Analyst, 5,* 127–136.

Rosenbaum, M., Franks, C. M., & Jaffe, Y. (1983). *Perspectives on behavior therapy in the eighties.* New York: Springer.

Segal, E. (1975). Psycholinguistics discovers the operant: A review of Roger Brown's *First Language. Journal of the Experimental Analysis of Behavior, 23,* 149–158.

Schwartz, B. (1982). Reinforcement-induced behavioral stereotypy: How not to teach people to discover rules. *Journal of Experimental Psychology: General, 111,* 23–59.

Skinner, B. F. (1953). *Science and human behavior.* New York: Macmillan.

Skinner, B. F. (1957). *Verbal behavior.* New York: Appleton-Century-Crofts.

Skinner, B. F. (1969). *Contingencies of reinforcement.* New York: Appleton-Century-Crofts.

Skinner, B. F. (1974). *About behaviorism.* New York: Knopf.

Skinner, B. F. (1977). Why I am not a cognitive psychologist. *Behaviorism, 5,* 1–10.

Thoreson, C. E., & Wilbur, C. S. (1976). Some encouraging thoughts about self-reinforcement. *Journal of Applied Behavior Analysis, 9,* 518–520.

Turk, D. C., Meichenbaum, D., & Genest, M. (1983). *Pain and behavioral medicine: A cognitive-behavioral perspective.* New York: Guilford Press.

Weiner, H. (1964). Conditioning history and human fixed-interval performance. *Journal of the Experimental Analysis of Behavior, 7,* 383–385.

Weiner, H. (1969). Controlling human fixed-interval performance. *Journal of the Experimental Analysis of Behavior, 12,* 349–373.

Weiner, H. (1970). Human behavioral persistence. *The Psychological Record, 20,* 445–456.

Zettle, R. D., & Hayes, S. C. (1984). Rule-governed behavior: A potential theoretical framework for cognitive behavior therapy. In P. C. Kendall (Ed.), *Advances in cognitive-behavioral research and therapy.* New York: Academic Press.

CHAPTER 10

Avoiding and Altering Rule-Control as a Strategy of Clinical Intervention

STEVEN C. HAYES, BARBARA S. KOHLENBERG, and SUSAN M. MELANCON

1. INTRODUCTION

If rule-governed behavior is as ubiquitous as it seems, it is only logical that many clinical disorders involve problems in verbal control of one kind or another. At least four types of problems can be discerned.

1.1. Types of Problems in Rule-Control

1.1.1. Problems in Self-Rule Formulation

A verbally competent person is both speaker and listener. It is quite possible to listen to one's own talk. This talk can then participate in the control of other behavior.

There are differences, of course, between following self-rules and rules made by others. In particular, the social contingencies involved in pliance (see Chapter 6 in this volume) cannot operate in the same manner when a person is listening to his/her own speech. Nevertheless, self-rule formation is probably quite important in behavioral control of impulsivity and other acts under greater control by direct contingencies.

Disorders of self-rule formulation could occur in at least two basic ways.

STEVEN C. HAYES, BARBARA S. KOHLENBERG, and SUSAN M. MELANCON • Department of Psychology, University of Nevada—Reno, Reno, Nevada 89557. Portions of this chapter were drawn from Hayes (1987) and Hayes and Melancon (in press).

First, a person could fail to formulate rules when it is worthwhile to do so. Second, a person could formulate rules but do so inaccurately or unrealistically. Much of the cognitive therapy literature can be interpreted as an attempt to train individuals in proper rule-formulation (see Poppen, Chapter 9 in this volume; Zettle & Hayes, 1982). An emphasis on developing accurate self-rules can also be discerned in insight-oriented therapy. In this case, a relationship is structured in which the client is encouraged to bring verbal behavior under the control of direct contact with experienced events and not states of reinforceability (e.g., hopes or fears) or audience control (e.g., attempting to please others).

1.1.2. Problems in Rule-Formulation of the Group

Many of the rules that guide our behavior are learned from others. In much the same manner that self-rule formulation can cause problems, problems can occur in the rule-formulation practices of the verbal community more generally. Particular cultures and subcultures may fail to develop adequate rules or may develop inaccurate ones. For example, a religious subculture might develop verbal rules about faith healing that prohibit adherents from seeking medical attention for life-threatening diseases. Similarly, a culture may fail to give any verbal guidance at all about important issues of health.

1.1.3. A Failure to Follow Rules

It is not enough to formulate worthwhile rules. They must also learn to be understood and followed. Without a repertoire of both aspects of rule-following, disordered behavior patterns seem likely. In some circumstances, it is desirable for rules to compete effectively with the destructive effects of some kinds of immediate contingency control. For example, a teenager may know that taking addictive drugs is likely to lead to extremely undesirable ends. Nevertheless, the immediate social contingencies and the immediate effects of the drug itself may draw the teenager into a pattern of drug addiction. The rule "do not take addictive drugs" is meant to establish an insensitivity to these direct contingencies. Without a sufficiently strong pattern of rule-following, the person is much more likely to have his or her behavior captured by immediate contingencies, even if the outcome is destructive.

Rule-following in this sense involves two distinguishable aspects: understanding the rule and the verbal activation of behavioral functions in terms of rule (see Chapter 6 in the present volume). Some clinical techniques have been oriented toward increased understanding, but most procedures assume that the person can organize events in terms of a rule. The focus of most clinical interventions, therefore, is establishing rule-following *per se* once a rule is understood.

Some of the techniques used with character-disordered or impulsive persons can be understood as an attempt to establish a greater degree of rule-following. For example, drug treatment programs such as Synanon are highly regimented, with many clearly stated rules of conduct. Compliance with the rules is promoted through group meetings focused on rule-infractions by group members. This intense social control can be understood as an attempt to establish pliance with regard to the rules of the house. Strong and consistent social contingencies are provided for rule-following, perhaps with the hope that a greater degree of insensitivity to undesirable and immediate contingencies will result.

1.1.4. Excessive Rule-Following

We come now to the focus of this chapter. Rule-governed behavior can never capture completely the subtlety of behavior controlled directly by experience. Driving a car after having read a book about driving is not the same as driving after having driven for many months. Interacting with members of the opposite sex after having read a book on it is not the same as such an interaction in a socially experienced individual.

It is not just a matter, however, of having enough experience. Some rules may be supported so pervasively by the verbal community that direct experience can nevertheless not overcome the effects of the rule. In other cases, the previous use of a rule may interfere with the control by direct experience such that the benefits of subsequent direct experience are attenuated.

The literature reviewed in this book makes the case that insensitivity to direct contingency control is a typical side effect of verbal control. But there are many times when control by direct contact with the world is desirable. In that context, it is remarkable how often therapists rely on direct instruction to produce therapeutic benefits. Directive therapies, such as Rational-Emotive Therapy (Ellis, 1962) and almost all of the behavior therapy techniques applied to adults (e.g., Lutzker & Martin, 1981; Rimm & Masters, 1979) rely heavily on directly instructing the client's behavior. Advances in our understanding of rule-governance is gradually cutting away at the foundation of many of these behavioral techniques.

Instead, "nonbehavioral" therapies began to appear to be more consistent with the basic behavioral literature. For example, Gestalt therapy (Perls, 1969; Perls, Hefferline, & Goodman, 1951) advocates the experiential aspects of learning; one must experience the "now" before real, lasting change can occur. Similarly, relationship-oriented psychotherapies (e.g., Strupp & Binder, 1984; Weiss & Sampson, 1986) also heavily emphasize the experiences that occur during the therapeutic relationship as being critical in the production of behavior change.

When instructional control is undesirable, two therapeutic courses seem available: avoid verbal control or alter it so as to diminish its insensitivity-producing effects. In this chapter, we will focus on both strategies. It is not, of course, that verbal control is itself harmful. Civilization itself is based on verbal control. Indeed, some of the methods described in this chapter themselves attempt to use the insensitivity-producing effects of rules in more useful ways. Their primary emphasis, however, is in the avoidance and alteration of rule-control.

One way in which a laboratory analysis shows its value is in the ways that it leads to new and effective methods of changing behavior. Thus, rather than interpret existing techniques in the language of rule-governed behavior, we will focus on new techniques being developed by behaviorists that are sensitive to the rule-governed/contingency-shaped distinction.

2. AVOIDING RULE-CONTROL: THE STRATEGY OF DIRECT SHAPING

We will consider two topics as examples of the direct shaping strategy. First, we will discuss the area of social skills training and show how the issues of rule-governance and contingency-shaped behavior apply. Some preliminary results of a direct shaping approach to social skills training will then be described. Second, a relationship-oriented, radical behavioral therapy called *Functional Analytic Psychotherapy* (Kohlenberg & Tsai, 1987) will be described and discussed in light of these distinctions.

2.1. Social Skills Training

Behavioral approaches to social skills training have traditionally been driven by the following assumptions. First, the individual being trained is viewed as being deficient or excessive in a set of particular skill areas. Second, it is assumed that the therapist/experimenter can identify and describe the social skills that are necessary for the client/subject to acquire or change. Third, it is assumed that the therapist then will be able to use verbal instructions (sometimes in conjunction with role playing and modeling) to establish the specified behaviors. Fourth, the therapist can further shape performance by giving feedback on the degree to which performances approximate the instructed ideal (Devany & Nelson, 1986) thus creating new, more effective behavior in the individual. Although this traditional "component skills" approach to social skills training has shown some success, it remains problematic for the following reasons.

2.1.1. Operationalizing the Target Behavior

The component skills approach to social skills training relies upon the notion that it is possible to operationalize the particular behavior that one wants to establish. Describing the specific components of "social skill" is often very difficult, however (Ciminero, Calhoun, & Adams, 1977; Conger & Conger, 1982). Because it is assumed that only when the target behavior can be operationalized can the therapist or experimenter then shape successive approximations to the desired behavior, literally hundreds of studies have been done over the last 20 years to identify the components of social skill (Rosenfarb, Hayes, & Linehan, in press). So far, only a handful of components have been identified that together account for only a fraction of the variance in social performances.

The problem seems to be that social behaviors are extremely complex and difficult to enumerate. Social skills may involve whole classes of behaviors that have functional similarities but few structural similarities. In addition to the form of the behaviors involved, complex issues of timing, situational control, and so on, make a list of the components of social skills difficult to develop.

Given our assumption that a response is meaningless independent of its context (Skinner, 1969), the specification of target behaviors is impossible without reference to context. When context is ignored, we can only rely on topographical descriptions of behavior; that is, on the structure rather than function of behavior. Such an approach distorts a behavioral perspective completely. A smile that appeared after being told "smile and I will give you a dime" is actually a different behavior than a smile that appears after seeing a letter in the mailbox from an old friend.

When dealing with some highly discriminable kinds of social difficulties, such as behaviors involving violence or self-destruction or poor hygiene, structural definitions may be adequate because a consistent social context may be assumed. Poor hygiene is likely to have similar results in a wide variety of social situations, and measurement of behavioral topographies may in this case not produce confusion.

Other acts are highly variable in form and effects are dependent upon context. For example, when one attempts to answer questions such as "how can I get close to people?" or "why do I attract people who eventually abandon me?", the difficulty with a reliance on structure becomes obvious. Thus, although the social skills literature traditionally has valued the topographical operationalization of target behaviors, there are many problems with this approach when trying to remain consistent with a functionalistic approach to the problem.

If one is committed to the measurement of context, the ungainly nature of a skills-deficit approach also becomes obvious. Even if it would be possible to name every component of social skill and relate each one to every conceivable context, the resulting rule-book would seemingly contain many thousands of rules and would be virtually impossible to teach. It may take generations to develop. Finally, because many social behaviors are conventional, it seems likely that the role of many components would change over time, so the rule-book would have to be updated continuously.

2.1.2. Generalization

An additional problem that has plagued the traditional behavioral social skills literature is that of generalization. Though behavior change is often seen within the context in which training occurred, it is difficult to get changes to generalize to other settings (Devany & Nelson, 1986; Gallassi & Gallassi, 1979).

2.1.3. Rule-Governed Training

Given the basic literature on rule-governance, it follows that if one attempts to instruct a particular behavior, then that behavior might become relatively insensitive to the many other contingencies that are operative at a given moment. Even if one could identify a particular set of behaviors that it might benefit an individual to acquire, establishing this set by verbal instructions could functionally render the behavior insensitive to a situation that differs from the training situation. In other words, the behavior could be under the control of the therapist's instructions, not the social situation that the individual is in (Azrin & Hayes, 1984).

In some respects, this leaves the component skills approach in a quandary. Even if the difficult task of identifying appropriate target behaviors can be overcome, instructing these target behaviors may induce an undesirable insensitivity to the effects of direct social experience. How can social skills be assessed and treated if the specific components are both unknown and uninstructable?

2.1.4. Contingency-Shaped Training

Several studies have emerged from our laboratory that have attempted to address the problem of training social skills, although remaining in contact with the issues described before. Our general strategy has been to expose clients to the conditions under which social skills can be acquired by direct experience.

Our first study focused on client's sensitivity to social cues indicating interest. We reasoned that if subjects could know when they were having a positive or negative impact on others, then they would be able to learn by direct experience which social behaviors had which effects.

We focused on cues of interest in heterosocial interactions (Azrin & Hayes, 1984). Male subjects were asked to view a videotaped conversation of a female with an unseen male. Subjects could see the female's face and body; the audio portion of the tape as turned off. After 1 minute, subjects rated how interested they thought that the female was in the male she was conversing with.

A variety of females were observed. In the original videotaping, the conversation between the male and female was halted every minute, and both were asked to confidentially rate their interest in their partner during the previous minute. By using the female's rating as a criterion, the male subjects' ratings could be assessed for their accuracy. This allowed an assessment of the males' sensitivity to social cues of interest. We did not know the specific cues good raters were responding to, but we did not need to know them in order to assess subjects' degree of social sensitivity.

An experiential treatment was developed based on the criterion ratings. After subjects rated a female's degree of interest in her unseen partner, half of the subjects received feedback as to how interested the woman really was, whereas the other half received no feedback.

The results suggest that as a result of training, the subjects improved in their ability to discriminate interest, that this ability generalized to previously unviewed females, and that subjects in the feedback condition displayed improvements in actual social skills in subsequent role-play situations. Importantly, this improvement occurred without any attempt to operationalize what behaviors constituted social sensitivity, and accordingly, no attempts were made to instruct these behaviors.

This study did not attempt to pit instructions against experience, but it did effectively demonstrate that a social skill can be assessed and trained without having to determine the components of the skill, and without using any verbal instructions about such components.

Rosenfarb, Hayes, and Linehan (in press) compared experiential and instructional social skills training in the treatment of adults with social difficulties. In this study, 36 adults received training designed to improve their assertiveness skills. In the context of repeated role playing of social scenes, one-third of the group received instructions as to how to become more assertive, one-third were helped to develop their own rules as to how to improve, and one-third received no rules and were not encouraged to develop their own. A fourth group served as a waiting list control. Half of the subjects across the three main conditions (rules, self-rules, and no rules) were also given noninstructional feedback about their performance; half were not given feedback. In the feedback condition, the experimenter simply stated his "gut reaction" about the quality of the role-played performance. No feedback was given on the behaviors the therapist liked or did not like.

The results of this study suggested that subjects receiving feedback improved more than subjects that did no receive feedback and were more likely to have developed behaviors that generalized to new situations. Instructions did not improve performance over no instructions.

In this study, subjects were able to learn effective social skills without instructions or directive verbal feedback. The experimenter need not know what components lead to a high rating. All that was required is that the experimenter be able to distinguish socially effective from ineffective performances in a global fashion. In fact, global social skills ratings are often highly reliable across raters, even when they are naive about formal definitions of social skill. Just by virtue of participation in the culture, most of us know good social skills when we see it. Thus, social skills were assessed and treated but without first having to known which skills needed to be improved.

This line of research is still in its early stages. It does show, however, that instructional approaches are not *necessary* in behavior therapy, however ubiquitous they may be. It is interesting that so much effort has been placed, in this case unsuccessfully, into the generation of rules of conduct for clinical use. The literature on rule-governance undermines the rationale for the effort; work such as that reported here undermines its need.

2.2. Functional Analytic Psychotherapy

Functional Analytic Psychotherapy is of interest because it is a treatment technique that consciously attempts to avoid a reliance on instruction. Instead, the therapeutic relationship itself is used to shape more effective behavior.

2.2.1. Theoretical Base

Kohlenberg and Tsai (1987) describe Functional Analytic Psychotherapy as an approach to psychotherapy that is derived directly from a Skinnerian conceptual framework. Unlike Ferster (1972) and Skinner (1953), who have written radical behavioral descriptions of psychoanalytic psychotherapy, Functional Analytic Psychotherapy significantly distinguishes itself from these early attempts to analyze psychotherapy in that it offers a new set of guidelines for the practice of psychotherapy that are tied to the authors' contact with the writings of B. F. Skinner (e.g., 1945, 1953, 1957).

Though the conceptual underpinnings of Functional Analytic Psychotherapy are strongly attributed to radical behaviorism, the techniques comprising it were also said to be contingency shaped. Kohlenberg and Tsai are each practicing clinical psychologists who noticed that over the years some of their clients showed dramatic and pervasive change, "far beyond the stated goals of therapy" and that for these clients, the therapeutic relationship was particularly intense. Functional Analytic Psychotherapy was developed in part then, in order to ". . . lead the therapist into a caring, genuine sensitive, involving, and emotional relationship with his or her client, while at the same time capitalizing on the clarity, logic, and precise definitions of radical behaviorism'' (Kohlenberg & Tsai, 1987, p. 389).

2.2.2. Guidelines and Rationale

Functional Analytic Psychotherapy emphasizes the role of reinforcement in changing operant behavior. Reinforcement, it is well known, is most effective when it occurs immediately following the particular behavior of interest. Therefore, Functional Analytic Psychotherapy procedures are oriented toward increasing the discriminability of the clinically relevant behaviors as they occur during the session, a necessary step in setting the stage for the behavior to be immediately reinforced.

The first basic assumption of Functional Analytic Psychotherapy is that treatment is most effective when the problem behaviors that bring the client into therapy also occur during the session. The second basic assumption is that the therapist must have the skills necessary to discriminate the clinically relevant behavior. The third assumption is that the therapists must actually have the client's goal behaviors in their own repertoire, thus enabling them to differentially reinforce the clients' approximations of the desired, often highly complex, goal behaviors.

2.2.3. Reinforcement

Borrowing the concepts from Ferster (1967) the authors suggest that whenever possible, natural and not arbitrary reinforcement should be used in the therapy environment. Ferster essentially suggested that reinforcement should match, as closely as possible, what would occur in the natural environment, so as to facilitate generalization when treatment stops and to avoid power struggles and resistance. Reinforcers that formally are as close to what is seen in the natural environment are identified by Ferster as natural. Reinforcers that are unlike what is naturally found in the environment as a consequence for a particular behavior are described as arbitrary reinforcement. Therefore, in the therapy environment, rewarding appropriate eye contact with money or tokens or by stating ''Good! I like it when you look at me!'' would be arbitrary, whereas rewarding the behavior with the increased attention of the therapist would be an example of a natural reinforcer. Accordingly, the therapist's drifting attention would be a natural consequence for poor eye contact, whereas a financial penalty or yelling ''no'' would be an arbitrary consequence.

Although reinforcement is extremely important in Functional Analytic Psychotherapy, the ability to discriminate the behaviors to be reinforced is equally important. Functional Analytic Psychotherapy stresses that there are several types of *clinically relevant behaviors* that the therapist must learn to discriminate.

2.2.4. Clinically Relevant Behaviors

There are three types of clinically relevant behaviors that are relevant to the practice of Functional Analytic Psychotherapy.

2.2.4a. Clinically Relevant Behavior 1. When actual instances of the behavior of interest occur in therapy, these are termed "Clinically Relevant Behavior 1s." For example, the authors describe a man whose main problem is that he avoids getting into love relationships. During the therapy hour, he watches the clock so he can end right on time, he cancels the next session after making an important self-disclosure, and he always decides ahead of time exactly what to talk about during the session. Through the course of treatment, these clinically relevant behaviors should decrease.

2.2.4b. Clinically Relevant Behavior 2. When individuals come into therapy primarily because they are deficient in certain repertoires, these low-rate or nonexistent repertoires are labeled as "Clinically Relevant Behavior 2s." For example, if a client feels badly because he is frequently ignored in conversation, he or she may have several types of repertoire deficiencies. If during the session, the therapist interrupts him or her or ignores him or her, the client could possibly develop the skill of discriminating the therapist's waning interest and then changing the topic or directing the therapist's attention back to the conversation. Clinically Relevant Behavior 2s are behaviors that would increase throughout the course of therapy.

2.2.4c. Clinically Relevant Behavior 3. This behavior refers to clients verbalizing about their own behavior and what appears to cause it. Clinically Relevant Behavior 3 involves observing one's own behavior and the reinforcing, discriminative, and eliciting stimlui that surround it. It also can include identifying events that occur in therapy as functionally equivalent to events that occur out of therapy. For example, "I am reacting to your suggesting to dress better in the same way I do to my lover criticizing me." Developing the behavior of describing functional relationships can help in obtaining reinforcement.

2.2.5. Rules of Therapy

In order to actually conduct Functional Analytic Psychotherapy, the authors offer five strategic rules of therapeutic technique. They are strategic rules in the sense that they do not proscribe a specific form of behavior but instead point to strategies to be acquired largely through direct experience. Rules such as "practice makes perfect" are rules of this sort and are themselves unlikely to induce harmful insensitivities in the clinician.

2.2.5a. Rule 1: Develop a Repertoire for Observing Possible Instances of Clinically Relevant Behaviors Occurring during the Therapy Session. The authors state that theoretically, this rule alone could be sufficient for successful treatment. The development of observing repertoires in a therapist is very difficult to instruct and is very likely contingency shaped.

2.2.5b. Rule 2: Construct a Therapeutic Environment That Will Enhance the Evocation of Clinically Relevant Behavior. In most cases, the authors argue, clinically relevant behaviors occur without the therapist having to take special measures. At times, however, special environments may need to be constructed. If clients report having relationship problems that only emerge when their spouses are present, for example, clinically relevant behaviors may appear in couples therapy but not individual therapy.

2.2.5c. Rule 3: Arrange for the Positive Reinforcement of Clinically Relevant Behavior 2. Given the sensitivity that the authors have to arbitrary/natural reinforcement issues, they hesitate to specify any particular forms of behavior on the part of the therapist that could potentially act as reinforcers. If they did so, they might actually interfere with the more "natural" reinforcers available to the therapist.

Therapists are members of the social community, in addition to being therapists. Therefore, the spontaneous responses they have to a client could be representative of the responses of individuals that the client interacts with outside of therapy. The private reactions of the therapist are, therefore, important data.

Although the therapeutic environment is in many respects identical to the client's daily environment, there are important differences. In the therapeutic environment, the therapist hopefully has the skills to amplify his or her private reactions in such a way as to most benefit the client. In doing so, the therapist is emitting verbal behavior that is "autoclitic" (Skinner, 1957)—it serves to "augment and sharpen the effect on the listener" (p. 369).

Given the importance of the therapist's private reactions in occasioning his or her own behavior in the session, certain features of the therapist become important, according to Kohlenberg and Tsai. First, the therapist must discriminate what to reinforce (Rule 1). Second, efforts should be made to match clients with therapists who are likely to be reinforced by progress toward the client's goal behaviors. For example, a female client interested in learning to be more self-disclosing in her personal relationships would do best with a therapist who has those skills in his or her own repertoire.

2.2.5d. Rule 4: Develop a Repertoire for Observing the Potential Reinforcing Properties of the Therapist's Behavior That Are Contingent on Occurrences of the Client's Clinically Relevant Behavior. If therapists have been emitting behavior that they think is acting as a reinforcer, it would be important for them to actually observe whether they are in fact increasing, decreasing, or having no effect on a particular client behavior. Feedback of this sort could lead to changes in the behaviors of the therapist that would render them more effective.

2.2.5e. Rule 5: Develop a Repertoire for Describing the Functional Relationships between Controlling Variables and the Client's Clinically Relevant Behavior. The authors suggest that strengthening verbal repertoires emitted by the client that describe functional relationships involving clinically relevant behaviors (occurring inside or outside of therapy) could be an important step in increasing the client's chances for obtaining reinforcement. The therapist can help the client build this kind of repertoire by themselves emitting statements of functional relationships concerning events in the therapy session. For example, saying to the client "whenever I ask about your feelings toward me, you change the topic" (Kohlenberg & Tsai, 1987, p. 411) or ". . . when I told you that I really care about you and wanted you to acknowledge my feelings, you reacted in an impersonal way. This reaction made me feel like my feelings don't count, and punished my telling you that I care. I think that's why you reacted the way you did, that is, you don't want me to bring up my caring and positive feelings about you" (Kohlenberg & Tsai, 1987, p. 412).

Statements of this sort would serve to create a context in which emotions were not viewed as random occurrences but rather as resulting from actual discriminable events, which could be reduced or increased if so desired. As with insight-oriented therapy, such procedures may develop a repertoire of more accurate self-rules, based on direct contact with the phenomena of interest.

2.2.6. Functional Analytic Psychotherapy and Rule-Governance

The procedures outlined here are designed to produce changes in client and in therapist behaviors that are largely shaped, not instructed. Rather than emulate much of previous behavior therapy that relies on instructional control, Functional Analytic Psychotherapy is oriented toward shaping and reinforcement. The therapist avoids utilizing "rules" to create changes in behavior, largely because rules may produce behavior that is functionally different from behavior that has been shaped.

The only kind of rule that is formally encouraged in this approach is the tracking of accurate tacts. Both the client and the therapist are encouraged to verbally describe the contingencies that surround particular experiences (Clinically Relevant Behavior 3s). They are encouraged to be in direct contact with experiences occurring in the session and to generate statements about the contingent relationships that appear to exist.

Functional Analytic Psychotherapy is a difficult therapy for many therapists, as it requires that the therapist produce effects in part by their "natural" reactions to the client's behavior. It requires that the therapist be quite involved with the client and that his or her private reactions to the client be examined continuously. This is quite different from other behavioral approaches to therapy, where the therapist can utilize instruction while remaining personally removed and distant from the session.

As previously discussed, much of the social skills literature is based on the notion that the particular behavior that one wants to establish or reduce can be operationalized. However, social skill can be affected without this occurring, as we have demonstrated (Azrin & Hayes, 1984; Rosenfarb, Hayes, & Linehan, in press).

Functional Analytic Psychotherapy deals with this issue by selecting therapists who already have the global goal behaviors of particular clients in their repertoires. The idea is that without having to define the components of, say, "being able to be intimate with others," therapists are more likely to be able to shape approximations toward this skill if they themselves are effective in this way. The therapist's own history and repertoire is used as a method for defining functional categories of behavior. To continue with the example, a structural, topographical description of particular behaviors needed for intimacy is not necessary because therapists can note reactions in themselves that the client's behavior produces. This enables them to reinforce behaviors that, for example, functionally produce intimacy rather then behaviors that have been structurally defined as a component of "intimate behavior."

Kohlenberg and Tsai's (1987) approach is designed to produce changes that go "far beyond the stated goals of therapy." So far, this has not been shown empirically. The rule-governance literature provides a conceptual support for the possibility, however. Instead of specific rules oriented toward specific problems, the product of this approach is at least designed to be a general skill of noting one's direct experience and generating self-rules that closely correspond with it. This general skill of course can be applied to any problem that life presents. Naturally, we cannot know before hand what a client will confront during the course of therapy or what will occur after therapy. Therefore, training an "approach" that can generalize to a wide variety of things one confronts is particularly valuable.

Skinner (1972) in his essay "Creating the Creative Artist" presents an analysis of producing creativity that may be analogous to the clinician creating the conditions required for a client to approach life in a flexible, creative, adaptive manner. Skinner suggests that "the young artist may be taught, for example, to tolerate effects he once rejected, to permit some features to stand for the sake of others, to stop painting in time, and so on" (p. 340). In other words, there are some elements of the process of creating something meaningful that can be taught, but the actual product that the artist produces is not something that was specifiable beforehand. Therapy, similarly, may be most generalizable when the goal is to shape an approach to life, some (but not all) aspects of which are difficult to specify.

Functional Analytic Psychotherapy is, as of yet, of unknown value. Its operating principles have, however, been informed by the current literature on rule-governance. Few behavioral techniques are sensitive to the downside of rule-governance, and little empirical work has yet been done on these techniques. Functional Analytic Psychotherapy is thus offered, not yet as a clear alternative, but as a challenge to the assumptions of existing behavior therapy techniques.

3. ALTERATION OF RULE-CONTROL: THE STRATEGY OF RECONTEXTUALIZATION

We turn now to techniques that have as their goal an alteration of the ways in which rules function. Some kind of rule control may need to be diminished; other types increased. In the approach that follows, we attempt to alter the ways in which rules function by altering the context in which rules occur.

3.1. Behavior–Behavior Relations

Most adult psychotherapies deal, implicitly or explicitly, with the role of client thoughts and feelings. To the extent that thoughts are recognized as behaviors, the question "what role do thoughts play in controlling human behavior?" would be changed to "what types of contingencies would lead one behavior to occur and to influence another behavior?" This reformulation has an enormous impact on the kinds of analyses that result.

Some authors (e.g., Killeen, 1984) have criticized the usefulness of calling private actions "behaviors," but there are strong reasons to do so. First, it emphasizes that it is the job of psychology to explain these events. If we seek to understand the behavior of an individual, considering thoughts to be behavior requires that we also understand thoughts. Second, it prevents incomplete explanations that are useless for prediction and control (see Hayes & Brownstein, 1986). We intuitively recognize that an explanation of one behavior by another of the same kind is inherently incomplete. For example, if we claimed that a person played Scrabble well because she played Trivial Pursuit well, we would immediately wonder why she played Trivial Pursuit well and why the two are related. Suppose, however, we seemed to change the realms of the two related events. Suppose we claimed that the person played good Scrabble because she had good verbal intelligence and was confident and bold. This explanation does not seem as obviously incomplete as the first. It looks as though the explanatory events are of a different kind than the explained event and thus are possibly complete. By using the term *behavior* for all organismic activity, this self-deception is made less likely.

There is a final reason to consider private actions to be behaviors. Once we get used to thinking of cognitive control as a matter of behavior–behavior relationships, we can begin to think of behavior–behavior relationships in contingency analysis terms. To do this requires that we understand the contingencies giving rise to each behavior *and* (and this is the crux of the matter) the relationship between them. Thus we must ask "what are the contingencies that support the relationship between thoughts and other forms of human action?" In this view, thoughts and self-rules do not *necessarily* produce any effect on other behaviors. It is only because of the context (the contingencies) that one form of behavior relates to another. What are the contingencies that lead verbal thoughts to control other forms of behavior? We point to three.

3.2. Contexts Relevant to Pathological Self-Rule Control

The most characteristic contexts in which client problems are embedded are (1) literality, (2) reason giving, and (3) the attempt to control. The first of these, literality, sets the stage for the others.

3.2.1. Literality

Through the processes described in Chapter 5 in this volume, words often come to be used as if they mean or *are* the things to which they *refer*. A word and the situation that it refers to can easily be confused. For example, "I'm sick" literally means that the situation of sickness has arrived. The even more direct fact, that the situation of *saying* "I'm sick" has arrived, virtually is buried in the avalanche of literal meaning.

If one member of a relational class (e.g., the "referent") is taken to be present when another member (e.g., a "word") is present, actions appropriate to the first are likely to be activated by the second. For example, the thought "I'm sick" may result in a child's asking to stay home from school, regardless of the actual state of his or her health. If mom is convinced by the child's words that she or he feels poorly, she or he will most likely be allowed to stay home. A behavior–behavior relation between saying things (e.g., thinking verbally) and overt action is thereby established by the "context of literality" created and supported by the verbal community at large.

We have extensive histories from the verbal community for maintaining a rough equivalence between words and events. We are encouraged to engage in formal analyses of situations and then to respond to these analyses. The verbal community is constantly tightening the equivalence between our talk and the world. Verbal stimuli are purely arbitrary stimuli, and there are few impediments to fairly tight equivalence classes emerging.

As an end result, when we think something, it is not always obvious that it is even a thought. In a sense, the relational classes involved are so tight that it is hard to see that the functions of one member of a class are in fact derived from those of other members. The insensitivity produced by verbal rules may in part be based on this very fact. One of the goals of *comprehensive distancing* is to "loosen" verbal equivalence classes, particularly in descriptive or analytical talk. Exactly why this is a goal will become clearer as the method and its underlying assumptions are described. Unlike other methods, however, that attempt to teach accurate tacting, the primary goal of Comprehensive Distancing is to help clients to see talk as an action that can be useful or not useful depending on the context.

3.2.2. *Reason Giving and Control*

In the context of literality, verbal reason giving acquires considerable potency. It is generally accepted by the social-verbal community that certain events can explain other events. For example, the agoraphobic tells her husband that she did not go to the grocery store today because she was too anxious. This explanation for her avoidance behavior is likely to generate sympathy support from the community at large because many people can identify with the experience of avoiding a situation where they might become afraid. Thus within the social-verbal community, a particular behavior–behavior relationship is established that appears to be of a causal nature: When I am anxious, it makes me avoid what is feared, and this avoidance makes the anxiety go away. "Anxiety" become an event that seemingly can make other behavioral events occur, but it does so in part because of the social support for this very conception.

Control is an extension of literality and reason giving. If anxiety can "cause" avoidance and avoidance is detrimental, then anxiety must be controlled in order to improve matters. This conception, too, is massively supported by the verbal community. The social support for controlling "bad thoughts" or "bad feelings" is itself part of the context in which these private actions precipitate other actions, namely attempts to get rid of these very thoughts and feelings.

3.3. The Problem and the Solution

"Getting rid of" is the client's "solution." In our view, it is instead one aspect of the problem. *Comprehensive Distancing* (Hayes, 1987) seeks to find a more workable solution by undermining the three contexts of literality, reason giving, and control. The hope is that by doing so, more direct processes of contingency control can have more of an impact and that unworkable but logical solutions can be abandoned. Additionally, certain worthwhile forms of rule-control may be made *more* likely.

Because each of the three relevant contexts are not only part of the client's perspective but also part of the social-verbal community's (including the therapist's), they are very difficult to challenge. In fact, the only way possible to do so is by behaving in ways that are not "logical," not "reasonable," and thus outside the verbal contexts the therapist is seeking to suspend.

3.3.1. Creative Hopelessness

In the first stage of Comprehensive Distancing, an attempt is made to establish a state of "creative hopelessness" in the client. The client typically comes into therapy with a set of identified problems, and most often, a set of logical verbal solutions to the problems. The therapist is then asked to assist the client in implementing these solutions (e.g., anxious clients wish to be calm). This identified set of problems and solutions arises from a set of practices established and maintained by the community of verbal organisms of which we all are a part. Creative hopelessness is our name for the condition in which the client's "solutions" begin to be seen as problems themselves, or at least, as impossible to implement. When all "solutions" are no longer solutions, the client feels hopeless, but it is a creative hopelessness because out of this context fundamentally new approaches are possible.

In this first part of therapy, the client is told that the "solution" he or she is proposing is part of his or her problem and that the therapist cannot possibly provide a technique to eliminate, control, or reduce the distressing emotions or reactions the client is experiencing. The situation *is* "hopeless," because even if the therapist could do what the client is asking, it would not yield the desired result.

In our view, the client *is* helpless and hopeless *within the context from which he or she currently is operating*. Clients are told they are not to blame, but that they are responsible, that is, able to respond. The many and varied ways the client has already tried to change, which have failed, are explored with the therapist. Because the things clients have already attempted and abandoned typically are logical, commonsense solutions, it becomes clear that some change beyond ordinary verbal logic is needed. Using metaphor, the therapist describes the "hopeless" dilemma in terms that identify the social-verbal system in which the client was trained, not the client personally, as the real problem. For example, a therapist might say:

THERAPIST: Let me give you a metaphor that might help see what I'm saying. The situation you are in is something like this. Imagine a large field. You are blindfolded, given some tools, and told to run through the field. Unknown to you, though, there are holes in this field. They are widely spaced in most places, but sooner or later you accidentally fall into one. Now when you fall into the hole, you start trying to get out. You don't know exactly what to do, so you take the tool that seems most useful, and you try to get out. Unfortunately, the tool you were given is a shovel. So you dig. And you dig. But digging is a thing that makes holes, not a way to get out of them. You might make the hole deeper, or larger, or there might be all kinds of passageways you can build, but you'll probably still be stuck in this hole. So you try other things. You might try to figure out exactly how you fell in the hole. "If I just hadn't turned left at the rise, I wouldn't be here," you might think. And of course that is literally true, but it doesn't make any difference. Even if you knew every step you took, it wouldn't get you out of the hole. So we're not going to spend a lot of time trying to figure out the details of your past—many of these will come up for other reasons, and we will deal with them, but not as a way to get you out of the hole you're in. Another thing you might do is that you might try to find a really great shovel. Maybe that's the problem. You need a gold-plated steam shovel. That's really why you're here. You think I have a gold-plated steam shovel. But I don't, and even if I did, it wouldn't do any good because shovels don't get people out of holes. To get out of a hole you need a ladder, not a shovel.

CLIENT: So what is the ladder? How do I get out?

THERAPIST: See, the reason I can't answer that now is that it wouldn't do any good until you really let go of this determination to dig your way out. Right now if you were given a ladder you'd try to dig with it. So let me go back to it and say that we can't begin to go on until you really start to face up to the fact that there is no way out, given the way you are holding it. It doesn't matter how you do it, you can't dig you way out. Digging faster won't work. Putting more effort into it won't work. And there is no room to do what will work until you put down the shovel. There is something else I want you to notice about this. In the metaphor, it is not the person's fault that he fell in the hole, and it's not his fault that he can't get out. If it hadn't been this hole, it might have been another. Fault and blame is when we add in social condemnation to try to motivate someone to change. You don't need that. You are already motivated to change. So it's not your fault. You are not to blame. You are, however, responsible in the sense of response ability. You had an ability to respond differently in the situation than you did. You just didn't know that you did. You didn't have to spend years digging furiously, as you have. If that's not true, then nothing can be done now, so don't try to avoid responsibility—just know that the ability to respond is not the same as blame. We have no need of blame here. The consequences themselves are plenty enough aversive already without having to dump social condemnation on top of them. I want you to know that it is very clear to me that you would like your life to work. If you known what to do, you would have done it.

Confusion is maintained deliberately to prevent the client from intellectualizing and compartmentalizing his or her dilemma into the same solutions and commonsense insights that have failed in the past. For example, the client is told that if he or she seems to be understanding what the therapist is saying, then indeed, he or she is *not* understanding it because within the logical verbal context from which he or she is operating, the therapist's real meaning cannot possibly be understood. Metaphor is used extensively to impress on the client that the therapist is *not* presenting a new and different belief system to be embraced literally.

3.3.2. Control

The second goal of Comprehensive Distancing is to focus on the issues of emotional and cognitive control. As mentioned earlier, by the time the client comes to therapy, he or she has been well trained to view many of his or her problems as related to a failure to control thoughts and feelings in his or her life (e.g., temper, anxiety, depression). This viewpoint has been supported by the social-verbal community at large, and recently, by many psychological theories that have had wide exposure among nonprofessional readers. For example, clients can pick up any magazine in the doctor's office and learn techniques to replace anxiety with relaxation, depressive thoughts with happy ones, a poor self-image with positive thinking, and so on.

We view such attempts to control private events (thoughts, feelings, opinions, etc.) as themselves causes of many major life difficulties. Clients are told that the rule "If you don't want it, get rid of it!" is ineffective in the world of private experience, despite its obvious reasonableness and cultural advantages in the physical world around them. Rather, in the world inside the skin, the rule can more accurately be stated, "If you aren't willing to have it, you've got it." Trying to get rid of anxiety will inevitably lead to thoughts about anxiety, thus producing the very thing the client is seeking to eliminate; trying not to be depressed is depressing. A metaphor is used to make this point:

THERAPIST: Suppose I had you wired up to a very fine polygraph. It is such a fine machine that there is simply no way you could possibly be anxious without my knowing it. Now imagine that I have given you a very simple task: Don't get anxious. However, to help motivate you I pull out a gun. I tell you that to help you work on this task I will hold the gun to your head. As long as you don't get anxious, I won't shoot you, but if you get anxious you will be shot. Can you see what would happen?

CLIENT: I'd be shot for sure.

THERAPIST: Right. There is no way you can follow this rule. If it is critical not to be anxious, guess what you get? This is not a far-fetched situation. It is exactly the situation you are in right now. Instead of a polygraph you have something even better: your own nervous system. Instead of a gun, you have your self-esteem or your success in life apparently on the line. So guess what you get? Haven't you noticed that about the most depressing thing to do is to try to stamp out your depression? Anger seems to make you mad—anxiety makes you anxious. It's a setup. We are applying a rule that works perfectly well in one situation into a situation in which the same rule is a disaster. And it's not just feelings. Suppose you have a thought you cannot permit. So you try not to think it. That really works great, doesn't it? Try it now. Don't think of jelly donuts; don't think of race cars; don't think of your mother. Guess what you get? In the world outside the skin the rule may be "If you don't want it, get rid of it," but inside the skin it seems to be something more like "If you are not willing to have it, you've got it."

The statement, "If you aren't willing to have it, you've got it," is impossible for the client to make use of literally. For example, the agoraphobic is told that if she expresses a willingness to have anxiety but only because such willingness will ultimately serve to eliminate anxiety, then she really is *unwilling,* and as a consequence anxiety is sure to continue. Thus paradoxical result itself attacks the literal basis upon which it depends.

3.3.3. "I" versus What "I" Do

The third goal identified in Comprehensive Distancing is that of helping the client to distinguish between the person he or she calls "I" and the problem behaviors that the client wants eliminated. The primary goal of Comprehensive Distancing is to establish a new social-verbal context within which verbalizations can function in new and more productive ways. Paradox is a great aid here because it attacks literal meaning. The attack, however, is itself based on literal meaning. A distinction between "I" and what "I" do is helpful by allowing the client to discern self-verbalizations more readily for what they are, not just what they say they are. That is, the distinction produces some "distance" between the person and his or her own thoughts. As when we step back from a painting to see it clearly, the purpose is not to diminish the thought but simply in part to see it *as* a thought. Thus the purpose of distancing is not avoidance but a richer, more varied, and more useful contact with one's own behavior.

The following analysis is drawn in part from the more detailed treatment in Hayes (1984, 1987). Let the word *seeing* represent all of the major things we do with regard to the world (feeling, moving, etc.). To nonverbal organisms, there is just the world and seeing. Seeing is controlled entirely by the direct contingencies (of survival and reinforcement). With the advent of verbal behavior, this changes. The availability of equivalence and other relational classes permits the social community to place past events in classes with present stimuli. A person can be asked such things as "what did you have for breakfast yesterday?" or "what did you do at the circus?" If the child answers incorrectly, the control over the response can be refined verbally, relying on relational classes learned in simpler situations. For example, if the child says she played with blocks at the circus, the question can say "no, you did that at school. What did you do at the circus? Did you see elephants?" Thus the verbal community establishes a generalized tendency to respond to one's own behavior verbally: not only seeing but what we might call "seeing *seeing*," or self-knowledge.

It is also critical to the verbal community, however, that this behavior (seeing *seeing*) occur from a given and consistent perspective, locus, or point of view. The verbal community must not only know that you see seeing but that you see seeing from the point of view of *you*. In this way, the verbal community creates a "sense of self" that has some very special properties.

The behavior of seeing *seeing* from a perspective might emerge in several ways. Children are taught deictic words (e.g., *here* and *there*) that do not refer to events but to the relation between events on the one hand and the child's point of view on the other. Children must be taught to distinguish their perspective from that of others Young children, when asked what they ate, may report what their brother ate. If seated across from a doll and asked what the doll sees, they may report what they themselves see, not what the doll would see. Finally, we are taught to respond generally to questions of the form "what did you *x*," where *x* is a wide variety of events such as eat, feel, do, watch, and so on. The events themselves constantly change. Only the locus of the observation does not. The invariant is that "you" is placed in sentences when reports are to be done from the point of view of you.

Thus the verbal community creates a kind of "content-less" behavior called seeing-seeing-from-perspective and gives it the name *you*. This behavior may even be the basis of the matter/spirit distinction so prevalent in our culture (Hayes, 1984). The term *you* is used in other ways as well (e.g., you as a physical organism), but the sense of the word *you* that is of special relevance to comprehensive distancing in this former sense.

Why might this make a difference? The behavior of observing thoughts from a perspective is quite different from the behavior of understanding and following self-rules. By helping the person distinguish between seeing-seeing-from-a-perspective and the things seen, it may make it more possible generate and understand a self-rule without also following that rule (cf. Ryle, 1949, p. 166). This is a difficult distinction, and it takes quite a bit of work in therapy to get it solidly established. A therapist monologue explains how distinguishing between *you* and what *you* do might be used in this way:

THERAPIST: As it is right now, it is very difficult, if not impossible to stay out of the struggle to get rid of "undesirable" thoughts or feelings. You are too much controlled by your own thoughts about what you need to do. The way we normally operate, we confuse the content of our own conditioning with the behavior of seeing the results of that conditioning. Because of that, when we think a thought, it is as if that is also now what is real, not just as a thought but as what the thought says it is. We that happens we are in what I call the *about* world. We get caught up in what the thoughts are about—not what they are. In other words, you aren't just noticing behavior called *thinking*, you are actually in the situation described by the thought. If you think you are bad, you are bad. Often you don't even notice that it is a thought. Right? So if you think a thought like "I can't stand this. I have to get out of here," it is not at all clear that what actually happened is that you experienced yourself thinking. You did not experience what the thought actually said. The form of the thought says one thing, but you actually only experienced that you thought that thought.

Here's a metaphor that may help. Imagine two people sitting in front of two identical computers. Given a particular set of programming, a given input will produce a given output. The programming of these computers is like what has happened to you in your life. Given a certain situation, a certain response is likely. Let's say that we type something in on the keyboard, and the output on the screen is "deep down you are a bad person." In one case, let's imagine that the person sitting in front of the computer is well aware of the distinction between himself and the computer. When the readout appears on the screen, it may be interesting, or maybe something to consider, or maybe something to show to others. It probably doesn't have to be changed, covered up, followed, not followed, disbelieved, and so on. The second person, however, is totally absorbed by the screen. Like a person at the movies, he has gotten so far into it he has forgotten that there is a distinction between him as an observer of the screen and what is on the screen. Readout like that I just mentioned would be far more unacceptable to this guy. To him it will probably be something to be denied, forgotten, changed, and so on. In other words, when you identify with the content of your private experiences, you will almost automatically be controlled by them, at least to the extent of trying to get rid of them.

Here is another metaphor that will help make the point. Imagine a chessboard that goes out indefinitely in all directions. On this board are lots of chess pieces, of all different colors. To keep it simple, let's just concentrate on the white pieces and the black pieces. Now in chess, the pieces are supposed to ally with their friends to beat up on their enemies. So the black pieces sort of hang out together and try to knock the white pieces off the board and vice versa. These pieces represent the content of your life: your thoughts, feelings, memories, attitudes, behavioral predispositions, bodily sensations, and so on. And if you notice, they do indeed hang out together. For example, the "positive" ones might cluster together—you know, the ones that say things like "I'm going to make it," and so on. And the negative ones work together too. So you'll notice that "bad" thoughts are associated with "bad" memories and "bad" feelings, and so on. Now the way we usually try to work it is that we nominate one of the teams as "our team." It is as if we get up on the back of the white queen and ride off to do battle with the black pieces. There is a big problem with that, however. As soon as we do this, whole great portions of us are our own enemy. In addition, if it is true that "if you are not willing to have it, you've got it," then as you battle with the undesirable pieces and try to knock them off the board, they loom larger and larger and larger. And that's in fact what has happened, isn't it? Anxiety, for example, has become more and more and more the central focus of your life. Within this metaphor, the sad thing is that when you act as if only part of your programming is acceptable, you must also go from who are to whom you are not. To be even more precise, you have to act as if you are no longer who you experience yourself to be. You have to forget that you are not the computer, in that last metaphor. Within this metaphor, can you see who "you" are?

CLIENT: I don't know. I always thought I was the pieces. Who else can I be?

THERAPIST: Well, think about it.

CLIENT: The board?

THERAPIST: Yeah. Do you see? Within that metaphor, *you* are the board. You are the context in which all these things can even be seen. If there was a thought and no one to see it, it'd be as if it wasn't there at all. Now you notice that a board, although it is being a board, can only do one of two things. It can hold what is put on it, and it can move everything (as when you pick up the board and move it in the middle of a game). Note also that it requires no effort to hold the pieces. If the board wanted to move the pieces around one at a time, however, it would have to go from the board level to the piece level. So if you get in the middle of the pieces in the name of moving the pieces, you have to forget that you are actually the board. And once you are on the piece level you have to fight, because at that level other pieces seem to threaten your very survival. That's why you can't logically force yourself not to struggle with your emotions. It's a lost cause. What you can do is to distinguish yourself as you experience yourself to be from the events you experience. That is, you can get clear that you are actually on the board level anyway. From that level it is possible to watch the war between your own pieces without actually getting hooked by them—that is, without having to take them literally, or without having to change them before you can get control over your life. It is only by realizing that you don't have control over the pieces and that you don't need it, that you can have control over your life.

In what sense is it possible that the socially created "you" can be independent from other behaviors? This is possible only because the behavior of seeing *seeing* from a perspective (this sense of "you") is itself content free. That is, it is a behavior that cannot itself be verbally seen as a thing by the person behaving in this way (Hayes, 1984). No sooner do you notice this behavior than the behavior has fundamentally changed. If we were to see our own perspective, from what perspective could we see it? Thus the sense of self established by the verbal community can be looked from, but cannot be looked at—or at least as soon as we do so, the behavior we are looking at is no longer occurring in the same place. This also means that "you" in this sense cannot be evaluated because only things can have good and bad qualities. This behavior cannot be viewed as a thing for the person engaging in it and thus cannot be evaluated. It may be part of what clinicians are talking about with such phrases as "you're OK as a birthright." Further, the sense of "being you" stays the same through life. It has to because all it is is the sense of viewing from perspective. If that were to change, you would no longer be you. This sense of unchangeability is important because it helps people experience negative thoughts and negative self-evaluations while at the same time knowing that a basic part of "you" will never change and is beyond evaluation.

The assumption of Comprehensive Distancing is that it is only when a distinction is made between this sense of *you* and the things in your life that it is possible consistently to do anything else with "undesirable" private events than to struggle with them, follow them, try to get rid of them, and so on. We have lots of socially established rules about self-worth. People want to be acceptable to themselves and others. Unfortunately, because of verbal evaluation at the level of content, no one is truly acceptable. We sometimes ask our clients to name one thing in the physical universe that they can not find fault with, always, at any given point in time. Usually they cannot. Then we ask, "so why should you ever be an exception?"

At this stage of therapy, we frequently do experiential exercises designed to help the client become more aware of awareness. We also adopt the somewhat awkward convention of framing statements in such a way as to make clear the distinction between the self and the behavior being emitted. For example, we instruct clients to say, "I'm having the thought that I can't go to the mall" (as opposed to simply stating, "I can't go to the mall"), or "I'm having the evaluation that I'm a bad person." This simple technique (which gestalt therapists have used to get clients to "own" their thoughts and feelings) very powerfully brings home to the client the distinction we are trying to make between the person he or she is and the things in his or her life.

3.3.4. *Letting Go of the Struggle*

In this phase of Comprehensive Distancing, we encourage clients to begin deliberately to experience thoughts and feelings that, if taken literally, must be avoided. There are many times when self-rules point to ineffective actions. Downhill skiing illustrates the point: When a person is on a steep slope, skiing downhill for the first time, the natural inclination is to lean back on the skis in order to slow down and keep in control of speed and steering. However, any experienced skier knows that, in fact, the opposite is true—the only way to gain maximum control over your speed and course is to lean *forward* into the slope. When we encourage clients to give up the struggle with control, we are *not* asking them to "grin and bear it" or "tough out" their symptoms until they are able to be endured. Rather, we are asking the client to lean into the symptoms; we encourage them not only to stop struggling but seemingly to embrace the very things that they most dread.

The only way it is possible for clients to cease struggling with depression, anxiety, self-deprecation, obsessions, and the like is if they can begin to view these things from a different context than is usual. We seek to loosen literality, undermine reason giving, and reduce control as the agenda. In this context, the client can recognize emotions or thoughts or bodily sensations *for what they are* (i.e., emotions, thoughts, body sensations), not for what they seem to be.

For example, the thought, "I am a bad person," is not the same as actually being a bad person. We ask the client to give up the struggle with the thought, as a thought, not to resign himself or herself to being a bad person. The feeling the agoraphobic has during a panic attack that she is going to go crazy is not the same as the actual experience of becoming psychotic. We ask the client to experience the *fear* of craziness, not actually to experience slipping into psychosis.

3.3.5. Commitment and Behavior Change

The fifth goal of Comprehensive Distancing is making a commitment to action. At this stage of therapy, the client has been led to view reasons as mere verbal behavior, not literal causes. A description of something is still just a way of speaking, and the value of any way to speaking is to be found in its function. The correspondence between the word and the thing is not the issue. If a client earnestly explains that things "really are" the way he or she has described them, the therapist is likely to ask, "and has this way of talking worked for you?" In other words, truth is not a matter of correspondence—it is a matter of utility.

Having altered the context in which client talk is used, certain other forms of talk can function in new ways. Verbal commitments become very important. Within this therapeutic context, the client who makes a commitment has no acceptable excuses for a failure to follow through. This stage of treatment is not punitive; there is no attempt to "punish" the recalcitrant client or trick him or her into keeping his or her commitments. Rather, a verbal environment has been created in therapy that allows no logical escape.

Although the insensitivity-producing effects of certain kinds of talk is harmful, in other cases, insensitivity is desirable. Commitments are an example. Promises usually work best when they are kept. Thus the goal of therapy at this point is practicing the successful making and keeping of verbal commitments. The commitments clients come to set for themselves often bear little resemblance to the presenting complaints that initially brought them into therapy. The size or labeled *importance* of each commitment is considered irrelevant to the process, so long as it is growth enhancing rather than growth inhibiting. In our opinion, this stage of therapy is possible only after the client has achieved some ability to distinguish "self" from his or her problem behaviors, and after reason giving and literality have lost their believability and power.

A commitment, of course, is a self-rule. A commitment to overt behavior change is a rule that at least theoretically can be followed. The effort to feel or think only certain things cannot be followed because many of these actions are not themselves under verbal control. Thus, we seek a discrimination between self-rules that cannot be followed effectively (i.e., rules of emotional avoidance) and self-rules that can be followed effectively (e.g., commitments to behavior change). The paradox is that, by reducing literality, verbal commitments of this kind seem to be made more effective and more impactful on behavior change.

3.4. Evidence of Efficacy

Comprehensive Distancing is a new procedure, consciously based on the behavior-analytic literature on equivalence and rule-governance and deliberately tied to contextualistic philosophy. The first formal report of the procedure was in 1987 (Hayes, 1987). There has been only a handful of attempts to evaluate the outcome of the procedure. What work has been done is supportive (see Hayes, 1987).

Comprehensive Distancing can be an effective treatment for depression. In the first study of its efficacy, it exceeded the effectiveness of Beck's cognitive therapy—widely acknowledged to be the most effective psychotherapy yet devised for depression (Zettle, 1984). It is also known that improvements in comprehensive distancing do not occur by reducing the frequency of depressive thoughts, as occurs in cognitive therapy. Rather, the believability of these thoughts diminishes radically (Zettle & Hayes, 1986). Comprehensive Distancing is also effective with anxiety disorders of various kinds (Hayes, 1987). The work is still quite preliminary, however, and it is not yet known if comprehensive distancing will prove to be more effective than other techniques. What is particularly interesting about Comprehensive Distancing at this point is not its known effectiveness but the fact that a therapy based on contemporary basic behavior-analytic research has deviated so massively from the mainstream of "behavioral" approaches to treatment that were based on the behavioral principles available in the 1950s and 1960s.

4. CONCLUSION

Behavior-analytic literature had a heavy influence on the field of applied psychology, especially applied behavior analysis. The range of behavior-analytic principles applied to human affairs, however, has been limited primarily to principles of direct contingency control; they have been applied primarily to children and to institutionalized populations. The more recent literature on rule-governance and relational classes is almost unknown outside of the basic area. These newer findings seem to have most direct relevance to verbal adults. They are useful in interpreting existing interventions in many areas (e.g., see Chapter 9 in this volume).

The purpose of the present chapter was to show that the kinds of basic analyses developed in this book can be useful in generating new ideas and interventions. It is perhaps a measure of the newness of the basic contributions being made by the attempt to analyze rule-governance that most of the novel clinical extensions deviate radically from what one might expect of behavioral interventions. Shaping social skills without instructions, using the therapeutic relationship to shape effective behavior, and using paradoxical verbal interventions to recontextualize client's thoughts are all very different from what is usually called *behavior therapy*. They all, in addition, bear notable resemblances to "nonbehavioral" interventions by clinicians such as Rogers, Frankl, or Perls.

Whether this trend is an anomaly or the harbinger of things to come is not yet clear. Most of these efforts are very preliminary, and may not prove themselves to be useful when subjected to further empirical evaluation. Still, it is interesting that the applied extensions of the rule-governance literature have taken this turn. If these extensions do hold up, it will strengthen the importance of the basic analysis by showing that new approaches are emerging from the basic behavior-analytic literature. Some of these principles may also help put in good theoretical order the messy area of adult psychotherapy. It is ironic, but basic behavior analysis may be building the kind of theoretical base that many of the "nonbehavioral" techniques have needed in order to tie clinical wisdom to scientifically validated principles.

5. REFERENCES

Azrin, R., & Hayes, S. C. (1984). The discrimination of interest within a heterosexual interaction: Training, generalization, and effects on social skills. *Behavior Therapy, 15*, 173–184.

Ciminero, A. R., Calhoun, S. K., and Adams, H. E. (1977). *Handbook of behavioral assessment*. New York: Wiley.

Conger, J. C., & Conger, A. J. (1982). Components of heterosocial competence. In J. P. Curran & P. M. Monti (Eds.), *Social skills training* (pp. 313–347). New York: Guilford.

Devany, J. M., & Nelson, R. O. (1986). Behavioral approaches to treatment. In H. C. Quay & J. S. Werry (Eds.), *Psychopathological disorders of childhood* (pp. 523–557). New York: Wiley.

Ellis, A. (1962). *Reason and emotion in psychotherapy*. Secaucus, NJ: Stuart.

Ferster, C. B. (1967). Arbitrary and natural reinforcement. *The Psychological Record, 22,* 1–16.

Ferster, C. B. (1972). An experimental analysis of clinical phenomena. *The Psychological Record, 22,* 1–16.

Gallassi, M. D., & Gallassi, J. P. (1979). Assertion: A critical review. *Psychotherapy: Theory, Research, and Practice, 15,* 16–29.

Hayes, S. C. (1984). Making sense of spirituality. *Behaviorism, 12,* 99–110.

Hayes, S. C. (1987). A contextual approach to therapeutic change. In N. Jacobson (Ed.), *Psychotherapists in clinical practice: Cognitive and behavioral perspectives* (pp. 327–387). New York: Guilford.

Hayes, S. C., & Brownstein, A. J. (1986). Mentalism, behavior-behavior relations, and a behavior analytic view of the purposes of science. *The Behavior Analyst 9,* 175–190.

Hayes, S. C., & Melancon, S. M. (in press). Comprehensive Distancing, paradox, and the treatment of emotional avoidance. In M. Ascher (Ed.), *Paradoxical procedures in psychotherapy*. New York: Guilford.

Killeen, P. (1984). Emergent behaviorism. *Behaviorism, 12,* 25–39.

Kohlenberg, R. J., & Tsai, M. (1987). Functional analytic psychotherapy. In N. Jacobson (Ed.), *Psychotherapists in clinical practice: Cognitive and behavioral perspectives* (pp. 388–443). New York: Guilford.

Lutzker, J. R., & Martin, J. A. (1981). *Behavior change*. Monterey, CA: Brooks/Cole.

Perls, F. S. (1969). *Gestalt therapy verbatim*. Lafayette, CA: Real People Press.

Perls, F. S., Hefferline, R., & Goodman, P. (1951). *Gestalt therapy*. New York: Dell.

Rimm, D. C., & Masters, J. C. (1979). *Behavior therapy*. New York: Academic Press.

Rosenfarb, I. S., Hayes, S. C., & Linehan, M. M. (in press). Instructions and experiential feedback in the treatment of social skills deficits in adults. *Psychotherapy: Theory, Research, and Practice*.

Ryle, G. (1949). *The concept of mind*. New York: Barnes & Noble.

Skinner, B. F. (1945). The operational analysis of psychological terms. *Psychological Review, 52,* 270–277.

Skinner, B. F. (1953). *Science and human behavior*. New York: Macmillan.

Skinner, B. F. (1957). *Verbal behavior*. New York: Appleton-Century-Crofts.

Skinner, B. F. (1969). *Contingencies of reinforcement: A theoretical analysis*. New York: Appleton-Century-Crofts.

Skinner, B. F. (1972). *Cumulative record*. New York: Appleton-Century-Crofts.

Strupp, H. H., & Binder, J. (1984). *Psychotherapy in a new key: A guide to time-limited dynamic psychotherapy*. New York: Basic Books.

Weiss, J., & Sampson, H. (1986). *The psychoanalytic process*. New York: Guilford.

Zettle, R. D. (1984). *Cognitive therapy of depression: A conceptual and empirical analysis of component and process issues*. Unpublished doctoral dissertation available from the University of North Carolina at Greensboro.

Zettle, R. D., & Hayes, S. C. (1982). Rule-governed behavior: A potential theoretical framework for cognitive behavior therapy. In P. C. Kendall (Ed.), *Advances in cognitive behavioral research and therapy* (Vol. 1, pp. 73–118). New York: Academic.

Zettle, R. D., & Hayes, S. C. (1986). Dysfunctional control by client verbal behavior: The context of reason giving. *The Analysis of Verbal Behavior, 4,* 30–38.

Index

Made in the USA
Monee, IL
13 September 2026

62976352R00227